AN INTRODUCTION TO PROGRAMMING

WITH JAVA™

APPLETS

Third Edition

An Introduction to Programming

with JAVA™ APPLETS

Third Edition

Elizabeth Sugar Boese
Colorado State University

JONES AND BARTLETT PUBLISHERS
Sudbury, Massachusetts
BOSTON   TORONTO   LONDON   SINGAPORE

World Headquarters

Jones and Bartlett Publishers
40 Tall Pine Drive
Sudbury, MA 01776
978-443-5000
info@jbpub.com
www.jbpub.com

Jones and Bartlett Publishers
Canada
6339 Ormindale Way
Mississauga, Ontario L5V 1J2
Canada

Jones and Bartlett Publishers
International
Barb House, Barb Mews
London W6 7PA
United Kingdom

Jones and Bartlett's books and products are available through most bookstores and online booksellers. To contact Jones and Bartlett Publishers directly, call 800-832-0034, fax 978-443-8000, or visit our website www.jbpub.com.

Substantial discounts on bulk quantities of Jones and Bartlett's publications are available to corporations, professional associations, and other qualified organizations. For details and specific discount information, contact the special sales department at Jones and Bartlett via the above contact information or send an email to specialsales@jbpub.com.

Production Credits
Publisher: David Pallai
Acquisitions Editor: Timothy Anderson
Editorial Assistant: Melissa Potter
Production Director: Amy Rose
Associate Production Editor: Melissa Elmore
Senior Marketing Manager: Andrea DeFronzo
V.P., Manufacturing and Inventory Control: Therese Connell
Text Design: Anne Spencer
Composition: Northeast Compositors, Inc.
Cover and Title Page Design: Scott Moden
Cover Image: © Cornelis Opstal/Dreamstime.com
Chapter Opener Image: © Bruce Rolff / ShutterStock, Inc.
Interior Images: Erica Beade, MBC Graphics; Java logo courtesy of Sun Microsystems
Printing and Binding: Courier Companies
Cover Printing: Courier Companies

Library of Congress Cataloging-in-Publication Data
Boese, Elizabeth Sugar.
 An introduction to programming with Java Applets / Elizabeth Sugar Boese. — 3rd ed.
  p. cm.
 ISBN 978-0-7637-5460-0 (pbk.)
 1. Java (Computer program language) 2. Web site development. I. Title.
 QA76.73.J38B62 2009
 006.7'6—dc22
                    2008048651

6048

Printed in the United States of America
13 12 11 10 09   10 9 8 7 6 5 4 3 2 1

Contents

● Preface

An Introduction to Programming with Java Applets is an introduction to the art of programming that focuses on giving readers the tools to create sophisticated programs fast. It assumes no prior programming knowledge and explains the necessary concepts to get first-time programmers started. For more seasoned programmers, the advanced material appears in "Advanced Concept" sections. It is intended to motivate and introduce readers to the fun of programming. Everything is based on graphics, and specifically applets, which can be posted on the Internet. The text also explains how and where to put applets on the Internet. This edition is updated for Java 6.0.

■ Why Choose This Book?

- The examples are all graphical Java applets, which can be put directly onto the Internet.
- The book is updated based on Java 6, using the capabilities of Swing components.
- All material is based on the standard Java API (Application Programming Interface), enabling the reader to understand examples from other books and the Internet without relying on custom libraries specific to a particular book.
- The book explains the essentials but delves deeper in separate "Advanced Concept" sections. This approach enables readers to learn the more interesting things that can be done in applets, instead of worrying about memory structures and parameter-passing details (unless the course requires it).
- The examples are creative, giving readers a chance to think outside the box. For example, readers will learn how to create fonts, how to have an image as a backdrop with components on top, and how to create a slideshow by using buttons or an automated rotation. There are also many business-focused examples.
- Each chapter contains summaries and exercises to practice.
- Supplements are also available, including solutions and PowerPoint slides with fill-in-the-blanks. Instructors can receive the slides with blanks filled in. The fill-in-the-blank style has been more successful in gaining students' attention during lectures and helps them learn how to study for what is important.

This material has been used successfully for more than five years in a nonmajors course at Colorado State University, as well as several other universities. Students are able to produce sophisticated and creative projects by the end of the semester. For example, student projects include a "Where's Waldo™" game; football statistics and details for every team; "Stephanie's Closet," where users can rotate shirts and/or pants to select what to wear; word search; sound mixer; Jeopardy!® game; hangman; photo albums; a memory game; and much more. To see some examples of what students have produced recently, go to: http://www.cs.colostate.edu/~boese/JavaApplets/studentProjects.html.

▆ Object or Procedural?

Teaching objects-first versus procedural programming is currently a huge debate for introductory courses. This book follows a natural approach—procedural with emphasis on using methods and creating classes when necessary (e.g., extending the JPanel class to create a custom component). Classes are presented on an as-needed basis; for example, when we need to create our own custom font, we need a separate class. The advanced sections enable readers to go into the concepts in more detail, covering core curriculum requirements for CS1.

▆ Topics

Chapter 1 introduces the programming process, including information about the different programming languages and Java applets. Chapter 2 explains the basics of drawing shapes and text on the applet. This chapter also discusses how to incorporate images on the applet, including the different image formats that Java supports. In Chapter 3 we explore the basics of variables, how to declare those variables, and how to segment the code into methods.

Chapter 4 builds on the fundamentals of variables explored in Chapter 3 and introduces components such as labels, buttons, lists, and text boxes. The chapter discusses the purpose of each component, as well as how to create each item within an applet. This chapter leads into Chapter 5, which explores the different layout managers used to display components and also discusses design strategies and guidelines.

Chapter 6 revisits data types and variables in more detail and reviews mathematical operations—including those that differ from the operations of which you may already be aware. Chapter 7 explores conditional structures such as the if, if-else, and switch statements, discussing methods to determine which statement should be used in different circumstances.

Chapter 8 introduces events and method stubs, and Chapter 9 explains repetition statements (loops).

Chapter 10 details the use of classes and how to extend the JPanel class to create custom components that will enhance the program. Chapter 11 explores some additional useful components and enhancements on components, including five different types of borders, audio files, and pop-up windows. Chapter 12 discusses arrays, tables, and `ArrayList`. Chapter 13 looks at threads and timers for slideshows and animation, explaining how to run two or more items simultaneously. We will also discuss when and why threads are sometimes preferred over timers.

Chapter 14 revisits multiple classes and discusses inheritance, a way to broaden functionality of classes and re-use code. Basics of game programming are introduced in Chapter 15, with details about Breakout™ (a simple game similar to Pong™) and dungeon games (ranging from straightforward games such as Pac-Man™, to detailed games such as Doom™). Chapter 16 talks about Internet applications, including `JEditorPane`, hosting applets on the Internet, emailing, and reading/writing files on the server with CGI programs.

Chapter 17 concludes the text with a discussion about Java and compares it to other languages; explains what object-oriented is; and describes some additional third-party libraries, `Graphics2D`, and Jar files. The appendices have a section on debugging techniques and a listing of the Java API.

◼ AWT versus Swing

AWT (Abstract Windowing Toolkit) contains the original classes for creating graphics. Swing is a newer set of graphics that replace many of the old classes in the AWT package. Although we still use some classes from AWT (e.g., layout managers, `Graphics`), we should not mix and match AWT components with Swing components. For example, `TextFields` (instead of Swing `JTextFields`) placed on `JTabbedPanes` do not display properly. To those who have programmed with AWT components: by following this book, you will be problem-free.

◼ Instance Variables

Sometimes it is incorrect to initialize instance variables at the top of the program (e.g., Image with the call to `getImage`). However, it is necessary to declare variables as instance variables to access them in multiple methods throughout our programs. To minimize confusion, we take the approach that variables should be declared only at the top and initialized within a method. We follow this approach for all variables to avoid confusion. There is no harm in this approach, and readers may find it much easier to follow.

◼ Supplemental Materials

Supplements are available at: http://java.frogandthefly.com and www.jbpub.com/catalog/9780763754600, including PowerPoint lecture slides, solutions, and test items.

◼ Suggestions?

If you have suggestions on how to improve this book or features that you would like added in the next edition, please provide feedback at http://computerscience.jbpub.com/javaapplets.

■ Acknowledgments

Huge thanks go out to the students who helped with their creative ideas and suggestions, to the publishers for accepting this book, and to you for buying it!

Credit goes to Luke Scanlon of 5311 Studios for several images and photos used in the book. I took all other photos.

I would like to thank the following reviewers for their input and suggestions: Jianmin Ma, Oxford College, and James Comer, Texas Christian University. Thanks also to the editorial and production teams at Jones and Bartlett Publishers: Amy Rose, Production Director; Tim Anderson, Acquisitions Editor; Melissa Elmore, Associate Production Editor; and Melissa Potter, Editorial Assistant.

Elizabeth Sugar Boese

Introduction to Programming

"I think there is a world market for maybe five computers."
—Thomas Watson, chairman of IBM, 1943

OUTLINE

1.1 Why Learn to Program?

We have all learned the basics of computation, such as $2 + 2 = 4$. We have learned how to compute more complex mathematical expressions, such as $5 \times (3 + 7) / 2$. We have also learned how to describe a calculation, such as *the area is the width multiplied by the height*.

Learning how to program is learning how to solve problems. First we must figure out what the problem is and then design a solution, implement the solution, test it, and fix errors. This approach takes a lot of practice and patience. Sometimes we will get error messages that tell us explicitly what the problem is, and sometimes we will get no error messages at all—and it does not work! This process can be somewhat frustrating, but it can also be rewarding when we figure out the solution.

Programming helps us develop critical-thinking and problem-solving skills. By learning how to program, we learn how to formulate problems, think creatively about possible solutions, and express a solution clearly and accurately. Problem solving is important for all disciplines:

- Mathematics   - Using formal languages; calculating of formulae
- Engineering   - Designing and assembling components, evaluating
                         between solutions
- Natural science   - Observing behavior of humans/animals/plants/
                         weather
  - Forming hypotheses and testing
  - Analyzing results from experiments
- Art   - Manipulating digital images/videos/sounds/movies
- History   - Recording, storing, indexing, searching, analyzing, and
                         retrieving historical documents and information
- All fields   - Discovering something new
                       - Exploring data and analysis

1.2 Programming Languages

Computers cannot understand the complexity and ambiguity of the English language. Instead, we need to write a computer program in the computer's language. A **program** is a set of instructions for the computer to execute. Programs are written in a programming language. A **programming language** is a grammar to designate information and specify instructions that a computer understands. The grammar is also referred to as the **syntax**, the set of rules and structure to be followed. Similar to when one learns a new foreign language, the computer has a particular grammar

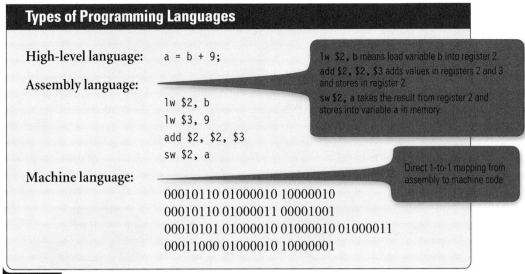

Types of Programming Languages

High-level language: a = b + 9;

Assembly language:

> lw $2, b means load variable b into register 2.
> add $2, $2, $3 adds values in registers 2 and 3
> and stores in register 2.
> sw $2, a takes the result from register 2 and
> stores into variable a in memory.

```
lw $2, b
lw $3, 9
add $2, $2, $3
sw $2, a
```

Machine language:

> Direct 1-to-1 mapping from
> assembly to machine code

```
00010110 01000010 10000010
00010110 01000011 00001001
00010101 01000010 01000010 01000011
00011000 01000010 10000001
```

FIGURE 1-1 Types of programming languages.

or syntax that must be followed to communicate properly. Programming languages are a lot less descriptive than English, but they do use English words.

There are three main types of languages that we are going to look at: machine, assembly, and high-level languages (see **FIGURE 1-1**). **Machine code** is the lowest level of programming languages; it is the only encoding that the computer understands—0s and 1s. Computers today store all information in a binary representation—as groups of 0s and 1s. Machine code differs for different machine types; for example, the machine code to add two values together will be different groups of 0s and 1s on an Intel system versus a SPARC station. **Assembly language** is a one-to-one mapping of the machine code to something more readable. For example, "lw $2, b" will load the value in a variable named b into register 2. **High-level language** allows us to simplify the program code with a higher level of abstraction than that of assembly code. An example of high-level code would be "x = y + 2;". Java is an example of a high-level language.

When we write in a high-level language, we still need to decompose it into machine code before the computer can execute its instructions. To do this, we take the **source code**, which is the program that we wrote, and run it through either a compiler or an interpreter. A **compiler** translates source code into a target language. Sometimes compilers translate source code into machine code, and sometimes they translate to another type of code. Programming languages such as C and C++ are run through compilers that translate the source code into machine code. This process is important because it means that the compiled C program can be executed only on machine types that it was compiled on. Other languages such as HTML and JavaScript are not compiled but rather interpreted. The source code for these programs is run through an interpreter. An **interpreter** translates the code into machine code and then executes the machine code.

1.3 How Java Works

Java source code (.java file)

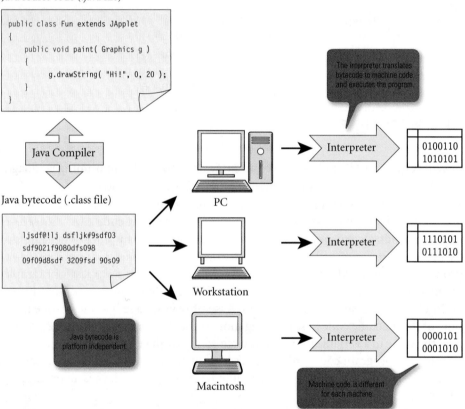

```
public class Fun extends JApplet
{
    public void paint( Graphics g )
    {
        g.drawString( "Hi!", 0, 20 );
    }
}
```

Java Compiler

Java bytecode (.class file)

```
ljsdf@!lj dsfljk#9sdf03
sdf9021f9080dfs098
09f09d8sdf 3209fsd 90s09
```

Java bytecode is platform independent.

PC

The interpreter translates bytecode to machine code and executes the program.

Interpreter → 0100110 1010101

Workstation

Interpreter → 1110101 0111010

Macintosh

Interpreter → 0000101 0001010

Machine code is different for each machine.

Java works a little differently from these other languages. Java source code is first compiled into **bytecode**. This bytecode can be distributed to any type of system: Macintosh, Windows, UNIX, etc. This bytecode is then run through an interpreter, the JVM (Java Virtual Machine), which translates the bytecode into machine code for the particular machine on which it will run. This is where the buzzword concepts "platform independent" and "write once, run anywhere" are derived.

These are two important catchphrases associated with Java: **platform independent** and **write once, run anywhere**. It is important to understand these phrases when talking about Java. Java is platform independent because the source code is compiled to bytecode, and it is the bytecode that can be used on any platform. This system works because each platform has an interpreter that can translate the bytecode to the machine code for that particular platform. So platform independence assumes the use of an interpreter, but the source code does not need to be recompiled on these machines. This concept leads to the phrase "write once, run anywhere." Java bytecode works on any platform. Other languages require the program to be modified so that it can be compiled for each platform.

The advantage of using interpreters is that we do not need a specific compiler for each machine; the code is platform independent, allowing it to be run on different machines. However, there are some disadvantages to using interpreters. Code is slower to execute—between 10 to 100 times slower than code compiled straight to machine code. Executing the code still requires an interpreter to be on the machine. Using interpreters also limits the abilities that can be programmed, because the code should be able to execute on all types of machines. Therefore, special machines such as those made by Silicon Graphics, Inc. (SGI), which are known for extra graphics abilities, are not able to exploit the graphic capabilities when programming in an interpreted language.

1.3.1 Where Did Java Come From?

Java was originally intended to make smart appliances, such as toasters and TVs. The idea was to create a small language that is easy to learn (unlike machine code) that could run on any kind of computer chip. This ability would enable a manufacturer of a smart appliance to upgrade the computer chip without having to rewrite the software to run it. However, Java never took off for electronic appliances, but it became a huge phenomenon with the advent of the World Wide Web.

1.3.2 The Internet and World Wide Web

A common misconception is that the World Wide Web (WWW) *is* the Internet, but in fact the Internet was around long before the WWW came into existence. In 1969, the U.S. Department of Defense connected four universities to form the first Internet. They wanted to make it easier to share information among researchers. By 1970, email was invented to communicate between people via computers on the Internet. In the 80s and early 90s, programs such as Gopher and WAIS were developed to navigate text files on the Internet.

The WWW came about in 1993 with the first web browsers that could display text and images from files on computers connected to the Internet. The WWW relies on the Hypertext Transfer Protocol (HTTP). A **protocol** is a set of rules, so HTTP is the set of rules governing how to handle web pages.

Web pages are identified by the **URL** (Uniform Resource Locator), which contains the protocol (e.g., http), the Internet address, and a path to the file. The Internet address usually starts with *www*. Part of the Internet address is the **domain name**, which can be bought and registered for a website. The domain name ends with a

top-level domain to identify its overall purpose and/or country of origin. For example, let us look at the following URL and dissect it:

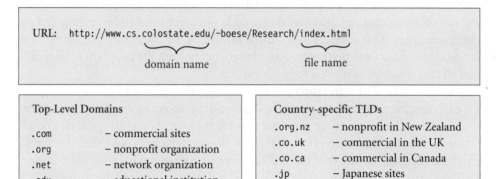

Web pages are intended to work on any computer platform, similar to Java programs. Java became an ideal language to adapt to the WWW as Java applets embedded within a web page.

1.4 Why Program in Java?

Java provides a programming tool for web pages because it has graphics capabilities, is machine independent (as described earlier), and is a relatively easy language to learn (compared with others). It can also be used to program over networks.

So why would we not use Java? Java is undergoing constant change, which requires learning and upgrading tools and software; the language is growing in size, adding complexity, and is slower to execute than languages such as C and C++.

Deciding the appropriate language for a program is based on many factors. Sometimes, for example, the decision is based on which languages the programmers already know, the efficiency and speed of a language, the graphics capabilities, and platform independence. For this course, we choose Java because it is still simpler than other languages, it has graphics capabilities, which makes it a bit more fun, and it allows us to create applets that we can put up on the Internet.

There are two different types of Java programs that we can create: applets and applications. Applets are Java programs embedded in a web page. Applications are stand-alone programs that can be run by themselves. In this course, we will be writing applets so that we can display them on the Internet. To create an applet, there are three different files that we will work with: the Java program (also called source code), which is what we will write; the bytecode, which is the output from the compiler; and the HTML file to display the applet. The source code is in a file with a **.java** file extension. The bytecode is in a file with a **.class** file extension. HTML files end with either an **.htm** or **.html** file extension.

1.5 The Java Applet

Java programs come in two forms: applications and applets. Applications run on their own, similar to Microsoft Word or the Netscape browser. Applets run inside a web page.

Our focus is on applets, so let us look at a simple example of an applet.

```java
import java.awt.*;
import javax.swing.*;
/** first program
 * @author  E.S.Boese
 * @version Fall 2007
 */
public class  MyFirstProgram  extends JApplet
{
    public void paint( Graphics g )
    {
        super.paint( g );
        g.drawString( "Hello World", 30, 20 );
    }
}
```

Let us break this program down into each part for discussion. There are four main parts in this program:

- Import statements
- Header comments
- `class` declaration
- `paint` method

1.5.1 Import Statements

There are two import statements at the top of the program:

```java
import  java.awt.*;
import  javax.swing.*;
```

Import statements allow us to reuse code that has already been written. There are classes that we can use so that we do not have to reinvent the wheel. There are many standard classes that come with every Java distribution, referred to as the Java API (application programming interface). For example, we want to create an applet and want the text to appear on the screen. Someone else has already written the code to draw things on the screen. We can use that class by referencing it: the `Graphics` class in our example. But when the compiler looks for this `Graphics.class` file, it needs to know where it is. We can tell the compiler where to look by specifying that it is in the `java.awt` **package**. The asterisk, or star (*), tells the compiler to look at all the classes in that package, because the package may contain many different classes. We could also be more specific and state exactly which class and package by using the following import statement:

```
import  java.awt.Graphics;
```

Both ways work, and neither is more efficient.

The second import statement tells the compiler to look for classes in the `javax.swing` package. This is where it will find the `JApplet` class. The `JApplet` class has the code to display our output within a web page.

Import statements need to go at the top of our program. This can be before or after comments and must be before the class declaration. The order of listing each one does not matter.

1.5.2 Header Comments

```
/** first program
 * @author  E.S.Boese
 * @version  Fall 2007
 */
```

The top of our program should always begin with a header comment. This comment area should include a description of the program, your name as the author, and the date that you created it. Comments are not executed as part of the program but are used as a documented record about the program for us humans to read. There is more information that we could provide here, but for now, we will keep it to these basics.

There are two types of comments in Java programs: **multiline comments** and **inline comments**. The preceding example used a multiline comment, designated with a slash-star (/*) to begin the comment and a star-slash (*/) to end the comment. Everything between the /* and */ is ignored when the program is executed. This format allows the comment to extend over multiple lines, as we see in this example.

Another type of comment is an inline comment, designated with two forward slashes (//). We will see this in our future examples. The // designates that the rest of the line (everything after the //) is to be ignored as a comment. The // can apply only to one line.

Technically, there is a third type of comment, which begins with a slash and two stars: /** and ends with the */. This form is used to designate **javadoc** comments, which can be used to easily create documentation as HTML web pages. This is what you see when you look online at the Java API code documentation. You can get this by running the command javadoc on your files.

■ 1.5.3 Class Declaration

```
public class MyFirstProgram extends JApplet
{


}
```

Each class that we create needs a class declaration. Here we define the name of the class. In our example, the name of the class is MyFirstProgram. This also means that the class is located in a file called MyFirstProgram.java. The class name and the file name must match—including uppercase and lowercase letters.

Because we are developing applets, we want to specify that our class is an applet. To do so, we say that our class extends the JApplet class. This way we *inherit* the functionality of an applet without rewriting the code to make an applet an applet.

We start out our class declaration with the word public to ensure that we can run the program directly. We are not going to go into much more depth about this at the moment.

> The name of the class must match the name of the file (with the .java extension). For example, a class named TradeTools must be in a file named TradeTools.java. Java is case sensitive, so the uppercase and lowercase letters must match.

> When we choose a name for our class, there are some rules about what types of characters we can use. We will explore this concept more in a later chapter, but for now you need to know that you cannot use spaces in the name of your class (and hence the name of your file).

■ 1.5.4 Paint Method

```
public void paint( Graphics g )
{
    super.paint( g );
    g.drawString ( "Hello World", 30, 20 );
}
```

> Each statement inside the method must end with a semicolon (;).

> Methods have open and close braces to define the beginning and ending of the method.

The paint method is where the meat of the program occurs. In our example, we want to draw the text for "Hello World" inside our applet. The Graphics class helps us accomplish this. We can call a **method** on the Graphics object. The method we call is the drawString method, which prints text. Each line inside the method (within the braces) ends with a semicolon. This convention is part of the Java syntax to designate the end of a statement and is required. If you leave off a semicolon, the compiler will complain to you with an error message.

To use the Graphics class, we have a **variable reference**: in our example, we used the name g. Now we can call *methods* on this object by calling g.<method>, where <method> is the name of a method such as drawString. When we call this method, we need to send it some **parameters**. Each parameter is separated with a comma. In our example, there are three parameters: "Hello World", 30, and 20. The first parameter, "Hello World", is the text that we want to print. The second parameter, 30, designates the *x* coordinate of where to draw the text, and the third parameter, 20, designates the *y* coordinate of where to draw the text.

The statement super.paint(g); forces the applet to first draw itself before doing our drawing code. This should be the first line in our paint method. The super keyword refers to our parent class, which because we extend the JApplet class is the JApplet class.

We will be talking more about methods, variables, and parameters in Chapter 3.

1.5.5 HTML File

The HTML file is essential for displaying applets—applets are intended to be embedded within web pages. This file needs to be in a separate file from our .java file with our source code. HTML files should also have an extension of .html. This book is not about writing HTML, so I will present only the essential HTML code to get an applet to display.

JavaClassName should match your class name inside your Java source code.

Width and height you want the applet.

You must have the end tag </APPLET>; otherwise, it will not show up!

```
<HTML>
  <BODY>
    <APPLET CODE=JavaClassName.class
          WIDTH = 400
          HEIGHT = 500 >
        </APPLET>
  </BODY>
</HTML>
```

> *Some IDEs such as Eclipse create the HTML file for us to run our applets. Therefore, while testing code within an IDE, we will not need to write our own HTML. However, once we want to put our applet up on the Internet, we will have to create an HTML file.*

1.5.6 Running an Example: Windows Machine

To set up our first applet, follow these steps on a computer running Windows.

    1. Open a command prompt.

       (Select Start → All Programs → Accessories → Command Prompt.)

2. We are going to use the basic editor Notepad to write our first program. If we want a program named `FirstProgram`, we need to add the .java extension to the file name, so we would type

   notepad FirstProgram.java

   > File names cannot have spaces.

3. Type in the following code, exactly how it appears:

```
/** First program with Java
   * @author: your name
   */
import java.awt.*;
import javax.swing.*;

public class FirstProgram extends JApplet
{
      String  text = "Cookie Monster";
      public void paint ( Graphics g )
      {
            super.paint( g );
            g.drawString ( text, 15, 20 );
      }
}
```

4. To save the file, make sure that Notepad does not add a .txt extension. Change the box that says "Save as Type:" to "All Files," and make sure that the file name includes the .java extension.

5. Close Notepad and return to the Command Prompt window.

6. Now we want to compile the program. The java compiler is called javac. Type

   javac FirstProgram.java

   If there are any syntax errors, they will be listed in the terminal window. If there are errors, we need to go back to Step 2 and correct the code until there are no errors when we compile the program.

7. When we run the source code through the compiler without errors, we get a bytecode file.

   If we get a listing of the directory, we should see the .class file listed:

   dir

   There should be the two files listed: `FirstProgram.java` and `FirstProgram.class`.

8. Now we need to create the HTML file to embed the applet. Using Notepad, open a new file named FirstProgram.html:

   notepad FirstProgram.html

9. Enter the following code exactly in this file:

```
<HTML>
<BODY>
   <APPLET  CODE="FirstProgram.class"  WIDTH=500   HEIGHT=400>
   </APPLET>
</BODY></HTML>
```

Java is case sensitive, so ensure that FirstProgram has a capital *F* and capital *P*, just as it is in the Java file.

10. Save this file as we did before, this time with the .html extension. Close Notepad.

11. To view the applet, we use the program named appletviewer:

appletviewer FirstProgram.html

A window should appear with "Cookie Monster" typed in it.

1.5.7 Running an Example: Linux and Macintosh Machines

To set up our first applet, perform the following steps on a Linux or Macintosh machine.

1. Open a terminal window.

2. We are going to use the basic editor pico to write our first program. If we want a program named FirstProgram, we need to add the .java extension, so we would type

pico FirstProgram.java

3. This editor is similar to Notepad on Windows. Type in the following code exactly how it appears:

```
/** First program with Java
  * @author: your name
  */
import java.awt.*;
import javax.swing.*;

public class FirstProgram extends JApplet
{
     String  text = "Cookie Monster";
     public void paint ( Graphics g )
     {
          super.paint( g );
          g.drawString ( text, 15, 20 );
     }
}
```

4. To save the file, hold down the control key (Ctrl) and press the letter o key.

5. To exit the pico environment, press Ctrl-x.

6. Now we want to compile the program. The java compiler is called **javac**. Type

```
javac FirstProgram.java
```

If there are any syntax errors, they will be listed in the terminal window. If there are errors, go back to Step 2 and correct the code until you get no errors when you compile the program.

7. When we run the source code through the compiler without errors, we get a bytecode file.

If we get a listing of the directory, we should see the .class file listed:

```
ls
```

(the lowercase letter *l* and the lowercase letter *s*)

There should be two files listed: `FirstProgram.java` and `FirstProgram.class`.

8. Now we need to create the HTML file to embed the applet. Using pico, open a new file named `FirstProgram.html`:

```
pico FirstProgram.html
```

9. Enter the following code exactly in this file:

```
<HTML>
<BODY>
  <APPLET  CODE="FirstProgram.class"   WIDTH=500   HEIGHT=400>
  </APPLET>
</BODY></HTML>
```

Java is case sensitive, so ensure that `FirstProgram` has a capital *F* and a capital *P*, just as it is in the java file.

10. Save this file as we did before.

11. To view the applet, we use the program named appletviewer:

appletviewer `FirstProgram.html`

A window should appear with "Cookie Monster" typed in it.

There are many other programs that we could use instead of Notepad or pico. For example, on Windows there are Crimson editor and EditPlus, and for Linux there are gedit and kwrite. An easier way to learn to program is to use a graphical IDE, such as Eclipse, BlueJ, and Gel.

If you get an error message "Command not found," then Java is not installed properly. Follow the instructions for the Java installation or download from java.sun.com.

Troubleshooting

Common errors:

Code will not compile.	Check spellings. The method header must be exact: `public void paint( Graphics g )`
	Be sure that there are semicolons after each import statement and after each statement within the method. Be sure that there is not a semicolon after `extends JApplet` nor after the method header: `public void paint( Graphics g )`.
	Make sure that the name of the class matches the name of the file, including uppercase and lowercase letters.
	Java is case sensitive, meaning that uppercase and lowercase letters are different. Make sure that your code matches that in the book.
Code compiles but I cannot see the text.	Make sure that the coordinates are within the region of the applet. When defining the *x* and *y* coordinates for drawing the string, if you use coordinates of (0,0) the text will appear just *above* the applet. Try (0,12) and you should see the text.
"Command not found" error when running javac or appletviewer	Java not installed properly. Follow the instructions for the Java installation or download Java from java.sun.com.

SUMMARY

- A **program** is a set of instructions for the computer to execute.
- The **syntax** is the grammar used by a programming language.
- A **programming language** is a grammar to designate information and instructions that a computer understands.
- **Machine code** is made up of 0s and 1s and is the only language that a computer understands. Programs in other languages need to be converted to machine language before a computer can execute it.
- **Assembly language** is a mapping of the machine code to something more readable, based on English words such as "load" and "add".
- **High-level language** allows us to simplify the program code with a higher level of abstraction than that of assembly code, such as "x = y + 2".
- **Source code** is the program that we write, usually in a high-level language such as Java.

- A **compiler** translates source code into a target language.
- An **interpreter** translates the code into machine code and then executes the machine code.
- When Java is compiled, the compiler creates an intermediate coding called **bytecode**.
- A programming language is considered to be **platform independent** if it can be interpreted/executed on different machine types (e.g., SunOS, MacOS, Linux, Windows) without changes.
- Applets are embedded within web pages. The .java file is the source code, the .class file is the bytecode, and the .html file (web page) specifies the .class file.
- Import statements are placed at the top of a program to designate the packages where other classes used by the program can be found.
- Header comments are listed at the beginning of a program to specify the author and date.
- Comments are not executed as part of the program and are used to explain things about the code. Comments either can begin with two forward slashes, //, to specify that the rest of one line is a comment, or can cross multiple lines by beginning with /* and ending with */.
- The class header starts all programs. This header needs to include

  ```
  public class nameOfProgram extends JApplet
  ```
- The `paint` method allows us to draw things on the applet.

EXERCISES

1. True or false? A Java compiler translates source code to machine code.
2. True or false? Java is an object-oriented language.
3. Java is considered to be **platform independent** because
   a. The source code can be compiled to machine code on any machine
   b. The bytecode can be interpreted on any machine
   c. The source code is the same independent of the machine that it is developed on
   d. The bytecode gets translated to source code on any machine
4. Approximately when did the Internet begin? The World Wide Web? Computers?
5. What is the difference between the Internet and the World Wide Web?
6. Why do we use the import statement?
7. True or false? Java source code gets compiled into a .class file, which is machine code.
8. True or false? Computers store all information by using decimal representation.

9. What is bytecode? How does it differ from machine code?

10. What is the definition of syntax?

11. How is the use of an IDE such as Eclipse useful for programming?

12. What is the difference between running Java programs versus C programs on different computer types? What more do we need to do with a C program?

13. What is a program?

14. What is an algorithm?

15. How do programs differ from algorithms?

16. There are three major programming language types: machine languages, assembly languages, and high-level languages. Give an example of each. How are they interrelated?

17. Match the following terms to their best-fitting definitions

    _____ Program   a. Grammar

    _____ Package   b. Data in context

    _____ Algorithm   c. Made up of 0s and 1s

    _____ Syntax   d. Steps to solve a problem

    _____ Machine language   e. What Java compiles to

    _____ Compiler   f. A mathematical computation

    _____ Byte code   g. Type of programming language

    _____ Assembly   h. Set of instructions for a computer

         i. Referenced using the import statement

         j. Process of viewing the source code

         k. Translates the source code into another code

18. True or false? Computers store all information by using binary representation.

19. True or false? Import statements can be listed anywhere in the program.

20. True or false? Comments are used by the interpreter to determine the instruction set.

21. What does it mean for a language to be portable? Define "platform independent" and what the Java motto "write once, run anywhere" means.

22. Explain the process of a Java program: source code, interpreter, compiler, bytecode, machine code. Draw a diagram.

23. If the name of our class is called CurrencyConverter, what is the name of the source code file? What is the name of the bytecode file?

24. What is the difference between inline comments and block comments?
25. What class do applets need to inherit from? What package is it in?
26. Put the following in numbered order of when they came into existence.

    _____ Java

    _____ WWW

    _____ Computers

    _____ Internet

27. Write a program that displays your name, the date, and a fun fact about yourself. Display each entry on a separate line.

If yes
before the
1 Sivan

Drawing Shapes and Text

2

Roses are #FF0000
Violets are #0000FF ...

2.1 Drawing Basics

We can draw things on an applet by writing a `paint` method. The `paint` method allows us access to a `Graphics` object, which is how we can specify what to draw and where to draw it. The `paint` method gets automatically called by the browser when it needs to draw the applet or redraw the screen if it has changed. An outline of a program with a `paint` method is listed in Example 2-1.

EXAMPLE 2-1

```
import   java.awt.*;          // access the Graphics object
import   javax.swing.*;       // access to JApplet

public class DrawEx extends JApplet
{
    public void paint( Graphics g )
    {
        super.paint( g );     // draw the applet
        // put your code here!
    }
}
```

The `Graphics` object allows us to call **methods** for drawing. We can draw circles, ellipses, squares, rectangles, and polygons, images, as well as write text.

2.2 Coordinate System

For all these drawing methods, we will need to specify where to draw by using an x and y coordinate system. The Java x–y coordinate system starts in the upper-left corner at (0,0). As we go right along the x axis, the x coordinate value goes up. As we go down along the y axis, the y coordinate value goes up. **FIGURE 2-1** shows the coordinate system.

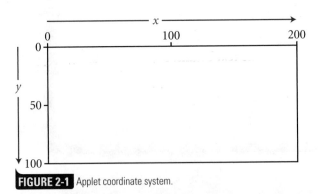

FIGURE 2-1 Applet coordinate system.

2.3 Drawing Text

We can draw text on an applet by using the drawString method inside our paint method. The drawString method requires the text and *x* and *y* coordinates to specify where the text should begin.

```
graphicsObj.drawString( String, x-coordinate, y-coordinate );
```

Example inside the paint method:

```
public void paint( Graphics grp )
{

        grp.drawString( "Some text to display", x, y );

}
```

> The name of the Graphics object must match: e.g., **grp**.

Our first example draws text in various locations in our applet. Notice what happens when we specify a location of (0,0) for our *x* and *y* coordinates, as shown in Example 2-2.

> Notice the "g" from "Worldling" hanging in view...

EXAMPLE 2-2

```
import java.awt.*; // access the Graphics object
import javax.swing.*;  // access to JApplet

public class Text1 extends JApplet
{
    public void paint( Graphics gr )
    {
        super.paint( gr );
        gr.drawString ( "Hello Worldling", 0, 0 );
        gr.drawString ( "Java rocks", 0, 50 );
        gr.drawString ( "Skiing is fun", 50, 50 );
        gr.drawString( "To be, or not 2 B", 50, 65 );
    }
}
```

The "Hello Worldling" is not visible in the applet because the *x* and *y* coordinates specify the bottom-left of where the text begins. So, if we are using 12-point font, our text begins at (0,0) and the top of our letters are at −12 in the *y* direction—not in the visible area for the applet! How would we fix this so that the text appears at the top of the applet?

Also notice how the text can be written on top of other text. If we do not want this overlap, it is up to us to place them such that they do not overlap. Example 2-3 shows where various coordinates display on the applet.

EXAMPLE 2-3

```java
import java.awt.*;
import javax.swing.*;
public class Coords extends JApplet
{
    public void paint( Graphics g )
    {
        super.paint( g );
        g.drawString( "(0,0)",        0,  0 );
        g.drawString( "(100,10)", 100, 10 );
        g.drawString( "(20,50)",   20, 50 );
        g.drawString( "(190,90)", 190, 90 );
    }
}
```

(0,0) bottom-left is at top of applet and text above it

Applet Viewer: Coords.class

Applet

(100,10)

(20,50)

(190,90)

Applet started.

To draw text beneath text we have already drawn, we keep the *x* value the same and increase the *y* value. The default font size is 12-pt, which means 12 pixels. Add 12 (or a little more for nice spacing between the two lines) to the *y* value and we will draw text beneath our other text.

2.3.1 Fonts

We can change the *font* of our text by specifying a particular font name, style, and size. The structure for creating a font is the following:

```java
Font fnt = new Font( type, style, size );
g.setFont( fnt );
```

or

Shortcut

```java
g.setFont( new Font( type, style, size ) );
```

Although we can try to reference some fancy fonts, they may not be available on other systems that run our applet. The main fonts that we can always depend on are "Serif", "SansSerif", "Monospaced", and "Dialog" (Dialog is the default font).

There are four styles that are available:

- Font.PLAIN
- Font.BOLD
- Font.ITALIC
- Font.BOLD + Font.ITALIC

This last style is a combination of both **bold** and *italic* to get ***boldItalic***.

A range of sizes are available, but regular text is usually either 10-pt or 12-pt font. Anything below size 8 is nearly impossible to read. So now we can create fonts, such as the following examples and Example 2-4:

```
Font small = new Font( "Serif", Font.PLAIN, 8 );
Font big = new Font( "SansSerif", Font.BOLD + Font.ITALIC, 36 );
```

To use these fonts, we can apply them to our components. So far, we have been working only with the `Graphics` component. To apply a particular font, we call the method `setFont` on the object.

EXAMPLE 2-4

```
import java.awt.*;
import javax.swing.*;

public class TextFonts extends JApplet
{
    public void paint ( Graphics g )
    {
        super.paint( g );
        g.drawString ("Hello World", 0, 10);
        Font small = new Font( "Serif", Font.PLAIN, 8 );
        g.setFont( small );
        g.drawString ("Java rocks", 0, 50 );
        g.drawString ( "Hiya", 60, 15 );
                    // font stays the same until we call setFont again
        Font big = new Font( "SansSerif", Font.BOLD + Font.ITALIC, 36 );
        g.setFont( big );
        g.drawString ( "Skiing is fun", 50, 50 );
    }
}
```

Example 2-5 shows the differences between the font types. Monospaced is similar to Courier—they are both *fixed-width* fonts. This means that each letter has the same amount of spacing; therefore, lowercase *i* has a lot of space on both sides. The others are all *variable-width* fonts, such that the letter *i* takes up only as much space as necessary. Variable-width fonts tend to be easier to read, but if we want to ensure the spacing then a fixed-width font may be desired.

EXAMPLE 2-5

```
import java.awt.*;
import javax.swing.*;
public class FontTypes extends JApplet
{
    public void paint ( Graphics g )
```

Example 2-5 (continued)

```
{
    super.paint( g );
    Font serf = new Font( "Serif", Font.PLAIN, 14 );
    g.setFont( serf );
    g.drawString ( "Serif", 10, 15 );
    g.setFont( new Font ("SansSerif", Font.PLAIN, 14) );
    g.drawString ( "Sans-Serif", 10, 30 );
    g.setFont( new Font ( "Dialog", Font.PLAIN, 14 ) );
    g.drawString ( "Dialog", 10, 45 );
    g.setFont( new Font ( "Monospaced", Font.PLAIN, 14 ) );
    g.drawString ( "Monospaced", 10, 60 );
}
}
```

[handwritten note: It goes before the g.drawString]

2.3.2 Color Basics

We can change the color when we draw shapes and text by creating `Color` objects. The simplest way to use colors is to reference one of the colors already created for Java programs. The following colors are available:

Color.BLACK	Color.BLUE	Color.CYAN	Color.DARK_GRAY
Color.GRAY	Color.GREEN	Color.LIGHT_GRAY	Color.MAGENTA
Color.ORANGE	Color.PINK	Color.RED	Color.WHITE
Color.YELLOW			

If we want to use a color, we call the method `setColor( color )` on the component for which we wish to change colors. Example 2-6 changes colors before each draw method.

EXAMPLE 2-6

```
import java.awt.*;
import javax.swing.*;
public class ColorEx extends JApplet
{
    public void paint ( Graphics g )
    {
        super.paint( g );
        g.setColor( Color.RED );
        g.drawString ( "Hello World", 0, 12 );
        g.setColor( Color.BLUE );
        g.drawString ( "Java rocks", 0, 50 );
        g.setColor( Color.CYAN );
        g.fillRect ( 50, 60, 40, 20 );
    }
}
```

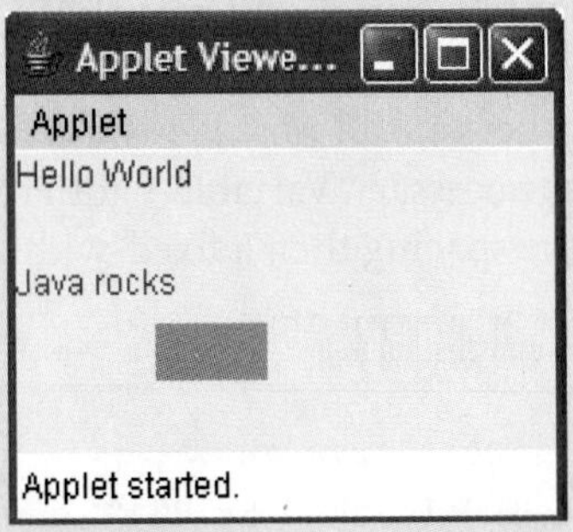

Applet Viewe...
Applet
Hello World

Java rocks

Applet started.

A good way to think about how this `setColor` method works is to imagine that we are using a marker. By default, we are holding onto a black marker, and anything that we are asked to draw we do with the black marker. As soon as we call `setColor` to change the color, for example to red, then we put down the black marker and now pick up the red marker. Now, anything that we are asked to draw will be in red until we call `setColor` to change to another color.

2.3.3 Custom Colors

We can also create custom colors. We do so by specifying how much red, green, and blue (RGB) that we want in our color.

```
Color mycolor = new Color( red, green, blue );
```

The maximum number for these values is 255, which means that we want a lot of that color. Therefore, we can analyze some colors as shown in the following. Example 2-7 shows how to call `setColor` to change the color used for drawing.

```
Color red = new Color( 255, 0, 0 );
Color gray = new Color( 128, 128, 128 );
Color yellow = new Color( 255, 255, 0 );
Color white = new Color( 255, 255, 255 );
Color black = new Color( 0, 0, 0 );
```

EXAMPLE 2-7

```
import java.awt.*;
import javax.swing.*;
public class ColorEx2 extends JApplet
{
    public void paint ( Graphics g )
    {
        g.setColor( new Color( 130, 130, 80 ) );
        g.drawString ( "Hello World", 0, 12 );
        g.setColor( new Color( 128, 0, 128 ) );
        g.drawString ( "Java rocks", 0, 50 );
        g.drawString ( "Rockin' to the music", 10, 70 );
    }
}
```

Applet ...

Applet
Hello World

Java rocks
  Rockin' to the music

Applet started.

The color stays the same until setColor is called again.

There are several ways to figure out the RGB combination for the color that we want. We could do the trial-and-error method of trying different values until we figure it out. An easier way would be to look for a color wheel on the Internet with the RGB values given. We can also use any graphics program such as Microsoft® Paint to tell us.

In MS Paint, select "Colors," then "Edit Colors...," and then click on the button "Define Custom Colors...." A dialog box appears, as depicted in **FIGURE 2-2**, that

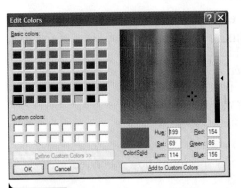

RGB values as displayed inside MS Paint

FIGURE 2-2 Microsoft Paint color dialog box.

displays a whole spectrum of colors. When we click on a color, it shows us the RGB values in the lower right-hand corner of the dialog box.

2.4 Drawing Shapes

2.4.1 Lines

We use the coordinate system to specify the x and y coordinates of where our line should start and the x and y coordinates for where the line should end. Because we are drawing on the applet, we need to reference our Graphics variable again.

The specification for the drawLine method follows:

```
drawLine( x, y,  x2, y2 )
```

Example 2-8 draws a diagonal line from the upper-left corner (0,0) to (50,50).

EXAMPLE 2-8

```
import java.awt.*;      // access the Graphics object
import javax.swing.*;   // access to JApplet
public class LineDiagonal extends JApplet
{
    public void paint( Graphics g )
    {
        super.paint( g );
        g.drawLine( 0, 0, 50, 50 );
    }
}
```

To draw a horizontal line, the y values need to stay the same:

```
g.drawLine( 10, 40, 70, 40 ); // draws horizontal line 40 pixels down
g.drawLine( 30, 10, 50, 10 ); // draws horizontal line 10 pixels down
```

To draw a vertical line, the *x* values need to stay the same:

```
g.drawLine( 40, 10, 40, 30 );   // draws vertical line 40 pixels right
g.drawLine( 30, 10, 30, 50 );   // draws vertical line 30 pixels right
```

Experiment with different values to see what type of lines you can draw. Remember that we can draw lines on top of other lines, shapes, or text.

2.4.2 Ovals and Circles

Let us start off by drawing an oval/ellipse. Ellipses are created using the method drawOval.

We need to send some parameters to the method to designate where we want our ellipse drawn, as well as the width and height. Again, we will need to call our methods on the Graphics variable. The specification for the drawOval method follows:

```
drawOval( x, y, width, height )
```

The *x* and *y* coordinates specify the location of the upper-left corner of the ellipse, not the middle of the ellipse. If we place our ellipse in the top-left corner of the applet, we could use an *x* and *y* coordinate of zero. Let us make a really wide oval with a width of 100 and a height of 10. Example 2-9 creates this wide oval.

EXAMPLE 2-9

```
import java.awt.*;      // access the Graphics object
import javax.swing.*;   // access to JApplet
public class Ellipse extends JApplet
{
        public void paint( Graphics g )
        {
                super.paint( g );
                g.drawOval( 0, 0, 100, 10 );
        }
}
```

Now, if we wanted to draw a circle, how would we change the preceding code? There is no method called drawCircle, so we have to use the drawOval method. But that is okay, because we know that circles are ovals with the same width and height. Modify the preceding program to make it draw a circle.

2.4.3 Rectangles and Squares

Similarly, we can draw rectangles and squares. The method we use is called drawRect, and we specify the *x* and *y* coordinates for the upper-left corner of the rectangle as well as a width and height to specify the dimensions.

```
drawRect ( x, y, width, height )
```

Just as for the circle, we can draw a square by specifying a rectangle with the same width and height. Example 2-10 demonstrates how to create a square.

EXAMPLE 2-10

```
import java.awt.*;       // access the Graphics object
import javax.swing.*;    // access to JApplet

public class Square extends JApplet
{
    public void paint ( Graphics g )
    {
        super.paint( g );
        g.drawRect ( 0, 0, 20, 20 );
    }
}
```

We can also draw a rounded rectangle by calling the drawRoundRect method.

2.4.4 Filling Shapes

Sometimes we want our shapes to be filled in with color. It is easy to fill in our shapes by simply changing the method call from draw to fill. *Note: This approach does not work on lines.*

For example, instead of drawRect we can call fillRect. The rest of the code is the same.

Examples:

```
g.drawRect( 0, 0, 20, 20 );     →   g.fillRect( 0, 0, 20, 20 );
g.drawOval( 0, 0, 100, 10 );    →   g.fillOval( 0, 0, 100, 10 );
```

We can draw multiple objects on the same applet by making multiple calls to these methods.

In Example 2-11, we change the location of each shape that we draw.

EXAMPLE 2-11

```
import java.awt.*;       // access the Graphics object
import javax.swing.*;    // access to JApplet

public class Shapes extends JApplet
{
    public void paint ( Graphics g )
    {
        super.paint( g );
        g.setColor( Color.GREEN );
```

```
        g.fillOval( 0, 0, 100, 10 );
        g.setColor( Color.BLUE );
        g.drawRect( 0, 0, 20, 20 );
        g.drawRect( 10, 10, 20, 20 );
        g.drawRect( 20, 20, 20, 20 );
        g.drawOval( 30, 30, 20, 20 );
    }
}
```

■ 2.4.5 Arcs

Arcs are a bit more difficult to get our heads around. When drawing an arc, we still need to specify the x and y coordinates as well as a width and a height. We also need to specify the starting angle and arching angle of the arc. The starting angle is based from the center of our x–y coordinates and width/height dimensions, with the angle of zero extending horizontally to the right. See **FIGURE 2-3** for examples of starting angles.

Then we also define the angle for the arc. **FIGURE 2-4** depicts different arc angles.

The code to create an arc is as follows:

```
drawArc( x, y, width, height, startingAngle, archingAngle )
```

Or, to create an arc that is filled in:

```
fillArc( x, y, width, height, startingAngle, archingAngle )
```

The width and height are based on the concept that an arc of a 360° angle is a full oval, like the ones we draw with drawOval. Example 2-12 demonstrates the use of the fillArc method by drawing a pie chart.

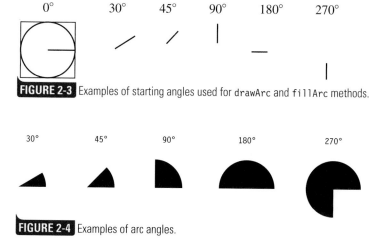

0°   30°   45°   90°   180°   270°

FIGURE 2-3 Examples of starting angles used for drawArc and fillArc methods.

30°   45°   90°   180°   270°

FIGURE 2-4 Examples of arc angles.

EXAMPLE 2-12

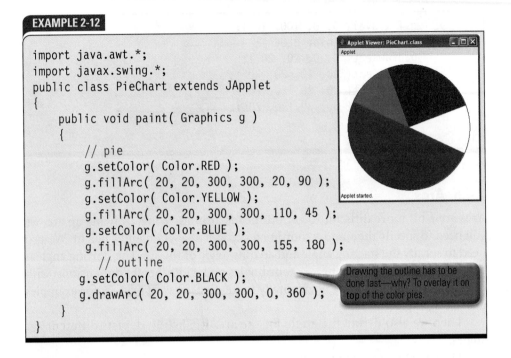

```java
import java.awt.*;
import javax.swing.*;
public class PieChart extends JApplet
{
    public void paint( Graphics g )
    {
        // pie
        g.setColor( Color.RED );
        g.fillArc( 20, 20, 300, 300, 20, 90 );
        g.setColor( Color.YELLOW );
        g.fillArc( 20, 20, 300, 300, 110, 45 );
        g.setColor( Color.BLUE );
        g.fillArc( 20, 20, 300, 300, 155, 180 );
            // outline
        g.setColor( Color.BLACK );
        g.drawArc( 20, 20, 300, 300, 0, 360 );
    }
}
```

Drawing the outline has to be done last—why? To overlay it on top of the color pies.

2.4.6 Polygons

Polygons can include any number of points. To create a polygon, first we declare and instantiate a Polygon object:

```java
Polygon  poly;
poly = new Polygon( );
```

Now we can add as many points as we want to our polygon. The order in which we add points to the polygon is important—think of it like playing connect the dots. The polygon will be created by drawing lines from one point to the next. We add points to the polygon by calling the addPoint method,

```java
poly.addPoint( x, y );
```

where x and y are our *x* and *y* coordinates for the point. When we are ready to draw a polygon, we can use either the draw or fill method from the Graphics class:

```java
drawPolygon( poly )
fillPolygon( poly )
```

Examples 2-13 and 2-14 show the same points in the polygon, but in different order.

EXAMPLE 2-13

```java
import java.awt.*;
import javax.swing.*;

public class Poly1 extends JApplet
{
  public void paint( Graphics g )
  {
    super.paint( g );
    Polygon pg = new Polygon( );
    pg.addPoint( 10, 10 );
    pg.addPoint( 50, 10 );
    pg.addPoint( 70, 80 );
    pg.addPoint( 50, 100 );
    pg.addPoint( 10, 30 );
    g.drawPolygon( pg );
  }
}
```

EXAMPLE 2-14

```java
import java.awt.*;
import javax.swing.*;

public class Poly2 extends JApplet
{
  public void paint( Graphics g )
  {
    super.paint( g );
    Polygon pg = new Polygon( );
    pg.addPoint( 10, 10 );
    pg.addPoint( 50, 100 );
    pg.addPoint( 10, 30 );
    pg.addPoint( 50, 10 );
    pg.addPoint( 70, 80 );
    g.drawPolygon( pg );
  }
}
```

2.5 Images

Images can be painted onto our applet with a call to the drawImage method, but first we need to load the image into the applet. To load the image, we call the method getImage and specify the location of where we are running the applet, which is obtained through a call to getCodeBase( ) and then the name of the image file. The name of the file should be a String variable or list the actual name of the file inside double quotes (e.g., "Lion.jpg").

```
Image  imageVariable  =  getImage( getCodeBase( ), filename );
```

To draw the image onto our applet, we call drawImage, specifying the image variable from the preceding code, the x and y coordinates of (0,0) (top-left corner) for where to draw it, and the keyword this.

```
drawImage( imageVariable, 0, 0, this )
```

Example 2-15 displays an image in an applet.

EXAMPLE 2-15

```
import java.awt.*;
import javax.swing.*;
public class ImageEx extends JApplet
{
  public void paint( Graphics g )
  {
    super.paint( g );
    Image  img = getImage( getCodeBase( ), "Lion.jpg" );
    g.drawImage( img, 0, 0, this );
  }
}
```

img is the variable that we declared in the previous line.

To scale the image to a different size, we call the method drawImage and send it additional information. This extra information includes the coordinates for where to draw the image (xd1, yd1); the coordinates of the bottom-right corner of where we want to draw the image (xd2, yd2), which defines the size to stretch the image; the coordinates of the top-left corner of the actual image where we want to start (xs1, ys1); and the coordinates of the bottom-right corner of the actual image (xs2, ys2). The coordinates on the source image allow us to crop the image. If we want the full source image, then we can use coordinates (0,0) for (xs1, ys2) and the width and height for (xs2, ys2) (shown in Example 2-16).

```
g.drawImage( imageVariable, xd1, yd1, xd2, yd2, xs1, ys1, xs2, ys2, this );
```

EXAMPLE 2-16

```
import java.awt.*;
import javax.swing.*;
public class ImageEx2 extends JApplet
{
    public void paint( Graphics g )
    {
        super.paint( g );
        Image  img = getImage( getCodeBase( ), "Lion.jpg" );
        g.drawImage( img, 0, 0, 500, 500, 0, 10, 1200, 1200, this );
    }
}
```

Now we can draw a picture of a photo and then call our drawing methods to draw on top of it. For example, in Example 2-17 we added some callouts to a photo that I took while dining in China.

EXAMPLE 2-17

```
import java.awt.*;
import javax.swing.*;
public class DrawOnImage extends JApplet
{
    public void paint( Graphics g )
    {
        super.paint( g );
        Image breakfast = getImage( getCodeBase( ), "China_Foods.jpg" );
        g.drawImage( breakfast, 0,0, this );
        Font bold16font = new Font( "Serif", Font.BOLD, 16 );  //text font
        g.setFont( bold16font );
        g.setColor( Color.green );          // eggs
        g.drawOval( 21, 180, 40, 40 );
        g.drawOval( 22, 181, 38, 38 );      // thicken the drawing
        g.drawLine( 42, 180, 50, 95 );      // line from eggs
        g.drawString( "Eggs for breakfast", 50, 95 );   // pointing to eggs
        g.setColor( Color.cyan );           // noodles
        g.drawOval( 35, 245, 90, 75 );
        g.drawLine( 120, 255, 190, 240 );
        g.drawString( "Noodles for every meal", 190, 245 );
```

(continues)

Example 2–17 (continued)

```
        g.setColor( Color.YELLOW );            // sauces
        g.drawRect( 70, 180, 90, 40 );
        g.drawLine( 115, 180, 130, 145 );
        g.drawString( "Amazing sauces", 130, 140 );
    }
}
```

■ 2.5.1 Image Types

A picture says a thousand words.
How much is that in pixels?

Creating for the Web requires the use of images, and creating Java applets is no exception. Images are an important part of portraying ideas and presenting our website. We can do a lot with image processing software, and we will cover some of the necessary basics. We can also do a lot of image processing by programming Java code, but it adds complexity that is unnecessary when it is easier to use an image processing software package like Microsoft® Paint, GIMP, Corel® Paint Shop Pro®, or Adobe® Photoshop®.

Java supports three major formats for images: .jpg, .gif, and .png.

.jpg JPEG stands for Joint Photographic Experts Group and has a file extension of either .jpg or .jpeg (both work the same way). It supports 24-bit colors, which is 2^{24} colors. JPG format is best for pictures of naturalistic artwork and photographs. This format does not work so well on lettering, simple cartoons, and black-and-white line drawings. JPG uses a compression algorithm to save the file as a smaller size, but this compression can cause a loss of detail.

.gif GIF stands for Graphics Interchange Format and is a proprietary image-encoding format. GIF supports only 8-bit colors, which amounts to only 256 colors. Therefore, this format is not optimal for photographs or realistic artwork. It does work well on lettering and simple sketches, but most importantly, it also supports transparency and animation. Transparency allows part of the image to be clear, such that the background shows through parts of the image. We can create transparent images in sophisticated programs such as GIMP, Paint Shop Pro®, and Photoshop®, as well as online sites such as http://stuff.mit.edu/tweb/map.html. For animation, the specific format is GIF89a, and it can also support interlacing. Animated images can be created through some graphics programs and other downloadable software.

.png PNG stands for Portable Network Graphics. PNG was created as a free compression algorithm once GIF became patented. It has better compression than .gif, usually resulting in smaller file sizes, and this format supports millions of colors. It also supports transparency but not animation.

2.5.2 Why Do We Care about the File Type?

There are several reasons why we should choose different file formats for different image types. As we discussed, some formats support transparency and animation, whereas others do not. Some can handle millions of colors, whereas others are restricted in the number of colors. Some of the compression algorithms can reduce the size of the file drastically, which can increase the loading speed of the image as well as decrease the amount of space required to store the image on the web server.

2.5.3 Changing the File Size

When we get images back from digital cameras or photo CDs, the images often are huge and fill our screens. The standard resolution for camera images is 1600 × 1200 pixels—which is usually bigger than the resolution of our screens (standard computer screen resolution is 1280 × 1024). This size is too big to display on the Internet. The best way to shrink the size of the photo, which also shrinks the size of the file, is to do so inside an image processing program.

To see the size of our image in Microsoft's Paint program, open our image and click on "Image" and then on "Attributes."

We should see a dialog box similar to the one shown in **FIGURE 2-5**. 640 × 400 pixels is probably the biggest size that we would want, or even smaller.

To resize an image in MS Paint, click on "Image" and then on "Stretch/Skew...."

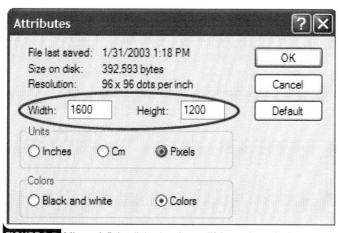

FIGURE 2-5 Microsoft Paint dialog box for modifying an image's size.

Change the "Stretch" only, and keep the percentage for width and height the same (this keeps the image proportionally correct). For a 1600 × 1200 photo, go to either 30% or 20%.

In our software programs, we sometimes see different terms such as dpi and ppi. DPI stands for "dots per inch" and is used for printing purposes. PPI stands for "pixels per inch" and is referenced for screen display.

2.5.4 Image Orientation

Some photos from digital cameras appear sideways on our computer. We can rotate them in any image processing program. For example, in MS Paint, click on "Image" and then select "Flip/Rotate...." In the dialog that appears (**FIGURE 2-6**), select "Rotate by angle...." Then select either "90" to rotate right or "270" to rotate left.

2.5.5 Pixels

We have been talking about pixels a lot—what exactly is a pixel? The easiest way to understand pixels is to see one up close. If we take an image and zoom in on it, we will see each pixel as a rectangle of one color. For example, if we zoom in on the image from **FIGURE 2-7**, we can see the individual pixels in the image in **FIGURE 2-8**.

You can do this yourself in any paint program. We can see that each pixel is one solid color. The more pixels that we use to display an image, the better the quality—because the pixel rectangles take up less space in the image.

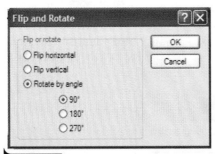

FIGURE 2-6 Microsoft Paint dialog box for rotating an image.

FIGURE 2-7 Original size of a photo versus zooming in (Figure 2-8), where individual pixels can be seen.

FIGURE 2-8 Zoomed-in image of Figure 2-7 that shows individual pixels.

This concept also explains why our drawings are ragged—we are seeing the rectangular pixels attempting to form curves. Anti-aliasing helps dither the colors between the curve color and the surrounding colors.

2.5.6 Anti-Aliasing

When we write text and draw on our applet, you might notice that the drawing is rather ragged and not smooth. We can fix this by turning on anti-aliasing when we are drawing. To see the difference with anti-aliasing, look at the two spaceship graphics in **FIGURE 2-9** and **FIGURE 2-10**.

To achieve anti-aliasing, we need to work with a Graphics2D object instead of a plain Graphics object. We do this by *casting* our Graphics object to Graphics2D:

```
public void paint( Graphics grph )
{
        Graphics2D  g2d = ( Graphics2D )grph;
}
```

Now we want to tell the program to turn anti-aliasing on,

```
g2d.setRenderingHint( RenderingHints.KEY_ANTIALIASING,
        RenderingHints.VALUE_ANTIALIAS_ON );
```

and then continue to add our drawing code, using the g2d variable that we defined.

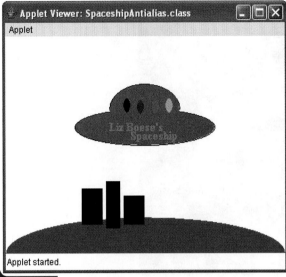

FIGURE 2-9 Drawing without anti-aliasing.

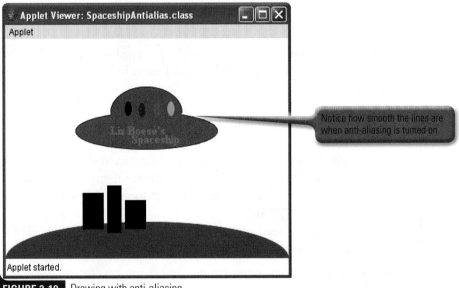

FIGURE 2-10 Drawing with anti-aliasing.

2.5.7 Image Transparency

There are different ways to make our images transparent. Transparent images must be saved as either .gif or .png. If you are familiar with a paint program, you can make your images transparent by using it (MS Paint does not do transparency).

One easy way to make images transparent is to use an online program. The only caveat is that you must have your image uploaded and available on the Internet.

You can read about this in Chapter 16 if you are not familiar with setting it up. One website that I have used throughout the years is at http://stuff.mit.edu/tweb/map .html, or you may try searching on the Internet. If you find an image that you want to use on the Internet, copy the URL of the image and feed it to the online website. If you have your own image that you want to make transparent, either use a graphics program or upload the image to a website, where it has a URL to access it.

2.6 Putting It Together

Table 2-1 summarizes the types of drawing that we can do on our Graphics object.

Table 2-1
Common Methods Used on Graphics Objects

Shape	Code
Lines	`drawLine( x, y, x2, y2 )`
Rectangles	`drawRect( x, y, width, height )`
	`fillRect( x, y, width, height )`
	`clearRect( x, y, width, height )`
Rounded rectangles	`drawRoundRect( x, y, width, height, arcWidth, arcHeight )`
	`fillRoundRect( x, y, width, height, arcWidth, arcHeight )`
3-D raised or lowered rectangles	Raised: `draw3DRect( x, y, width, height, true )`
	Lowered: `draw3DRect( x, y, width, height, false )`
	Raised: `fill3DRect( x, y, width, height, true )`
	Lowered: `fill3DRect( x, y, width, height, false )`
Ovals	`drawOval( x, y, width, height )`
	`fillOval( x, y, width, height )`
Arcs	`drawArc( x, y, width, height, startAngle, arcAngle )`
	`fillArc( x, y, width, height, startAngle, arcAngle )`
Polygons	`drawPolygon( Polygon )`
	`fillPolygon( Polygon )`
Images	`drawImage( Image, x, y, this )`
	`drawImage( Image, xd1, yd1, xd2, yd2, xs1, ys1, xs2, ys2, this)`

FIGURE 2-11 depicts a grid view of the Java coordinate system. Each point along the *x*-axis (horizontal) and *y*-axis (vertical) is labeled at 10-pixel increments. To draw the rectangle, we specify the *x* and *y* coordinates of where it begins (10, 20) and

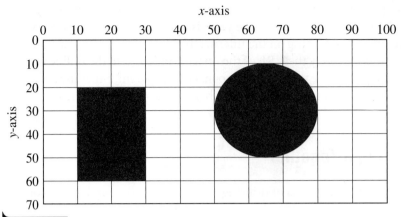

FIGURE 2-11 Grid overlay example of drawing on the applet coordinate system.

then specify the width of 20 pixels and height of 40 pixels. The red rectangle can be drawn using the fill method fillRect as follows:

```
g.setColor( Color.RED );
g.fillRect ( 10, 20, 20, 40 );   // x, y, width, height
```

The blue circle is drawn similarly, with the *x* coordinate as the top-left corner of where we want to begin the circle (50) and the *y* coordinate at the top-left corner as well (10). The width of the circle is 30 pixels, and the height is 40 pixels.

```
g.setColor( Color.BLUE );
g.fillOval( 50, 10, 30, 40 );   // x, y, width, height
```

We can create our own coordinated shapes by drawing two or more shapes on top of each other in the same color. When displayed, it appears as if it is one shape. Example 2-18 illustrates this.

EXAMPLE 2-18

```
import java.awt.*;
import javax.swing.*;
public class Overlap extends JApplet
{
      public void paint ( Graphics g )
      {
            super.paint( g );
            g.setColor( Color.BLUE );
            g.fillOval( 10, 10, 50, 50 );
            g.fillRect( 50, 10, 50, 50 );
      }
}
```

Troubleshooting

Common errors:

Polygon looks weird.	Remember that the order in which you add your points to the polygon will dictate how the connect-the-dots are connected and therefore what the polygon will look like.
Transparency will not work.	Only .png and .gif support transparency (and .png is not always supported in older versions of Windows). Make sure that the extension on your image file is not .jpg.
Image is too big.	Use a graphics program to shrink your image.
Drawing on top of the image does not appear.	Be sure that the order in which you draw things is correct. Remember that drawing is sequential and that the later things you draw will be drawn on top of things you have already drawn. Therefore, if you are drawing on top of an image, make sure that you draw the image *first* before you start drawing things on top of it.
Anti-aliasing is not working.	Make sure that you are using the new variable name that you declared for all subsequent drawing method calls. If you are still using the variable name from the method header for the Graphics object, then the anti-aliasing is not applied.
I left off the super.paint(g) and my program still works. Do I need it?	Most applets will work just fine without the call to super.paint. However, this is good practice because it will sometimes help to ensure that the applet is drawn correctly.

SUMMARY

- The coordinate system starts in the upper-left corner with $(0, 0)$.
- Drawing shapes is accomplished by calling methods on the Graphics object inside the paint method.
- Lines are drawn using drawLine: drawLine(x, y, x2, y2).
- Horizontal lines are drawn with two different x values and the y values unchanged.
- Vertical lines are drawn with the x values unchanged and different y values.
- Circles and ellipses are drawn using drawOval: drawOval(x, y, width, height) or colored in using fillOval.
- Circles have the same value for the width and height of the oval.
- Rectangles and squares are drawn using drawRect: drawRect(x, y, width, height) or colored in using fillRect.
- Squares have the same value for both the width and height of the rectangle.

- Arcs are drawn using drawArc: drawArc(x, y, width, height, startAngle, arcAngle) or colored in using fillArc.
- Polygons are drawn by creating a Polygon object, adding points to the Polygon object with addPoint, and then drawn by calling drawPolygon or fillPolygon on the Graphics object.
- Draw/fill methods on the Graphics object are drawn in order of the program, where subsequent drawings are drawn on top of the previously drawn ones.
- Colors can be set by calling the method setColor on the Graphics object: setColor(Color).
- There is a set of colors that can be referenced as Color.name (e.g., Color.RED).
- Custom colors can be created by specifying the amount of red, green, and blue: Color newColor = new Color(red, green, blue);.
- Text can be drawn by calling drawString on the Graphics object: drawString(string, x, y).
- Fonts are created by specifying the type (e.g., "Serif"), style (e.g., Font.BOLD or Font.PLAIN), and the size in pixels: Font fnt = new Font("Serif", Font.PLAIN, 12);.
- Font of bold and italic can be specified with a style of Font.BOLD + Font.ITALIC.
- Set the font for drawing by calling the setFont method on the Graphics object.
- Java supports three main image formats: .jpg, .gif, and .png.
- .jpg is a good image format for photographs and naturalistic artwork.
- .gif is used for simple line/cartoon drawings, animation, and transparency.
- .png is good for both photographs and simple drawings, and it can handle transparency.
- Image file size is important to minimize the download time of the applet.
- Pixels are individual rectangular regions of the screen that display one color.
- The more pixels used to represent an image, the better the quality.
- Anti-aliasing helps smooth out curves.
- To use anti-aliasing, we need to use the Graphics2D class.
- PPI stands for pixels per inch and is referenced for screen viewing.
- DPI stands for dots per inch and is referenced for printing.

EXERCISES

1. In a window that is 100 × 100 pixels, position (95, 95) is nearest to which corner?

2. If we draw a rectangle with the same value for width and height, what did we draw?

   a. Parallelogram   b. Square
   c. Rounded square   d. Rounded rectangle
   e. Polygon   f. Hexagon

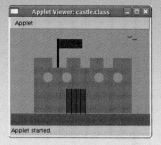

3. What two steps are necessary to paint an image?

4. True or false? The paint method is called automatically by the browser whenever it needs to redraw the screen.

5. How do we create a new font that is both bold and italic?

6. In what package is the `Graphics` object?

7. True or false? To draw a circle, call the method `drawCirc` and send the (x, y) coordinates and the radius of the circle.

8. Take the `"Hello World"` example and center the text.

9. Draw a car. Draw a house. Draw a self-portrait. Draw Pac-Man™. Draw a spaceship.

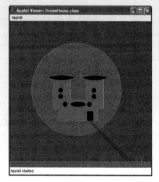

10. Draw a smiley face or a pirate face. Draw a farm house with animals.

11. Draw a bar graph (histogram). Draw different chart types on the same data values.

12. Write out a multiline blog. If you are unsure what a blog is, use a search engine to find the term.

13. True or false? We can create colors by specifying the amount of red, blue, and yellow.

14. In the arc example, what would happen if we drew the outline before filling in each pie section?

15. What colors do the following statements produce?

    ```
    Color mycolor = new Color( 255, 0, 255 );
    Color mycolor = new Color( 0, 0, 255 );
    Color mycolor = new Color( 128, 128, 128 );
    ```

16. Write a program that displays a photo of yourself and display your name in large text on top of the image.

17. Write a program that is your own personal logo. Use several shapes, both filled and outlined, in your design.

18. Correct the errors in the following program (best to rewrite it). There are about 15 errors. Find as many as you can.

```
//    ******************************
My First Applet – I'm so proud!   ***/
Import java.swing;

Public class MyfirstApplet
{
    private void paint ( graphics theGraphics );
    {
    graphics.drawstring( 'chocolate', 20 )
}
```

19. Which image format(s) is best for photographs?
20. Which image format(s) supports animated images?
21. Which image format(s) supports transparency?
22. Why do we care what type of image a file is saved as?
23. What are two ways to decrease the size of an image?
24. Which three major image formats does the Web fully support?
25. True or false? ppi is used for printing, dpi is used for screen display.
26. True or false? We cannot change the size of an image within the Java code.
27. True or false? Anti-aliasing makes the text in an image appear smoother.
28. True or false? Images with transparency can be saved as .jpg.
29. What is the purpose of using anti-aliasing on images?
30. Does anti-aliasing work on text?
31. True or false? Photographs are best saved as .gif.
32. Find a simple image (not a photograph) and make one of the colors transparent. Draw it on an applet in two areas with different backgrounds.

Variables and Methods

3

Variables vary ...
after all, change is the status quo.

3.1 Variables

A variable is a name for a spot in memory. We can store values in memory by referencing a variable name. But first we need to *declare* the variable.

■ 3.1.1 Declaration

We declare a variable by specifying a **data type** and **variable name**. We have already used a variable when we referenced a `Graphics` object.

```
Graphics g
```

`Graphics` is the data type and `g` is our variable name.

There are other data types that we can use in our programs. There are eight **primitive data types** in Java:

Integers: `byte, short, int, long`

Real values: `float, double`

Boolean: `boolean`

Characters: `char`

These data types are considered to be **primitive** because these are the only things that are *not* objects. Primitive data types can keep track of only one value, whereas an object can keep track of many things.

Integers are whole numbers that could be negative, positive, or 0. We cannot use commas when declaring our numbers. Examples of integers: -528, 0, 12973, -2. Although there are four data types for integers, we usually work with the `int` data type.

Real values are floating-point numbers that are either negative or positive. Real number examples: -41.238, 0, 12.34447, 9.234e102. Although there are two data types for real values, we usually work with the `double` data type.

Boolean values can contain only one of two values: either `true` or `false`. When we assign either `true` or `false`, we do *not* put the value in quotes. `true` and `false` are *reserved words* in Java, which means that they have special meaning in the Java syntax.

Characters are represented inside single quotes. We can store only one character inside a `char` data type.

Here are some examples of declaring primitive data types:

```
int numPeople;
int age, numCredits, yearInSchool;
boolean isHappy;
char middleInitial;
double gpa;
```

> **Declaration** includes the *data type* and then a *variable name*.

We can declare variables together as in the second example, where age, numCredits, and yearInSchool are all declared to be of type int. Each declaration needs to end with a semicolon.

When we are not using a primitive data type, we will be using an object data type. The most common object data type is String. We can declare strings as follows:

```
String str;
```

We will work with many other objects besides Graphics and String once we get to Chapter 4.

For choosing variable names, we can use any combination of letters, numbers, the underscore character (_), or the dollar sign ($). However, we cannot begin a variable name with a number. There is not really a limit on how many characters we use for a variable name (within reason). It is best to be as descriptive as possible for the name, so that you and anyone helping or maintaining the code you wrote can figure it out easily. Usually, variable names begin with a lowercase letter, and any word we add to create a phrase would start with a capital letter to make it easier to read. Because we cannot use spaces in our variable names, we could instead use the underscore character to separate the words.

3.1.2 Initialization

We initialize a variable when we assign it a value for the first time. This step is usually done at the same time as we declare our variables. Instead of just declaring them, we also assign them an initial value.

Examples:

Initialization is an assignment of a variable for the first time.

```
int numPeople = 17;
boolean isHappy = true;
char middleInitial = 'S';
int age = 21, numCredits = 15, yearInSchool= 1;
double gpa = 3.6;
```

We can create strings in one of two ways:

```
String str = "Cookie Monster likes cookies";
String str = new String( "Cookie Monster likes cookies" );
```

Both of the preceding lines have the same effect—creating a String object with the characters "Cookie Monster likes cookies."

3.1.3 Assignment

We perform an assignment when we change the value of a variable. This process is similar to *variable initialization* except that we do not declare the variable's type.

Examples:

Assignment changes the value of a variable. The variable is always left of the equal sign.

```
numPeople = 22;
age = 25;
```

```
gpa= 3.3
isHappy = false;
middleInitial = 'E';
str = "I like cookies too";
str = new String( "Life is a bowl of chocolate" );
```

3.1.4 Reference

We can refer to our variables that we create by referencing them with the name that we declared. Be sure not to put the variable name in double quotes; otherwise, it will print the variable name instead of the value that the variable is referencing.

```
String name = "Elizabeth S. Boese";
g.drawString ( name, 0, 12 );      // prints Elizabeth S. Boese
g.drawString ( "name", 0, 12 );    // prints name
```

We can also reference our variables inside equations:

```
gpa = gradeValue * numCredits / 100;
```

Strings are common to programs and there are some methods that we may want to call on our `String` variables. When we call a method on a string, we need to refer to the variable.

```
String str = "Java";
```

`str.toUpperCase( )`   returns a copy of the string in all uppercase letters (e.g., "JAVA")

`str.toLowerCase( )`   returns a copy of the string in all lowercase letters (e.g., "java")

`str.length( )`   returns the number of characters in the string (e.g., 4)

`str.charAt( index )`   returns the character at position `index` in the string, where the first character is at index 0

3.1.5 Locations and Scope

When we write our programs, there are two ways that we can *declare* our variables: as instance variables or local variables. **Instance variables** are declared at the top of the program just after the class header and open brace. **Local variables** are declared inside methods, such as the `paint` method. Local variables consist of variables declared inside the method as well as those declared in the **parameters** for the method. In Example 3-1, x and y are instance variables and `text` and `grph` are local variables.

EXAMPLE 3-1

```java
import java.awt.*;
import javax.swing.*;
public class HiWorld extends JApplet
{            // declare instance variables here
   int x;
   int y;
   public void paint ( Graphics grph )
   {
      super.paint( grph );
      x = 0;          // initialize the instance variables
      y = 12;
      String text = "Hello World";          // local variable
      grph.drawString ( text, x, y );
   }
}
```

We will want to declare most of our variables as *instance variables*. Doing so allows us to reference those variables throughout the class. Variables that we declare inside a method can be referenced only inside that method. This fact will become essential once we get to the chapter on events.

In Example 3-2 we convert the HiWorld example to one using methods. We cannot access the variable text inside the anotherMethod method because text was declared inside the paint method and is accessible only inside that paint method. However, we can access the variable x inside anotherMethod because x is an instance variable.

EXAMPLE 3-2

```java
import java.awt.*;
import javax.swing.*;
public class HiWorldWithMethods extends JApplet
{
  // declare instance variables here
  int x = 0;
  int y = 12;
  public void paint ( Graphics grph )
  {
    super.paint( grph );
    String text = "Hello World";    // local variable
    grph.drawString ( text, x, y );
    anotherMethod( grph );
  }
```

(continues)

Example 3-2 (continued)

```
public void anotherMethod( Graphics g )
{
   g.drawString ( text, x, 50 );    // will not work!
}
}
```
Cannot reference the variable text because its scope is only within the paint method.

3.2 Methods

We can create multiple methods in our program, as we saw in the last example. A **method** is a set of statements grouped together that can be called, or *invoked*, by the program. The statements within the method are designated inside the braces. Each method needs its own set of braces to designate the beginning and ending of that method.

In Example 3-2, we *invoked* the anotherMethod method inside the paint method. We do so by specifying the name of the method being called, here, anotherMethod; placing the parentheses; and sending any data as *parameters*. In our example, there was one parameter that was sent: grph. A copy of grph is copied into the method's parameter's variable name: g. Doing so allows the anotherMethod method to also call the drawString method on the Graphics object.

Our example also shows two different type of method calls:

- Within a class
- In another class

The method call to anotherMethod called a method inside the same class. We can see the definition of the method anotherMethod in this class. The drawString method, on the other hand, was a call to a method inside a different class—the Graphics class. This time we do not see the definition of the drawString method in this class. We can invoke the drawString method only by specifying which object to call it on: here, the Graphics object designated by the variable grph inside the paint method and g inside the anotherMethod method.

3.2.1 Method Structure

Declaring methods requires us to follow Java's syntax structure for methods. We first specify the method header, which is the first line of the method before the braces:

```
accessModifier returnType methodName ( parameter(s) )
```

Parameters are specified with data type and variable name.

Examples:

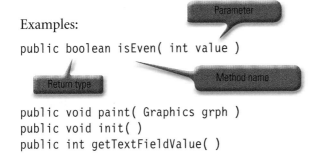

```
public boolean isEven( int value )
```

```
public void paint( Graphics grph )
public void init( )
public int getTextFieldValue( )
```

After the method header we add the open and close braces. The `public` is an access modifier that specifies that other classes can access this method. At this point, simply accept the fact that *most* methods should be declared `public`.

The `void` keyword specifies the *return type* for the method. A return type of `void` means that the method is not returning anything. Even though the method does not return a value, we still need a placeholder for the return type, which is why we use the word `void`. We could return a `String`, `int`, `double`, `boolean`, `char`, `Graphics` object, etc. However, we can return only *one* thing.

`paint` is an example name of a method. We can name our methods almost anything we like, following a few rules that also apply to variable names (see Chapter 6). When we are drawing on our applet, we must name one method `paint` because this is the method that is automatically called by the browser when it needs to draw the applet.

The parameters inside parentheses can contain any number of variable declarations. If we do not want any parameters, we still need to include the parentheses, but we can leave empty space inside of them. When we specify a parameter, we must *declare* the variable—define the data type and the variable name. If we need multiple parameters, separate each declaration with a comma. For example:

```
public void paintWindow( Graphics g, int x, int y)
```

We can put as many statements as we want within each method. Sometimes methods contain only one line of code—for example, to return the value of a variable. Sometimes we have 10 or 50 lines of code within a method. Although we can put an unlimited number of statements within a method, the general guideline is to put only as many lines within a method that are viewable on the screen without scrolling. This rule makes it easier to read our code and look for errors when we can see an entire method within the same screen.

Example 3-3 shows the flow of the program when methods get called. When we call the `getAdd` method, we send two values, 2 and 7, which are stored in local variables num1 and num2. Inside the method, the numbers 2 and 7 are added together and the resulting value is returned. This value is then assigned to the variable named `addition`. Because this method returns a value, we specify the data type that will be returned in the method header.

```
public int getAdd( int num1, int num2 )
```

EXAMPLE 3-3

```java
import java.awt.*;
import javax.swing.*;

public class Calculate extends JApplet
{
  public void paint ( Graphics g )
  {
    super.paint( g );
    int addition = getAdd( 2, 7 );
    String added = "2 + 7 = " + addition;
    g.drawString ( added, 0, 12 );

    String subtracted = "2 - 7 = " + getSubtract( 2, 7 );
    g.drawString ( subtracted, 0, 24 );
  }
  public int getAdd( int num1, int num2 )
  {
    return num1 + num2;
  }
  public int getSubtract( int num1, int num2 )
  {
    return num1 - num2;
  }
}
```

The call to getAdd returns the value 9. addition is initialized to 9.

num1 is initialized to 2. num2 is initialized to 7.

Step 1

Step 2

3.2.2 Why Have Methods?

Using methods is essential when programming. Sometimes it is required, such as the methods we call on our Graphics object (drawString, fillOval) and when processing events. But we also want to use methods to help organize our code to make it easier to read, as well as to enable us to reuse code that we have already written. There are many reasons to use methods:

- Organize a program (easier to read)
- Modularize repeated code
- Make code accessible to other objects
- Handle events

Organize a Program   As our programs grow bigger, it gets harder to read through a program with many lines of code. By grouping related code segments into methods and naming the methods with something descriptive, we make the program much easier to follow. Example 3-4 shows two ways to write a program to draw a house: one without methods and one with several methods. At a quick glance, the program on the left is more difficult to follow—we need to read through the code to figure out which code draws the tree, which draws the windows, etc. However, the code on the right is much clearer to read at a glance by looking at the method names that segment the code.

EXAMPLE 3-4

```
import java.awt.*;
import javax.swing.*;
public class House
            extends JApplet
{
  public void paint(Graphics g )
  {
    super.paint( g );
    g.setColor( Color.pink );
    g.fillRect( 100, 100, 200, 200 );
    g.setColor( Color.black );
    Polygon poly=new Polygon( );
    poly.addPoint( 100, 100 );
    poly.addPoint( 200, 50 );
    poly.addPoint( 300, 100 );
    g.fillPolygon(poly);

    g.setColor( Color.blue );
    g.fillRect( 200, 230, 40, 70 );
    g.fillRect( 120, 150, 20, 30 );
    g.fillRect( 150, 150, 20, 30 );
    g.fillRect( 200, 150, 20, 30 );
    g.fillRect( 230, 150, 20, 30 );
    g.setColor(Color.black);
    g.fillRect(400,130,30,170);
    g.setColor( Color.green );
    g.fillOval( 370, 80, 100, 100 );
    g.fillRect( 0, 295, 500, 5 );
  }
}
```

```
import java.awt.*;
import javax.swing.*;
public class HouseMethods extends JApplet
{
    int  WINDOW_WIDTH = 20;
    int  WINDOW_HEIGHT = 30;
    public void paint (Graphics g )
    {
      super.paint( g );
      paintHouse( g );
      paintLandscape( g );
    }
    public void paintHouse( Graphics grph )
    {
      grph.setColor( Color.pink );
      grph.fillRect( 100, 100, 200, 200 );
      grph.setColor( Color.black );
      Polygon poly = new Polygon( );
      poly.addPoint( 100, 100 );
      poly.addPoint( 200, 50 );
      poly.addPoint( 300, 100 );
      grph.fillPolygon(poly);
      grph.setColor( Color.blue );
      grph.fillRect( 200, 230, 40, 70 );
                                    // windows
      paintWindow( grph, 120, 150 );
      paintWindow( grph, 150, 150 );
      paintWindow( grph, 200, 150 );
      paintWindow( grph, 230, 150 );
    }
    public void paintWindow(
                Graphics gp, int x, int y )
    {
      gp.setColor( Color.blue );
      gp.fillRect( x, y, WINDOW_WIDTH,
                        WINDOW_HEIGHT);
    }
    public void paintLandscape( Graphics g )
    {
      g.setColor( Color.black );
      g.fillRect( 400, 130, 30, 170 );
      g.setColor( Color.green );
      g.fillOval( 370, 80, 100, 100 );
      g.fillRect( 0, 295, 500, 5 );
    }
}
```

Example 3-4 shows drawing a house can be easy to work with the code if we have an error or want to add new features. For example, if the tree stump is off center from the trees, we can easily find the few lines of code in the method paintLandscape that we need to modify.

Modularize Repeated Code   Sometimes a program has sections of code that are the same or nearly the same. These sections are ideal for placement inside a method. We can use the parameters to the method to customize the code fragment.

Example 3-5 creates a portion of a checkerboard of black and white squares. Which program will be easier and faster to modify to create a full-sized checkerboard? Which program will be easier and faster to modify the sizes to make the squares twice as big?

EXAMPLE 3-5

```java
import javax.swing.*;
import java.awt.*;

public class Checkerboard
              extends JApplet
{
  public void paint (Graphics g)
  {
    super.paint( g );
    // row 1
    g.fillRect( 20, 20, 10, 10 );
    g.fillRect( 40, 20, 10, 10 );
    g.fillRect( 60, 20, 10, 10 );
    g.fillRect( 80, 20, 10, 10 );
    g.fillRect( 100, 20, 10, 10 );

    // row 2
    g.fillRect( 30, 30, 10, 10 );
    g.fillRect( 50, 30, 10, 10 );
    g.fillRect( 70, 30, 10, 10 );
    g.fillRect( 90, 30, 10, 10 );
    g.fillRect( 110, 30, 10, 10 );
  }
}
```

```java
import javax.swing.*;
import java.awt.*;

public class Checkerboard2 extends JApplet
{
    public void paint ( Graphics g )
    {
        super.paint( g );
        drawRows( g, 20, 20 );
        drawRows( g, 30, 30 );
    }
    public void drawRows( Graphics graphics,
                          int x, int y )
    {
        graphics.fillRect( x, y, 10, 10 );
        graphics.fillRect( x+20, y, 10, 10 );
        graphics.fillRect( x+40, y, 10, 10 );
        graphics.fillRect( x+60, y, 10, 10 );
        graphics.fillRect( x+80, y, 10, 10 );
    }
}
```

Applet V...

Applet

Applet started.

For Access by Other Objects   We have used many methods defined in another class: drawString, fillRect, setColor. All these methods are defined in the Graphics class. When we call the drawString method, for example, the program will go inside the Graphics class and look for the method named drawString. It will run the statements listed within this method and ignore the code within the other methods. This is how the program distinguishes between statements to execute.

Example: The Graphics class defined some methods for us to use:

```
drawString (...
fillRect ( ...
setColor(...
```

If these were not methods, we would not be able to draw anything.

When using methods defined in another class, we need to tell the compiler where to find these methods—which class are they in? This information is important because you may have two classes that define the same method name. We can distinguish between them by calling the method on the class itself (e.g., Math.sqrt) or on an *instance* of the class (e.g., Graphics g, where g is a declared variable of the data type Graphics). We use the period to separate the class name or class instance from the method name. For example, if we have a Graphics instance named grp:

```
grp.drawString ( "hi", 0, 12 );
grp.setColor( Color.BLUE );
int  positiveVal = Math.abs( -55 ); // returns the absolute value
```

There are also special types of methods called **constructors** that create an instance of an object. These methods are called when the new operator is used. Although we have not used these methods yet, we will use them extensively throughout the rest of the book. For example, when we want to create a new instance of a button, we can call the following:

```
JButton  myButton;
myButton = new JButton( "text on button" );
```

After the keyword new, the method name matches the name of the data type. The new operator and the method name matching the data type is how we can recognize that we are calling a *constructor* method instead of a normal method. We will discuss JButton in more detail in Chapter 4.

Event Handling   Events are incidents that occur that automatically call particular methods. Example events include a mouse click, a mouse move, a button click, and a list selection. We need to write the required methods to handle the events, which are specified by the Java paradigm. These methods are then automatically called when the event occurs; for example, when the user clicks on a button, the method actionPerformed is automatically called. We will discuss events in more detail in Chapter 8.

Troubleshooting

Common errors:

Code will not compile.	Look at your instance versus local variables. Make sure that you are not referencing a local variable that is declared inside a different method.
	Ensure that you spelled the name of the method the same way for the name of the method and for when you call the method.
	Ensure that there are no semicolons at the end of each method header.
	Strings are designated within double quotes, and `char` data types define a single character within single quotes.
	When assigning a `boolean` data type to either `true` or `false`, be sure that there are no quotes around the Java keywords: `true` or `false`.
The code in my method does not seem to execute.	Make sure that you call your method. The `paint` method gets called automatically, so make sure that you invoke the methods you write inside the `paint` method so that they execute.

SUMMARY

- Variables are declared by specifying the data type and a name.
- `boolean` values are either `true` or `false`.
- Integers (positive, negative, or zero) are stored in the data type `int`.
- Floating-point numbers in Java default to the data type `double`. Integer numbers in Java default to `int`.
- Declare variables at the top of the class under the class header so that the scope of reference for the variable is anywhere within the class. These are called *instance variables*.
- Local variables are those declared inside a method or as a parameter for a method. The scope of a local variable is only within the method.
- Method headers contain the access modifier (usually public), return data type, method name, and parameters listed in parentheses.
- Parameters in a method header require the data type and name for each variable, separating multiple parameters with a comma.
- Methods defined in the same class (or inherited class, e.g., `JApplet`) can be invoked by calling the method name and any parameters.
- Methods defined in other classes need to be called on an instance of that class, such as a `Graphics` object variable reference grp: `grp.drawString( . . . )`, or on the class, such as `math.sqrt(number)`.

- Methods are useful for organizing a program to be easier to read, to modularize repeated code, to make code accessible to other objects, and for handling events.

EXERCISES

1. Declare a character variable named `initial`. Declare a `boolean` variable named `done` and initialize it to `false`.

2. Declare variables for a birthday: the month, day, and year. Assign each variable to your own birthdate.

3. In the following method header, what is the data type that is returned?

```
public void getInteger( char value )
```

4. In the following method header, what is the data type that is returned?

```
public double calcAvg( int x, int y, char value )
```

5. True or false? A method is a section of a program whose statements are executed only when the method is called.

6. True or false? Methods that do not return anything do not need a return data type in the method header.

7. True or false? If we have redundant code, we should try to put it into a method and have each code section call the method instead.

8. True or false? A method is a section of a program that causes the computer to take some action.

9. True or false? If no parameters are necessary for a method, leave off the parentheses in the method header.

10. True or false? If there are multiple parameters that are all of type `int`, we could put the data type `int` once and list each variable name separated with commas.

11. What are the benefits of creating methods?

12. Write the method header for a method named `convertToKM` that takes an `int` as a parameter, which is the number of miles, and returns a `double` value for the converted value in kilometers.

13. Which of the following reasons are why we create methods? Choose all that apply.
    a. Code is easier to read
    b. Program is less likely to crash
    c. Can group repeated code sections
    d. To order the code sequentially

Swing Components

Adding components to an applet is like adding magnets to the fridge—easy to move around. Writing in the paint method is like finger painting your fridge—permanently placed.

4.1 Swing

Swing is the name for a graphics library that has more enhanced graphics than the AWT library. Swing components can be accessed by importing the `javax.swing` package at the top of our program:

```
import javax.swing.*;
```

Most components in the Swing package (**FIGURE 4-1** and **FIGURE 4-2**) begin with the capital letter *J* to distinguish them from their predecessors in the AWT package. Swing components allow more flexibility over the look and feel of the components and allow extra functionality, such as support for tooltips. We can also ensure that our Swing components look the same on all platforms, whereas AWT components will look different (e.g., the checkbox may be a square or diamond depending on the operating system). The disadvantage of using Swing components is that the extra functionality also means more complexity.

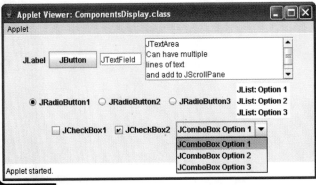

FIGURE 4-1 Example display of various Swing components.

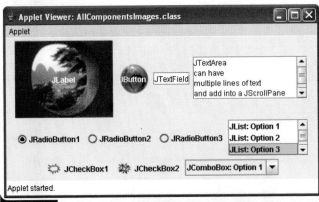

FIGURE 4-2 Example display of various Swing components with images.

4.2 Adding Components

JLabel is an example of a component that we can place on our applets. When we called the drawString method in the paint method in Chapter 2, we were painting *directly* on the applet. With components, we *place* them on the applet and can modify their location on the basis of a **layout manager**, which we will discuss in more detail in Chapter 5. Here is one way to look at it. With the paint method, you are taking a marker and drawing on your fridge. With components, you have magnets that you place on the fridge, and these can be easily moved.

The general structure of an applet follows:

```
comments with you as author and purpose of the applet
import statements
public class name extends JApplet
{
        instance variables (declare components)
        public void init( )
        {
                set layout manager for applet
                create/modify components
                add components to the applet
        }
}
```

When working with components, we need to be careful of where we *declare* our components. We want to declare our components at the top of the class after the class header and first brace so that we can access those components in any method we create. This concept has to do with the *scope* of a variable. This approach will be required when we get to events, but even now it will be helpful to us when we use several methods to help divide up our tasks (for examples, see Chapter 3).

Component variable declarations include the **data type** and a **variable name**. Examples include:

```
Image    image;
ImageIcon   imgIcon;
JLabel   myName;
JTextArea   message;
```

> Declaring a variable means specifying a data type (e.g., int, JLabel) and a variable name.

Our class then should appear as Example 4-1, declaring our variables at the top and initializing them (setting them equal to something) inside the init method.

EXAMPLE 4-1

```
import javax.swing.*;
public class Components extends JApplet
{          // declare components here
   JLabel title;
   JTextField fullName;
   public void init( )
   {
       // initialize  variables  here
       title = new JLabel( "My Lovely Applet" );
       fullName = new JTextField( 20 );
   }
}
```

> We have not added the components to the applet yet, so if you run this program, nothing is displayed.

Now we need to figure out how to add them to the applet. We need to specify a particular layout for managing how the components are to appear on the applet. In the next chapter we will learn about the different options for layout managers; right now we will use a basic one named FlowLayout, which simply adds the components in order and places them centered at the top. When it runs out of room on a line, it goes to the next line. To set the layout, we need to make a call to the method setLayout.

```
setLayout( layoutManager );
```

Because we will use the FlowLayout manager for this chapter, we need

```
setLayout( new FlowLayout( ) );
```

> There is further discussion on setLayout in Chapter 5.

This line should be placed after the opening brace of our init method, as shown in Example 4-2.

EXAMPLE 4-2

```
import java.awt.*;
import javax.swing.*;
public class Components extends JApplet
{
   // declare components here
   JLabel title;
   JTextField fullName;

   public void init( )
   {
       // set the layout manager
       setLayout( new FlowLayout( ) );
```

Applet Viewer: Components.class
Applet
                    My Lovely Applet
Applet started.

```
        // initialize variables here
        title = new JLabel( "My Lovely Applet" );
        fullName = new JTextField( 20 );

        // add components to the applet
        add( title );
        add( fullName );
    }
}
```

> The order in which we call the add method is the order in which the components are displayed.

Now let us take a look at the components that we can add to our applet. We will start off with the JLabel.

4.3 JLabel

JLabel is a component into which we can put text and/or images. It is simply a label, and a user cannot click on it or select or change the text from the label.

To create a label, we call the constructor method for JLabel with appropriate parameters.

```
JLabel variableName;
```

> Three ways to create a JLabel: text, image, or both text and an image.

```
variableName = new JLabel( String );
variableName = new JLabel( ImageIcon );
variableName = new JLabel( String, ImageIcon, horizontalAlignment );
```

where the horizontalAlignment can be one of the following:

```
JLabel.LEFT       JLabel.RIGHT       JLabel.CENTER
```

to determine where the text and/or image in the label should be positioned with respect to the layout manager. *Note: Until we use layout managers other than* FlowLayout, *these alignments will have no visible effect.* Examples follow and appear in Example 4-2.

```
JLabel myName, mythought, meLabel;

myName = new JLabel( "Cookie Monster" );
mythought = new JLabel( "This label has a lot of text" );
meLabel = new JLabel( "Me, Myself and I" );
```

JLabels are not editable by the user; they are intended to simply be text on the applet. In Example 4-3 we create two labels and add them to the applet. *If you resize the applet to be very wide, both labels will appear on the same line—this is based on our layout manager* FlowLayout.

EXAMPLE 4-3

```
import java.awt.*;
import javax.swing.*;

public class JLabelEx1 extends JApplet
{
    JLabel label1, label2;
    public void init ( )
    {
        setLayout( new FlowLayout( ) );
        label1 = new JLabel( "Java is fun to learn" );
        label2 = new JLabel( "But I like skiing too!" );

        // add labels to applet
        add( label1 );
        add( label2 );
    }
}
```

When working with the text in a JLabel, as well as in many of the components that we will look at, we can customize it by using HTML tags. HTML is the language used to create web pages, and we can use some of the syntax inside our Swing components. HTML basics include the following and are demonstrated in Example 4-4.

Basic HTML:

- The text must start with the tag <HTML>.
-
—go to the next line.
- <P>—create a blank line (works similar to the <BR> tag).
- <B>the text</B>—put the text in bold: **the text**.
- <I>the text</I>—put the text in italics: *the text*.
- <B><I>the text</I></B>—put the text in bold and italics: ***the text***.
- <CENTER>the text</CENTER>—center the text. Works best on multiline HTML text.
- <FONT COLOR=Red>the text</FONT>—change the text to the color red: the text.
- <FONT SIZE=+1>the text</FONT>—change the text to one size bigger: the text.
- <FONT SIZE=5>text</FONT>—change text size to 5 (sizes go from 1 to 7).
- <FONT SIZE=-1>the text</FONT>—change the text to be one size smaller: the text.

> HTML tags are not case sensitive!

FIGURE 4-3 JLabel example using HTML code.

Example using HTML code in JLabel, as shown in **FIGURE 4-3**:

```
JLabel   fox, name;
fox = new JLabel( "<HTML><FONT SIZE=+5>T</FONT>"
    + "he <FONT COLOR=RED>fox</FONT>"
    + "<BR>jumped<BR>"
    + "<B>over</B> da <I>moon.</I>" );
name = new JLabel( "<HTML><B><I>GOOOOD MORNING!!!</I></B>");
```

> Using + with two strings appends them together (Chapter 6).

> When creating String literals (text within double quotes), we cannot have the double quotes around the String on separate lines because Java would not know how much space to put in to wrap it. However, we can add Strings together by having one String on the first line with the beginning and ending double quotes, then a plus sign, and then the second String inside double quotes on the next line.

Example 4-4 shows the use of HTML tags to customize the text.

EXAMPLE 4-4

```
import java.awt.*;
import javax.swing.*;
public class JLabelEx extends JApplet
{
    JLabel label1, label2;

    public void init( )
    {
        setLayout( new FlowLayout( ) );
```

(continues)

Example 4-4 (continued)

```
        //Create the first label.
        label1 = new JLabel( "<HTML>Text<BR>on<BR>"
                + "separate Lines", JLabel.CENTER );

        //Create the other labels.
        label2 = new JLabel( "<HTML><FONT COLOR=RED>Cookie"
                            + "</FONT>Monster" );

        //Add the labels.
        add( label1 );
        add( label2 );
    }
}
```

If we want the text to be centered within the label, JLabel.CENTER will not work (it only centers the label as a whole within the placed location per the layout manager). We use the HTML tag CENTER to center the text within the label (**FIGURE 4-4**).

```
JLabel mylabel = new JLabel( "<html><center>Text<BR>on<BR>"
        + "separate Lines</center>" );
```

4.3.1 Images

We can also put images inside a JLabel. We can have a JLabel either with just an image or with an image and text (or just text). To do so, we need to create an ImageIcon object. Then we can add the ImageIcon to the JLabel. Therefore, there are four steps to adding an image to an applet:

> Four steps to adding an image to an applet

1. Create an Image object with the name of the image file.
2. Create an ImageIcon with the Image object we just created.
3. Add the ImageIcon to the JLabel (or other component).
4. Add the JLabel (or other component) to the applet.

FIGURE 4-4 JLabel example using HTML code to center the text on multiple lines.

Step 1: Create an Image **object with the name of the image file.**   First we *declare* a variable to hold our image in the instance variable section at the top of our code. In the following example, we have

```
Image img;
```

Then inside the init method, we can grab the image by calling the getImage method. When we call this method, we need to specify where exactly the image is. For this book, we will store all our images in the same place as our source code. This approach is the easiest and works when we transfer our final applets to the Internet. To specify the location, we want to reference the fully specified location by calling the method getCodeBase( ). The method getCodeBase( ) will automatically figure out where your code is, whether you are running the program locally on your computer or on the Internet.

The last part of this step is to reference the name of the image file. Be careful with uppercase and lowercase letters—running on Windows allows us to use either, but running our applet on a Linux or UNIX system requires us have correct cases. Avoid using spaces and punctuation in your file names because this will mess things up later when we add our applets to the Internet.

```
img = getImage( getCodeBase( ), "door.jpg" );
```

> We cannot call the getImage method at the top of the program where we declare our instance variables. It will not work! We should declare our variables at the top only.

Step 2: Create an ImageIcon **with the** Image **object previously created.**   First we *declare* a variable to hold our ImageIcon object in the instance variable section at the top of our code. In the following example, we have

```
ImageIcon imgIcon;
```

Then inside the init method, we can *instantiate* an ImageIcon object by calling the new operator and sending as a parameter our Image object:

```
imgIcon = new ImageIcon( img );
```

Step 3: Add the ImageIcon **to the** JLabel.   First we *declare* a variable to hold our JLabel in the instance variable section at the top of our code. In the following example, we have

```
JLabel label;
```

Then inside the init method, we can *instantiate* our JLabel object by calling the new operator and sending as a parameter our ImageIcon object:

```
label = new JLabel( imgIcon );
```

We can also put images in JButton, JList, JRadioButton, and other components by following this same structure. See examples in their respective sections.

Step 4: Add the JLabel to the applet.   To add the JLabel to the applet, we first need to make sure that we have set our layout manager:

```
setLayout( new FlowLayout( ) );
```

Then we add our JLabel component by using the add method:

```
add( label );
```

> We cannot add an Image or an ImageIcon object directly to the applet or JPanel; we need to stash it into a component such as a JLabel or JButton.

Example 4-5 displays just an image in a JLabel with no text, and Example 4-6 displays an image with text in the JLabel.

EXAMPLE 4-5

```
import java.awt.*;
import javax.swing.*;
public class JLabelWithImage extends JApplet
{
    Image img;
    ImageIcon imgIcon;
    JLabel label;

    public void init( )
    {
        img = getImage( getCodeBase( ), "door.jpg" );
        imgIcon = new ImageIcon( img );
        label = new JLabel( imgIcon );
        setLayout( new FlowLayout( ) );
        add( label );
    }
}
```

Applet View...
Applet

Applet started.

EXAMPLE 4-6

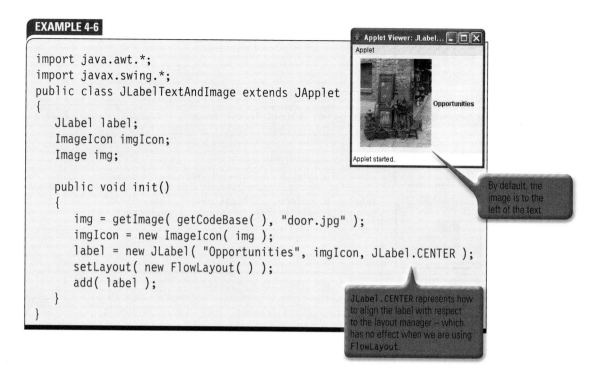

```
import java.awt.*;
import javax.swing.*;
public class JLabelTextAndImage extends JApplet
{
    JLabel label;
    ImageIcon imgIcon;
    Image img;

    public void init()
    {
        img = getImage( getCodeBase( ), "door.jpg" );
        imgIcon = new ImageIcon( img );
        label = new JLabel( "Opportunities", imgIcon, JLabel.CENTER );
        setLayout( new FlowLayout( ) );
        add( label );
    }
}
```

> By default, the image is to the left of the text.

> JLabel.CENTER represents how to align the label with respect to the layout manager – which has no effect when we are using FlowLayout.

We can also adjust where the text is with respect to the image by using one of the following methods,

```
setHorizontalTextPosition( textPosition )
setVerticalTextPosition( textPosition )
```

where `textPosition` is one of the following:

Horizontal

- JLabel.LEFT
- JLabel.CENTER
- JLabel.RIGHT

Vertical

- JLabel.TOP
- JLabel.CENTER
- JLabel.BOTTOM

TABLE 4-1 shows the output based on the lines entered. When we create the JLabel with the call to new JLabel, the position specified is for alignment of the text and image with respect to the layout manager and has no effect on the text or image when we are using the FlowLayout manager. The default for text alignment is right-aligned horizontally and centered vertically with respect to the image.

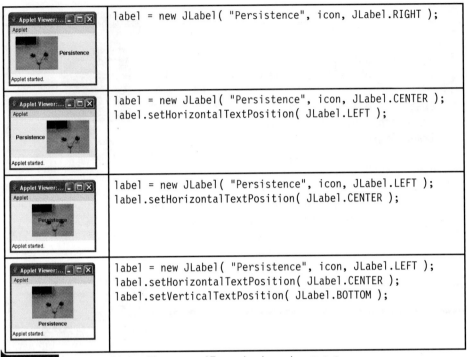

	`label = new JLabel( "Persistence", icon, JLabel.RIGHT );`
	`label = new JLabel( "Persistence", icon, JLabel.CENTER );` `label.setHorizontalTextPosition( JLabel.LEFT );`
	`label = new JLabel( "Persistence", icon, JLabel.LEFT );` `label.setHorizontalTextPosition( JLabel.CENTER );`

	`label = new JLabel( "Persistence", icon, JLabel.LEFT );`
	`label.setHorizontalTextPosition( JLabel.CENTER );`
	`label.setVerticalTextPosition( JLabel.BOTTOM );`

TABLE 4-1   Examples of Various Placements of Text and an Image in a `JLabel`

A shortcut for adding images is to combine the step of creating an `ImageIcon` and adding it to the button. For example:

```
Image img;
JLabel myLabel;
img = getImage( getCodeBase( ), "img.gif" );
myLabel = new JLabel( new ImageIcon( img ) );
```

However, you cannot use the shortcut
```
myLabel = new JLabel( new ImageIcon( "img.gif") );
```
Although this will seem to work while testing on your own computer, it will not run on the Internet.

4.4 JButton

We can add buttons to the applet by creating JButton objects. We specify a new button object in one of the following ways:

```
JButton btn;

btn = new JButton( String );          // creates button with text
btn = new JButton( ImageIcon );       // creates button with image
btn = new JButton( String, ImageIcon ); // creates button with text
                                      //    and image
```

where ImageIcon is created from the Image object. Examples include:

```
JButton btn
btn = new JButton( "Cookie Monster" );

Image img = getImage( getCodeBase( ), "happy.gif" );
ImageIcon ic = new ImageIcon( img );

btn = new JButton( ic );
btn = new JButton( "Coffee rules", ic );
```

Example 4-7 creates three JButtons and adds them to the applet by using FlowLayout.

EXAMPLE 4-7

```
import java.awt.*;
import javax.swing.*;
public class JButtonEx extends JApplet
{
    JButton one;
    JButton two;
    JButton three;
    public void init( )
    {
        setLayout( new FlowLayout( ) );
        one = new JButton( "one" );
        two = new JButton( "two" );
        three = new JButton( "three" );
        add( one );
        add( two );
        add( three );
    }
}
```

Right now, our buttons do not do anything interesting—they just appear on our applet. We will learn how to do things when the button is clicked when we cover events.

We can extend Example 4-7 to add images to the buttons. In Example 4-8, we will leave the first button as is with just text on it. On the second button we will just add an image. For the third button we will show how to add both text and an image to the button.

EXAMPLE 4-8

```java
import java.awt.*;
import javax.swing.*;
public class JButtonImg extends JApplet
{
    JButton one, two, three;
    Image img;
    ImageIcon icon;
    public void init( )
    {
        setLayout( new FlowLayout( ) );
        one = new JButton( "one" );
        img = getImage( getCodeBase( ), "buttonPoland.png" );
        icon = new ImageIcon( img );
        two = new JButton( icon );
        img = getImage( getCodeBase( ), "buttonYellowstone.png" );
        three = new JButton( "three", new ImageIcon( img ) );
        add( one );        add( two );        add( three );
    }
}
```

Example 4-9 is the same program as Example 4-8 but uses methods.

EXAMPLE 4-9

```java
import java.awt.*;
import javax.swing.*;
public class JButtonImgMethods extends JApplet
{
    JButton one, two, three;
    Image img;
    ImageIcon icon;
    public void init( )
    {
        setLayout( new FlowLayout( ) );
        setupButtons( );
    }
    public void setupButtons( )
    {
        one = new JButton( "one" );
        img = getImage( getCodeBase( ), " buttonPoland.png" );
        icon = new ImageIcon( img );
        two = new JButton( icon );
```

```
        img = getImage( getCodeBase( ), " buttonYellowstone.png " );
        three = new JButton( "three", new ImageIcon( img ) );
        add( one );        add( two );        add( three );
    }
}
```

We can customize the layout of the text and image in our buttons in a similar way in which we did it for JLabels. We can adjust where the text is with respect to the image, using methods named

```
setHorizontalTextPosition( textPosition )
setVerticalTextPosition( textPosition )
```

For example, adding the following line to the preceding code example will put the text to the left of the image (**FIGURE 4-5**):

```
button.setHorizontalTextPosition( JButton.LEFT )
```

To put the text below the image, use the following code (**FIGURE 4-6**):

```
button.setHorizontalTextPosition( JButton.CENTER )
button.setVerticalTextPosition( JButton.BOTTOM )
```

Buttons also have additional customizations that we can apply. These include modifying the aesthetics of the button as well as which image is to be displayed depending on the state of the button. The following examples and **TABLE 4-2** assume that we have created a button and an ImageIcon for the Image.

```
Image img;
ImageIcon imgIcon;
JButton myButton;

img = getImage( getCodeBase( ), "idea.png" );
imgIcon = new ImageIcon( img );
myButton = new JButton( imgIcon );
```

FIGURE 4-5 JButton with text to the left of the image.

FIGURE 4-6 JButton with text centered below the image.

	[Default]
	`mybutton.setBorderPainted( false );`
	`mybutton.setContentAreaFilled( false );`
	`mybutton.setBorderPainted( false );` `mybutton.setContentAreaFilled( false );`
	`mybutton.setMargin( new Insets( 0, 0, 0, 0 ) );` *Where first 0 is top margin, second 0 is left, third 0 is bottom margin,* *and last 0 is right.*
	`mybutton.setRolloverIcon( rolloverImageIcon );` *Changes the image displayed on the button when the mouse rolls over* *the button.*
	`mybutton.setEnabled( false );` *User cannot select the button, and a different image is displayed.*
	`mybutton.setDisabledIcon( disabledImageIcon );`
	`mybutton.setFocusPainted( false );` *Removes a border around text/image when focused/user selects it.*

TABLE 4-2   Examples of Methods to Use on `JButton`s

 Text Components

There are three types of text components where users can enter information:

- JTextField
- JPasswordField
- JTextArea

The JTextField allows only one line of text. JPasswordField also allows only one line of text, and when the user types in this box, the letters are displayed with the star echo character to ensure privacy. JTextArea allows the user to enter multiple lines of text (e.g., a comment field).

4.5.1 JTextField

We can create a JTextField component several ways:

Create a text field with no text, default width of zero characters.

```
JTextField field1;
field1 = new JTextField( );
```
Default to zero characters wide.

Create a text field with text inside the text field; the width will be the exact size of the text.

```
JTextField field2;
field2 = new JTextField( "Hello" );
```

Create a text field with default text and specified width (number of columns).

```
JTextField field3;
field3 = new JTextField( "Hello", 5 );
```

> When determining the width, remember that each column is approximately the size of the letter *W* in the current font. Therefore, when we are using a variable-width font, the columns will not match up to the number of characters in the text field.

Example 4-10 demonstrates five example JTextFields.

EXAMPLE 4-10

```java
import java.awt.*;
import javax.swing.*;
public class JTextFieldEx extends JApplet
{
   JTextField tf1, tf2, field1, field2, field3;
   public void init( )
   {
      setLayout( new FlowLayout( ) );
      tf1 = new JTextField( );
      tf2 = new JTextField( " ", 20 );
      field1 = new JTextField( );
      field2 = new JTextField( "Hello" );
      field3 = new JTextField( "Hello", 5 );

      add( tf1 );      add( tf2 );
      add( field1 ); add( field2 );
      add( field3 );
   }
}
```

4.5.2 JPasswordField

The password field is identical to the JTextField, except that the characters typed into the field are replaced with the star character (*) to maintain some privacy for users entering sensitive information, such as passwords.

4.5.3 JTextArea

A text area allows users to enter multiple lines of information. This is useful when we want the user to enter comments or a description or such text. When creating a text area, we need to specify the number of rows and columns. We can create a text area either with default text or without it.

Create a text area with 3 rows and 20 columns, no text inside:

```java
JTextArea area;
area = new JTextArea( 3, 20 );
```

Create a text area with 5 rows and 10 columns, text inside:

```java
JTextArea area;
area = new JTextArea( "Enter message here", 5, 10 );
```

When adding `JTextArea` components to the applet, we need to display them inside a `JScrollPane` to ensure that they display correctly. Then we add the `JScrollPane` to the applet.

```
JScrollPane scrollPane;
scrollPane = new JScrollPane( textareaComponent );
add( scrollPane );
```

Example 4-11 illustrates three different ways to create text areas.

EXAMPLE 4-11

```
import java.awt.*;
import javax.swing.*;
public class JTextAreaEx extends JApplet
{
    JTextArea ta1, ta2, ta3;
    JScrollPane pane;
    public void init( )
    {
        setLayout( new FlowLayout( ) );
        ta1 = new JTextArea( );
        ta2 = new JTextArea( 4, 20 );
        ta3 = new JTextArea( "I like java." );
        add( ta1 );
        pane = new JScrollPane( ta2 );
        add( pane );
        ta3.setBackground( Color.RED );
        ta3.setForeground( Color.CYAN );
        add( ta3 );
    }
}
```

Applet Viewer: JTextAreaEx.class

Applet

like java

Applet started.

> Put `JTextArea` components inside a `JScrollPane` and add the `JScrollPane` to the applet to ensure that the `JTextArea` displays properly.

We can have the text area wrap within the columns set. To set wrapping enabled, call the `setLineWrap` method on a text area.

```
ta3.setLineWrap( true );
```

We can also specify to wrap only on word boundaries by calling the `setWrapStyleWord` method:

```
ta3.setWrapStyleWord( true );
```

> JTextArea components do not display HTML. We can still force it to display text on multiple lines by using the newline character, which is \n (backslash n).
>
> If we want to display HTML in a text area, we need to use JTextPane or JEditorPane.

 ## 4.6   JCheckBox

JCheckBox is another component that we can add to our applets. Essentially, a checkbox displays one of two states: checked or not checked. We usually use checkboxes for options that are not coupled so that users can select independently from other options available. We can create a checkbox in several ways, depending on whether we want text and/or an image displayed.

```
JCheckBox cb;

cb = new JCheckBox( String );
cb = new JCheckBox( ImageIcon );            // image instead of check-
                                            //   box, no text with it
cb = new JCheckBox( String, ImageIcon ); // image with text on right
```

Examples include:

```
JCheckBox cb;
Image img;
ImageIcon icon;

cb = new JCheckBox( "text" );
img = getImage( getCodeBase( ), "lightbulb.png" );
icon = new ImageIcon( img );
cb = new JCheckBox( "red", icon );
```

If we want to use images, they replace the checkbox. So, we need an image for when the checkbox is selected and when it is not selected. When we call the constructor with an ImageIcon object, it designates the image for when it is not selected.

```
JCheckBox cb;
Image img;
ImageIcon icon;

img = getImage( getCodeBase( ), "gocart.png" );
icon = new ImageIcon( img );

cb = new JCheckBox( icon );
```

or

```
cb = new JCheckBox( "text", icon );
```

To set the image for when the checkbox is selected, we need to call setSelectionIcon:

```
cb1.setSelectedIcon( selectedIC );
```

Example 4-12 demonstrates a simple applet adding three checkboxes. Example 4-13 shows the same three checkboxes and adds images for each checkbox and for the selected checkbox. The selected image icon has the full image of both the checkbox and the selected image.

EXAMPLE 4-12

```
import java.awt.*;
import javax.swing.*;
public class JCheckBoxEx extends JApplet
{
    JCheckBox cb1, cb2, cb3;
    public void init( )
    {
        setLayout( new FlowLayout( ) );
        cb1 = new JCheckBox( "red" );
        cb2 = new JCheckBox( "blue" );
        cb3 = new JCheckBox( "pink" );
        add( cb1 );
        add( cb2 );
        add( cb3 );
    }
}
```

To remove the border around the text when highlighted, call .setFocusPainted(false) on each checkbox.

EXAMPLE 4-13

```
import java.awt.*;
import javax.swing.*;
public class JCheckBoxEx2 extends JApplet
{
    Image notsel, selected;
    ImageIcon notselIC, selectedIC;
    JCheckBox cb1, cb2, cb3;
    public void init( )
```

(continues)

Example 4-13 (continued)

```
    {
        notsel = getImage( getCodeBase( ), "checkbox.png" );
        notselIC = new ImageIcon( notsel );
        selected = getImage( getCodeBase( ), "checkboxSelected.png" );
        selectedIC = new ImageIcon( selected );

        cb1 = new JCheckBox( "red", notselIC );
        cb1.setSelectedIcon( selectedIC );
        cb2 = new JCheckBox( "blue", notselIC );
        cb2.setSelectedIcon( selectedIC );
        cb3 = new JCheckBox( "pink", notselIC );
        cb3.setSelectedIcon( selectedIC );

        setLayout( new FlowLayout( ) );
        add( cb1 );   add( cb2 );   add( cb3 );
    }
}
```

Call `.setFocusPainted(false)` on each checkbox to prevent a border drawn around the component when it has focus.

4.7   JRadioButton

JRadioButton is another component that allows users to select or deselect. Essentially, a radio button displays a group of options with only one selected. Within a group the options are mutually exclusive. When a radio button is selected in a group, the button that is currently selected is automatically toggled to be unselected.

We can create radio buttons as follows:

```
JRadioButton rb;
rb = new JRadioButton( String );
```

Example:

```
JRadioButton rb1, rb2;
rb1 = new JRadioButton( "text" );
rb2 = new JRadioButton( "happy" );
```

Then we also have to associate the buttons with a particular group:

```
ButtonGroup grp;
grp = new ButtonGroup( );
grp.add( rb1 );
grp.add( rb2 );
```

Example 4-14 creates three mutually exclusive radio buttons.

EXAMPLE 4-14

```
import java.awt.*;
import javax.swing.*;
public class JRadioButtonEx extends JApplet
{
    JRadioButton jb1, jb2, jb3;
    ButtonGroup group;
    public void init( )
    {
        setLayout( new FlowLayout( ) );
        jb1 = new JRadioButton( "red" );
        jb2 = new JRadioButton( "blue" );
        jb3 = new JRadioButton( "pink" );
        group = new ButtonGroup( );
        group.add( jb1 );
        group.add( jb2 );
        group.add( jb3 );
        add( jb1 );         add( jb2 );         add( jb3 );
    }
}
```

There is no shortcut for adding all the radio buttons or adding the `ButtonGroup` variable. This design allows full flexibility for you to decide where and how to display each button.

Example 4-15 demonstrates how to have two different groups of radio buttons. Each set of radio buttons is added to its specific `ButtonGroup`. This example also shows how to create a method to handle the images for all the buttons.

EXAMPLE 4-15

```
import java.awt.*;
import javax.swing.*;
public class JRadioMultiGroups extends JApplet
{
   JRadioButton jb1, jb2, jb3, happy, mellow, sad;
   ButtonGroup colors, mood;
   Image img;
   ImageIcon icon;
   public void init( )
   {
       setLayout( new FlowLayout( ) );
       jb1 = new JRadioButton( "red" );
       jb2 = new JRadioButton( "blue" );
       jb3 = new JRadioButton( "pink" );
       happy = new JRadioButton( "Happy" );
       mellow = new JRadioButton( "Mellow" );
       sad = new JRadioButton( "Sad" );

       addButtonIcons( jb1 );       addButtonIcons( jb2 );
       addButtonIcons( jb3 );       addButtonIcons( happy );
       addButtonIcons( mellow ); addButtonIcons( sad );

       colors = new ButtonGroup( );
       colors.add( jb1 );   colors.add( jb2 );   colors.add( jb3 );

       mood = new ButtonGroup( );
       mood.add( happy );   mood.add( mellow );   mood.add( sad );

       add( jb1 );     add( jb2 );     add( jb3 );
       add( happy );   add( mellow ); add( sad );
   }
   public void addButtonIcons( JRadioButton btn )
   {
       img = getImage( getCodeBase( ), "radioButtonRing.png" );
       icon = new ImageIcon( img );
       btn.setIcon( icon );
       img = getImage( getCodeBase( ), "radioButtonSelected.png" );
       icon = new ImageIcon( img );
       btn.setSelectedIcon( icon );
   }
}
```

4.8 JComboBox

JComboBox is another component that we can add to our applets. A combo box is a drop-down list of items where the user can select one (and only one) option. List items can be text, images, or text with an image. Scrollbars will automatically be added to the drop-down list if about seven or more items are in the list (this number can be modified by calling the setPreferredSize method).

To create a new combo box:

```
JComboBox comboBox;
comboBox = new JComboBox( );
```

To add items to the combobox, we call the addItem method. We can add text or ImageIcon objects. Example 4-16 adds a combo box to the applet.

EXAMPLE 4-16

```
import java.awt.*;
import javax.swing.*;
public class JComboEx extends JApplet
{
    JComboBox majors;
    public void init( )
    {
        setLayout( new FlowLayout( ) );
        majors = new JComboBox( );
        majors.addItem( "CS" );
        majors.addItem( "Math" );
        majors.addItem( "History" );
        majors.addItem( "Leisure Studies" );
        majors.addItem( "Psych" );
        add( majors );
    }
}
```

Useful Methods

```
       void setEditable( boolean yesno )
```
allows users to enter text (true) or only select from list (false)

Example: `combolist.setEditable( false );`

`int getItemCount( )`   returns the number of items in the list

Example: `int numItemsInList = combolist.getItemCount( );`

`int getSelectedIndex( )`   returns the index of the selected item

Example: `int selectedIndex = combolist.getSelectedItem( );`

`void removeItem( Object obj )`   removes the object from the list
`void removeItemAt( int index )`   removes the object at the specified index

4.9   JList

JList is another component that we can add to our applets. Essentially, a JList displays many items from which the user can select one (or more). List items can be text, images, or buttons.

We will create lists with a simple list model.

```
DefaultListModel model;
JList list;
model = new DefaultListModel( );
list = new JList( model );
```

There are two ways to add text or images to the list, demonstrated in Examples 4-17 and 4-18:

- The `addElement( thing )` method to add the thing to the end of the list
- The `add( index, thing )` method to add the thing to the list at the specified index

Note: indices start at index 0.

We can set the type of selection allowed as either:

- Single selection: only one item can be selected at a time (default)
  `list.setSelectionMode( ListSelectionModel.SINGLE_SELECTION );` or
- Multiple selection: user can select one or more items at the same time

  `list.setSelectionMode(`
  `                ListSelectionModel.MULTIPLE_INTERVAL_SELECTION );`

EXAMPLE 4-17

```
import java.awt.*;
import javax.swing.*;
public class JListWithAddElement extends JApplet
{
    DefaultListModel model;
    JList majors;
    public void init( )
```

Applet ...

Applet

   CS
   Math
   History
   Leisure Studies
   Psych

Applet started.

```
{
    model = new DefaultListModel( );
    majors = new JList( model );
    model.addElement( "CS" );
    model.addElement( "Math" );
    model.addElement( "History" );
    model.addElement( "Leisure Studies" );
    model.addElement( "Psych" );
    setLayout( new FlowLayout( ) );
    add( majors );
}
}
```

addElement adds each item to the end of the list.

EXAMPLE 4-18

```
import java.awt.*;
import javax.swing.*;
public class JListEx extends JApplet
{
    DefaultListModel model;
    JList majors;
    public void init( )
    {
        model = new DefaultListModel( );
        majors = new JList( model );

        model.add( 0, "CS" );
        model.add( 1, "Math" );
        model.add( 2, "History" );
        model.add( 3, "Leisure Studies" );
        model.add( 4, "Psych" );

        setLayout( new FlowLayout( ) );
        add( majors );
    }
}
```

Lists start at index 0.

add method requires us to specify the index location of each element.

Useful Methods

int getSelectedIndex( )	returns the index of the item that is selected
Object getSelectedValue( )	returns the object that is selected
void setSelectionMode(int mode)	single or multiselect items in list

where mode can be:

```
ListSelectionModel.SINGLE_SELECTION
ListSelectionModel.MULTIPLE_INTERVAL_SELECTION (default)
```

4.9.1 Scrollbars

To get scrollbars on the list, we need to put the list inside a JScrollPane.

```
JScrollPane pane;
pane = new JScrollPane( list );
```

Example 4-19 shows a program with JList inside a JScrollPane to show scroll-bars.

EXAMPLE 4-19

```java
import java.awt.*;
import javax.swing.*;
public class JListExScrollPane extends JApplet
{
    DefaultListModel model = new DefaultListModel( );
    JList majors = new JList( model );
    public void init( )
    {
        setLayout( new FlowLayout( ) );
        model = new DefaultListModel( );
        majors = new JList( model );
        model.addElement( "CS" );
        model.addElement( "Math" );
        model.addElement( "History" );
        model.addElement( "Leisure Studies" );
        model.addElement( "Psych" );

        majors.setVisibleRowCount( 3 );
        JScrollPane spane = new JScrollPane( majors );
        add( spane );
    }
}
```

4.9.2 Images

We can also add images into the list. To do this, create ImageIcon objects as we have done before (see JLabel examples). Then add the ImageIcon object into the list. In Example 4-20, we add both text and images into the same list.

EXAMPLE 4-20

```java
import java.awt.*;
import javax.swing.*;
public class JListExImage extends JApplet
{
    DefaultListModel model;
    JList majors;
    Image img;
    ImageIcon icon;

    public void init( )
    {
        model = new DefaultListModel( );
        majors = new JList( model );
        img = getImage( getCodeBase( ), "buttonPoland.png" );
        icon = new ImageIcon( img );
        model.add( 0, icon );

        model.add( 1, "Europe" );

        img = getImage( getCodeBase( ), "buttonLaos.png" );
        icon = new ImageIcon( img );
        model.add( 2, icon );

        model.add( 3, "Asia" );

        img = getImage( getCodeBase( ), "buttonGirl.png" );
        icon = new ImageIcon( img );
        model.add( 4, icon );

        setLayout( new FlowLayout( ) );

        majors.setVisibleRowCount( 3 );
        JScrollPane spane = new JScrollPane( majors );
        add( spane );
    }
}
```

4.10 Components

When we create components such as the JLabel, there are additional methods that we can access through the hierarchy of inheritance. JLabel inherits from the Component class, which has other methods that we can use as well. This applies to many other components that we will be covering too, because they also inherit from the Component class.

The hierarchy looks similar to the following:

```
Component
      |
      |--JButton
      |--JComboBox
      |--JLabel
      |--JList
      |--JTextField
      |--JTextArea
```

4.10.1 Colors

We can change the coloring scheme of our components by using one of the following methods on our components (**FIGURE 4-7**):

setBackground(Color)   sets the background color of the component

setForeground(Color)   sets the text color of the component

setOpaque(false)   makes the component transparent for background color to display through

setOpaque(true)   makes a solid background, useful for setBackground method

Example:

```
JLabel name;
name = new JLabel( "Mr. Cookie Monster" );
name.setOpaque( true ); // necessary for background color
name.setBackground( Color.BLUE );
name.setForeground( Color.YELLOW );
```

FIGURE 4-7 JLabel with custom background color.

setBackground will not work on the JApplet directly. Either fill in a rectangle the size of the applet inside the paint method or create a JPanel and add all components to this JPanel and call setBackground on the JPanel.

setBackground may require us to first call setOpaque(true) on the component—some components such as JLabel default to transparent (opaque = false).

Example 4-21 illustrates two ways to get the background colors of a component to work. We create a panel and set the background color (because we cannot setBackground directly on the applet). We then add three checkboxes. The first one is simply added to the panel. The second one sets the background color of the checkbox to match the color of the panel. The third checkbox just changes its opaqueness to false to allow for transparency so that the panel's color shows through.

EXAMPLE 4-21

```java
import java.awt.*;
import javax.swing.*;
public class OpaqueEx extends JApplet
{
    JCheckBox cb1, cb2, cb3;
    JPanel pane;
    public void init( )
    {
        setLayout( new FlowLayout( ) );
        pane = new JPanel( );
        pane.setBackground( Color.ORANGE );
        cb1 = new JCheckBox( "periwinkle" );
        cb2 = new JCheckBox( "snowflake" );
        cb2.setBackground( Color.ORANGE );
        cb3 = new JCheckBox( "magenta" );
        cb3.setOpaque( false );
        pane.add( cb1 );      pane.add( cb2 );      pane.add( cb3 );
        add( pane );
    }
}
```

Applet Viewer: OpaqueEx.class

Applet

☐ periwinkle   ☐ snowflake   ☐ magenta

Applet started.

To remove the border around the text when highlighted, call .setFocusPainted(false) on each radio button.

Font We can also change the font of the text in our component by calling

setFont(Font)

Example:

```
JLabel name;
name = new JLabel( "Mr. Cookie Monster" );
Font bigFont = new Font( "Serif", Font.BOLD, 36 );
name.setFont( bigFont );
```

or

```
name.setFont( new Font( "Serif", Font.BOLD, 36 ) );
```

or

```
name = new JLabel( "<HTML><FONT SIZE=16>Mr. Cookie Monster</FONT>" ) );
```

Enabled   Sometimes we want a component to be disabled, displaying it as grayed out—and for items such as buttons and lists, to disallow users from clicking on them. To do this, we can call the following method on our component:

```
setEnabled( boolean )
```

Example:

```
JButton submit;

submit = new JButton( "Submit it!" );
submit.setEnabled( false );
```

Example 4-22 demonstrates examples of disabled buttons.

EXAMPLE 4-22

```
import java.awt.*;
import javax.swing.*;
public class setEnabledEx extends JApplet
{
   JButton one;
   JButton two;
   JButton three;
   public void init( )
   {
     setLayout( new FlowLayout( ) );
     one = new JButton( "one" );
     two = new JButton( "two" );
     three = new JButton( "three" );
     one.setEnabled( false );
     three.setEnabled( false );
     add( one );    add( two );    add( three );
   }
}
```

Applet Viewer:...

Applet

one   **two**   three

Applet started.

Users cannot select disabled buttons.

4.11 Examples with Methods

Although we went through many simple examples to explore each component, now we will see how we create a complicated applet with multiple components and ensure that we make use of methods to keep the code more readable. Examples 4-23 and 4-24 use multiple methods to add a variety of components to the applet.

EXAMPLE 4-23

```java
import java.awt.*;
import javax.swing.*;
public class components extends JApplet
{
    JLabel l_address;
    JTextField street, city, state, zip;
    JTextArea ta_message;
    JButton b_go;
    JCheckBox cb_lucky, cb_happy;
    ButtonGroup bg_mood = new ButtonGroup( );
    JRadioButton rb_lucky2, rb_happy2;
    public void init( )
    {
        setLayout( new FlowLayout( ) );
        setupAddressInfo( );
        setupSelections( );
        ta_message = new JTextArea( " ", 3, 50 );
        add( ta_message );
    }
    public void setupAddressInfo( )
    {
        l_address = new JLabel( "Address: " );
        street = new JTextField( );
        city = new JTextField( 50 );
        state = new JTextField( "CO", 2 );
        zip = new JTextField( "80521" );
        add( l_address );   add( street );
        add( city );    add( state );    add( zip );
    }
    public void setupSelections( )
    {
        b_go = new JButton( "Go!" );
        cb_lucky = new JCheckBox( "Lucky?" );
        cb_happy = new JCheckBox( "Happy?", true );
        bg_mood = new ButtonGroup( );
```

(continues)

Example 4-23 (continued)

```
        rb_lucky2 = new JRadioButton( "Lucky2" );
        rb_happy2 = new JRadioButton( "Happy2", true );
        add( b_go );
        add( cb_lucky );
        add( cb_happy );
        bg_mood.add( rb_lucky2 );
        bg_mood.add( rb_happy2 );
        add( rb_lucky2 );
        add( rb_happy2 );
    }
}
```

EXAMPLE 4-24

```
import java.awt.*;
import javax.swing.*;
public class ComponentsWithMethods extends JApplet
{
    // instance data
    JLabel name, imageLabel1, imageLabel2, imageLabel3;
    JTextField tfield;
    JButton button;
    Image img;
    ImageIcon ic;
    public void init( )
    {
        setLayout( new FlowLayout( ) );
        setupName( );
        setupButton( );
        setupImage( imageLabel1, "door.jpg" );
        setupImage( imageLabel2, "flowers.jpg" );
        setupImage( imageLabel3, "Statue.jpg" );
    }
    public void setupName( )
    {
        // sets up the name label and text field
        name = new JLabel( "Name: " );
        tfield = new JTextField( 5 );
        add( name );
        add( tfield );
    }
```

Each call to setupImage sends to the method which label should be set up and added to the applet.

```
    public void setupButton( )
    {
        button = new JButton( "GO" );
        add( button );
    }
    public void setupImage( JLabel lab, String myimage)
    {
        img = getImage( getCodeBase( ), myimage );
        ic = new ImageIcon( img );
        lab = new JLabel( ic );
        add( lab );
    }
}
```

Troubleshooting

Common errors:

Code will not compile.	Make sure that you reference each variable in exactly the same way—remember that Java is case sensitive too.
	Ensure that there are no semicolons at the end of each method header.
	Check to make sure that you are calling the right methods on your variables on the basis of the data type. For example, to add something to a JComboBox call .addItem, and for JList call .addElement or .add with the index number.
The code in my method does not seem to execute.	Make sure that you call your method. The init method gets called automatically, so make sure that you invoke the methods you write inside the init method so that they execute.
I added many components, but only the last one is showing up.	Be sure to call setLayout(new FlowLayout( )) at the beginning of your init method.
My JTextArea keeps expanding when a user types inside it.	JTextArea should be placed within a JScrollPane, then add the JScrollPane to the applet.
My JTextArea is in a JScrollPane, but the scrollbars are not appearing.	By default the scrollbars appear only when necessary. If they should be appearing, then make sure that you added the JScrollPane variable to the applet (and not the JTextArea variable).
How do I get rid of the border around the radio button/checkbox/button?	On your component, call the method .setFocusPainted(false).

(continued)

The background color on my component does not work.	Certain components are by default transparent, such as JLabel. First call .setOpaque(true) on the component and then the background color will show.
The applet works fine with my IDE/appletviewer, but when I add it to the Internet the applet will not initialize.	When adding images, you must first call getImage and store this into an Image object; then instantiate the ImageIcon with the Image variable as a parameter. This is the only way that images will work on the Internet.

SUMMARY

- Swing components are in the javax.swing package and usually begin with the letter J.
- Declare components at the top of the class, after the class header and first brace.
- Swing components are added to the applet by calling the add method.
- Most Swing components allow us to use HTML tags to customize the appearance.
- JLabel is simple text displayed on the applet. The user cannot click on it or change it.
- Image and ImageIcon objects cannot be added directly to the applet or JPanel. First put them into a JLabel or other component and then add that to the applet/JPanel.
- The alignment on JLabel is used to align the component within the allocated space on the basis of the layout manager. To center a multiline text label, use the HTML <CENTER> tag.
- The alignment of text with respect to an image in a JLabel can be changed by calling the setHorizontalTextPosition method.
- There are four steps to adding images: (1) create an Image object by using getImage, (2) create an ImageIcon of the image, (3) add the ImageIcon to a Swing component, and (4) add the component to the applet.
- Radio buttons are grouped together in a ButtonGroup. Multiple ButtonGroups can be used in an applet. The user can select only one item from each ButtonGroup.
- Checkboxes are used when users can select zero or more options. Radio buttons are used when users are to select only one from the group.
- JComboBox is a drop-down list that can be user editable.
- Swing components can have their text color changed by calling the .setForeground method on the component.
- Swing components can allow the background color to come through by making it transparent by calling the .setOpaque method on the component and sending it the Boolean value false.

- Call `.setFocusPainted( false )` on components to avoid a border painted around the component with focus.

1. What package do we need to import to use Swing components?
2. Which component codes for a drop-down box?
3. Which letter do most Swing components begin with?
4. How many items can be true in a `ButtonGroup`?
5. What type of component should we use if we want a field where the user could enter a few lines of a text message?
6. True or false? We can have text on top of an image inside a `JButton`.
7. Write the `String` required to make a single `JLabel` with "`Hello`" on the first line and "`World`" on the next line.
8. What three types of image formats does Java support?
9. What are the four steps to add an image to an applet?
10. True or false? After a call to `getImage` to create the `Image` object from a file, we can add the `Image` object directly onto the applet.
11. What method do we call on a `JButton` to set the image for when a mouse rolls over the button?
12. Given the following button, write a one-line code statement to change the color of the text to blue.

    ```
    JButton javaRocks = new JButton( "I love Java" );
    ```

13. How do we make a button with an image on it have no border around it?
14. True or false? The `init` method is called automatically by the browser whenever an applet is started.
15. How do we create radio buttons?
16. How do we get scrollbars on a `JTextArea`? On a `JList`?
17. How do we allow users to enter text into a `JComboBox`?
18. What method can we call to disable a `JList`? A `JTextField`? A `JButton`?
19. What method can we call to remove an element from a `JList`? A `JComboBox`?
20. What does the method `getItemCount` return?
21. True or false? Images can be displayed in a `JList`.
22. True or false? Images can be displayed in a `JComboBox`.
23. How do we set a `JList` to allow only one selection?
24. What is the difference between a group of `JCheckBox` and a group of `JRadioButton`?
25. What is the difference between `JList` and `JComboBox`?

26. Which Java components can produce text on multiple lines? How? Are there multiple ways to achieve this result, based on the type of components?

27. How does a `JLabel` differ from using the `paint` method? How are they similar?

28. Can a `JLabel` contain both text and images?

29. Create a `JLabel` with the text in both bold and italic.

30. Can a `JLabel` have HTML tags embedded?

31. How do we get the text to appear on multiple lines inside a `JLabel`?

32. If you are using HTML tags, what has to be the first thing inside the string?

33. Can we add an `ImageIcon` directly to the applet?

34. True or false? `JLabel` can contain text with multiple colors.

35. True or false? A `ButtonGroup` is necessary to group `JCheckBox` components together.

36. Put the following steps in order to add an image to the applet.

    _____ Create a `JLabel`

    _____ Create an `ImageIcon`

    _____ Call `getImage`

37. Create an applet that has three sets of radio button groups asking the user for her favorite color, movie, and TV show.

38. Create an applet with five navigational buttons: Home, About Me, Photos, Portfolio, and Friends. Make a button background image (use transparency as necessary), display each button with your image, and remove all decorations that Java displays (e.g., border, background, focus, etc.). Use the same image for all five buttons, centering the text of each button on top of the image.

39. Create an applet that is a party invitation. Include a text field for users to enter their name, a checkbox to designate whether they are planning on attending, a drop-down list of what they will bring (appetizer, main dish, dessert), radio buttons for how many guests they will bring (0, 1, 2), and a text area for them to describe their costume.

40. Create an applet that displays a library of all your music. Include a list with each song listed, a drop-down list for different genres, and buttons to play/stop a song.

41. Create an applet of all your favorites: movies, bands, artists, people, and quotes. Select appropriate components to display each.

GUI
Design

I would love to change the world,
if only somebody would give me the source code!

OUTLINE

- Layout Managers
  - FlowLayout
  - BorderLayout
  - GridLayout
  - BoxLayout
- Warnings
- Structuring with Methods
- Design
  - Design Examples
  - Design Guidelines
- Case Study
- Troubleshooting
- Summary
- Exercises

5.1 Layout Managers

Layout managers allow us to control where and how components are displayed. They divide the space of a container into regions and arrange the components in these regions. Different layout managers have different effects on the components—some layout managers will stretch components to fill the space allocated to it, and some layout managers allow the components to be whatever size they prefer.

We can add greater control by also using extra panels to nest components within layouts. A panel is a container into which we can put components, such as additional buttons and labels. The applet itself is a container, which is how we added components in the previous chapter. We also want to make use of a panel, JPanel, as another container to hold components.

To create a JPanel, we can specify the layout manager either when we instantiate it or by calling the method setLayout, like we did with our applet:

```
JPanel  pane;

pane  =  new JPanel( new FlowLayout( ) );
```

or

```
pane  =  new JPanel( );
pane.setLayout( new FlowLayout( ) );
```

Then we can add components to our JPanel by specifying which JPanel and calling the add method:

```
pane.add( myButton );
pane.add( myLabel );
```

The last thing we need is to remember to add the panel to the applet. We do this in the same way that we add other components such as buttons and labels:

```
add( pane );
```

When working with containers, be it the applet or JPanels, we can add as many components or other containers as we wish—there are no limits (until we run out of memory).

▪ 5.1.1 FlowLayout

FlowLayout is the easiest layout manager to work with. We have been using FlowLayout in our previous examples to keep it simple. Let us now analyze this layout scheme in more detail.

The way our components are laid out on the screen in FlowLayout is by placing them centered at the top of our applet. As we add more components, we run out of room in that "row," and therefore the remaining components are added beneath the first row, starting out centered again.

Example 5-1 is shown in **FIGURE 5-1**, **FIGURE 5-2**, and **FIGURE 5-3** in different applet sizes. Notice how the components wrap depending on the size of the applet.

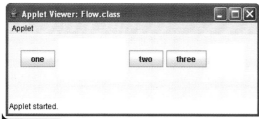

FIGURE 5-1 Example 5-1 displayed with a width of 400 pixels and height of 100 pixels.

FIGURE 5-2 Example 5-1 displayed with a width of 150 pixels and height of 200 pixels.

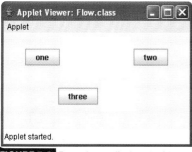

FIGURE 5-3 Example 5-1 displayed with a width of 300 pixels and height of 150 pixels.

EXAMPLE 5-1

```java
import java.awt.*;
import javax.swing.*;
public class FlowEx extends JApplet
{
    JButton one, two, three;
    JTextArea ta1, ta2;
    public void init( )
    {
        setLayout( new FlowLayout( ) );
        one = new JButton( "one" );
        two = new JButton( "two" );
        three = new JButton( "three" );
        ta1 = new JTextArea( 4, 10 );
        ta2 = new JTextArea( 3, 5 );
        add( one );
        add( ta1 );
        add( two );
        add( three );
        add( ta2 );
    }
}
```

We can customize this layout a little by specifying that we want our components aligned to either the left or right. We can do this when we declare the FlowLayout manager by specifying

- FlowLayout.LEFT
- FlowLayout.RIGHT
- FlowLayout.CENTER (default)

Example:

```java
setLayout( new FlowLayout( FlowLayout.RIGHT ) );
```

By changing this line in the program Example 5-1, we can see the output in **FIGURE 5-4** based on a 300 × 200 applet.

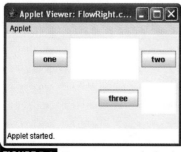

FIGURE 5-4 FlowLayout example that is right-aligned.

Advanced Concept

FlowLayout does not support an easy method for vertical alignment of components. If, for example, we wanted to center three buttons vertically on a JPanel (see next section) in BorderLayout.CENTER (see next section), we would need to calculate the dimensions of the JPanel and set the vertical gap on the JPanel. However, we cannot calculate the dimensions of a component until after all the components are on the applet and displayed. This means that we need to put our code to calculate the dimension and change the vertical gap in a different method, the start method, which is called when everything is ready in the applet. Example 5-2 demonstrates how to get three buttons to show up centered vertically:

EXAMPLE 5-2

```
import java.awt.*;
import javax.swing.*;
public class FlowVertEx extends JApplet
{
    JButton one, two, three;
    FlowLayout flow = new FlowLayout( );
    JPanel pane = new JPanel( );
    public void init( )
    {
        one = new JButton( "one" );
        two = new JButton( "two" );
        three = new JButton( "three" );
        pane.add( one );
        pane.add( two );
        pane.add( three );
        add( pane );
    }
    public void start( )
    {
        flow.setVgap( ( int )( pane.getSize( ).getHeight( )/2 ) -
                ( int ) ( one.getHeight( )/2 ) );
        pane.setLayout( flow );
    }
}
```

> setVgap method takes integers;
> getHeight returns a double, so
> we must *cast* final value to int

Applet Viewer: FlowVertEx.class

Applet

    one   two   three

Applet started.

■ 5.1.2 BorderLayout

BorderLayout allows us to align components within five areas:

- NORTH
- SOUTH
- WEST
- EAST
- CENTER

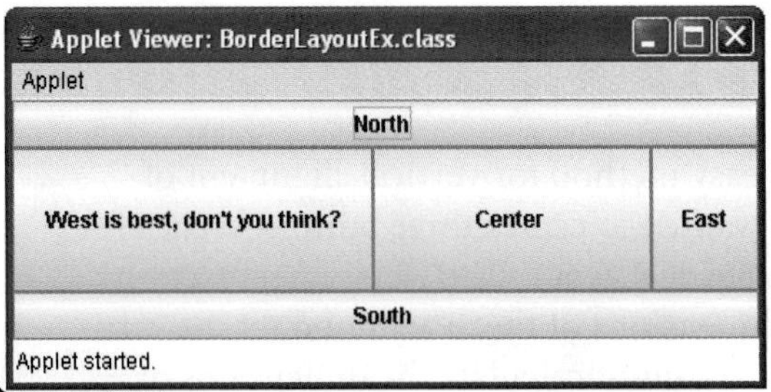

FIGURE 5-5 BorderLayout example demonstrating all five regions.

The layout scheme appears in **FIGURE 5-5**. The code is in Example 5-3.

EXAMPLE 5-3

```
import java.awt.*;
import javax.swing.*;
public class BorderLayoutEx extends JApplet
{
    JButton b1, b2, b3, b4, b5;
    public void init( )
    {
        setLayout( new BorderLayout( ) );
        b1 = new JButton( "North" );
        b2 = new JButton( "South" );
        b3 = new JButton( "West is best, don't you think?" );
        b4 = new JButton( "East" );
        b5 = new JButton( "Center" );

        add( b1, BorderLayout.NORTH );
        add( b2, BorderLayout.SOUTH );
        add( b3, BorderLayout.WEST );
        add( b4, BorderLayout.EAST );
        add( b5, BorderLayout.CENTER );
    }
}
```

When using the BorderLayout, we first need to specify that we want to use this layout manager. We can do so by calling the method setLayout, as follows:

```
setLayout( new BorderLayout( ) );
```

Once we set the layout for our applet to BorderLayout, we now have to specify where to add the components. When we call the add method, we specify which component we want to add to the applet, as well as the location (**FIGURE 5-6**).

The format for the add method:

```
add( component, location );
```

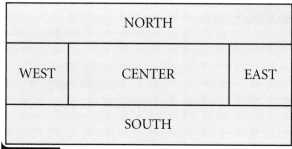

FIGURE 5-6 The five regions of `BorderLayout`.

The locations that we can specify for `BorderLayout` are:

- `BorderLayout.NORTH`
- `BorderLayout.SOUTH`
- `BorderLayout.EAST`
- `BorderLayout.WEST`
- `BorderLayout.CENTER`

There are some peculiarities that we need to look at: how components are stretched to fill the space and limitations and rules for adding components to each space. When we add components to a container by using `BorderLayout`, they stretch in different ways ...

- Components added to the NORTH and SOUTH stretch the entire horizontal width but take up only as much space vertically as necessary. (See preceding example; only enough space horizontally for the text on the buttons.)
- Components added to the WEST and EAST stretch the vertical height between the components in the NORTH and SOUTH, but take up only as much space horizontally as necessary. (See preceding example; only enough space vertically for the text on the buttons.)
- Components added to the CENTER will stretch to fill in whatever remaining space is available. *Note:* if there is nothing added to the center, we may have a hole in our applet!

If we modify the previous example and comment out the line

```
add( b5, BorderLayout.CENTER );
```

from the preceding program, the applet displays as shown in **FIGURE 5-7**. Notice the hole in the center region. Only the center region will stretch in both directions to fill any empty space. Therefore, we will probably always want to put at least *something* in the center region.

The second peculiarity concerns how many components we can add to each area. We can add only one component into each area: NORTH, SOUTH, WEST, EAST, and CENTER. This is where things become complex. If we wanted to have a label and a button in the WEST side of our applet, we can do this by placing those two components into a JPanel and then add the JPanel to the applet to the WEST side.

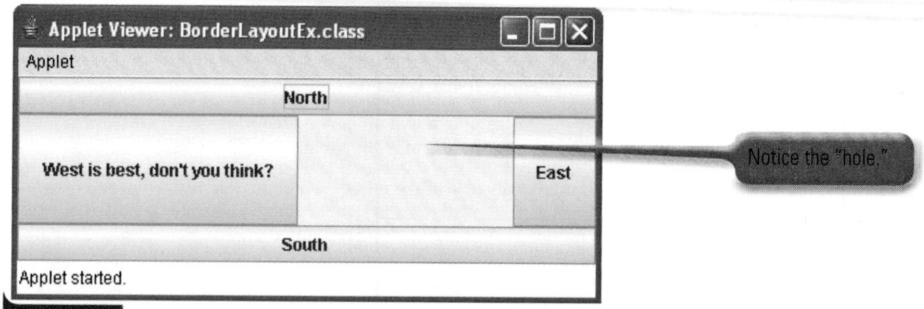

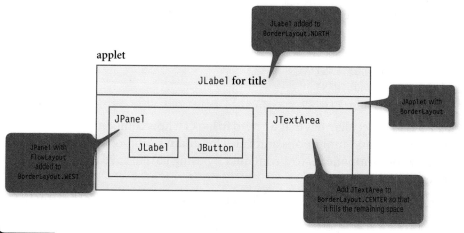

FIGURE 5-7 Example of a hole in BorderLayout when the center region is not filled.

FIGURE 5-8 Example of nesting components using a JPanel.

What is a JPanel? A JPanel is a component that is a surface pane onto which we can add components. Because we can put only one component into each area of BorderLayout, we can work around this limit by placing multiple components onto a JPanel and then add the JPanel into the area in the BorderLayout. **FIGURE 5-8** depicts this nesting of components. Example 5-4 uses a JPanel for nesting components:

EXAMPLE 5-4

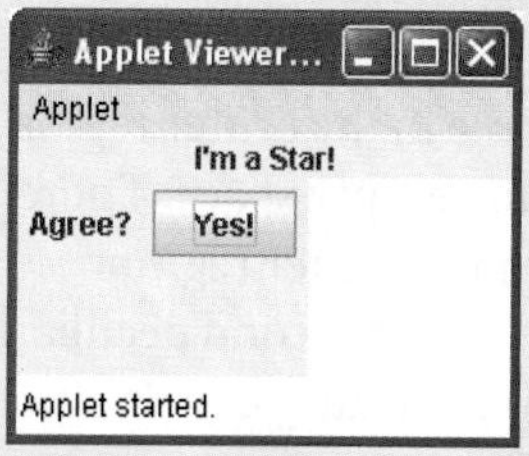

```
import java.awt.*;
import javax.swing.*;
public class Nesting extends JApplet
{
    JLabel title, agree;
    JButton yes;
    JTextArea msg;
    public void init( )
```

```
{
    setLayout( new BorderLayout( ) );    // set layout
        // create components
    title = new JLabel( "I'm a Star!", JLabel.CENTER );
    agree = new JLabel( "Agree?" );
    yes = new JButton( "Yes!" );
    msg = new JTextArea( 2, 10 );
    JPanel pane = new JPanel( new FlowLayout( ) );
        // create nested panel
    pane.add( agree );
    pane.add( yes );
    add( pane, BorderLayout.WEST );     // add panel to WEST side
    add( title, BorderLayout.NORTH );   // add title to NORTH
    add( msg, BorderLayout.EAST );      // add text area to EAST
                                        //   side
}
}
```

We cannot see the JPanel; it is there mostly to help us organize our components on the applet. However, we could make the JPanel more obvious by changing its color. If we add the following line to the preceding example, we will see exactly where the JPanel is (**FIGURE 5-9**):

```
pane.setBackground( Color.RED );
```

Nesting JPanel components is the secret for customizing the appearance of our applet. But how are components arranged inside JPanel? By default, JPanel is set to use the FlowLayout manager. If we want to change the layout manager for a JPanel, we can do so in two different ways.

- When creating the JPanel:

```
JPanel pane;
pane = new JPanel( new BorderLayout( ) );
```

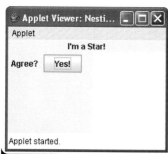

FIGURE 5-9 Example of changing the background color of a JPanel.

- By calling the setLayout method:

```
pane.setLayout( new BorderLayout( ) );
```

We can use any of the layout managers either on our applet or in a JPanel (including the ones we have yet to learn).

> We can put only one component in each of the five regions of BorderLayout!
> *Hint:* use JPanels to nest components and add the single JPanel to the region.

Let us go back again and take a look at our JLabel. Remember that there were options for alignment on a JLabel? For FlowLayout, the size of the label is the exact size to encompass the text, so the alignment is irrelevant. However, with BorderLayout, the size of the label stretches to fill the region. Now we can make use of our alignment in JLabel. The default alignment for JLabel is left-justified if there is only. The default for JLabel if there is only an image is to be center-justified. JLabels with both text and an image require us to specify the alignment when we create the JLabel.

In Example 5-5, we can see JLabels in the NORTH and SOUTH as left-aligned. WEST and EAST alignment are irrelevant because the width is the same size as the label's text.

EXAMPLE 5-5

```java
import java.awt.*;
import javax.swing.*;
public class BorderLayoutJLabel extends JApplet
{
    JLabel n1, n2, n3, n4, n5;

    public void init( )
    {
        setLayout( new BorderLayout( ) );
        n1 = new JLabel( "North" );
        n1.setOpaque( true );
        n1.setBackground( Color.GREEN );
        n2 = new JLabel( "South" );
        n3 = new JLabel( "West is best, don't you think?" );
        n4 = new JLabel( "East" );
        n5 = new JLabel( "Center" );
        add( n1, BorderLayout.NORTH );
        add( n2, BorderLayout.SOUTH );
```

```
        add( n3, BorderLayout.WEST );
        add( n4, BorderLayout.EAST );
        add( n5, BorderLayout.CENTER );
    }
}
```

5.1.3 GridLayout

GridLayout sets up a spreadsheet-like grid of cells, where each cell has the same width and same height. (Width may not be the same as the height.)

When using the GridLayout, we first need to specify that we want to use this layout manager. We can do so by calling the method setLayout and specifying the number of rows and columns, as follows:

```
setLayout( new GridLayout( numRows, numColumns ) );
```

Once we set the layout for our applet to GridLayout, we now have to add the components. When we call the add method, we specify which component we want to add to the applet. The format for the add method:

```
add( component );
```

GridLayout adds each component to the cells from the top in left-to-right order. It also stretches out each component to fill the entire space of the cell. Example 5-6 sets the applet with 3 rows and 2 columns, and demonstrates a nested JPanel in the last cell which contains two buttons.

EXAMPLE 5-6

```
import java.awt.*;
import javax.swing.*;
public class GridLayoutEx extends JApplet
{
    JButton b1, b2, b3, b4, b5, a, b;
    JPanel pane;

    public void init( )
    {
        setLayout( new GridLayout( 3, 2) );
        b1 = new JButton( "First" );
        b2 = new JButton( "Two" );
        b3 = new JButton( "Three" );
        b4 = new JButton( "Four" );
        b5 = new JButton( "Five" );
        add( b1 );
        add( b2 );
        add( b3 );
```

(continues)

Example 5-6 (continued)

```
            add( b4 );
            add( b5 );
            pane = new JPanel( );
            pane.setLayout( new BorderLayout( ) );
            a = new JButton( "go" );
            b = new JButton( "there" );
            pane.add( a, BorderLayout.NORTH );
            pane.add( b, BorderLayout.CENTER );
            add( pane );
        }
    }
```

> The JPanel *pane* has two buttons: "go" and "there."

We can add spacing between each component by adding the horizontal and vertical spacing when we create the GridLayout (**FIGURE 5-10**). In Example 5-6, change the setLayout method call to be the following:

```
setLayout( new GridLayout( 3, 2, 15, 5 ) );
```

The parameters designate the number of rows (3), number of columns (2), and the number of pixels for spacing between components horizontally (15) and vertically (51) (**FIGURE 5-10** and **FIGURE 5-11** when the JPanel is not added, thereby leaving a blank spot).

FIGURE 5-10 Example of GridLayout with horizontal and vertical spacing between cells.

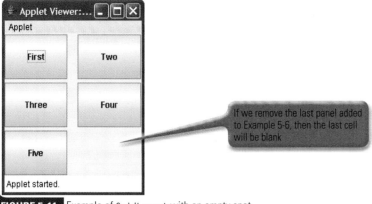

If we remove the last panel added to Example 5-6, then the last cell will be blank

FIGURE 5-11 Example of GridLayout with an empty spot.

5.1.4 BoxLayout

BoxLayout sets up a gridlike structure in either a row or a column. BoxLayout differs from GridLayout in that it is only one row or column, and the components added to the cells are not stretched to fill in the space. BoxLayout is good for creating toolbars.

When using the BoxLayout, we first need to specify that we want to use this layout manager. We can do so by calling the method setLayout and specifying whether to create a row or column, as follows for the applet:

Row

```
setLayout( new BoxLayout( getContentPane( ), BoxLayout.X_AXIS ) );
```

Column

```
setLayout( new BoxLayout( getContentPane( ), BoxLayout.Y_AXIS ) );
```

Once we set the layout for our applet to BoxLayout, we now have to add the components. When we call the add method, we specify which component we want to add to the applet. The format for the add method:

```
add( component );
```

BoxLayout adds each component to the cells in order either from top to bottom if set to Y_AXIS or in left-to-right order if set to X_AXIS. Example 5-7 demonstrates the use of BoxLayout.

EXAMPLE 5-7

```
import javax.swing.*;
public class BoxLayoutEx extends JApplet
{
    JButton one, two, three;

    public void init( )
    {
        one = new JButton( "one" );
        two = new JButton( "two" );
        three = new JButton( "buckle my shoe" );

        setLayout( new BoxLayout( getContentPane( ),
                   BoxLayout.Y_AXIS ) );
        add( one );
        add( two );
        add( three );
    }
}
```

Using BoxLayout in a JPanel is a little tricky. First we need to declare the JPanel. Then we can call the method setLayout on the JPanel and instantiate a new Box-Layout. When we do this, we need to specify the JPanel again as well as the axis. For example:

```
JPanel verticalPanel = new JPanel( );
verticalPanel.setLayout( new BoxLayout( verticalPanel,
                         BoxLayout.Y_AXIS ) );
```

Example 5-8 makes use of two BoxLayouts; one on a JPanel and one on the applet.

EXAMPLE 5-8

```
import javax.swing.*;
public class BoxLayoutExInJPanel extends JApplet
{
    JButton one, two, three;
    JPanel verticalPanel;
    public void init( )
    {
        setLayout( new BoxLayout( getContentPane( ), BoxLayout.X_AXIS ) );
        one = new JButton( "one" );
        two = new JButton( "two" );
        three = new JButton( "buckle my shoe" );
        verticalPanel = new JPanel( );
```

```
        verticalPanel.setLayout( new BoxLayout(verticalPanel,
                               BoxLayout.Y_AXIS) );
        verticalPanel.add( new JButton( "abc" ) ) ;
        verticalPanel.add( new JButton( "def" ) );
        verticalPanel.add( new JButton( "ghi" ) );
        add( verticalPanel );
        add( one );
        add( two );
        add( three );
    }
}
```

5.2 Warnings

We have to be careful about adding components. If we attempt to add a component that is already contained elsewhere, it will be removed and reinserted. For example, in Example 5-9, button1 will be displayed only in the EAST section.

EXAMPLE 5-9

```
import java.awt.*;
import javax.swing.*;
public class Warning2 extends JApplet
{
    JButton button1, button2;
    public void  init( )
    {
        button1 = new JButton( "one" );
        button2 = new JButton( "two" );
        JPanel panel = new JPanel( );
        panel.setLayout( new BorderLayout( ) );
        panel.add( button1, BorderLayout.NORTH );
        panel.add( button2, BorderLayout.WEST );
        panel.add( button1, BorderLayout.EAST );
        add( panel );
    }
}
```

Another warning is that we can put only one component into a region with some of the layout managers. For example, if we try to add two components to the NORTH of BorderLayout, only the last component added will be displayed (Example 5-10).

EXAMPLE 5-10

```java
import java.awt.*;
import javax.swing.*;
public class Warning1 extends JApplet
{
    JButton button1, button2;
    public void init( )
    {
        button1 = new JButton( "one" );
        button2 = new JButton( "two" );
        JPanel panel = new JPanel( );
        panel.setLayout( new BorderLayout( ) );
        panel.add( button1, BorderLayout.NORTH );
        panel.add( button2, BorderLayout.NORTH );
        add( panel );
    }
}
```

To change the background color of the applet, create a JPanel and call
.setBackground on the JPanel, add the JPanel to the BorderLayout.CENTER of
the applet, and add all components to the JPanel.

5.3 Structuring with Methods

Now is a good time to see a structured approach to using methods for layouts. By
using a BorderLayout type of structure, we can divide up the applet into the five
regions and create methods to set up each region. Example 5-11 sets up a general
structure of a class with methods that we can use for many projects.

EXAMPLE 5-11

```java
import java.awt.*;
import javax.swing.*;
public class Structure extends JApplet
{
        // Declare all your variables HERE!
        // this includes all your components!
    JPanel  title,  leftside,  rightside,  center,  bottom;
    public void init( )
```

```
    {
        setLayout( new BorderLayout( ) );
        setupTitle( );
        setupLeftSide( );
        setupRightSide( );
        setupCenter( );
        setupBottom( );
    }
    public void setupTitle( )
    {
        // add title at the top of applet
    }
    public void setupLeftSide( )
    {
        // set the layout manager for the left side panel
        // set background color on this panel
        // add components on this panel
        // add this panel to the applet
    }
    public void setupRightSide( )
    {
        // set the layout manager for the right side panel
        // set background color on this panel
        // add components on this panel
        // add this panel to the applet
    }
    public void setupCenter( )
    {   // set the layout manager for the center panel
        // set background color on this panel
        // add components on this panel
        // add this panel to the applet
    }
    public void setupBottom( )
    {
        // set the layout manager for the bottom panel
        // set background color on this panel
        // add components on this panel
        // add this panel to the applet
    }
}
```

5.4 Design

When we work with applets, we need to first design how the GUI (graphical user interface) should look. The first step is to determine the purpose of the applet—is it for your company, your personal résumé, your list of favorite recipes, your favorite football team statistics, etc.? Once we figure out what we want to do, the next step is to lay it out on paper (you can also use various computer programs to do this, but that approach can take a lot more time than simply sketching it on paper). Sometimes it helps to look at other programs to get ideas of what to do. Fortunately, the Internet is an excellent source for design—with many good and bad examples. We can use these as templates for our own design ideas.

5.4.1 Design Examples

A drawing example is shown in **FIGURE 5-12**. Each component is labeled as the type of component, and all JPanels are specified with their layout managers. It is much easier to figure this out on paper before attempting to program it—even for expert programmers!

Let us look at another example. **FIGURE 5-13** depicts how would achieve the result for **FIGURE 5-14**. For practice, try programming this GUI. This example shows different colors for different panels to make it easier to see how we could divide up the layout. We can see how the overall aspects of the applet are based on BorderLayout, with a title in the north and checkboxes in the south. The left side then appears to have a GridLayout with two rows of the same size. In the bottom one, it looks like we can use GridLayout again for the three labels and drop-down boxes.

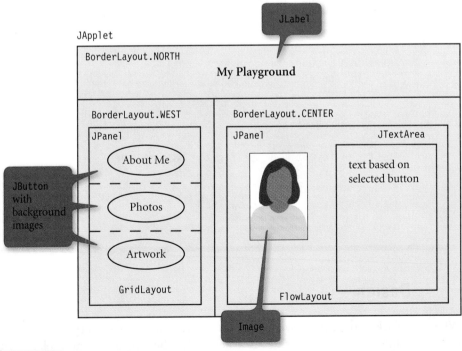

FIGURE 5-12 Example layout of components and layout managers.

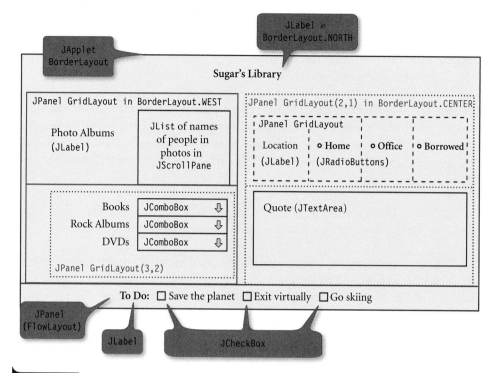

FIGURE 5-13 Example layout of Figure 5-14.

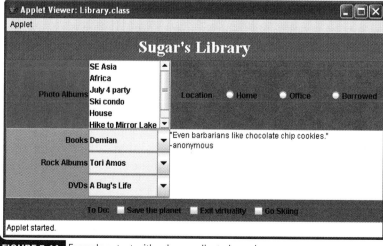

FIGURE 5-14 Example output with color coordinated panels.

■ 5.4.2 Design Guidelines

Although designing may seem easy, the process is actually complex if we want good design. There are many theories on good design, and we will look at a few of them related to website design.

One page: Websites (and applets that run on them) are best if the user does not have to scroll on the page. Unfortunately, this guideline is hard to follow because everyone has different-sized monitors and uses different resolutions. However, we can keep this in mind when we choose how much to display and choose the size of our images.

Navigation: Users should be able to navigate easily to different areas. With applets, we can use JTabbedPane to allow users to access different screens easily.

Recognition versus recall: It is easier for a user to recall something by selecting it in a list as opposed to having to type it in (which also leads to errors). Use drop-down lists for selections with many standard items (e.g., state code) or radio buttons for smaller sets of selections.

Consistency: Keep buttons in consistent locations (e.g., OK and Cancel), use the same color scheme (otherwise the user's eyes go nuts focusing), etc.

Progress indicators: Update the user about what is going on when processing something big, such as when loading many images. Use a status notice or a progress bar.

Who are you?: Users that surf the net, and especially those who buy from a website, like to see some humanity associated with the site. Adding an "About Us" information page on the people behind the company and/or design of the website helps users feel more comfortable and secure with your website. For professional websites, it is also important to provide contact information such as an email address and/or phone number.

Not too much!: Some developers get carried away with the nifty things that they can do—one of the best examples is the use of too many animated graphics. Anything that moves or is animated catches users' eyes and draws them up there. If they are trying to read an article on your site, it is difficult when their eyes are constantly drawn to different areas on the screen.

Readable text: Substantial text that is either too small or too large is hard to read, as is text wider than 80 characters. Beyond 80 characters, users have a hard time finding their place as they go to the next line.

case study

In the remaining chapters, we will develop a program for a coffee club. We will follow the Software Engineering methodology of the Software Development Life Cycle (SDLC). The SDLC consists of four main phases: requirements, design, implementation, and testing. The requirements phase is when we discuss with the client their wants and needs. Usually a requirements document is written up to document the client's specifications. The second phase is design, where the programmers develop solution ideas to meet the client's needs. No programming is involved in this phase. Instead, the GUI will be drawn out and potential solutions will be sketched out, designating layout managers, extra JPanels, and all the necessary components. The design phase may also include descriptions about how to implement the solution without actually writing any programming code. Once a solution is designed, we proceed to the implementation phase, where the program is written in a programming language. The testing phase is partially accomplished by the programmers as they write the code and test to ensure that their piece works. Once the system is complete, a full testing cycle is run as if the client were using the system. This step is necessary because sometimes programs will break after a particular sequence of instructions or after running for a while. All these phases are iterative; as we start at the requirements and proceed into the design phase, we may need to go back to the client for clarification and modify the requirements before working again through the design phase. Sometimes projects will go through all four phases and be in the testing phase when something comes up that necessitates modifying the requirements again, working through a modified design, implementing the modification, and repeating the testing.

First we begin with a client's request. For our examples, our clients are providing us a sketch of what they want their program to look like and some simple directives of how it should work. This is similar to the homework assignments you get. In industry, we would fully document every single feature and how it should work to use for legal purposes in determining whether the final software product actually delivers what the company promised for the pay.

Our first example is from a coffee club company. They want to sell a monthly membership where their customers will get a gourmet coffee, regional gift, and information sheets each month. They have four main views of the applet: Home, Join the Club, FAQ, and Contact Us. **FIGURE 5-15** and **FIGURE 5-16** are two screenshots of how the client wants the overall look and feel to be for the applet.

case study, cont.

The client is not providing screen shots for the "Join the Club" and "Contact Us" buttons but wants you to come up with something that looks professional. For our purposes, I will leave that as an exercise for you. We will walk through the design phase for setting up these two screenshots, and in later chapters we will look at various ways to implement it.

Our first step is to sketch out how we can design a layout for these screens. We will work through the main screen. Because we have a screenshot, we will use that as our basis for sketching our design and draw our design on top. Overall, our applet can make use of BorderLayout because the logo would work well in BorderLayout.NORTH, the buttons with the image in a GridLayout in BorderLayout.WEST, and the copyright information listed in BorderLayout.SOUTH. The inside of the main center section takes a little work. At first glance, it appears that there are many JLabels necessary to get this to work. But in actuality, we can create lists and the lines by using HTML codes inside our JLabel so we can put the top half of the screen all into one JLabel. The HTML code for the horizontal lines is the <HR> tag, and for lists we use <UL> to start an unordered list and the <LI> tag for each list item. The bottom section then has an image, text, and another image. We could design this with three JLabels inside a separate JPanel by using GridLayout. **FIGURE 5-17** is a sketch that shows our design idea.

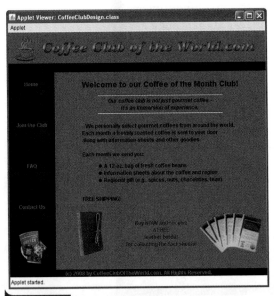

FIGURE 5-15 Case study Coffee Club home page.

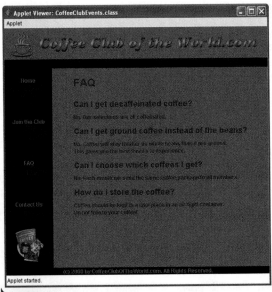

FIGURE 5-16 Case study Coffee Club FAQ page.

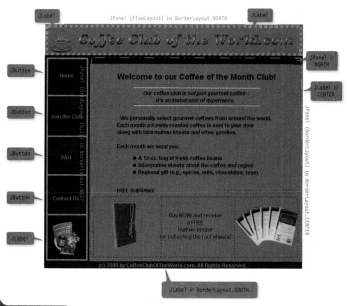

FIGURE 5-17 Case study Coffee Club layout.

case study, cont.

Now that we have a design from which to work, we can start to implement the GUI. The first step is to copy the Structure class to set us up for using BorderLayout. We can remove the code for the right side because we are not using it. The code is developed in Example 5-12.

EXAMPLE 5-12

```
import java.awt.*;
import javax.swing.*;
public class CoffeeClubDesign extends JApplet
{
    JButton home, join, faq, contact;
    Image img;
    JLabel title, logo, copyright, ntbkImg, ntbkDesc, infoSheets, welcomeMsg;
    Color tanColor = new Color( 204, 153, 51 );
    Color darkColor = new Color( 51, 17, 0 );
    Color bkgrdColor = new Color ( 17, 8, 0 );
    JPanel leftside, top, center, welcomePanel, separator, freeNotebook;
```

(continues)

```
public void init( )
{
   setLayout( new BorderLayout( ) );
   doTitle( );
   doLeftSide( );
   doBottom( );
   doCenter( );
}
public void setupButton( JButton b )     // method to set up each button
{
      b.setContentAreaFilled( false );
      b.setBorderPainted( false );
      b.setFocusPainted( false );
      b.setForeground( tanColor );
      leftside.add( b );
}
public void doTitle( )
{
   img = getImage( getCodeBase( ), "coffeeLogoMetal.png" );
   logo = new JLabel( new ImageIcon(img) );
   img = getImage( getCodeBase( ), "logoName.png" );
   title = new JLabel( new ImageIcon(img) );
   top = new JPanel( new FlowLayout( ) );
   top.add( logo );
   top.add( title );
   top.setBackground ( tanColor );
   add( top, BorderLayout.NORTH );
}
public void doLeftSide( )
{
   // left side menu
   leftside = new JPanel( new GridLayout( 5, 1 ) );
   leftside.setBackground ( darkColor );
   home = new JButton( "Home" );
   join = new JButton( "Join the Club" );
   faq = new JButton( "FAQ" );
   contact = new JButton( "Contact Us" );
   setupButton( home );
   setupButton( join );
   setupButton( faq );
   setupButton( contact );
   JLabel basket = new JLabel( new ImageIcon( getImage( getCodeBase( ),
                                    "coffeeBasket.png" ) ) );
   leftside.add( basket );
   add( leftside, BorderLayout.WEST );

}
```

```
public void doBottom( )
{
   copyright=new JLabel( "<HTML><SMALL>(c)2008 by CoffeeClubOfTheWorld.com."
      + "  All Rights Reserved.", JLabel.CENTER );
   copyright.setForeground( tanColor );
   copyright.setOpaque( true );
   copyright.setBackground( darkColor );
   add( copyright, BorderLayout.SOUTH );
}
public void doCenter( )
{
   center = new JPanel ( new BorderLayout( ) );
   center.setBackground( tanColor );
   // add dark separator as a blank-colored panel in NORTH of center panel
   separator = new JPanel( );
   separator.setBackground ( darkColor );
   separator.setPreferredSize( new Dimension( 10, 20 ) );
   center.add( separator, BorderLayout.NORTH );

   welcomePanel = new JPanel( new FlowLayout( ) );
   welcomePanel.setOpaque( false );
   welcomeMsg = new JLabel( "<html><center>"
      + "<H2>Welcome to our Coffee of the Month Club! </h2>"
      + "<HR WIDTH=80%><I>Our coffee club is not just gourmet coffee — "
      + "<BR>it's an immersion of experience. <HR WIDTH=80%><BR>"
      + "We personally select gourmet coffees from around the world. <BR>"
      + "</CENTER>Each month a freshly roasted coffee is sent to your door"
      + "<BR>along with information sheets and other goodies."
      + "<BR><BR>Each month we send you:"
      + "<UL><LI>A 12-oz. bag of fresh coffee beans"
      + "<LI>Information sheets about the coffee and region"
      + "<LI>Regional gift (e.g., spices, nuts, chocolates, teas)"
      + "</UL><BR><B>FREE SHIPPING!</B><BR><BR>");
   welcomeMsg.setForeground( darkColor );
   welcomePanel.add( welcomeMsg );
   // create the bottom free notebook offer
   freeNotebook = new JPanel( new GridLayout( 1, 3 ) );
   freeNotebook.setOpaque( false );
   ntbkImg = new JLabel(
      new ImageIcon( getImage( getCodeBase( ), "ntbk.png" ) ) );
   ntbkDesc = new JLabel(
      "<HTML><CENTER>Buy NOW and receive<BR> a FREE<BR>"
      + "leather binder <BR>for collecting the fact sheets!" );
```

String can go across multiple lines, using + to append.

(continues)

case study, cont.

```
        infoSheets = new JLabel( new ImageIcon( getImage( getCodeBase( ),
        "InfoSheets.png" ) ) );
        freeNotebook.add( ntbkImg );
        freeNotebook.add( ntbkDesc );
        freeNotebook.add( infoSheets );
        welcomePanel.add( freeNotebook, BorderLayout.SOUTH );
        center.add( welcomePanel, BorderLayout.CENTER );
        add( center, BorderLayout.CENTER );
    }
}
```

Troubleshooting

Common errors:

Code will not compile.	Make sure that you reference each variable in exactly the same way—remember that Java is case sensitive too.
	When creating a new GridLayout, specify the number of rows and columns.
	When adding components, be sure to specify the location if using BorderLayout.
Only one component is showing up.	Applets use BorderLayout by default. If you do not specify a location for each component, it defaults to adding the component to BorderLayout.CENTER. Because only one component can be displayed in each region of BorderLayout, only the last one you add to the applet is being displayed. Modify each add method call to include the location.
I tried to add a component to two locations in Border-Layout and it appears only once.	Components can be displayed in only one location. The last place added in the code is the location of where it is displayed.
There is a hole in the middle of the applet.	When using BorderLayout, it is best to add something to BorderLayout.CENTER because it will stretch in both directions to cover all remaining space. If you add things only to WEST and EAST, there may be a gap in the center of your applet. Put your WEST or EAST panel in BorderLayout.CENTER instead.
My panel is not showing up in the location I wanted it.	Make sure that you actually added the JPanel to the applet or other JPanel where it should be displayed.

SUMMARY

- Layout managers determine how and where components are to be displayed.
- Some layout managers will stretch components to fill the space.
- Call the setLayout method to change the layout of a container.
- JPanels can be nested inside other JPanels and the applet.
- The default layout for the JApplet is BorderLayout. The default layout for JPanel is FlowLayout.
- GridLayout makes each cell of equal size: same widths, same heights. The width is not necessarily the same as the height.
- The number of rows and columns must be specified when creating a GridLayout (e.g., setLayout(new GridLayout(numRows, numCols));).
- BorderLayout has only five regions: NORTH, SOUTH, WEST, EAST, and CENTER. Each region follows specific rules on how it stretches its components.
- If nothing is added to the center in BorderLayout, a gap *might* appear in the applet.
- When you add components to a container with BorderLayout, the location must be specified with the component in the add method (e.g., add(component, BorderLayout.EAST);).
- The default alignment for JLabel if there is only text is to be left-justified. The default for JLabel if there is only an image is to be center-justified. JLabels with both text and an image require us to specify the alignment when we create the JLabel.
- Attempting to add a component that is already contained elsewhere will cause that component to be removed and reinserted.
- Only one component can be added to each region in BorderLayout and GridLayout. To fit multiple components in a particular region, add them to a separate JPanel and then add this JPanel to the region.
- Structuring code can be done based on regions of the applet based on the layout manager in use.
- Design is an important step *before* starting to program.
- Design of the GUI should be sketched out, fully specifying all JPanels with their layout managers.
- All components should also be displayed with the appropriate text and Java component type.
- Good design includes following standard practices and being consistent.
- Designs should not have too much in a single view.

1. True or false? The default layout for a JPanel is NullLayout.

2. Which layout managers position everything on the basis of equal-sized rows and columns?

3. Which layout manager positions everything on the basis of north, south, east, west, and center positioning?

4. True or false? FlowLayout defaults to laying out components centered both horizontally and vertically.

5. True or false? FlowLayout, GridLayout, and BorderLayout resize objects to stretch either horizontally or vertically (or both).

6. Given the following code, draw out how it should look when I run it: **Be sure to draw out the size and location of each item.**

```java
import java.awt.*;
import javax.swing.*;
public class layoutsEx extends JApplet
{
    JLabel l_cat ;
    JTextField tf_age;
    JButton b_go;
    JCheckBox cb_fun;
    public void init( )
    {
        setLayout( new BorderLayout( ) );
        l_cat = new JLabel( "Cat:", JLabel.RIGHT );
        tf_age = new JTextField( 2 );
        b_go = new JButton( "Go" );
        cb_fun = new JCheckBox( "Fun?" );
        add( l_cat, BorderLayout.NORTH );
        add( tf_age, BorderLayout.CENTER );
        JPanel p2 = new JPanel( );
        p2.add( b_go );
        add( p2, BorderLayout.EAST );
        JPanel p3 = new JPanel( );
        p3.add( cb_fun );
        add( p3, BorderLayout.SOUTH );
    }
}
```

7. True or false? We can nest JPanels inside another JPanel.

8. True or false? A layout manager is an object that determines how components are arranged in a container.

9. True or false? When using BorderLayout, we can add only one thing to each of the five sections.

10. What is the code to set the layout for the applet to two rows and three columns?

11. True or false? If we add a component that is already contained elsewhere, it will be displayed in two locations.

12. Develop a program using various layout managers and JPanels for the following:

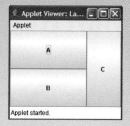

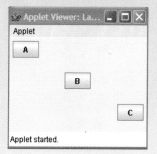

13. Create an applet that has three sets of radio button groups asking the user for his favorite color, movie, and TV show. Add a title at the top: "What's your favorite?" Display appropriately.

14. Create an applet that is a party invitation. Include a text field for users to enter their name, a checkbox to designate whether they are planning on attending, a drop-down list of what they will bring (appetizer, main dish, dessert), radio buttons for how many guests they will bring (0, 1, 2), and a text area for them to describe their costume. Display appropriately with labels associated with each component and a title at the top of the applet.

15. Create an applet that displays a library of all your music. Include a list with each song listed, a drop-down list for different genres, and buttons to play/stop a song.

16. Create an applet of all your favorites: movies, bands, artists, people, quotes. Select appropriate components to display each.

17. For the first drawing example in this chapter, create sketches for when the other two buttons get selected: Photos and Artwork. What should be displayed? How should it be laid out? How many art pieces should be displayed at a time? How will the user get to see the rest of them?

18. Lay out a full design for any corporate web page on the Internet.

19. Lay out a full design for your mail program.

20. What are some good practices in design of web pages?

21. What is the problem if the text is more than 80 characters across?

22. Sketch out a design for a company website. Find one on the Internet and draw out how you would implement it in Java.

23. Sketch out a design for your own personal website. Include your résumé, portfolio, or information about your friends.

24. Sketch out a design for your school's main website.

Data Types and Operators

6

They aren't all just objects to me;
some of them are primitive.

Variables

What is a *variable*? Remember from Chapter 3 that a variable is data that is referenced by a named identifier. What is an *identifier*? It is anything that we name, such as the name of a class, the name of a method that we create, or the name of a variable.

The first thing that we do with variables is *declare* them. We do this by specifying the data type (e.g., JButton, Graphics, JLabel) and then specify a name for us to reference it.

Examples include:

```
JButton submit;
JTextField tf_street;
Graphics grp;
```

We can name our variables almost anything that we want because there is no real limit to the length of the variable name. However, we do have to conform to a few rules concerning our variable names.

■ 6.1.1 Rules

1. Can contain any letter, number, the underscore (_) or dollar sign ($).
2. Cannot begin with a number.
3. Must not be a Java *reserved word* (*Java keyword*); see Table 6-1 (e.g., public, class, void).
4. Cannot have any spaces.

Some conventions that most programmers follow include the following:

1. Constants are in all uppercase letters (e.g., MAX_SCORE) and are declared with keyword final.
2. Classes are named in mixed case, with the first letter a capital letter (e.g., MyFirstApplet).
3. Methods are named in mixed case as well, but the first letter is usually lowercase (e.g., paintComponent, setupButtons).
4. Variables are named in mixed case with the first letter lowercase. These names should be meaningful, such that a person reading the variable name can decipher what data is stored in the variable. The alphabet is not acceptable—a, b, c, d, ... Good examples are: firstName, lastName, midtermGrade, labGrade, qtyShirts, and qtyShorts.
5. Be consistent—e.g., Frequency as freq or fqy or fq (tempFqy, hitFqy, cntFqy).

6.1.2 Java-Reserved Words

There are many reserved words in Java, meaning that we cannot use them as identifiers because they already have special meaning as part of the Java syntax. **TABLE 6-1** is a list of Java-reserved words:

TABLE 6-1   Java-Reserved Words

abstract	continue	for	new	switch
assert	default	goto	package	synchronized
boolean	do	if	private	this
break	double	implements	protected	throw
byte	else	import	public	throws
case	enum	instanceof	return	transient
catch	extends	int	short	try
char	final	interface	static	void
class	finally	long	strictfp	volatile
const	float	native	super	while

6.1.3 Data Types

Java is an *object-oriented* language, meaning that all the data types we work with are *objects*—except for the eight primitive data types. The difference is that a primitive data type can keep track of only one value, whereas objects may keep track of multiple data of various data types as well as having methods that we can call on it. For the most part, we will be concerned only with the four primitive data types that are used most frequently:

int   for whole numbers (negative and positive)

double   real numbers (negative and positive)

char   single characters

boolean holds either the Java-reserved word `true` or `false`

The eight primitive data types are shown in **TABLE 6-2**.
Examples of usage:

> Primitive data types can store only one value and have no methods we can call on them.

```
int age = 13;
double gpa = 3.76
char firstInitial = 'E';
boolean isHappy = true;
```

TABLE 6-2   The Eight Primitive Data Types

	Data Type	Description	Number of Bits Used to Represent the Number
Integers	byte	Byte-length integer	8-Bit
	short	Short integer	16-Bit
	int	Integer	32-Bit
	long	Long integer	64-Bit
Reals	float	Single-precision floating point	32-Bit
	double	Double-precision floating point	64-Bit
	char	A single character	16-Bit Unicode character
	boolean	Holds either the value true or false	1-Bit

Examples of objects:

> Object data types can store multiple values and have methods associated with them.

```
String name = "Cookie Monster";
JLabel title = new JLabel( name );
JButton submit ;
```

With objects, we can call methods on them:

```
String value = nameTextField.getText( );
```

6.1.4 Instance Variables

Instance variables are those that are declared at the top of the class, just inside the brace after our class header. This is where we want to *declare* our variables, not necessarily *initialize* them. Remember, declaring a variable means that we specify the data type and the variable—we do not set it equal to anything. Following this approach will become important as we work with images and events.

Instance variables are accessible throughout our class. This way, we can reference variables inside any methods that we create. If we declare a variable inside a method, then we have access to that variable inside that method only. Because we usually we want most of our variables to be instance variables, we need not worry about whether we can access them. Example 6-1 shows where we declare our instance variables and how we can reference them inside our methods.

EXAMPLE 6-1

```
import java.awt.*;
import javax.swing.*;
public class int2String extends JApplet
{
    JLabel name;                          Instance variables are
    JButton go;                           declared here.
    public void init( )
    {
        setLayout( new FlowLayout( ) );
        name = new JLabel( "Cookie Monster" );
        go = new JButton( "GO!" );         We can reference instance vari-
        add( name );                       ables throughout our program.
        add( go );
    }
}
```

EXAMPLE 6-2

```
import java.awt.*;
import javax.swing.*;
public class Fun extends JApplet
{
    public void init( )
    {
        JButton b_submit = new JButton( "Submit" );
        JTextField tf_state = new JTextField( "great", 10 );
        doLeftSide( );
    }
    public void doLeftSide(  )
    {
        JPanel p = new JPanel( new FlowLayout( ) );
        p.add( b_submit );
        p.add( tf_state );
    }
}
```

A problematic example is shown in Example 6-2: What is wrong and what happens? This is a common mistake that new programmers make. The problem is that the variables b_submit and tf_state are declared inside the init method and therefore are accessible only inside the init method. When we try to reference these variables inside the doLeftSide method, it does not know anything about these variables. To fix this code, we need to declare these variables at the top of the class.

6.2 Math Operators

Mathematical expressions are essential in programming. To express mathematical equations in Java, we can make use of methods in the Math class and many provided operators. Java operators include arithmetic, relational, and conditional operators.

■ 6.2.1 Math Class

The Math class contains some methods that can be useful to us in our programs. This way we do not have to reinvent the wheel on performing common functions such as determining the absolute value of a number or finding trigonometric values. **TABLE 6-3** shows some common math functions that are available in the Math class.

TABLE 6-3 Math Class Methods

Math Class Method	Example	Description
number abs(number)	double posX = Math.abs(x);	Returns the absolute value of the number, where the data type will match int or double
double ceil(double)	double x = Math.ceil(y);	Returns the number rounded to the next higher integer value
double exp(double)	double x = Math.exp(double)	Returns Euler's number, e raised to the power of a double value
double floor(double)	double x = Math.floor(y);	Returns the number rounded down to the next lower integer value
double log(double)	double x = Math.log(y);	Returns the natural logarithm (base e) of a double
double pow(double1, double2)	double x = Math.pow(x, y);	Returns the value of x^y
double sqrt(double)	Double x = Math.sqrt(y);	Returns the square root of a double

Advanced Concept

The methods we reference in the Math class are declared static, which allows us to call the methods without instantiating an instance of the Math class. For example, usually we would need to write code such as

```
Math m = new Math( );
m.sqrt( 43.2 );
```

We do not do this for the methods in the Math class because they are declared with the keyword static. The static keyword designates that the method can be accessed simply by calling the method on the class, such as Math.sqrt(25).

If we wanted to make our own methods static in our classes, we can do so by adding the static keyword in the method header. Methods can be declared static only when they are either fully encompassed modular methods or methods to access shared class variables, which are declared static. In other words, they cannot access instance variables. The following example demonstrates how to declare a method static:

```
public static double sqrt( double x )
```

6.2.2 Arithmetic Operators

Mathematical operations are important in many programs. The standard mathematical operations are available, but some may be a twist from what you know (**TABLE 6-4**). For example, the plus sign is used for adding numbers as well as concatenating Strings. In fact, anytime a String and a number are added with the plus sign, it forces the number to concatenate to the String.

Another twist is Java division. When we divide two *integer* numbers, we end up with an integer result—the remainder is dropped. However, if we use division on two double values, the result is what you would think.

TABLE 6-4 Mathematical Operations

Operator	Java Code	Description
+	op1 + op2	Adds op1 and op2; also used to concatenate strings
-	op1 - op2	Subtracts op2 from op1
*	op1 * op2	Multiplies op1 by op2
/	op1 / op2	Divides op1 by op2
%	op1 % op2	Computes the remainder of dividing op1 by op2

The modulus operator is sometimes a new concept to students. The percent sign, %, represents the modulus operator. It computes the remainder of dividing the two operands. Essentially, it returns the value thrown away during integer division. Examples:

```
int   x = 7 + 2 * 3;           // equals 13
int   y = 14 / 5;              // equals 2
int   z = 14 % 5;             // equals 4
double yy = 14.0 / 5;          // equals 2.8
String a = "Hello" + "World";  // equals "HelloWorld"
String result = "x is " + x;   // equals "x is 13"
```

When would the use of the modulus function be useful? When do you use this technique in your daily life?

Arithmetic Operator Shortcuts   Our assignment statements can include the variable on both sides of the equal sign:

```
int x = 5;
x = x * 2;  // x gets the value 10
```

A shortcut way to express this is to apply the operator before the equal sign and leave off the variable on the right side:

```
int x = 5;
x *= 2;     // x gets the value 10
```

TABLE 6-5 shows the shortcuts for each operator.

■ 6.2.3 Relational Operators

Relational operators are used to compare two operands. Although you may be familiar with some of these, take notice of the Java syntax. For example, to see if two operands are the same, Java uses two equal signs together. We cannot use a single equals statement because that is reserved for assignment of a value to a variable. All the relational operators return a boolean value, either `true` or `false`. This system will be useful to us when we start using conditionals and loops. **TABLE 6-6** describes the relational operators.

TABLE 6-5   Mathematical Operator Shortcuts

Operator	Java Code	Expansion
+=	x += 3;	x = x + 3;
-=	x -= 3;	x = x - 3;
*=	x *= 3;	x = x * 3;
/=	x /= 3;	x = x / 3;
%=	x %= 3;	x = x % 3;

TABLE 6-6 Relational Operators

Operator	Use	Description
>	op1 > op2	Returns `true` if op1 is greater than op2
>=	op1 >= op2	Returns `true` if op1 is greater than or equal to op2
<	op1 < op2	Returns `true` if op1 is less than op2
<=	op1 <= op2	Returns `true` if op1 is less than or equal to op2
==	op1 == op2	Returns `true` if op1 and op2 are equal
!=	op1 != op2	Returns `true` if op1 and op2 are not equal

> The symbols ≤ and ≥ are not in Java! (Remember—they are not on our keyboards!)

Examples:

```
int x = 3;
boolean g = (x >= 10);    // equals false
boolean h = ( x != 3 );   // equals false
boolean j  = ( x == 3 );  // equals true
```

Let us practice the math operators so far and create a method that determines whether an integer value is even or odd. If we name our method isEven, then we should return true if it is even and return false if it is an odd number. Remember that true and false are boolean values. Therefore, our method header should contain the following:

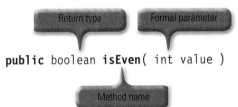

```
public boolean isEven( int value )
```

To fill in the method body, we need to figure out a way to determine whether an int is even or odd. Doing so can be tricky, but once you see some examples like this one you will start thinking in line with a computer. Remember how the % operator works? The modulus operator % gives us the remainder after dividing two numbers. What are all even numbers divisible by? Two. So if we divide by 2 and get a zero for a remainder, then the number is even.

So how do we implement this in code?

```
return  value % 2 == 0;
```

> Need **two equal signs** to check equality, not one.

We can also use parentheses to enforce the order of operations.

```
return ( value % 2 ) == 0;
```

Warning! When we check for equality on numbers, we cannot use the == operator on floating-point data types. The problem is that some floating-point numbers cannot be accurately stored in memory, so an approximation occurs. Example 6-3 demonstrates this problem.

EXAMPLE 6-3

```
import java.awt.*;
import javax.swing.*;
public class ProbDblPrecision extends JApplet
{
    JLabel value;
    public void init( )
    {
        double val = 1.0/5 + 1.0/5 + 1.0/5 - 0.6;
        value = new JLabel( "val should be zero but is = " + val );
        add( value );
    }
}
```

Applet Viewer: ProbDblPrecision.class
Applet
val should be zero but is = 1.1102230246251565E-16
Applet started.

We need a different solution for checking whether a floating point value is *nearly equivalent* to a particular value. We can do this by checking to see if the difference between the two values is within a specified tolerance of error. In our solution, we can make use of the absolute value function in the Math class to find the absolute value of the difference and determine whether this value is less than the tolerance. The following example shows a solution:

```
Math.abs( val1 - val2 ) < 0.0001
```

Object data types such as Strings are also problematic for a different reason. Variables that are object data types are actually reference pointers to somewhere in memory where the object itself is stored. Because two objects (e.g., Strings) may have the same value but are stored in two different places in memory, the == will return false even though the values each object contains are the same. Therefore, we need to use the .equals method on the two strings. **FIGURE 6-1** is an example of how memory may look and why the == operators may fail even though the two strings have the same value.

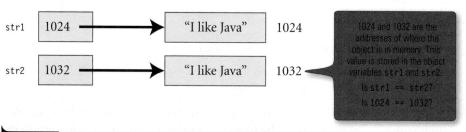

FIGURE 6-1 Object Variables Store an Address in the Variable Reference.

We cannot compare `Strings` or other objects by using the relational operators. If we want to determine whether two objects are equal, we need to use the `.equals` method.
  Example:

```
String name = "Elizabeth";
boolean isEqual = name.equals( "elizabeth" );
```

In this example, `isEqual` would be `false` because "E" is different from "e". If it were `name.equals( "Elizabeth" )`, it would then be `true`.

6.2.4 Conditional Operators

Conditional operators work on boolean operators to determine a boolean result (**TABLE 6-7**).
  Examples:

How do we express $0 < x < 10$ in Java? $0 < x < 10$ does not work. We need to use $0 < x$ && $x < 10$.

```
int x = 5;
int y = 10;
boolean a = ( x == 5 && y < 10 );   // equals false
boolean b = ( x == 5 || y < 10 );   // equals true
boolean c = ( a && b );             // equals false
boolean d = !c;                     // equals true
boolean e = ( 0 < x && x <= 10 );   // equals true
```

In the preceding examples, a is `false` because y is not less than 10, and because it is an AND operation (`&&`), both x==5 and y<10 have to be true for it to be true. b is true because only one of the operands needs to be true, and x==5 is true.

To evaluate conditional operators, we sometimes set up truth tables to define all the possibilities that could occur. Each row represents a possible state in the program based on each of the variables. The variables used evaluate to either `true` or `false`. The number of rows is based on the number of variables involved. If there are two variables (e.g., A and B) then there are four possible permutations: A is `false` and B is `false`, or A is `false` and B is `true`, or A is `true` and B is `false`, or A is `true` and B is `true`. Then we create a column for different conditional operator combinations. To

TABLE 6-7 Conditional Operators

Operator	English	Use	Description
&&	AND	op1 && op2	Returns `true` if op1 and op2 are both `true`
||	OR	op1 || op2	Returns `true` if either op1 or op2 is `true`
!	NOT	!op	Returns `true` if op is `false`

make it easier to fill out, we sometimes represent true as *T* and false as *F*. **TABLE 6-8** demonstrates an example truth table.

TABLE 6-8   Truth Table Showing All Permutations of Two Variables

VARIABLES

A	B	!A	!B	A && B	A || B	A && !B	!(A || !B)
F	F	T	T	F	F	F	F
F	T	T	F	F	T	F	T
T	F	F	T	F	T	T	F
T	T	F	F	T	T	F	F

6.3 Order of Operations

Determining the order of operations in a combination expression is based on the following:

1. ( ) parentheses first
2. Unary operators (+, -, !)
3. *, /, %
4. +, -
5. <   <=   >   >=   instanceof
6. ==   !=
7. &&
8. ||
9. =

Examples:

$$3 * (2 + (3 - 4 * 2 + (5\text{-}1))) =$$
$$3 * (2 + (3 - 4 * 2 + 4)) =$$
$$3 * (2 + (3 - 8 + 4)) =$$
$$3 * (2 + (-1)) =$$
$$3 * 1 = 3$$

$$5 + 2 >= 7 \&\& 5 - 2 != 0$$
$$7 >= 7 \&\& 3 != 0$$
$$\text{true} \&\& \text{true}$$
$$\text{true}$$

```
boolean isGood  =  5 + 2 >= 7 && 5 - 2 != 0;
        isGood is equal to true
```

6.4 **instanceof Operator**

The instanceof operator tests whether a variable is a particular class type, such as JButton or JCheckBox. We can check only on objects—we cannot check if something is an instance of a primitive data type (e.g., int, boolean). We will make use of this instanceof operator when we get to events.

Examples:

```
obj instanceof JButton
obj instanceof JCheckBox
obj instanceof JFrame
```

6.5 **Converting Data Types**

Sometimes we want to convert one type to another type; for example, if we want to append an int to a JTextArea, we need to convert it to a String before we can do so. This chapter covers some of the common conversions that we need to know.

■ 6.5.1 Converting int to String

We can connect an int to a String by calling the method valueOf from the String class:

```
int value = 5;
String strValue = String.valueOf( value );
```

Example 6-4 demonstrates an applet converting numbers to String to be able to add them to a JComboBox.

EXAMPLE 6-4

```
import java.awt.*;
import javax.swing.*;
public class int2String extends JApplet
{
    JComboBox list;
    int num1, num2, num3;

    public void init( )
    {
        setLayout( new FlowLayout( ) );
        num1 = 10;
        num2 = 20;
        num3 = 30;
```

Applet

10 ▼

10
20
30

Applet started.

(continues)

Example 6-4 (continued)

```
        setupList( );
    }
    public void setupList( )
    {
        list = new JComboBox( );
        list.addItem( String.valueOf(num1) );
        list.addItem( String.valueOf(num2) );
        list.addItem( String.valueOf(num3) );
        add( list );
    }
}
```

■ 6.5.2 Converting `String` to `int` or `double`

To convert a `String` to an `int`, we use the method `parseInt` from the `Integer` class. There is a similar method for the `double` data type in the `Double` class.

```
int value = Integer.parseInt( String );
double dval = Double.parseDouble( String );
```

Examples:

```
String text = "52";
int num = Integer.parseInt( text );
double cost = Double.parseDouble( textFieldCost.getText( ) );
```

Converting from a `String` to a number is important for tasks where we need to read a value from a `JTextField` or `JComboBox` where the user entered a value that we need to convert to a number so that we can perform mathematical operations on it.

■ 6.5.3 Converting `Object` to a Specific Type

Sometimes when we call particular methods, they return `Object` types instead of the actual type like `String` or `ImageIcon`. What we need to do is called **casting**: cast the `Object` type to a specific type like `String` or `ImageIcon`.

The way we cast an `Object` to another type is to specify the new data type in parentheses before the `Object`. We can only do data casting from object types to other data types; casting does not work on primitive data types.

```
String str = (String )obj;
ImageIcon str = (ImageIcon )obj;
JButton button = (JButton )obj;
```

This approach can be useful when grabbing elements out of a JList or JComboBox:

```
ImageIcon icon = ( ImageIcon ) list.getSelectedValue( );
String txt = ( String ) combobox.getSelectedItem( );
```

This method is also useful inside our event listener methods, after we pull out the object type:

```
Object src = event.getSource( );
JButton button = ( JButton )src;
```

Fun Interlude—Java-Reserved Words

Circle the 20 Java-reserved words hidden in the following puzzle.

```
v a e s l w h i w e t u r n e x t e n e d i o
v o l s e f a i s t h i e t r x n u o p s r l
r u i t r t u r x e f r w e p o t r r u e s p
o u p d f a l u s i c h e n w l i p l s s r w
w p e r l c l p u b l i s d x t e m t r c u e
s r p u b l i c s o a h l f w h i l e r h i p
s o t h w a x m e l s u p n f r t c t a u p o
u t f a l s i n p r i v a t e o t p u p a w v
p e c l a s u p e l s n e s n w r e r r e x d
e c l e f t i p i i e o x e l s e i s a d v e
t r u x t a t i e x s m t s k i t e o x w r r
a s t e f t l s a r u r e s k i u r l s e u o
x v d x s i s s s s p i n n e x r e a e p b t
p r o t e c t e d i r g d x t u n u s u e l e
f a m e r s s s b f a l s e h s e e s m r i c
p l c n l u a f o x t l w x i d n e t x s c t
a s m f t r e r o n o h r t s u p e p m o i d
a p c o o k i e m o n s t e s t a t t r u x l
x w v n w e l i b x u b l u a e a l r e o a k
i l o v e t o s k i p l p t l e c h d p x t f
t x e x t h r w s s l n e t x e s t m a l s e
```

Troubleshooting

Common errors:

My code will not compile.	Make sure that you reference each variable exactly the same, and remember that Java is case sensitive.
	Variables, methods, and class names cannot have spaces or other special characters. Make sure that you follow the rules listed in the chapter for naming.
I keep getting a null pointer exception.	Make sure that you *declare* your variables only once at the top in the instance variable declaration section. If you *declare* it again inside a method, there will be two of those variables in memory.
I get a number exception error.	When reading values that the user enters in text components, the getText method call returns the value as a `String`. If you want to use it as a number, call `Integer.parseInt` or `Double.parseDouble`. When changing or setting numerical values into components, first convert the number to a string with `String.valueOf( number )`.
Expression is not working.	Verify your use of relational and logical operators. `&&` for AND results in `true` only if both sides evaluate to true; `||` for OR results in true if either side is `true`.

SUMMARY

- Variable names can contain any combination of letters and numbers, the _, and the $ as long as the first character does not begin with a number.
- Identifiers include any variable name, class name, and method name that the programmer defines.
- Identifiers cannot be a Java-reserved word.
- Java-reserved words have special meaning in the Java programming language.
- The Math class contains many useful methods.
- There are eight primitive data types in Java. The most commonly used ones are int for integers, double for floating-point values, char for characters, and boolean for true or false values.
- Division of two integers results in an integer; any fractional part is discarded.
- The % operator gets the remainder from integer division.
- For comparing Strings, the == operator may not work; instead, use the .equals method.
- Order of operations for expressions is similar to that for math. The = is evaluated last.
- The instanceof operator checks to see if a variable instance is of a particular type of object. It cannot be used on primitive data types.

- Truth tables show all states of a program on the basis of the variable values.
- Numbers can be converted to Strings by calling String.valueOf(number).
- Strings can be converted to a number by calling Integer.parseInt(String) to get an integer or Double.parseDouble(String) for a double.
- Data types of type Object need to be cast to a specific data type such as String or JButton. Doing so is necessary when getting items out of a JList or JComboBox.

EXERCISES

1. Which operator would you use to determine whether a number is even?
2. Which operator would you use to determine if a number is divisible by 3?
3. What is the result when you add a number to a String, e.g., 25 + "1010"?
4. What can you not use for a variable name?
5. Is it required that you name your variables beginning with a lowercase letter?
6. What is the line of code to calculate the square root of 99?
7. What is the code to determine the absolute value of an integer named amt?
8. What is the main integer data type used?
9. True or false? Java-reserved words can be used for class names but not variable names.
10. What two values can a boolean be equal to? Do you put quotes around the values?
11. Why declare variables at the top of the class and not inside the methods?
12. What is a good example in real life for using the modulus function?
13. What is the difference between relational and conditional operators?
14. True or false? The expression p && q will be true if either or both are true.
15. True or false? Variables declared inside a method can be referenced anywhere in the class.
16. What is the final value of xVal in the following Java code? xVal = 12 / 7;
17. What is the final value of xVal in the following Java code? xVal = 12 % 7;
18. How do you convert a String to an int? From an int to a String?
19. Can you use the instanceof operator on a char?
20. How would you represent "not equal" in Java?

21. Fill in the following truth table.

A	B	A || !B	!(A && ! B)
F	F		
F	T		
T	F		
T	T		

Conditionals

7

What if?

Conditionals

Conditional statements allow us to choose which statements we would like to execute. Usually the *flow of control* of a program follows line by line through the code. Conditional statements allow us to skip a statement or statements on the basis of some condition. A condition must evaluate to either `true` or `false`—boolean values. The conditional structures in Java are `if`, `if-else`, and the `switch` structure.

 `if` **Structure**

The `if` statement allows us to select which statements we would like to execute (FIGURE 7-1). This allows us to have some statements that may or may not execute. The format of the `if` statement is as follows:

```
if  ( booleanExpression )
{
        statements;
}
```

where `booleanExpression` is any expression that evaluates to either `true` or `false` and the statements are any number of Java statements. If the `booleanExpression` evaluates to `true`, then the statements are executed. If the `booleanExpression` evaluates to `false`, then the statements are skipped.

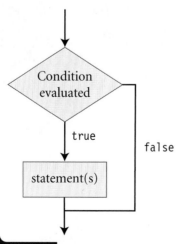

FIGURE 7-1 Flow diagram of an `if` statement.

> Note: The braces are optional if there is only one statement under the if but are required if we want more than one statement for the if.

An example of an if structure:

```
if ( value > maxAllowed )
   warning.setText( "Warning! Value exceeds the maximum allowed." );
```

We commonly have boolean expressions that make use of relational or logical operators. We can use these operators discussed in the previous chapter. For example:

```
if ( value <= 0 || value > 10 )
   warn.setText( "Value out of range. Enter a # between 1 & 10." );

if ( total != 100 )
   status.setText( "Total does not add up to 100." );

if ( ! hasPermission )
   status.setText( "You don't have permission to access." );
```

hasPermission is a variable of type boolean.

In the preceding examples we can decipher the data types that would work for the variables involved in each boolean expression. value and total could be any integer or floating-point data type, and hasPermission has to be a boolean because the not operator ! works only on boolean values.

We can also use some of the methods provided from our components. For example, we can check to see whether our radio buttons and checkboxes are selected with a call to the isSelected method on the components.

```
if ( ! chkboxIsAttending.isSelected( ) )
   msg.setText( "You aren't coming?" );
```

Some of our components have multiple states. For example, a JList may have three options that can be selected. To figure out which one was selected, we first determine which option is selected and then check to see if it is equal to one of the three options. If we have a JList named myList with the options "red," "blue," and "green," we can customize a message to the user on the basis of the selection with the following code:

```
String selection = ( String )myList.getSelectedValue( );
if ( selection.equals( "red" ) )
   msg.setText( "Red is HOT!" );
if ( selection.equals( "blue" ) )
   msg.setText( "Blue is cool" );
if ( selection.equals( "green" ) )
   msg.setText( "Green's my favorite color too!" );
```

When we compare strings to other strings we need to use the `.equals` method instead of the `==` operator. Although the `==` operator works most of the time, it is inconsistent based on how memory is allocated. The `.equals` method verifies character by character to see whether the two strings are identical (and is case sensitive).

This last example leads us to another conditional structure we can use, called the `if-else` structure. Assuming that our `JList` allows only one option to be selected at a time, a more proper structure would check each option until it finds one that matches and then quit checking for other matches. This is what the `if-else` structure does.

7.2.1 `if-else` Structure

The `if-else` structure allows us to choose between different statements on the basis of which condition is true (**FIGURE 7-2**). We can have an option of two sets of statements with an `if-else` statement, where the first group of statements (`statementsA`) is executed if the `booleanExpression` evaluates to `true` and the `statementsB` are executed if the `booleanExpression` evaluates to `false`:

```
if ( booleanExpression )
{
    statementsA;
}
else
{
    statementsB;
}
```

> Either statementsA or statementsB will be executed—not both, and not neither.

Example 7-1 demonstrates a checkbox that displays "You're so happy!" if the checkbox is selected and displays "Why not happy?" if it is not selected.

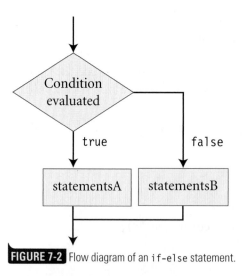

FIGURE 7-2 Flow diagram of an `if-else` statement.

Note: *The braces are optional for either the* if *or the* else *clause if there is only one statement, but they are required if we want more than one statement.*

EXAMPLE 7-1

```java
import java.awt.*;
import javax.swing.*;
public class Check extends JApplet
{
   JCheckBox isHappy;
   JTextArea textarea;

   public void init( )
   {
      setLayout( new FlowLayout( ) );
      isHappy = new JCheckBox( "Happy?", true );
      textarea = new JTextArea( 3, 10 );

      if ( isHappy.isSelected ( ) )
        textarea.setText( "You're so happy!" );
      else
      {
          textarea.setText( "Why not happy?" );
      }
      add( isHappy );
      add( textarea );
   }
}
```

Note: we have not learned how to do events yet, so the saying does not change when we click on the checkbox. We can make more interesting programs once we learn events, but it is critical that we first learn how to use the if statement for processing events.

We can use the operators that we learned in the previous chapter for our boolean expressions (**TABLE 7-1**).

Going back to our JList example from the previous section, we can incorporate the three if statements into an if-else structure. To do so, we need to extend our else statement to an else if.

```java
String selection = ( String )myList.getSelectedValue( );
if ( selection.equals( "red" ) )
   msg.setText( "Red is HOT!" );
else if ( selection.equals( "blue" ) )
   msg.setText( "Blue is cool" );
else if ( selection.equals( "green" ) )
   msg.setText( "Green's my favorite color too!" );
else
   msg.setText( "Nothing's selected!" );
```

TABLE 7-1 Examples of `boolean` expressions in `if` and `if-else` structures.

If A is greater than or equal to B, set the text area to say "A is great".	```if (A >= B) textArea.setText("A is great");```
If C is not equal to zero, then display "Good to Go" in the text area.	```if (C != 0) textArea.setText("Good to Go");```
If the text the user entered in the `textField` is equal to "Cookie Monster", then display "WELCOME Cookie Monster!" in the text area (on two separate lines); otherwise, display "Who are you?" in the text area.	```String text = textField.getText( ); if (text.equals("Cookie Monster") { String display = "<HTML>WELCOME " + name + "!"; textarea.setText(display); } else textarea.setText("Who are you?");```

The `if-else` structure allows us to have a default `else` case to handle the situation where none of the options are selected. As we start at the top of the `if-else` structure, once one of the `boolean` expressions evaluates to `true`, the rest of the `if` statements and the final `else` within the `if-else` structure are skipped. If none of the `boolean` expressions evaluates to `true`, the final `else` clause will be executed.

For an example, we will write a method that determines whether the first character in a `String` is a vowel. First we need to determine how to structure the method, so let us start by defining the method header. We need to take a `String` as a parameter and return either `true` or `false` depending on whether the `String` begins with a vowel. We will need a `boolean` variable because we will need to return this `true` or `false` value. So we start with the following method stub:

```
public boolean beginsVowel( String str )
{
     boolean isVowel;

     return isVowel;
}
```

Now we need to implement the body of the method. We need to start by getting the first character in the `String`. Remember that there is a method called `charAt` that we can call on strings and specify the index of the character we want. Java starts counting at zero, so the first character in the string is at index 0. This method returns a `char` to us. Our string is named `str`, which we defined inside our method header parameters.

```
char firstLetter = str.charAt( 0 );
```

There are several ways that we could implement the if statement to check for each vowel. One way we can do this is by using many instances of the OR operator, ||. Checking for equality on char data types can be done with the == operator. For example:

```
public boolean beginsVowel( String str )
{
        char firstLetter = str.charAt( 0 );
        boolean isVowel;
        if ( firstLetter == 'A' || firstLetter == 'a' ||
                        firstLetter == 'E' || firstLetter == 'e' ||
                        firstLetter == 'I' || firstLetter == 'i' ||
                        firstLetter == 'O' || firstLetter == 'o' ||
                        firstLetter == 'U' || firstLetter == 'u' )
                isVowel = true;
        else
                isVowel = false;
        return isVowel;
}
```

> Note: an easier way might have been to first convert the string to uppercase or lowercase letters, then our if statement would have five fewer equality checks. Can you think of any other ways to implement this example?

7.2.2 Comparing Data Types

Usually when we want to compare two data values, we think of using the == to check for equality between two values. This approach works all the time on primitive data types (e.g., int, double, char, boolean), but when we are dealing with object data types we need to be careful about what we are actually comparing. To understand what is going on, we need to take a quick look at how these values are stored in memory. When we declare a variable, a spot in memory is reserved for us to put the value of the variable. Memory is accessed through address numbers, but that is difficult for us to remember; hence, we use variable names to reference those spots in memory. If we declare a primitive data type, the value that we assign to our variable goes directly into that spot in memory. However, all object variables are *references* to another spot in memory where the actual object is stored. **FIGURE 7-3** depicts these differences.

When we use the == operator, we are comparing if the spot in memory for the variable is equal to the other variable's value. For primitive data types, doing so always results in evaluating whether the two variables contain the same value. When working with object data types, the == operator will return to us whether or not the variables are *referencing* the same spot in memory—in other words, is the address

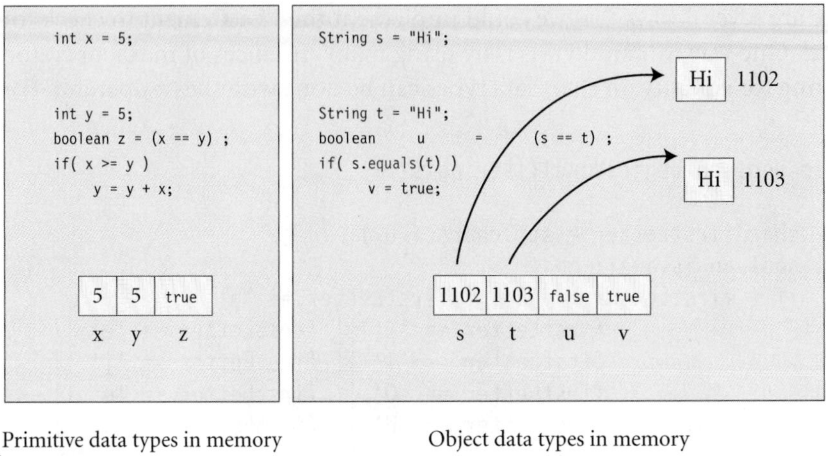

Primitive data types in memory   Object data types in memory

FIGURE 7-3 Comparison of memory between primitive and object data types.

stored in each variable the same? This does *not* return whether the two objects happen to have the same value. This is an important distinction. Therefore, when we want to determine whether the two objects have the same *value*, we call the .equals method instead of using the == operator.

So when do we use == versus using the .equals method? The first rule is to always use == when comparing primitive data types. We can also use the == operator when we get to events and want to determine whether a particular component (JButton/JCheckBox/JRadioButton) triggered an event. However, when *comparing* two Strings we always want to use the .equals method. For example, say that we have a JTextField named tf_userName and we want to see if the user typed in the value "Terry". We can call the .getText( ) method on our JTextField component to get the String the user typed in and then call the .equals method on the string to see if it matches with "Terry". If it does match, we will display a "welcome back" message in the same JTextField; otherwise, we will display an error message.

```
String userEntered = tf_userName.getText( );
if ( userEntered.equals( "Terry" ) )
      tf_userName.setText( "Welcome back Terry!" );
else
      tf_userName.setText( "Error: I don't know you!" );
```

7.2.3 Nesting if Statements

The statements inside an if statement can be almost any statement—including another if statement. This allows us to make another decision after the first decision is made. For example, if we need to find the maximum value among three numbers, we could nest some if statements:

```
if ( x > y )
{
   if ( x > z )
   {
        maxValue = x;
   }
   else                      // if x is bigger than y but not z, then z
                             //   must be the biggest
        maxValue = z;
}
else if ( y > z )          // we only get here if y is >= to x
{
   maxValue = y;
}
else
   maxValue = z;
```

What happens if x is 5 and y is 5 and z is 8? If x is 5, y is 2, and z is 6? What happens if the braces are removed?

Another example where we may use nested if statements is when we get to events and we want to determine mouse clicks on two separate images. Because images are put inside a JLabel to display on an applet, we would first check to see which of the two images the user is clicking on and then determine whether the *x* and *y* coordinates are within a particular region. This way, the *x* and *y* coordinates could overlap some in each image, but we will still be able to distinguish what we should do based on which image is clicked. This is a great introduction to events that we will cover in the next chapter.

```
if ( eventTrigger == firstImage )
{
   if ( region.contains( x1Coordinate, y1Coordinate ) )
   {
        // do something
   }
   else if ( region.contains( x2Coordinate, y2Coordinate ) )
   {
        // do something else
   }
}
else if ( eventTrigger == secondImage )
{
   if ( region.contains( x1Coordinate, y1Coordinate ) )
   {
        // do something based on second image clicked
   }
}
```

7.3 `switch` Statements

The `switch` statement is another conditional structure that we can use. It can be easier to read than an `if-else` structure, but it has some limitations. The `switch` statement can only compare integer and character values to a set of *cases*. Therefore, we cannot use the `switch` statement for `doubles`, `Strings`, or other objects.

The `switch` statement evaluates an expression in parentheses that must be either an `int` or `char`. The structure requires braces around the set of cases. Each case identifier ends with a colon, `:`, before the statements are listed. The keyword `break` is used to transfer the flow of control of the program to the end of the `switch` statement, skipping all other statements and cases listed below. Without the `break` statement, the program will continue through the statements below until either a `break` statement is executed or the end of the `switch` structure is reached. The last case in the `switch` structure can be a default case to handle the situation when none of the cases above matches the expression in parentheses at the beginning of the `switch` statement. The `break` and `default` statements are not required within the `switch` structure.

In the following example, we take the numerical grade entered by the user in the `JTextField` named `tf_grade`, convert it to an integer, and store that value in the variable `grade`. If the number is between 0 and 100, if we divide by 10 (integer division, so the remainder is truncated) and we end up with an integer value between 0 and 10. This makes it easy for us to display a custom message back to the user that is based on the achievement level. If the user got a 100% or anything in the ninetieth percentile, we want to display the same message; therefore, we do not put a break statement between those two case statements.

```
int grade = Integer.parseInt( tf_grade.getText( ) );
switch( grade/10 )
{
    case 10:
    case 9:
        tf_grade.setText( "You ROCK!" );
        break;
    case 8:
        tf_grade.setText( "Doin' good" );
        break;
    case 7:
        tf_grade.setText( "Rather average" );
        break;
    default:
        tf_grade.setText( "Study more!" );
}
```

Let us go back and redo the example from the `if-else` section on writing a method that returns whether the first letter is a vowel. By using a `switch` statement, we can have each case of a vowel character fall through to the same statement to set the isVowel variable to true. The default case can be used to set the value to false.

```java
public boolean beginsVowel( String str )
{
    boolean isVowel;
    char firstLetter = str.charAt( 0 );
    switch( firstLetter )
    {
        case 'A':   case 'a':
        case 'E':   case 'e':
        case 'I':   case 'i':
        case 'O':   case 'o':
        case 'U':   case 'u':
                isVowel = true;
                break;
        default:
                isVowel = false;
    }
    return isVowel;
}
```

7.4 Programming Tidbits

The following are some programming tidbits. When writing if-else structures, we want to avoid creating an empty if section just so we can use the else section. For example, if we wanted to do something only when the checkbox was *not* selected in Example 7-1, we could write

```java
if ( isHappy.isSelected( ) )
{

}
else
{
    textArea.setText( "Why not happy?" );
}
```

A better way to write this code is to make use of the not operator, !:

```java
if ( ! isHappy.isSelected( ) )
{
    textArea.setText( "Why not happy?" );
}
```

Another example we will see is when we want to see whether something is true or false. We could write the code to see if a variable is equal to true or false as follows:

```
if (  myVariable == true )
   ...

if ( myVariable !=  false )
   ...
```

When we write an expression inside the parentheses of the if statement, it has to evaluate to true or false. If our variable is already either true or false, then we need not add code to see if it is == true or == false. For checking to see if it is true, we just put our variable inside parentheses. For checking to see if it is false, we can use the not operator, !, again. For example, we could change the preceding code to read as follows:

```
if ( myVariable )
   ...

if ( ! myVariable )
   ...
```

7.5 Comparing if-else and switch

When should we use an if instead of a switch, and vice versa? The first thing to determine is what the data type is that we are working with. Remember that the switch can be used only on expressions that evaluate to int or char. If the data type is anything other than int or char, then we will need to use an if structure. If the data type is int or char, then we should next ask if the values are within a range such that an if statement may be easier to specify than listing each case value for a switch statement. For example, if we were to write a method to check if the user entered a proper number for the month in the year, the if structure is easier to write than the switch statement:

```
public String checkMonth( )
{
   String str = txtField_month.getText( );
   int month = Integer.parseInt( str );
   String result;
   if( month >=1 && month <= 12 )
     result = "Valid";
   else
     result = "Invalid";
   return result;
}
```

```
public String checkMonth( )
{
   String str = txtField_month.getText( );
   int month = Integer.parseInt( str );
   String result;
   switch( month )
   {
       case 1:  case 2:  case 3:  case 4:
       case 5:  case 6:  case 7:  case 8:
       case 9: case 10:  case 11: case 12:
           result = "Valid";
           break;
       default:
           result = "Invalid";
   }
   return result;
}
```

7.6 Example: Seasonal Weather

We can make use of if statements to create an applet that changes based on the season and time of day. We will display a house, and if it is winter, have snow falling and snow on the ground. For spring, we will have green grass and rain. In the summer we will show green grass and blue skies. For fall we will show that our grass is brown. We will also customize our sky to depict daytime or nighttime. **FIGURE 7-4** shows what our applet should do depending on the season and time of day.

We can use the Calendar class to determine the time of the year and create a custom applet drawing. The Calendar class allows us to access the current date and time. The Calendar class is from the java.util package, so we also need an additional import statement at the top of our program.

```
import java.util.*;
```

To use the Calendar class, we can get the current time by calling getInstance:

```
Calendar rightNow;
rightNow = Calendar.getInstance( );
```

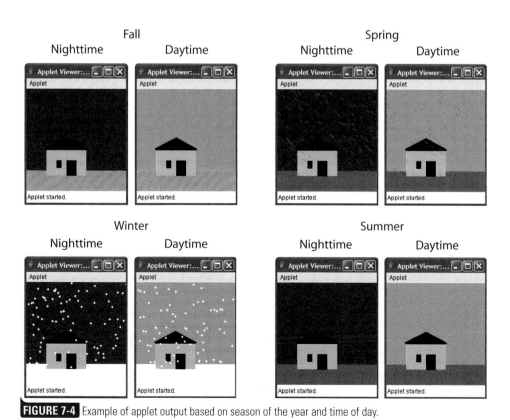

FIGURE 7-4 Example of applet output based on season of the year and time of day.

To get the current month or hour from our `Calendar` instance, we call:

```
int hour, month;
hour = rightNow.get( Calendar.HOUR_OF_DAY );
month = rightNow.get( Calendar.MONTH );
```

> HOUR_OF_DAY returns a value between 0 and 23 from the 24-hour clock.

Other options in the `Calendar` class include the following:

`Calendar.HOUR`	the hour on 12-hour clock
`Calendar.MINUTE`	the minutes
`Calendar.SECOND`	the seconds
`Calendar.MILLISECOND`	the milliseconds
`Calendar.HOUR_OF_DAY`	the hour based on 24-hour clock: 0...23
`Calendar.TIME`	the time in milliseconds after Jan. 1, 1970 GMT
`Calendar.DATE`	the day within the month
`Calendar.MONTH`	the month
`Calendar.YEAR`	the year
`Calendar.DAY_OF_MONTH`	the day of the month
`Calendar.DAY_OF_YEAR`	the day within the year
`Calendar.WEEK_OF_MONTH`	the week within the month
`Calendar.WEEK_OF_YEAR`	the week within the year

To create our weather program, we need three instance variables: `int`s for the month and hour of the day, and a `Calendar` object to determine the current time. To make our program easier to manage, let us set up some methods to handle drawing different scenes. We need methods for drawing the house, sky, snow, and rain. Let us get started with an outline for our `WeatherClip` class in Example 7-2.

EXAMPLE 7-2

```
import java.awt.*;
import javax.swing.*;
import java.util.*;
public class WeatherClip extends JApplet
{
    Calendar rightNow;
    int month, hour;
    public void paint( Graphics g )
    {
        rightNow = Calendar.getInstance( );
        hour = rightNow.get( Calendar.HOUR_OF_DAY );
        month = rightNow.get( Calendar.MONTH );
```

```
        drawSky( g );
        drawHouse( g );
    }
    public void drawHouse( Graphics g )
    {
        g.setColor( Color.BLACK );
        g.fillArc( 30, 50, 100, 90, 210, 120 );   // draw roof on
                                                   //    house
        g.setColor( Color.PINK );
        g.fillRect( 40, 120, 80, 50 );        // draw the main house
        g.setColor( Color.BLACK );
        g.fillRect( 60, 140, 10, 15 );        // draw a window
        g.fillRect( 80, 140, 20, 30 );        // draw the door
    }
    public void drawSnow( Graphics gr )       {
    }
    public  void drawRain( Graphics gr )      {
    }
    public void drawSky( Graphics g )       {
    }
}
```

Let us start by working on the drawSky method. In this method we need to check the hour of the day, which is one of the instance variables that we set. If this value is between 8 AM and 8 PM inclusive, then it is daytime and we want our sky to be cyan. If the hour is before 8 AM or after 8 PM, we should make our sky look dark with a dark blue. Once we set the color for the sky, then we can fill in a rectangular area for the sky. We can draw the sky with the following if statement:

```
public void drawSky( Graphics g )
{
    if ( hour >= 8 && hour <= 20 )
        g.setColor( Color.CYAN );
    else
        g.setColor( new Color( 25, 25, 112 ) );
    g.fillRect( 0, 0, 200, 160 );
}
```

> hour is an instance variable that we declared at the top of our program, so we can access it inside our drawSky method.

Now we might want to customize daytime in winter with a gray sky. Winter months include December, January, and February. So if it is daytime (if evaluates to true), then we will nest another if statement to check to see if it is wintertime. If it is, then we will set the color to gray; if it is not, we will set the color to cyan. Example 7-3 is the final code for our drawSky method:

EXAMPLE 7-3

```
public void drawSky( Graphics g )
{
    if ( hour >= 8 && hour <= 20 )                           // daytime
    {
        if ( month == 12 || month == 1 || month == 2 )   // winter months
            g.setColor( new Color( 138, 173, 217 ) );    // gray color
        else
            g.setColor( Color.CYAN );
    }
    else
        g.setColor( new Color( 25, 25, 112 ) );
    g.fillRect( 0, 0, 200, 160 );
}
```

It is time that we test our program to see if it works. It is important to work incrementally on a big program and make sure that everything works as you go.

To test that the sky really works, let us add some debugging lines in our WeatherClip class to test winter, summer, daytime, and night. After we get the actual month and hour of the day, let us temporarily reassign these values so that we can test our program. Let us set the month to January and the hour to 11. Run the program again and verify that the color is gray. Change the values again for the month of May and set the hour to 22. Run the program again and verify that the color is cyan. We will use these temporary assignments to continue to check that our program is fully operational (because we do not want to wait a full year to keep checking it). Once we are sure that all the seasons and day/night settings paint correctly, we can comment out these two lines of code.

```
rightNow = Calendar.getInstance( );
hour = rightNow.get( Calendar.HOUR_OF_DAY );
month = rightNow.get( Calendar.MONTH );
month = 1;   // FOR DEBUGGING
hour = 12;   // FOR DEBUGGING
```

After we have drawn the sky and the house, we can draw in the ground and any rain or snow, if appropriate. This is a good opportunity to make use of a switch statement. Because we have three cases (months) for each season, we could create three case statements that drop into the same set of statements. We add the following code to the end of our paint method.

```
switch( month )
{
   case 12:   case 1:  case 2:   // WINTER
                                 // ground is white
      drawSnow( g );
      break;
   case 3: case 4: case 5:       // SPRING
                                 // ground is green
      drawRain( g );
      break;
   case 6: case 7: case 8:       // SUMMER
                                 // ground is green

      break;
   case 9: case 10: case 11:     // FALL
                                 // ground is brown

      break;
}
```

Within each set of cases for a particular season, we add the code to draw in the ground: white for winter, brown for fall, and green for spring and summer. In winter we will also call the method drawSnow, and in spring we will call the method drawRain.

Implementing the drawSnow and drawRain methods are very similar. They both rely on selecting random numbers for (x, y) coordinates to draw a raindrop or snowflake. Using the Random class requires us to import the java.util package, but we have already added that to our code for the Calendar class. Now we can maintain an instance variable of type Random at the top of our WeatherClip class and create an instance of the Random class at the beginning of our paint method:

```
random = new Random( );
```

Inside our drawSnow and drawRain methods, we can get a random number for our coordinates by calling the nextInt method on our Random variable. To restrict the values it returns to ones that would fit within the dimensions of our applet, we send as a parameter the maximum value it should return (actually it will return a number between 0 and $N - 1$, where N is the number we send as a parameter).

```
random.nextInt( 200 );
```

Now we can draw snow as many times as we like. Because we have not covered loops yet, we will have to copy and paste the line to randomly draw a raindrop or snowflake many times to get a lot of precipitation. Our drawSnow method now appears as follows:

```
public void drawSnow( Graphics gr )
{
    gr.setColor( Color.WHITE );
    gr.fillOval( random.nextInt(200), random.nextInt(200), 5, 5 );
```

```
        gr.fillOval( random.nextInt(200), random.nextInt(200), 5, 5 );
        gr.fillOval( random.nextInt(200), random.nextInt(200), 5, 5 );
    }
```

The drawRain method is similar except that it draws lines in a gray color. Because lines require the (x, y) coordinates of the start and end of the line, we need to store the random numbers into a variable to be able to calculate the endpoint.

```
public void drawRain( Graphics gr )
{
        gr.setColor( Color.GRAY );
        int x = random.nextInt( 200 );
        int y = random.nextInt( 200 );
        gr.drawLine( x, y, x-5, y-5 );
        x = random.nextInt( 200 );
        y = random.nextInt( 200 );
        gr.drawLine( x, y, x-5, y-5 );
}
```

When we learn loops, we will make a lot of rain and snow easily.

Our final program appears in Example 7-4.

EXAMPLE 7-4

```
import java.awt.*;
import javax.swing.*;
import java.util.*;
public class WeatherClip extends JApplet
{
    Calendar rightNow;
    int month, hour;
    Random random;
    public void paint( Graphics g )
    {
        rightNow = Calendar.getInstance( );
        hour = rightNow.get( Calendar.HOUR_OF_DAY );
        month = rightNow.get( Calendar.MONTH );
        random = new Random( );

// month = 1;    // FOR DEBUGGING
// hour = 12;    // FOR DEBUGGING

        drawSky( g );
        drawHouse( g );
```

```
         switch( month )
         {
                case 12:   case 1:   case 2:           // WINTER
                        g.setColor( Color.WHITE );
                        g.fillRect( 0, 160, 200, 40 );   // ground is white
                        drawSnow( g );
                        break;
                case 3:    case 4:   case 5:           // SPRING
                        g.setColor( Color.GREEN );
                        g.fillRect( 0, 160, 200, 40 );   // ground is green
                        drawRain( g );
                        break;
                case 6:    case 7:   case 8:           // SUMMER
                        g.setColor( Color.GREEN );
                        g.fillRect( 0, 160, 200, 40 );   // ground is green
                        break;
                case 9:    case 10:   case 11:          // FALL
                        g.setColor( new Color( 222, 184, 135 ) );
                        g.fillRect( 0, 160, 200, 40 );   // ground is brown
                        break;
         }
    }
    public void drawHouse( Graphics g )
    {
         g.setColor( Color.BLACK );
         g.fillArc( 30, 50, 100, 90, 210, 120 );        // draw roof on house
         g.setColor( Color.PINK );
         g.fillRect( 40, 120, 80, 50 );                 // draw the main house
         g.setColor( Color.BLACK );
         g.fillRect( 60, 140, 10, 15 );                 // draw a window
         g.fillRect( 80, 140, 20, 30 );                 // draw the door
    }
    public void drawSnow( Graphics gr )
    {
         gr.setColor( Color.WHITE );
             // right now draws only three snowflakes — use loops for more
         gr.fillOval( random.nextInt( 200 ), random.nextInt( 200 ), 5, 5 );
         gr.fillOval( random.nextInt( 200 ), random.nextInt( 200 ), 5, 5 );
         gr.fillOval( random.nextInt( 200 ), random.nextInt( 200 ), 5, 5 );
    }
    public void drawRain( Graphics gr )
```

(continues)

Example 7-4 (continued)

```
    {
            gr.setColor( Color.GRAY );
            int x = random.nextInt( 200 );
            int y = random.nextInt( 200 );
            gr.drawLine( x, y, x-5, y-5 );
            x = random.nextInt( 200 );
            y = random.nextInt( 200 );
            gr.drawLine( x, y, x-5, y-5 );
    }
    public void drawSky( Graphics g )
    {
        if ( hour >= 8 && hour <= 20 )
        {
            if ( month == 12 || month == 1 || month == 2 )   // winter
                g.setColor( new Color( 138, 173, 217 ) );    // gray
            else
                g.setColor( Color.CYAN );
        }
        else
            g.setColor( new Color( 25, 25, 112 ) );   // night: dark blue
        g.fillRect( 0, 0, 200, 160 );
    }
}
```

> When we learn loops, we will make a lot of of rain and snow easily.

Add to the program a tree that has a few leaves in spring, a lot of green leaves in summer, multicolored leaves in fall, and no leaves in winter.

Troubleshooting

Common errors:

My code will not compile.	Make sure that you reference each variable exactly the same, and remember that Java is case sensitive.
	When writing the condition in your if, remember that the structure "0 < x < 10" does not work in Java: separate it properly as 0 < x && x < 10.
How do I test my program when using month/day/year/season/etc.?	When testing your program, add a line of code that you will delete later that assigns the appropriate variable to different values to test. See the weather example (Section 7.5) and assignment of month and time-of-day variables.
The code in my else clause keeps executing and it should not.	If you have multiple if statements ending with an else clause, make sure after the first if the other ifs are "else if", and then end with the else. This ensures the else clause executes only if all the other if statements fail.

The if statement is not working.	One way to debug your if statement is to add print statements to each section. Remember to add braces, { }, if you do not have them already, to group statements within each clause.
	Verify your use of relational and logical operators. && for AND results in true only if both sides evaluate to true; || for OR results in true if either side is true.
When I use == for comparing two Strings, it always returns false.	The == operator compares whether two variables are pointing to the same object in memory—it does not work to compare whether two strings are the same. Use .equals instead.

SUMMARY

- Conditional statements allow us to choose which statements to execute.
- The if statement evaluates a boolean expression. If the boolean expression evaluates to true, the statements within the if statement are executed.
- Boolean expressions can include combinations of relational and logical operators as long as the final expression evaluates to either true or false.
- Braces are used to designate a block of statements attached to an if or else statement.
- An if-else structure executes the statements in the else block if the boolean expression evaluates to false.
- Each else requires a matching if.
- Strings and other objects should be compared to each other by using the .equals method and not by using the == operator.
- switch statements evaluate either an integer or character value.
- Each case statement in a switch structure must be followed by a colon.
- The break and default statements in a switch structure are optional.
- if-else and switch structures can be nested inside each other.
- If a method returns a boolean value, it is not necessary to add a check: == true (e.g., if (btn.isVisible( ))).
- The Calendar class can be used to get an instance of the current day/time.

EXERCISES

1. True or false? An else clause is always matched to the nearest available unmatched if.
2. True or false? Braces are required with if structures.
3. True or false? An else clause is required with every if statement.
4. True or false? In Java, the statement if (x = y) is a valid construct of an if statement.

5. What is the value of the variable xyz after the following code segment?

```
int x = 5;
int y = -2;
if ( x > 0 )
     if ( y > 0 )
              xyz = 1;
else
     xyz = 2;
```

6. True or false? The statement if (ale = bez) evaluates to true if ale and bez have the same value.

7. True or false? Any if-else statement can be expressed in a switch structure.

8. True or false? Any switch statement can be expressed in an if-else structure.

9. True or false? The break statement is required for all cases in a switch structure.

10. True or false? The default statement is required in a switch structure.

11. Write a switch statement that takes an integer value for a student's grade out of 100 points and displays a label with the letter grade based on the following:

90–100	A
80–89	B
70–79	C
60–69	D
Anything else	F

12. What would be a more descriptive name for the following method?

```
public int myMethod( int a, int b )
{
     if( a >= b )
           return b;
     else
           return a;
}
```

13. What is wrong in the following code?

```
boolean isEqual;
double m = 1.22 + 1.07;
if( m == 2.29 )
       isEqual = true;
else
       isEqual = false;
```

14. Does the ordering of `if-else` segments matter? Why or why not?

15. Does the ordering of `switch case` segments matter? Why or why not?

16. Is the `break` keyword required in `switch` statements? What happens if the `break` statement is not in a `switch` statement?

17. Is the `default` keyword required in a `switch` statement?

18. Can you put the `default` keyword first in the `switch` statement? Try it and see how it works.

19. Why can `Strings` not be used in a `switch` statement?
    Hint: see the section on `==` *vs* `.equals( )` *on objects.*

20. Write a method named `isEven` that takes an `int` parameter between 1 and 10 and returns whether the number is even or odd. Implement both the `if-else` structure and a `switch` statement. Which is easier? Which is easier to implement if the `int` parameter could be between 1 and 10000?

21. Write a method named `getMin` that takes two `int` parameters and returns the lesser of the two values. Then write a second method that takes three `int` parameters and returns the minimum of all three values. In the second method, be sure to call your first method in your solution.

22. Write a method named `getMonth` that takes a number between 1 and 12 as a parameter and returns a `String` of the full name of the month (e.g., 3 should return "March"). Write it first with an `if-else` structure and then again with a `switch` statement.

23. We want to check a date entered by the user for validity. Write a program that prompts the user for the date as an integer between 1 and 31 and then an integer month between 1 and 12. We will assume that the year is 2005 (which is not a leap year). Print out whether the month/day combination is valid.

24. Write a method called `getMonthAsString` that takes three integers as parameters (`month`, `day`, and `year`) and returns a `String` formatted as "`Month, day, year`" (e.g., "`November 25, 2009`").

25. Write a method named `isEqual` that takes two double values as parameters and returns `true` if they are essentially equal, or within 0.0001 of each other.

26. Extend the Weather Clip program (see Section 7.5) to draw a tree that is bare in winter, has buds in spring, has green leaves in summer, and has colored leaves in fall (for leaves, you can keep it simple by drawing lots of circles—somewhat abstract art).

27. Write a class that maintains information about a date. The month, day, and year need to be stored as integer instance variables. Write a constructor that takes an `int` for each of these values and initializes them. Add the following additional methods:

    a. `getEuropeanDate` that returns the date as "`DD MMM YYYY`" (e.g., "`25 Nov 2007`")

b. `getAmericanDate` that returns the date as "`MMM DD, YYYY`" (e.g., "Nov 25, 2007")

c. `getIntDate` that takes a `char` as a parameter to designate the delimiter and returns the date as "`MM-DD-YY`" (e.g., "11-25-07" or "11/25/07")

Events

8

To listen, or not to listen—
that is what we must decide ...

Events

Now we get to learn how to handle events. An event is a situation when something occurs that we can decide to respond to. Usually an event corresponds to actions by the user, but not always. For example, an event occurs when the user clicks on a button, selects one of the radio buttons, selects or deselects a checkbox, selects an item from a list, types text into a text field or text area, clicks on the mouse, or even clicks on a key or combination of keys.

When working with events, we set up listeners to specify that we are interested in particular types of events. For example, if we want to listen to button clicks, we need to work with the `ActionListener`. If we are listening for mouse events, we implement either the `MouseListener` or the `MouseMotionListener` (or both). Common listeners are listed in **TABLE 8-1**.

TABLE 8-1   Common Listeners and Their Event Triggers

Listener	Event Triggers
`ActionListener`	Button clicks
`ItemListener`	Selecting/deselecting a `JCheckBox`, selecting/deselecting a `JRadioButton`, selecting from `JComboBox`
`ListSelectionListener`	Selecting from a `JList`
`KeyListener`	Any key on the keyboard pressed
`FocusListener`	User's focus enters or leaves the component
`MouseListener`	Mouse entered the component, exited the component, mouse button pressed, mouse button released, mouse button clicked
`MouseMotionListener`	Mouse moved, mouse dragged

We can capture these events and handle them by using the following procedure. There are four things we need to do to get events to work in our applets:

1. Import the events package.

   ```
   import java.awt.event.*;
   ```

2. Implement the appropriate listener(s).

   This is specified at the end of the class header, using the keyword `implements`.

   ```
   public class XYZ extends JApplet implements ActionListener
   ```

You can specify multiple listeners by separating each with a comma.

```
public class XYZ extends JApplet implements ItemListener,
    MouseListener
```

3. Add listeners to the components.

```
submitButton.addActionListener( this );
combobox.addItemListener( this );
panel.addMouseListener( this );
textfield.addFocusListener( this );
```

The this Java keyword specifies that the class that we are currently writing is the class that wants to listen for events from the component specified.

4. Write the required listener method(s).

Each listener that we implement (from Step 2) requires a particular set of methods that we are required to write.

The list of methods for the common listeners are listed in **TABLE 8-2**.

Implementing the required listener methods requires some thought and usually makes use of if-else structures. The first thing we want to do, no matter which method we are writing, is to figure out the source of the event. First create a variable to store the object:

```
Object source = parameter.getSource( );
```

where *parameter* is the variable name that we used in the method header. (For example: in public void mousePressed(MouseEvent me) the variable is me, so the line above would have me.getSource( )).

TABLE 8-2 Event Listeners and Their Required Methods

Event Listener	Required Methods
ActionListener	public void actionPerformed(ActionEvent ae)
ItemListener	public void itemStateChanged(ItemEvent ie)
ListSelectionListener	public void valueChanged(ListSelectionEvent e)
KeyListener	public void keyReleased(KeyEvent ke) public void keyTyped(KeyEvent ke) public void keyPressed(KeyEvent ke)
FocusListener	public void focusGained(FocusEvent fe) public void focusLost(FocusEvent fe)
MouseEvent	public void mouseClicked(MouseEvent me) public void mousePressed(MouseEvent me) public void mouseReleased(MouseEvent me) public void mouseEntered(MouseEvent me) public void mouseExited(MouseEvent me)
MouseMotionListener	public void mouseMoved(MouseMovedEvent me) public void mouseDragged(MouseMovedEvent me)

The next thing we want to do is determine which component caused the event. For example, if we have three buttons on our applet, it helps to know which button was the one that the user selected. We can do this by using the == operator. We will see examples of this in the following sections.

8.1.1 ActionEvents

The ActionListener handles the button clicks on JButtons. Whenever the user clicks on a button, an ActionEvent occurs and the program automatically calls the actionPerformed method. If we do not write an actionPerformed method, the program will go to an actionPerformed method in the JApplet class (the class we extend or inherit), which does nothing. To do something on the basis of a button click, we need to specify that our class implements the ActionListener, add our class as an ActionListener for each button that we want to handle, and write the actionPerformed method.

Steps for ActionListener:

1. Import the events package.

   ```
   import java.awt.event.*;
   ```

2. Implement the appropriate listener(s).

   ```
   public class XYZ extends JApplet implements ActionListener
   ```

3. Add listeners to the components.

   ```
   submitButton.addActionListener( this );
   otherButton.addItemListener( this );
   ```

4. Write the required listener method(s).

   ```
   public void actionPerformed( ActionEvent ae )
   {
           Object src = ae.getSource( );
   }
   ```

Example 8-1 demonstrates the ActionListener on two buttons that each modify the text displayed in a JTextField.

EXAMPLE 8-1

```
import java.awt.*;
import javax.swing.*;
import java.awt.event.*;
public class IfButton extends JApplet
                implements ActionListener
{
    JButton go, stop;
    JTextField textf;
    public void init( )
```

First run:

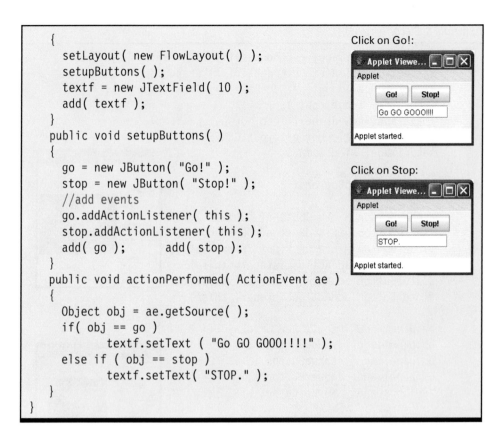

```
{
  setLayout( new FlowLayout( ) );
  setupButtons( );
  textf = new JTextField( 10 );
  add( textf );
}
public void setupButtons( )
{
  go = new JButton( "Go!" );
  stop = new JButton( "Stop!" );
  //add events
  go.addActionListener( this );
  stop.addActionListener( this );
  add( go );       add( stop );
}
public void actionPerformed( ActionEvent ae )
{
  Object obj = ae.getSource( );
  if( obj == go )
        textf.setText ( "Go GO GOO!!!!" );
  else if ( obj == stop )
        textf.setText( "STOP." );
}
}
```

Click on Go!:

Click on Stop:

Example 8-2 uses JButtons, which chang the image displayed when clicked.

EXAMPLE 8-2

```
import java.awt.*;
import javax.swing.*;
import java.awt.event.*;
public class ButtonImages extends JApplet  implements ActionListener
{
   JButton windowButton, statueButton, flowerButton;
   Image windowImg, statueImg, flowerImg;
   ImageIcon icon;
   JLabel imagelabel;
   JPanel butpanel;
   public void init( )
   {
      setLayout( new BorderLayout( ) );
      setupButtons( );
```

(continues)

Example 8-2 (continued)

```
    windowImg=getImage( getCodeBase( ), "ChinaWindow.jpg" );
    statueImg=getImage( getCodeBase( ),"Statue.jpg" );
    flowerImg=getImage( getCodeBase( ),"flowers.jpg" );
    icon = new ImageIcon( );
    imagelabel=new JLabel( icon, JLabel.CENTER );
    add( imagelabel, BorderLayout.CENTER );
    setupImage( windowImg );
}
public void setupButtons( )
{
    windowButton = new JButton( "China" );
    statueButton = new JButton( "Germany" );
    flowerButton = new JButton( "Slovakia" );
    windowButton.addActionListener( this );
    statueButton.addActionListener( this );
    flowerButton.addActionListener( this );

    butpanel=new JPanel( new GridLayout( 3, 1 ) );
    butpanel.add( windowButton );
    butpanel.add( statueButton );
    butpanel.add( flowerButton );
    add( butpanel, BorderLayout.WEST );
}
public void setupImage( Image img )
{
    icon.setImage( img );
    imagelabel.setIcon( icon );
    repaint( );
}
public void actionPerformed( ActionEvent ae )
{
    Object source = ae.getSource( );
    if( source == windowButton )
            setupImage( windowImg );
    else if( source == statueButton )
            setupImage( statueImg );
    else if( source == flowerButton )
            setupImage( flowerImg );
}
}
```

> You must call repaint for it to display the change.

In Example 8-3, we want the user to enter something to search for, and if we find it in the list, we will highlight it. The call to `.setSelectedValue` will automatically scroll to the item's location in the list.

EXAMPLE 8-3

```java
import java.awt.*;
import javax.swing.*;
import java.awt.event.*;
import java.util.*;
public class SearchTFScroll extends JApplet implements ActionListener
{
   JLabel searchLabel;
   JTextField searchField;
   JPanel searchPanel;
   JButton searchButton;
   JList list;
   DefaultListModel model;
   JScrollPane scrollPane;
   public void init( )
   {
      setLayout( new BorderLayout( ) );
      searchLabel= new JLabel( "Search for:" );
      searchField = new JTextField( 10 );
      searchPanel = new JPanel( );
      searchButton = new JButton( "search" );
      model = new DefaultListModel( );
      list = new JList( model );
      addListItems( );
      scrollPane = new JScrollPane( list );
      searchButton.addActionListener( this );
      searchPanel.add( searchLabel );
      searchPanel.add( searchField );
      searchPanel.add( searchButton );
      add( scrollPane, BorderLayout.CENTER );
      add( searchPanel, BorderLayout.NORTH );
   }
   public void addListItems( )
   {
      model.addElement( "apples" );
      model.addElement( "bananas" );        model.addElement( "blackberries" );
      model.addElement( "blueberries" );     model.addElement( "carrots" );
      model.addElement( "capers" );          model.addElement( "cauliflower" );
      model.addElement( "cucumber" );        model.addElement( "kiwifruit" );
   }
   public void actionPerformed( ActionEvent e )
```

(continues)

Example 8-3 (continued)

```
{
    String field = searchField.getText( );
    if (field != null)
        findNode( field );
}
public void findNode( String field )
{
    list.clearSelection( );
    list.setSelectedValue( field, true );
}
}
```

8.1.2 ItemEvents

ItemListener listens for events pertaining to selecting or deselecting a JCheckBox, selecting or deselecting a JRadioButton, or selecting from a JComboBox. Example 8-4 demonstrates the steps listed using a JCheckBox, and Example 8-5 shows the steps with a JRadioButton that ignores all deselection events.

Steps for ItemListener:

1. Import the events package.

   ```
   import java.awt.event.*;
   ```

2. Implement the appropriate listener(s).

   ```
   public class XYZ extends JApplet implements ItemListener
   ```

3. Add listeners to the components.

   ```
   combobox.addItemListener( this );
   ```

4. Write the required listener method(s).

   ```
   public void itemStateChanged( ItemEvent ie )
   {
           Object src = ie.getSource( );
   }
   ```

EXAMPLE 8-4

```
import java.awt.*;
import javax.swing.*;
import java.awt.event.*;
public class CheckEvent extends JApplet
        implements ItemListener
{
    JCheckBox isHappy;
    JTextArea textarea;
```

Select checkbox:

```
    public void init( )
    {
        setLayout( new FlowLayout( ) );

        isHappy = new JCheckBox( "Happy?", true );
        textarea = new JTextArea( 3, 10 );
        // add listener
        isHappy.addItemListener( this );
        add( isHappy );
        add( textarea );
    }
    public void itemStateChanged( ItemEvent ie )
    {
        Object source = ie.getSource( );
        if( source == isHappy && isHappy.isSelected( ) )
            textarea.setText( "You're so happy!" );
        else if( source == isHappy && ! isHappy.isSelected ( ) )
            textarea.setText( "Why not happy?" );
    }
}
```

Deselect checkbox:

EXAMPLE 8-5

```
import java.awt.*;
import javax.swing.*;
import java.awt.event.*;

public class JRadioEvent extends JApplet
                implements ItemListener
{
    ButtonGroup grp;
    JRadioButton red, fuchsia, pink;
    JTextArea ta;
    public void init( )
    {
        setLayout( new FlowLayout( ) );
        ta = new JTextArea( 5, 10 );
        setupButtons( );
        addListeners( );
        add( red );
        add( fuchsia );
        add( pink );
        add( ta );
    }
```

Select "fuchsia":

(continues)

Example 8-5 (continued)

Select "pink":

```java
public void setupButtons( )
{
  red = new JRadioButton( "red" );
  fuchsia = new JRadioButton( "fuchsia" );
  pink = new JRadioButton( "pink" );
  grp = new ButtonGroup( );
  grp.add( red );
  grp.add( fuchsia );
  grp.add( pink );
}
public void addListeners( )
{
    red.addItemListener( this );
    fuchsia.addItemListener( this );
    pink.addItemListener( this );
}

public void itemStateChanged( ItemEvent ie )
{
    Object o = ie.getSource( );
    if ( ie.getStateChange( ) == ItemEvent.DESELECTED )
        return;      // ignore if deselecting
    if( o == red )
        ta.append( "We like red \n" );
    else if( o == fuchsia )
        ta.append( "We like fuchsia \n" );
    else if( o == pink )
        ta.append( "We prefer pink \n" );
}
}
```

8.1.3 `ListSelectionEvents`

`ListSelectionEvents` occur when the user selects from a `JList`. Example 8-6 shows the steps necessary to implement a `JList` with events. Steps for `ItemListener`:

1. Import the events package.

   ```java
   import javax.swing.event.*;
   ```

2. Implement the appropriate listener(s).

   ```java
   public class XYZ extends JApplet implements ListSelectionListener
   ```

3. Add listeners to the components.

   ```java
   list.addListSelectionListener( this );
   ```

4. Write the required listener method(s).

```
public void valueChanged( ListSelectionEvent le )
{
        Object src = le.getSource( );
}
```

EXAMPLE 8-6

```
import java.awt.*;
import javax.swing.*;
import javax.swing.event.*;
public class JListEvent extends JApplet
                    implements ListSelectionListener
{
    JList list;
    DefaultListModel model;
    JLabel dessert;
    public void init( )
    {
      model = new DefaultListModel( );
      list = new JList( model );
      model.addElement( "apple" );
      model.addElement( "banana" );
      model.addElement( "pear" );
      list.addListSelectionListener( this );
      JScrollPane pane = new JScrollPane( list );
      dessert = new JLabel( );
      setLayout( new FlowLayout( ) );
      add( pane );  add( dessert );
    }
    public void valueChanged( ListSelectionEvent le )
    {
      int index = list.getSelectedIndex( );
      if ( index == 0 )
         dessert.setText( "We're having apple pie!" );
      else if ( index == 1 )
         dessert.setText( "Banana split anyone?" );
      else if ( index == 2 )
         dessert.setText( "Pear for the pair?" );
    }
}
```

When applet first run:

Select "apple":

Select "banana":

■ 8.1.4 KeyEvents

Key events are used when we want to keep track of when the user types any keys on the keyboard. Doing so is especially fun for controlling characters in a game environment. To listen for key events, we need the import statement as before, and we need to specify that we are implementing the KeyListener:

```
import java.awt.*;
import javax.swing.*;
import java.awt.event.*;
public class KeyEventEx extends JApplet implements KeyListener
```

We also need to state that we are interested in all key events performed on the applet. To do this, we add the key listener:

```
public void init( )
{
        addKeyListener( this );
}
```

Usually we want to listen for key events when the focus is anywhere within the applet, so we do not need to call the addKeyListener method on a specific object. Instead, we call addKeyListener on the entire applet. We could, however, listen for KeyEvents only when the focus is on a specific JPanel by calling the method on our JPanel:

```
JPanel pane = new JPanel( );
pane.addKeyListener( this );
```

Listening for key events requires us to write three methods:

```
public void keyReleased( KeyEvent ke )  { }
public void keyTyped( KeyEvent ke )     { }
public void keyPressed( KeyEvent ke )   { }
```

We would probably be interested only in the keyPressed method, so we can leave the other two methods as *stubs*. A method stub contains the method header and the braces but nothing for the body of the method (inside the braces). We just list the method stubs as follows:

```
public void keyReleased( KeyEvent ke )  { }
public void keyTyped( KeyEvent ke )     { }
```

Inside the keyPressed method we will do something on the basis of which key was pressed. We do not need to get the source of the event like we do in the actionPerformed method—instead, we want to know which key was pressed. To figure this out, we ask for the key code:

```
public void keyPressed( KeyEvent ke )
{
        int code = ke.getKeyCode( );
}
```

Now we can check to see if it matches to a particular key. For example, we can look at the following:

up arrow	KeyEvent.VK_UP	left arrow	KeyEvent.VK_LEFT
down arrow	KeyEvent.VK_DOWN	right arrow	KeyEvent.VK_RIGHT

To see if a particular letter was pressed, check the KeyEvent.VK_[letter], where [letter] is any letter A through Z (in uppercase). For numbers on a keypad, use KeyEvent.VK_NUMPAD[#], where [#] is any number 0 through 9. Numbers not on the keypad can be accessed with KeyEvent.VK_[#]. Other useful key codes include VK_ADD, VK_SUBTRACT, VK_MULTIPLY, VK_DIVIDE, VK_ENTER, VK_PERIOD, VK_SPACE, VK_TAB, VK_SHIFT, VK_ALT, and VK_CONTROL.

One last thing we need to do is set the applet as the focus so that it can start listening for key events:

```
setFocusable( true );
```

In Example 8-7, we can move around an animated GIF image by pressing arrow keys on the keyboard. Because we want to control where the image is, we will use the null layout manager, which allows us to call the method setLocation on our JLabel with the image so that we can specify the exact (x, y) coordinates for the image. The (x, y) coordinate specifies the upper-left corner of the label/image. To handle the key events, the user can press the arrow keys to get the image to move. The speed variable makes it easy for us to change how fast the image moves—how many pixels it should move in either the x or y direction each time an arrow key is pressed.

EXAMPLE 8-7

```
import java.awt.*;
import javax.swing.*;
import java.awt.event.*;
public class KeyEventAnimation extends JApplet implements KeyListener
{
  Image img;
  JLabel penny;
  int x = 0, y = 0, speed = 10; // ( x, y ) coordinates and how many pixels
  JPanel pane;                  // move
  public void init( )
  {
    pane = new JPanel( );
    pane.setLayout( null );
    pane.setBackground( Color.WHITE );
    img = getImage( getCodeBase( ), "Walk.gif" );
    player = new JLabel( new ImageIcon( img ) );
    player.setSize( img.getWidth( this ), img.getHeight( this ) );
```
(continues)

Example 8-7 (continued)

```
    addKeyListener( this );
    pane.add( player, 0, 0 );
    add( pane, BorderLayout.CENTER );
    setFocusable( true );
}
public void keyReleased( KeyEvent ke ) { }
public void keyTyped( KeyEvent ke ) { }
public void keyPressed( KeyEvent ke )
{
    int code = ke.getKeyCode( );
    if ( code == KeyEvent.VK_UP )
        y -= speed;
    else if ( code == KeyEvent.VK_DOWN )
        y += speed;
    else if ( code == KeyEvent.VK_LEFT )
        x -= speed;
    else if ( code == KeyEvent.VK_RIGHT )
        x += speed;
    player.setLocation( x, y );
}
}
```

Image courtesy of Luke Scanlon, 5311 Studios.

8.1.5 FocusEvents

There are several different solutions to handling changes in text components such as JTextField, JTextArea, and JPasswordField. One method is to write a KeyListener on the components and handle events according to the methods provided with the KeyListener. Another option: if we want to handle the event only when the user presses the Enter key after typing inside the text component, we could add the ActionListener to the component, which will automatically call the actionPerformed method when the Enter key is pressed. A third option is to handle the event when the user's focus leaves the component. This approach is ideal for validating user input. Here we work with the FocusListener, and we write two required methods: focusGained and focusLost. Example 8-8 demonstrates the following steps listed using a JTextField and JTextArea with the FocusListener.

Steps for FocusListener:

1. Import the events package.

   ```
   import java.awt.event.*;
   ```

2. Implement the appropriate listener(s).

   ```
   public class XYZ extends JApplet implements FocusListener
   ```

3. Add listeners to the components.

   ```
   textComponent.addFocusListener( this );
   ```

4. Write the required listener method(s).

```
public void focusGained( FocusEvent fe )
public void focusLost( FocusEvent fe )
```

EXAMPLE 8-8

```
import java.awt.*;
import javax.swing.*;
import java.awt.event.*;
public class TextChange extends JApplet implements FocusListener
{
    JLabel status;      // starts out empty, displays error messages
    JTextField email;
    JTextArea mesg;
    JScrollPane scroll;
    public void init( )
    {
        setLayout( new FlowLayout( ) );
        status = new JLabel( );
        status.setForeground( Color.RED );
        email = new JTextField( 15 );
        mesg = new JTextArea( 4, 10 );
        scroll = new JScrollPane( mesg );
        email.addFocusListener( this );
        mesg.addFocusListener( this );
        add( email );
        add( scroll );
        add( status );
    }
    public void focusGained( FocusEvent fe ) { } // method stub
    public void focusLost( FocusEvent fe )
    {
        Object src = fe.getSource( );
        if ( src == email )
        {
            String userText = email.getText( );
            if ( ! userText.contains( "@" ) )
                status.setText( "Must provide a valid email address." );
            else
                status.setText( "" );  // everything is fine
        }
```

(continues)

Example 8-8 (continued)

```
      else if ( src == mesg )
      {
        String mesgText = mesg.getText( );
        if ( mesgText.length( ) < 1 )
          status.setText( "Must provide a message" );
        else
          status.setText( "" );  // everything is fine
      }
   }
}
```

■ 8.1.6 MouseEvents

There are two types of listeners to deal with mouse events: MouseListener and MouseMotionListener. The event types and methods required to write for each listener are listed in **TABLE 8-3**. Each method takes a MouseEvent as a parameter.

To listen for mouse events, we need the import statement as before, and we need to specify that we are implementing either the MouseListener or the MouseMotionListener.

```
import java.awt.*;
import javax.swing.*;
import java.awt.event.*;
public class MouseEx extends JApplet implements MouseListener
{
```

We also need to state that we are interested in all mouse events performed on the applet. To do this, we add the MouseListener to the applet:

```
public void init( )
{
      addMouseListener( this );
}
```

TABLE 8-3 MouseListener and MouseMotionListener Events and Methods

Listener	Methods Required	Event Types
MouseListener	mouseEntered mouseExited mousePressed mouseReleased mouseClicked	Mouse entered the component Mouse exited the component Mouse button pressed Mouse button released Mouse button clicked
MouseMotionListener	mouseMoved mouseDragged	Mouse moved Mouse dragged while button held down

Usually we want to listen for mouse events when the focus is anywhere within the applet, so we do not need to call the addMouseListener method on a specific object. Instead, we call addMouseListener on the entire applet. We could, however, listen for MouseEvents only when the focus is on a specific JPanel by calling the method on our JPanel:

```
JPanel pane = new JPanel( );
pane.addMouseListener( this );
```

Implementing the MouseListener requires us to write five methods, demonstrated in Example 8-9:

```
public void mouseEntered( MouseEvent me )      { }
public void mouseExited( MouseEvent me )       { }
public void mousePressed( MouseEvent me )      { }
public void mouseReleased( MouseEvent me )     { }
public void mouseClicked( MouseEvent me )      { }
```

We probably do not want to use all the methods required, so we can leave the other methods as *stubs*. Inside our methods that we do want to implement, we can find out the *x* and *y* coordinates of the mouse at the time of the event. To do this, we call the methods getX( ) and getY( ) on our MouseEvent variable.

```
public void mousePressed( MouseEvent me )
{
        int x = me.getX( );
        int y = me.getY( );
}
```

EXAMPLE 8-9

```
import java.awt.*;
import javax.swing.*;
import java.awt.event.*;
public class MouseEvents extends JApplet implements MouseListener, MouseMotionListener
{
  JTextArea msg;
  JScrollPane spane;
  public void init( )
  {
      addMouseListener( this );
      addMouseMotionListener( this );
      msg = new JTextArea( 10, 20 );
      spane = new JScrollPane( msg );
      setLayout( new FlowLayout( ) );
      add( spane );
  }
  public void mouseEntered( MouseEvent me )
  {
      msg.append( "\nMouse entered applet at: x=" + me.getX( ) + " y=" + me.getY( ) );
  }
```

Applet Viewer: MouseEvent...

Applet

Mouse entered applet at: x=275 y=183
Mouse moved at: x=275 y=183
Mouse moved at: x=274 y=182
Mouse moved at: x=272 y=181
Mouse moved at: x=270 y=180
Mouse moved at: x=269 y=179

Applet started.

(continues)

Example 8-9 (continued)

```java
public void mouseExited( MouseEvent me )
{
    msg.append( "\nMouse exited applet at: x=" + me.getX( ) + " y=" + me.getY( ) );
}
public void mousePressed( MouseEvent me )
{
    msg.append( "\nMouse button pressed at: x=" + me.getX( ) + " y=" + me.getY( ) );
}
public void mouseReleased( MouseEvent me )
{
    msg.append( "\nMouse button released at: x=" + me.getX( ) + " y=" + me.getY( ) );
}
public void mouseClicked( MouseEvent me )
{
    msg.append( "\nMouse button clicked at: x=" + me.getX( ) + " y=" + me.getY( ) );
}
public void mouseMoved( MouseEvent me )
{
    msg.append( "\nMouse moved at: x=" + me.getX( ) + " y=" + me.getY( ) );
}
public void mouseDragged( MouseEvent me )
{
    msg.append( "\nMouse dragged at: x=" + me.getX( ) + " y=" + me.getY( ) );
}
}
```

8.2 Method Stubs

When our code states that we implement one of these listeners, we are required to write *all* the required methods. Sometimes we do not care to handle any of the events for some of these methods. We can instead write a *method stub*. A **method stub** is a method with nothing in the body of the method. For example, if we wanted to print out only when the mouse entered and exited the applet, we would change the code from Example 8-9 to what we have in Example 8-10.

EXAMPLE 8-10

```java
import java.awt.*;
import javax.swing.*;
import java.awt.event.*;
public class MouseEventsWithStubs extends JApplet implements MouseListener
{
    JTextArea msg;
    JScrollPane spane;
    public void init( )
```

```
    {
        addMouseListener( this );

        msg = new JTextArea( 10, 20 );
        spane = new JScrollPane( msg );

        setLayout( new FlowLayout( ) );
        add( spane );
    }
    public void mouseEntered( MouseEvent me )
    {
        msg.append( "\nMouse entered applet at: x=" + me.getX( ) + " y=" + me.getY( ) );
    }
    public void mouseExited( MouseEvent me )
    {
        msg.append( "\nMouse exited applet at: x=" + me.getX( ) + " y=" + me.getY( ) );
    }
    public void mousePressed( MouseEvent me )     {    }
    public void mouseReleased( MouseEvent me )    {    }
    public void mouseClicked( MouseEvent me )      {    }
}
```

In Example 8-10, we wrote *method stubs* for the mousePressed, mouseReleased, and mouseClicked methods. We are required to have the methods written in the program, but we do nothing inside the method.

We can listen to mouse events either on the applet itself (as in the preceding examples) or on a particular component. Doing so could be useful if we wanted to handle mouse events on a helper class that we create, such as the Smiley example from Chapter 10 in which we extend the JPanel class.

Example 8-11 uses the MouseListener and MouseMotionListener.

EXAMPLE 8-11

```
import java.awt.*;
import javax.swing.*;
import java.awt.event.*;

public class Scribble extends JApplet
        implements MouseListener, MouseMotionListener
{
    int last_x, last_y;
```

(continues)

Example 8-11 (continued)

```
public void init( )
{
    addMouseListener( this );
    addMouseMotionListener( this );
}

public void mousePressed( MouseEvent me )
{
    last_x = me.getX( );
    last_y = me.getY( );
}

public void mouseDragged( MouseEvent me )
{
    Graphics g = this.getGraphics( );
    int x = me.getX( );
    int y = me.getY( );
    g.drawLine( last_x, last_y, x, y );
    last_x = x;
    last_y = y;
}

// Method stubs for methods that we do not need
public void mouseReleased( MouseEvent me ) {  }
public void mouseClicked( MouseEvent me ) {  }
public void mouseEntered( MouseEvent me ) {  }
public void mouseExited( MouseEvent me ) {  }
public void mouseMoved( MouseEvent e ) {  }
}
```

Another example using mouse events is Example 8-12, where the eyeballs follow the mouse around the applet.

EXAMPLE 8-12

```
import java.awt.*;
import javax.swing.*;
import java.awt.event.*;
public class MouseEyes extends JApplet implements MouseMotionListener
{
    int mouseX, mouseY;   // track current location of mouse
```

```
public void init( )
{
    addMouseMotionListener( this );
}
public void paint( Graphics g )
{
    g.clearRect( 0, 0, getWidth( ), getHeight( ) );
    int eyeWidth = 40;
    int eyeHeight = 80;
    g.setColor( Color.WHITE );                      // color the whites of the eyes
    g.fillOval( 0, 0, eyeWidth, eyeHeight );
    g.fillOval( eyeWidth, 0, eyeWidth, eyeHeight );
    g.setColor( Color.BLACK );                      // draw outline
    g.drawOval( 0, 0, eyeWidth, eyeHeight );        // left eye
    g.drawOval( 1, 1, eyeWidth-2, eyeHeight-2 );
    g.drawOval( eyeWidth, 0, eyeWidth, eyeHeight );  // right eye
    g.drawOval( eyeWidth+1, 1, eyeWidth-2, eyeHeight-2);

        // eyes, ( x, y ) as percentage of where mouse is
    int eyeX = ( mouseX * 100 / getWidth( ) ) * eyeWidth / 100;  // eyeball
    int eyeY = ( mouseY * 100 / getHeight( ) ) * eyeHeight / 100;
    g.fillOval( eyeX, eyeY, 10, 10 );
    g.fillOval( eyeX+eyeWidth, eyeY, 10, 10 );
}
public void mouseMoved( MouseEvent me )  // track current location of mouse
{
    mouseX = me.getX( );
    mouseY = me.getY( );
    repaint( );
}
public void mouseDragged( MouseEvent me ) { }
}
```

Example 8-13 shows how we can be annoying by causing the button to move randomly around the applet as soon as the mouse gets near it.

EXAMPLE 8-13

```java
/** Program that moves a button whenever the mouse
 * gets near it. */
import java.awt.*;
import javax.swing.*;
import java.awt.event.*;
import java.util.*;

public class Annoying extends JApplet implements MouseMotionListener
{
    JButton winner = new JButton( "Click me and win a million" );
                    // need a Random object to randomly select new x and y coordinates
                    //   when we move the button to a new location
        Random random = new Random( );
                    // Rectangle object that determines the x and y coordinates
                    //   that trigger a move of the button.
                    // The coordinates are 10 pixels bigger than the actual button,
                    //   such that if the mouse gets within 10 pixels of the button, the
                    //   button will move.
    Rectangle rectangle = new Rectangle( );

    public void init( )
    {
                    // null layout so we can place the button in an exact location
        setLayout( null );
                    // Because we are using the null layout, we have to set the bounds
                    //   on our button: x and y coordinates ( 100, 200 ), width of 200, and
                    //   height of 20.
        winner.setBounds( 100, 200, 200, 20 );
                    // rectangle holds the buffer area, 10 pixels bigger than the button
                    // records the x and y coordinates ( 90, 190 ), width 220, and height
                    //   40.
        rectangle.setBounds( 90, 190, 220, 40);        // "too close" boundary

        addMouseMotionListener( this );
        add( winner );

    }
    public void mouseMoved( MouseEvent me )
    {
        int x = me.getX( );
        int y = me.getY( );
        if ( rectangle.contains( x, y )  ) // method returns true if ( x, y ) inside
                                           //   rectangle
        {
                    // Move the button to a new spot.
                    // to make sure it does not go off screen, the max x is 300
            winner.setLocation( random.nextInt( 300 ), random.nextInt( 490 ) );
                    // reset the boundary for the rectangle, such that it is a 10-pixel
                    //   buffer from the new location of the button
```

Applet Viewer: Annoying.class

Applet

Click me and win a million

Applet started.

```
                 rectangle.setBounds( winner.getX( )-10, winner.getY( )-10,
                            winner.getWidth( )+20, winner.getHeight( )+20 );
        }
    }
    public void mouseDragged( MouseEvent me )  {  }
}
```

8.3 Adding and Removing Components Dynamically

Now that we can dynamically change things according to certain events, we can make bigger and more complex applets. This leads to the desire to change the main area of the applet on the basis of a selection, such as a button or list option. To ensure that the graphics are redrawn properly, the easiest way to do this is to use a JPanel where you can remove all items by calling the removeAll method on it and then add new items to the JPanel. We also need to call the validate and repaint methods to ensure that the screen is redrawn with the new components. Example 8-14 illustrates how to achieve this.

EXAMPLE 8-14

```
import java.awt.*;
import java.awt.event.*;
import javax.swing.*;
public class ClearPanelEx extends JApplet implements ActionListener
{
    JLabel title;
    JButton productInfo, aboutUs;
    JPanel mainPanel;        // use this JPanel for everything in BorderLayout.CENTER
    JPanel productPanel, aboutUsPanel;
    public void init( )
    {
        setLayout( new BorderLayout( ) );
        title = new JLabel("<HTML><B><FONT COLOR=RED>Waxing For You!", JLabel.CENTER);
        add( title, BorderLayout.NORTH );
        setupButtons( );
        setupProductPanel( );
        setupAboutUsPanel( );
        mainPanel = new JPanel( new BorderLayout( ) );
        JLabel tmpMsg = new JLabel( "<HTML><CENTER>Welcome<BR><BR> to our<BR><BR>Home!",
                                                            JLabel.CENTER);
        tmpMsg.setFont( new Font( "Serif", Font.BOLD, 18 ) );
        mainPanel.add( tmpMsg, BorderLayout.CENTER );
        add( mainPanel, BorderLayout.CENTER );
    }
    public void setupAboutUsPanel( )
    {
        aboutUsPanel = new JPanel( new GridLayout( 2, 1 ) );
```

(continues)

Example 8-14 (continued)

```
        Image img = getImage( getCodeBase( ), "tuning.jpg" );
        ImageIcon icon = new ImageIcon( img );
        aboutUsPanel.add( new JLabel( icon ) );
        JLabel text = new JLabel( "<HTML><CENTER><B>About Us</B><BR><BR> We are a family-"
            + "run business <BR>that has been waxing since 1997. <BR> We take pride"
            + " in our work <BR>and guarantee that you will love our work!",
                JLabel.CENTER );
        aboutUsPanel.add( text );
    }
    public void setupProductPanel( )
    {
        productPanel = new JPanel( new BorderLayout( ) );
        JLabel prodinfo = new JLabel( "<HTML><CENTER><B>Product Info</B><BR> <BR>"
            + "We use only high-quality wax.<BR> We layer each wax over hours<BR>"
            + "to ensure that it soaks in and sticks.<BR>Guaranteed! ", JLabel.CENTER );
        productPanel.add( prodinfo, BorderLayout.CENTER );
    }
    public void setupButtons( )
    {
        productInfo = new JButton( "Info" );
        aboutUs = new JButton( "About Us" );
        productInfo.addActionListener( this );
        aboutUs.addActionListener( this );
        JPanel west = new JPanel( new GridLayout( 2, 1 ) );
        west.add( productInfo );
        west.add( aboutUs );
        add( west, BorderLayout.WEST );
    }
    public void actionPerformed( ActionEvent ae )
    {
        Object src = ae.getSource( );
        if ( src == productInfo )
        {
            mainPanel.removeAll( );
            mainPanel.add( productPanel, BorderLayout.CENTER );
        }
        else if ( src == aboutUs )
        {
            mainPanel.removeAll( );
            mainPanel.add( aboutUsPanel, BorderLayout.CENTER );
        }
        mainPanel.validate( );
        mainPanel.repaint( );
    }
}
```

Courtesy of Luke Scanlon, 5311 Studios.

case study

Now we can add events to our case study of the coffee club applet. Just as in our last example, we want to click one of the buttons and use the extra layer panel to remove all components in the center region so that we can add the new panel to be displayed. Example 8-15 has highlighted code to show the new code added to get events to work on our coffee club case study.

EXAMPLE 8-15

```java
import java.awt.*;
import javax.swing.*;
import java.awt.event.*;
public class CoffeeClubEvents extends JApplet implements ActionListener
{
    JButton home, join, faq, contact;
    Image img;
    JLabel title, logo, copyright, ntbkImg, ntbkDesc, infoSheets, welcomeMsg;
    JLabel basket;
    Color tanColor = new Color( 204, 153, 51 );
    Color darkColor = new Color( 51, 17, 0 );
    Color bkgrdColor = new Color ( 17, 8, 0 );
    JPanel leftside, top, center, welcome, separator, freeNotebook, faqPanel;
    public void init( )
    {
        setLayout( new BorderLayout( ) );
        doTitle( );
        doLeftSide( );
        doBottom( );
        doCenter( );
        setupFAQPanel( );
    }
    public void setupButton( JButton b )
    {
        b.setContentAreaFilled( false );
        b.setBorderPainted( false );
        b.setFocusable( false );
        b.setForeground( tanColor );
        b.addActionListener( this );
        leftside.add( b );
    }
    public void doTitle( )
    {
        img = getImage( getCodeBase( ), "coffeeLogoMetal.png" );
        logo = new JLabel( new ImageIcon( img ) );
        img = getImage( getCodeBase( ), "logoName.png" );
        title = new JLabel( new ImageIcon( img ) );
        top = new JPanel( new FlowLayout( ) );
        top.add( logo );
```

(continues)

case study, cont.

Example 8-15 (continued)

```
      top.add( title );
      top.setBackground ( tanColor );
      add( top, BorderLayout.NORTH );
   }
   public void doLeftSide( )
   {
      // left side menu
      leftside = new JPanel( new GridLayout( 5, 1 ) );
      leftside.setBackground ( darkColor );
      home = new JButton( "Home" );
      join = new JButton( "Join the Club" );
      faq = new JButton( "FAQ" );
      contact = new JButton( "Contact Us" );
      setupButton( home );
      setupButton( join );
      setupButton( faq );
      setupButton( contact );
      basket = new JLabel( new ImageIcon( getImage( getCodeBase( ),"basket.png" ) ) );
      leftside.add( basket );
      add( leftside, BorderLayout.WEST );
   }
   public void doBottom( )
   {
      // String can go across multiple lines: use + to append
      copyright = new JLabel( "<HTML>(c) 2008 by CoffeeClubOfTheWorld.com."
         + "  All Rights Reserved.", JLabel.CENTER );
      copyright.setForeground( tanColor );
      copyright.setOpaque( true );
      copyright.setBackground( darkColor );
      add( copyright, BorderLayout.SOUTH );
   }
   public void doCenter( )
   {
      center = new JPanel ( new BorderLayout( ) );
      center.setBackground( tanColor );
      // add dark separator as blank-colored panel in NORTH of center panel
      separator = new JPanel( );
      separator.setBackground ( darkColor );
      separator.setPreferredSize( new Dimension( 10, 20 ) );
      center.add( separator, BorderLayout.NORTH );

      welcome = new JPanel( new FlowLayout( ) );
      welcome.setOpaque( false );
      welcomeMsg = new JLabel( "<html><center>"
         + "<H2>Welcome to our Coffee of the Month Club! </h2>"
         + "<HR WIDTH=80%><I>Our coffee club is not just gourmet coffee —"
         + "<BR>it's an immersion of experience. <HR WIDTH=80%><BR>"
         + "We personally select gourmet coffees from around the world. <BR>"
```

```
      + "</CENTER>Each month a freshly roasted coffee is sent to your door"
      + "<BR>along with an info page about the coffee and other goodies."
      + "<BR><BR>Each month we send you:"
      + "<UL><LI>A 12-oz. bag of fresh coffee beans"
      + "<LI>Information sheets about the coffee and region"
      + "<LI> A regional gift each month (e.g., spices, nuts, chocolates, ...)"
      + "</UL><BR><B>FREE SHIPPING!</B><BR> <BR>");
   welcomeMsg.setForeground( darkColor );
   welcome.add( welcomeMsg );
   // create the bottom free notebook offer
   freeNotebook = new JPanel( new GridLayout( 1, 3 ) );
   freeNotebook.setOpaque( false );
   ntbkImg = new JLabel( new ImageIcon( getImage( getCodeBase( ), "ntbk.png" ) ) );
   ntbkDesc = new JLabel( "<HTML><CENTER>Buy NOW and receive<BR> a FREE"
      + "<BR>leather binder <BR>for collecting the fact sheets!" );
   infoSheets = new JLabel( new ImageIcon( getImage( getCodeBase( ),
                 "InfoSheets.png" ) ) );
   freeNotebook.add( ntbkImg );
   freeNotebook.add( ntbkDesc );
   freeNotebook.add( infoSheets );
   welcome.add( freeNotebook, BorderLayout.SOUTH );
   center.add( welcome, BorderLayout.CENTER );
   add( center, BorderLayout.CENTER );
}
public void setupFAQPanel( )
{
   /* put this into a method so that it is done only once, and then we
      need only one line inside the if statement of the actionPerformed method */
   JLabel faqText = new JLabel( "<HTML><H1>FAQ</H1>"
      + "<H2>Can I get decaffeinated coffee?</H2>"
      + "No. Our selections are all caffeinated."
      + "<H2>Can I get ground coffee instead of the beans?</H2>"
      + "No. Coffee will stay fresher as whole beans than if preground."
      + "<BR>This gives you the best flavors to experience."
      + "<H2>Can I choose which coffees I get?</H2>"
      + "No. Each month we send the same coffee package to all members."
      + "<H2>How do I store the coffee?</H2>"
      + "Coffee should be kept in a cool place in an airtight container."
      + "<BR>Do not freeze your coffee!" );
   faqPanel = new JPanel( new FlowLayout( ) );
   faqPanel.setOpaque( false );
   faqPanel.add( faqText );
}
public void actionPerformed( ActionEvent ae )
{
   Object src = ae.getSource( );
   center.removeAll( );
   // add dark separator as a blank-colored panel in NORTH of center panel
   separator = new JPanel( );
```

(continues)

case study, cont.

Example 8-15 (continued)

```
    separator.setBackground ( darkColor );
    separator.setPreferredSize( new Dimension( 10, 20 ) );
    center.add( separator, BorderLayout.NORTH );
    if ( src == home )
    {
      center.add( welcome, BorderLayout.CENTER );
    }
    else if ( src == faq )
    {
      center.add( faqPanel, BorderLayout.CENTER );
    }
    center.repaint( );
    validate( );
    repaint( );
  }
}
```

Now you can add your own code to extend this program. Implement the other two buttons.

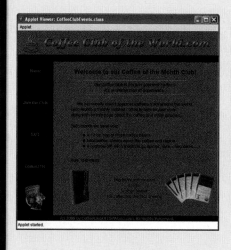
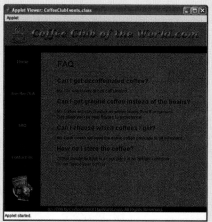

Troubleshooting

Common errors:

My code will not compile.	Java is case sensitive, so check each step for adding events to ensure that each item is spelled correctly.
	Once you specify that your class implements a particular listener, you are then required to write the methods required for that listener. Remember that you can create method stubs for the methods that you do not need to use.
	If you specify that you are listening for a particular event by adding that listener to one of your components, make sure that you also specified that you implemented that listener in your class header.
I have the methods implemented, but the actual event does not trigger to call any of those methods.	Make sure that you add the listener to the component. For example, if listening for button clicks, be sure to call on your button `.addActionListener( this )`.
I added the `ActionListener` on my checkbox/radiobutton, but it does not work.	`JCheckBox` and `JRadioButtons` use the `ItemListener`, not `ActionListener`.
I am listening for key presses on the applet, but it is not working.	Be sure to call `setFocusable( true )` on the applet itself or on the component to activate it listening for those events.

SUMMARY

- An event is when something triggers and we have the option of whether or not to handle it.
- Events require four steps to work: importing the `java.awt.event` package, specifying which listeners to implement in the class header, adding listeners to the applet or components, and writing the appropriate methods required of the implemented listener.
- Button clicks cause `ActionEvents` handled by the `ActionListener` and require the `actionPerformed` method to be written.
- `ItemEvents` are caused by selecting/deselecting a `JCheckBox`/`JComboBox`/ `JRadioButton` and require the `itemStateChanged` method.
- `ListSelectionEvents` are caused by selecting from a `JList`.
- `MouseEvents` are caused by the mouse entering/exiting the component or by the button being pressed/released/clicked.
- `MouseMotionEvents` are caused by the mouse being moved or dragged.
- `KeyEvents` occur when the user clicks on any key on the keyboard.
- `FocusEvents` occur when the user's focus either enters or leaves a component.

- For each event, a call to getSource( ) will return an Object reference to the object that caused the event.
- A *method stub* is a method with no body. Because many methods are required for implementing certain listeners, several methods may be listed in the code as a method stub.

EXERCISES

1. What are the four things that you need to handle events?
2. What two things must your program do to respond to a particular type of event?
3. True or false? Clicking a mouse button generates a KeyEvent.
4. Which listener is used to handle events when the user changes the option in a drop-down list?
5. What is the method to get the text from the selected item in a JTextField component?
6. What method sets the text in a JTextArea component?
7. What is the difference between MouseEvent and MouseMotionEvent?
8. How many methods do you need to code when implementing the MouseListener?
9. How do you implement two listeners, e.g., ActionListener and ItemListener?
10. What do you do with methods that you do not care about when implementing a listener? For example, if you implement the MouseMotionListener and want to do something only when the mouse is moved and not when the mouse is dragged, what do you do with the mouseDragged method?
11. Match the following events with the appropriate type of listener.

    a. ____ button clicks   1. ActionListener
    b. ____ mouse entered the component   2. ItemListener
    c. ____ user selects a new item from JComboBox   3. MouseListener
    d. ____ user drags the mouse   4. MouseMotionListener
    e. ____ user deselects a JCheckBox   5. KeyListener

12. Write a mini version of the MasterMind game. Use three JButtons or JCheckBoxes with images. Allow three image options: a red, green, and blue ball. As the user selects each ball, the color changes (display a different image on the button/checkbox) from red to green, green to blue, and blue back to red. Randomly select an answer for each of the buttons/

checkboxes. Once the user clicks on the "Try me!" button, check to see if the button colors match the answer.

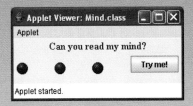 

13. Write a Tic-Tac-Toe game. Set up a GridLayout with JButtons. Use images for the X, O, and empty squares. Allow two users to play against each other. Notify the winner by setting text on a JLabel at the bottom of the applet.

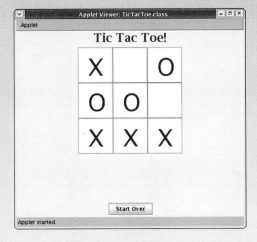

14. Modify the KeyEventAnimation class to display different images according to the direction that the figure is moving.

15. Create a "Where's Waldo" puzzle by dividing the screen into small images on buttons. Align the images so that it looks like a seamless picture to the user.

16. Create a board game by using a null layout manager. Move the pieces by calling setLocation on them.

17. Create a family tree as an image and use MouseClicked to display more information for each person.

Loops

Why did the programmer get stuck in the shower?
Because the shampoo bottle said, "Lather, Rinse, Repeat"

Repeating Statements

Loops allow us to execute a statement(s) multiple times. How many times the statements are executed depends on the boolean expression. The statements are executed over and over again while the boolean expression evaluates to `true`; once it evaluates to `false`, the program continues.

Java has three types of loops:

- `while` loop
- `for` loop
- `do . . . while` loop

Although we could probably get away with programming a loop with any of the loop types, there is a reason why there are three different types. As programmers, we should select the right kind of loop for the situation. Before we figure this out, let us first look at each one.

■ 9.1.1 `while` Loop

The `while` loop is as follows:

```
while( booleanExpression )
        oneStatement;
```

If we want multiple statements within the `while` loop, we add braces:

```
while( booleanExpression )
{
        statements;
        statements;
}
```

Before executing the statements inside the loop, the program evaluates the `booleanExpression`. If it evaluates to `false`, then the statements inside the loop are skipped. If, however, the boolean expression evaluates to `true`, then the statements are executed and the boolean expression is evaluated again. The following procedure is repeated until the boolean expression evaluates to `false`:

1. Evaluate the boolean expression.
2. If the boolean expression evaluates to `true`,
    a. Execute all the statements within the loop.
    b. Go to step 1.
3. If the boolean expression evaluates to `false`, skip the statements in the loop and continue with the program.

Example 9-1 paints rectangles inside rectangles by calculating where the next rectangle should be while inside a `while` loop.

EXAMPLE 9-1

```
import java.awt.*;
import javax.swing.*;

public class DrawRectsLoop extends JApplet
{
    int x = 0;
    int y = 0;
    int width = 300;
    int height = 200;
    int spacing = 20;

    public void paint ( Graphics g )
    {
        while( width > spacing && height > spacing )
        {
            g.drawRect( x, y, width, height );
            x = x + spacing;
            y = y + spacing;
            width = width - 2*spacing;
            height = height - 2*spacing;
        }
    }
}
```

Applet Viewer: DrawRectsLoop.class
Applet
Applet started.

What would happen if you change the boolean expression such that the width and height are both greater than or equal to zero instead of spacing?

9.1.2 for Loop

The for loop is as follows:

```
for( initialization; booleanExpression; incrementer )
        statement;
```

If we want multiple statements within the for loop, we add braces:

```
for( initialization; booleanExpression; incrementer )
{
        statement;
}
```

Here the initialization is usually setting a variable to an initial value, such as

```
int i = 0;
```

the booleanExpression is the same as the while loop, evaluating to either true or false; and the incrementer is used to either increment or decrement our initial value:

```
i = i+1;
```

Example 9-2 demonstrates the use of a for loop to populate a JComboBox with the numbers from 1 through 10.

EXAMPLE 9-2

```
import java.awt.*;
import javax.swing.*;
public class DropFor1to10 extends JApplet
{
   JComboBox list = new JComboBox( );
   public void init( )
   {
      setLayout( new FlowLayout( ) );
      setupList( );
   }
   public void setupList( )
   {
      for ( int i=1; i<=10; i++ )
      {
         list.addItem( String.valueOf( i ) );
      }
      add( list );
   }
}
```

Example: populate a JComboBox with numbers 1 through 10.

In Example 9-3 we use a for loop to fill the applet with alternating stripes. We need to make use of two methods on the applet to determine the size:

```
this.getWidth( ); // returns the width of the component or applet
this.getHeight( );// returns the height of the component or applet
```

EXAMPLE 9-3

```
import java.awt.*;
import javax.swing.*;
public class Stripes extends JApplet
{
   public void paint( Graphics g )
   {
      int stripes = 0;
      int width = 30;
```

```
        int height = this.getHeight( );
        int appletWidth = this.getWidth( );
        for (int x=0; x < appletWidth; x+=width)
        {
            if (stripes%2 == 0)
            {
                g.setColor(Color.RED);
            }
            else
            {
                g.setColor(Color.CYAN);
            }
            g.fillRect(x, 0, width, height);
            stripes = stripes + 1;
        }
    }
}
```

> this.getHeight( ) returns the height of the applet.

> Use modulus % operator to check if even (no remainder = 0) to alternate colors.

In Example 9-4, we make use of converting a String in a JTextField to a number, loop from 1 to that number, and convert each number in our loop to a String to display in the JTextArea.

EXAMPLE 9-4

```
import java.awt.*;
import javax.swing.*;
import java.awt.event.*;

public class Conversions extends JApplet implements ActionListener
{
    JTextArea textarea;
    JTextField enter;
    JLabel label;
    JButton go;
    JScrollPane spane;

    public void init( )
    {
        setLayout( new FlowLayout( ) );
        label = new JLabel( "Enter the number you want me to count to:" );
        enter = new JTextField( 5 );
        textarea = new JTextArea( 7, 6 );
        spane = new JScrollPane( textarea );
```

(continues)

Example 9-4 (continued)

```
        go = new JButton( "GO!" );
        go.addActionListener( this );
        add(label);    add(enter);    add(spane);    add( go );
    }

    public void actionPerformed( ActionEvent ae )
    {
        Object src = ae.getSource( );
        if ( src == go )
        {
            String text = enter.getText( );
            if ( text.length( ) > 0 )
            {
                int num = Integer.parseInt( text );
                textarea.setText( "" );
                for ( int i=1; i<=num; i++ )
                {
                    textarea.append( String.valueOf(i) );
                    textarea.append( "\n" );
                }
            }
            else
                textarea.setText( "Please enter something first!" );
        }
    }
}
```

Example 9-5 populates a JTextArea with items copied from a JList. This could also be implemented based on events, with buttons to add all items from the list into a grocery cart.

EXAMPLE 9-5

```
import java.awt.*;
import javax.swing.*;
public class List2TA extends JApplet
{
    JList list;
    DefaultListModel model;
    JTextArea textarea;
    public void init( )
```

```
    {
        setLayout( new FlowLayout( ) );
        setupList( );
        textarea = new JTextArea( 5, 10 );
        add( textarea );
        addListItemsToTextarea( );
    }
    public void setupList( )
    {
        model = new DefaultListModel( );
        list = new JList( model );
        model.addElement( "Milk" );
        model.addElement( "Cookies" );
        model.addElement( "Eggs" );
        add( list );
    }
    public void addListItemsToTextarea( )
    {
        // getSize returns the number of items in the list
        for( int i=0; i<model.getSize( ); i++ )
        {
                // grab the item at index i
            textarea.append( (String )model.get(i) );
            textarea.append( "\n" );
        }
    }
}
```

In Example 9-5 we were able to copy the values in the JList into the JTextArea. To get this example to work, we need to reexamine some of the components introduced earlier. When working with the JList, remember that we have to add the items in the list to a DefaultListModel object.

To find out how many items are in the JList, we call a method named getSize( ) on the DefaultListModel object.

To get each item out of the list, we call the method get(index) on the DefaultListModel, where the parameter specifies which one in the list (remember that Java starts counting at zero, so the first one in the list is at 0). Therefore, our loop starts at 0 and continues while the i variable counter is less than the number of elements in the list. When we call the get method, it is returned to us as an Object. Because we want it to be a String specifically, we need to *cast* it to a String, which is why the String in parentheses is there.

```
( String ) model.get( i )
```

◼ 9.1.3 do Loop

The do loop is as follows:

```
do
{
        statement(s);
} while( booleanExpression );
```

The do loop is similar to a while loop, except that it is guaranteed to execute the statements in the loop at least once. I will not cover the do loop in any more detail because we can program any loop into a for or while loop.

9.2 Which Loop to Use?

To determine which loop to use, the guideline is the following:

IF you know the number of times to go through the loop,
  USE the for loop
ELSE IF you need to execute the statements in the loop at least once,
  USE the do loop
ELSE
  USE the while loop

9.3 Animation

We can also create our own animation by using loops in the paint method. By using the method clearRect on the Graphics object, we can erase a section that has been painted and then repaint it at a different *x* and *y* location. Example 9-6 demonstrates animation using a while loop in the paint method.

EXAMPLE 9-6

```
/* Demonstrate loops with animation */
import java.awt.*;
import javax.swing.*;
public class Animate extends JApplet
{
    int x, y, size, move, speed, count;
    public void paint ( Graphics g )
```

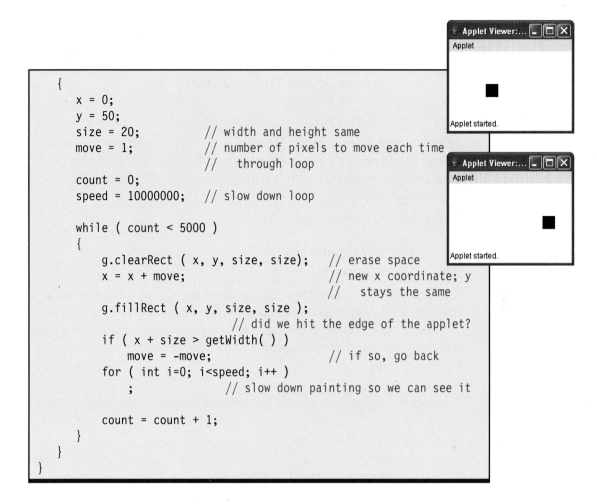

```
{
    x = 0;
    y = 50;
    size = 20;          // width and height same
    move = 1;           // number of pixels to move each time
                        //    through loop
    count = 0;
    speed = 10000000;   // slow down loop

    while ( count < 5000 )
    {
        g.clearRect ( x, y, size, size);   // erase space
        x = x + move;                      // new x coordinate; y
                                           //    stays the same
        g.fillRect ( x, y, size, size );
                            // did we hit the edge of the applet?
        if ( x + size > getWidth( ) )
            move = -move;                  // if so, go back
        for ( int i=0; i<speed; i++ )
            ;                   // slow down painting so we can see it

        count = count + 1;
    }
}
}
```

Although this example should make use of Threads and/or Timer to create the animation, this works for now even though the animation forces us to wait to do anything until it finishes. We could also draw an image instead of a square by using the drawImage method call from Chapter 2.

This looks really good with animated GIFs of a character walking. Just be sure to use different images for each direction that the character is walking so he is not walking backward. There are plenty of images available to use on the Internet.

 Careful

Some things to be careful with when working with loops:

- Off-by-one error:
  Example: want to add values 1 through 10 to the textarea.

  ```
  for( int i=1; i<10; i=i+1 )
          textarea.append( String.valueOf(i) );
  ```

- Braces for multiple statements:

```
int i=10;
while( i < 100 )
        textarea.append( String.valueOf(i) );
        textarea.append( "\n" );
        i = i + 10;
```

the `textarea.append( "\n" );` and `i = i + 10;` is not part of the `while` loop, even though the indentation makes it look like it is. Remember to use braces if you want multiple statements as part of the loop.

- Semicolon syntax:

```
for( int i=1; i<=10; i=i+1 );
{
        textarea.append( "Hello" );
}
```

You will not get an error message. However, because of the semicolon at the end of the `for` loop declaration, this designates that there is nothing inside the loop. It will go through the loop nine times doing nothing and then go down and do the append to the `textarea` once.

- Infinite Loops

Example 1: no braces, so only the one line under the `while` is part of the loop

```
int i=10;
while( i<100 )
        textarea.append( String.valueOf(i) );
        i=i+1;
```

Example 2: semicolon at the end of the `while` loop declaration

```
int i=10;
while( i<100 );
{
        textarea.append( String.valueOf(i) );
        i=i+1;
}
```

The semicolon should not be at the end of the `while` loop declaration; this designates that the loop is empty—do nothing inside the loop. This example then ends up in an infinite loop, because the boolean expression `i < 100` is always `true`.

Converting Binary to Decimal

Let us write a program named BinToDec that takes a binary number as a String variable consisting of 0s and 1s and converts it to a decimal value. First we need to learn how to convert a binary number to a decimal before we can attempt to program it in Java. Let us start by looking at decimal representation. Decimal uses base 10, so values are based on multiples of 10.

$$4096 = 4 \times 1000 + 0 \times 100 + 9 \times 10 + 6 \times 1$$

This could also be represented as

$$4096 = 4 \times 10^3 + 0 \times 10^2 + 9 \times 10^1 + 6 \times 10^0$$

In binary we use base 2. So a binary number can be represented as

$$
\begin{aligned}
1011 &= 1 \times 2^3 + 0 \times 2^2 + 1 \times 2^1 + 1 \times 2^0 \\
&= 1 \times 8 + 0 \times 4 + 1 \times 2 + 1 \times 1 \\
&= 8 + 0 + 2 + 1 \\
&= 11
\end{aligned}
$$

An algorithm for converting the number follows:

```
SET numBits to the number of bits in the binary number
    (HINT: how many characters in the string?)
SET power as the number of bits in the binary number minus one
SET sum to zero

LOOP for as many bits in the number
    SET bit to be the value at the next position (as an integer)
    SET term to be the value of the bit × 2^power
    ADD term to the sum
    SET power to power minus 1
END loop
RETURN decimal value of sum
```

An algorithm is a set of steps to solve a problem. The preceding algorithm is written in *pseudocode*, which is not quite proper English and not quite programming code. The words in uppercase are types of instructional statements. There are no steadfast rules on what these keywords should be, but we tend to use words that represent the process that should take place. The pseudocode could be useful for programming into any computer language—it is not specific to Java.

Advanced Concept, cont.

For our solution from the preceding algorithm, we end up with Example 9-7.

EXAMPLE 9-7

```java
import java.awt.*;
import javax.swing.*;
import java.awt.event.*;
public class BinToDec extends JApplet implements ActionListener
{
    JTextField binaryNum;
    JLabel label, dec;
    JButton go;
    public void init( )
    {
        setLayout( new FlowLayout( ) );
        label = new JLabel( "Enter a binary number" );
        binaryNum = new JTextField( 10 );
        dec = new JLabel( "" );
        go = new JButton( "convert" );
        go.addActionListener( this );
        add( label );      add( binaryNum );
        add( go );         add( dec );
    }
    public void actionPerformed( ActionEvent ae )
    {
        String bin = binaryNum.getText( );
        int numBits = bin.length( );
        int power = numBits - 1;
        int sum = 0;
        for( int i=0; i<numBits; i++ )
        {
                int bit = Integer.parseInt( bin.substring( i, i+1 ) );
                int term = ( int )( bit * Math.pow( 2, power ) );
                sum += term;
                power--;
        }
        dec.setText( String.valueOf( sum ) );
    }
}
```

Applet Viewer: BinToDec.class

Applet

Enter a binary number `101`   convert   5

Applet started.

Now it is your turn—write a program that converts binary back to decimal, or work with other bases such as octal or hexadecimal.

Troubleshooting

Common errors:

My code will not compile.	Any variable that you declare inside your loop (inside the braces or in the initializer section of the `for` loop) is a local variable to that loop and cannot be accessed after the loop finishes. If this is the case, you can declare the variable just before the loop instead of inside of it.
	When writing the condition in your loop, remember that the structure "0 < x < 10" does not work in Java: separate it properly as `0 < x && x < 10`.
I am stuck in an infinite loop.	Make sure that there is no semicolon at the end of the loop declaration. Only the `do . . . while` loop has a semicolon at the end of the `while`.
	If you intend to have more than one statement as part of your loop, make sure that you use braces to designate the group of statements that belong inside the loop.
	Try printing out the incrementer inside your loop to make sure that it is heading toward making the condition become `false`. You can do this by writing `System.our.println( incrementerVariable );`. The output shows up in the console window.
The condition always results in `true`/`false`.	If you have a boolean variable that you are checking to see if it is equal to either `true` or `false`, make sure that you use two equals signs on checking for equality: `variableName == true` or `variableName == false`. Using only one `=` assigns the variable to the value instead of checking for equality.
	Verify your use of relational and logical operators. `&&` for AND results in `true` only if both sides evaluate to `true`; `||` for OR results in `true` if either side is `true`.

SUMMARY

- Repetition statements (loops) allow us to repeat statements multiple times.
- There are three loops in Java: `while`, `for`, and `do . . . while`.
- We can use relational and conditional operators and complex expressions for our loops so long as the expression evaluates to a boolean value.
- Braces on `while` and `for` loops allow more than one statement to be executed in the body of the loop.
- The `for` loop is used when the number of iterations necessary is known or easily deciphered.
- The `do . . . while` loop is used when we want the body of the loop to execute at least once.
- The braces are required for a `do . . . while` loop.

- Semicolons should not be placed after the `while` and `for` loops (but are required at the end of a `do . . . while` loop).
- Once the condition evaluates to `false`, the body of a loop is skipped and control of the program continues to the point after the loop.
- An *infinite loop* is a loop whose condition never evaluates to `true`, and the program is stuck executing inside the loop forever.
- Loops can be nested inside other loops or inside `if-else/switch` structures.
- To determine which loop to use, the guideline is the following:

> IF you know the number of times to go through the loop,
>> USE the `for` loop
>
> ELSE IF you need to execute the statements in the loop at least once,
>> USE the `do` loop
>
> ELSE
>> USE the `while` loop

EXERCISES

1. True or false? Braces are required with loop structures.
2. Given the following code, answer the next two questions:

```
int val = 1;
for( int i=0;  i<4;  i++ )
        val += i;
```

   How many times does the initialization part of the `for` loop get run?

   What is the final value of the variable `val`?

3. What three types of loops does Java support?
4. True or false? A loop can be used to create animation.
5. True or false? Loops allow us to repeat statements until a condition evaluates to `true`.
6. List the values that are in the `JComboBox` from the following code segment:

```
JComboBox list = new JComboBox( );
for( int x=15; x<60; x = x+15 )
{
        list.addItem( String.valueOf( x ) );
}
```

7. How many times does the body of the following loop execute?

```
int count = 10;
while( count < 50 )
        count = count + 5;
```

8. True or false? You can you write a loop in the `paint` method but not the `init` method.

9. Write a code fragment that copies each element in a `JList` named `songs` to a `JTextArea` named `available`, with each song from the `JList` displayed on a separate line inside the `JTextArea`.

10. Write a code fragment that creates a histogram inside a `JTextArea` named `histogram` based on the values listed in a `JComboBox` named `grades`. For example, if the values in `grades` are: 8, 8, 5, 9, 7, display an asterisk (*) for each point.

```
8 : ********
8 : ********
5 : *****
9 : *********
7 : *******
```

11. What is wrong with the following code?

```
int x = 5;
while( x < 100 )
        textarea.append( String.valueOf(x) );
        x = x + 5;
```

12. What is wrong with the following code?

```
for( int x=1; x<=10; x=x+1 );
{
        textarea.append( "Hello" );
}
```

13. What does the following code fragment do?

```
int sum = 0;
for( int i=0; i < 100; i++ )
        sum += i;
```

14. What is the final value of the variable x when the loop finishes?

```
int  w = 4, x = 0, y = 3, z = 5;
for( int i=0; i<z; i++ )
    x = x + i;
```

15. What is the final value of the variable x when the loop finishes?

```
int  w = 4, x = 0, y = 3, z = 5;
for( int i=0; i&lt;z; i++ )
    x = x * i;
```

16. What is the final value of the variable z when the loop finishes?

```
int z = 1999;
do{
        z = z - 100;
} while( z > 0 );
```

17. Give an example of an off-by-one error when writing loops.

18. Which loop should you use in the following situations?
    a. Display odd numbers between 1 and 100
    b. Guessing game that prompts the user for a value and ends when the user guesses the randomly chosen value
    c. Display even numbers between 1 and 1000
    d. Printing the characters in a string backward (e.g., "Hello" prints as "olleH")

19. Write a code fragment that adds the numbers 1 through 10 to a JComboBox named `rating`.

20. Write a method named `power` that takes two integers, x and y, and returns the value x^y.

21. Write a method named `spacer` that takes a String as a parameter and returns a new String with a space between each character (e.g., `spacer( "Java ROCKS!" )` returns "J a v a   R O C K S !").

22. Write a method named `numReverse` that takes an integer as a parameter and returns the digits of the number in reverse (e.g., `numReverse( 1234 )` returns 4321). *Hint: make use of integer division and the remainder %
operator.*

23. Write a method named `palindrome` that takes a String as a parameter and returns the boolean value `true` if the String is a palindrome and `false` if not (e.g., `palindrome( "racecar" )` returns true). A palindrome is a string that is the same whether read forward or backward.

24. Write a method named `stripVowels` that takes a String as a parameter and returns the String without the vowels (e.g., `stripVowels( "Java is fun" )` returns "Jv s fn").

25. Write a method named `numVowels` that takes a String as a parameter and returns the number of vowels in the string (e.g., `numVowels( "Java" )` returns 2).

26. Modify the Weather program from Section 7.6 to use loops and have 100 snowflakes in winter and 100 raindrops in spring.

27. Create a program similar to the Weather program (Section 7.6) that draws a photo of your house and randomly chooses whether it is raining

or not. Be sure to make use of good methods to make it easier to program. Make the snowflakes randomly different sizes.

Classes

Got class?

10.1 Using Classes

Java is an object-oriented language, meaning that we organize our code into separate *classes* so that we can instantiate *objects*. So far we have used many classes that someone else wrote and put together into either the java.awt package or the javax.swing package. Examples of these classes are JButton, JLabel, Graphics, and Color. Now we can learn how to create our own classes.

Why create our own classes? Doing so allows us to greatly enhance our programs with customized classes that we define, as well as modularize a big program into smaller parts. We can create our own custom buttons or fancy labels, or we can create a class that we can use over and over again like the labels and text fields necessary for prompting users for their address (e.g., billing, school, home, shipping). We can also create classes that we use to store information instead of displaying it, such as an inventory of our music collection. We could set it up with a class for each album, listing the title, artist(s), year, and song tracks. By creating our own classes, we can expand our programs into anything that we can imagine.

To get started with creating our own classes, we will be working with two files—one for the applet and one for the new class that we are creating. Remember from when we started programming that each class needs to be in a file with the file name matching the name of the class and ending with the .java extension. So now we will create two classes in two separate files following this format. Then we will reference the new class inside the class that extends JApplet, just like how we reference Color and JLabel inside our applet classes that we have done so far. When we create our second class, however, we will not have it extend the JApplet. This means that we will not be able to put it directly into a web page and view it—instead, it will extend JPanel (or another component) and we will reference it in our class that does extend JApplet. Because of this, we usually call this second class a helper class.

When we create our own class, we often want it to be our own custom component. The easiest way to do this is to have our helper class extend the JPanel class. This approach enables our new class to have all the functionality of the JPanel class in addition to whatever customizations we add to it. Our new class inherits the drawing methods from Chapter 2; it also uses layout managers and adds components to the JPanel as we did in Chapter 5.

10.2 Extending JPanel

We have been using the JPanel class as a container to hold other components. But this class also allows us to create customized drawn components. We do so by writing a *separate class* that extends the JPanel class. Then we can create objects of this new class inside our applet program.

To set up this second class, create a new class that extends JPanel.

```
import java.awt.*;
import javax.swing.*;

public class Smiley extends JPanel
{

}
```

Inside this class, we can write a paintComponent method similar to the paint method from Chapter 2. One big difference is that inside this paintComponent method, we must first call our parent's (a JPanel) paintComponent method. We can do this with a call to super.paintComponent and send it the variable for the Graphics object:

```
import java.awt.*;
import javax.swing.*;

public class Smiley extends JPanel
{
     public void paintComponent ( Graphics gr )
     {
          super.paintComponent( gr );

     }
}
```

> Note: We must use the **paintComponent** method instead of the **paint** method when we create a class that extends a component such as **JPanel**.

Inside this paintComponent method, we can call methods on the Graphics object—just like we did in Chapter 2. We can also work with 2D graphics with Graphics2D.

```
Graphics2D  g2d = (Graphics2D )gr;
```

In Example 10-1 we draw a smiley face in a class that extends JPanel.

EXAMPLE 10-1

```
import java.awt.*;
import javax.swing.*;
public class Smiley extends JPanel
{
    public void paintComponent ( Graphics g )
    {
        super.paintComponent( g );
        g.setColor( Color.yellow );      // face
        g.fillOval( 10, 10, 200, 200 );

        g.setColor( Color.black );       // outline of face
        g.drawOval( 10, 10, 200, 200 );

        g.fillRect( 50, 75, 50, 5 );     // left eye
        g.setColor( Color.blue );        // right eye
        g.fillOval( 130, 50, 30, 50 );

        g.setColor( Color.red );         // mouth
        g.fillArc( 70, 100, 100, 70, 180, 180 );
    }
}
```

> We cannot run this class because it is not an applet—instead, create an instance of this in another class that does extend JApplet.

Now we can use the Smiley class in our applet class just like we use JLabels and JButtons. We do so by first creating a Smiley object:

```
Smiley smiles;
smiles = new Smiley( );
```

> When you see new Smiley( ) that means we are creating an *instance* of the Smiley class.

Then we need to call a method, setPreferredSize(new Dimension(width, height)), on our Smiley object. If we do not call this method, the default width and height is zero. So even if we add it to the applet, we would not be able to see it because the size would be zero.

```
smiles.setPreferredSize( new Dimension( 300, 300 ) );
```

Finally, we can add it to the applet.

```
add( smiles );
```

Example 10-2 shows the applet class with the Smiley object and other components as well.

EXAMPLE 10-2

```java
import java.awt.*;
import javax.swing.*;

public class SmileyApplet  extends JApplet
{
    Smiley smiles;
    JButton button;
    JTextField tf;
    public void init( )
    {
        smiles = new Smiley( ); // create a Smiley object
                // MUST set size or size will be zero!
        smiles.setPreferredSize( new Dimension( 300, 300 ) );
        button = new JButton( "go!" );   // create button and text
                                         // field
        tf = new JTextField( 10 );
        setLayout( new FlowLayout( ) ); // add to applet
        add( button );
        add( smiles );
        add( tf );
    }
}
```

JPanel is good for creating our own components, such as a thermometer, dial, fancy button, customized font, smiley face, or any other drawing that we want as a component among our other components on our applet. We can also create multiple Smiley objects by declaring multiple variables of type Smiley and instantiating each as a separate object.

```java
Smiley smiles1, smiles2, smiles3;
Smiles1 = new Smiley( );
smiles2 = new Smiley( );
smiles3 = new Smiley( );
smiles1.setPreferredSize( new Dimension( 300, 300 ) );
smiles2.setPreferredSize( new Dimension( 300, 300 ) );
smiles3.setPreferredSize( new Dimension( 300, 300 ) );
add( smiles1 );   add( smiles2 );  add( smiles3 );
```

When adding a JPanel object to our applet, we must call the setPreferredSize method on the JPanel object; otherwise, it will display with a width and height of zero.

We cannot run as an applet any class that extends `JPanel`—it is not an applet. We can only add it to a class that extends `JApplet`.

◼ 10.2.1 Customizing Our Class

Now that we can create multiple instances of our `Smiley` class and add them to our applet, it would be nice if we could customize each instance. For example, it would be nice if each instance could be a different size and if we could change the colors. Let us start with the task of customizing the color of the face.

If we look back at our code for the `Smiley` class, inside the `paintComponent` method we *hard-coded* the face color of our smiley face. *Hard-coded* means that we specified the actual values without making use of variables that are easily changed. We will start by changing this value into a variable. This leads us to our first question—do we want to declare the variable as a *local* or *instance* variable? (Refer to Chapter 3.) To answer this question, we need to decide what our solution will be. If we follow the conventions that we have seen before where we can change colors on components by calling a method called `setColor`, then we will need to create our own method called `setColor`. The purpose of this method should be to simply set the variable for the color to the new value. Because it does not need to return any information to the caller, we will specify a return type of `void`. Our method should look like the following:

```
public void setColor( Color newColor )
{
        faceColor = newColor;
}
```

Now we need to have the variable `faceColor` declared somewhere. Remember, if we declare it as a local variable then we can refer to it only in the same method where it was declared. Because we want to be able to set its value within the `setColor` method and reference it to set the color of the `Graphics` object in the `paintComponent` method, we will need to declare the variable as an instance variable. Our final version of the `Smiley` class with color customization is listed in Example 10-3.

EXAMPLE 10-3

```
import java.awt.*;
import javax.swing.*;
public class Smiley extends JPanel
{
    Color faceColor;   // declare variable as an instance variable
    public void paintComponent ( Graphics g )
```

```
    {
        super.paintComponent( g );
        g.setColor( faceColor );        // face
        g.fillOval( 10, 10, 200, 200 );
        g.setColor( Color.black );      // outline of face
        g.drawOval( 10, 10, 200, 200 );
        g.fillRect( 50, 75, 50, 5 );    // left eye
        g.setColor( Color.blue );       // right eye
        g.fillOval( 130, 50, 30, 50 );
        g.setColor( Color.red );        // mouth
        g.fillArc( 70, 100, 100, 70, 180, 180 );
    }
    public void setColor( Color newColor )
    {
        faceColor = newColor;
    }
}
```

In our applet class we can now customize each Smiley object by calling the setColor method:

```
Smiley smiles1, smiles2;
Smiles1 = new Smiley( );
smiles2 = new Smiley( );
smiles1.setPreferredSize( new Dimension( 300, 300 ) );
smiles2.setPreferredSize( new Dimension( 300, 300 ) );
smiles1.setColor( Color.ORANGE );
smiles2.setColor( Color.MAGENTA );
add( smiles1 );    add( smiles2 );
```

Now let us take a look at customizing the size. We could follow the same approach that we did for changing the color, but we could also use a different solution involving the *constructor* method. The constructor method is the method that automatically gets called when we create an instance, which is when the new operator is used (e.g., new Smiley ( )). We can customize our constructor to take two parameters—one for the width, and one for the height. If we store this information in instance variables similar to our faceColor variable, we can reference them in the paintComponent method as well. The constructor method follows—constructors do not specify a return type, and the name of the method must match the name of the class.

```
public Smiley( int w, int h )
{
        width = w;
        height = h;
}
```

We are not quite done yet. If we change the size of the smiley face, we also need to change the location of our eyes, nose, and mouth. So now we need to calculate, with respect to the width and height, where these features should be located and how big they should be. Example 10-4 creates instance variables for the width and height of our component and modifies all the code for drawing our smiley face to be relative to the width and height available.

EXAMPLE 10-4

```java
import java.awt.*;
import javax.swing.*;
public class Smiley extends JPanel
{
   Color faceColor;   // declare variable as an instance variable
   int  width, height;
   public Smiley( int w, int h )
   {
      width = w;
      height = h;
      setPreferredSize( new Dimension( width, height ) );
                            // change size here instead of applet
   }
   public void paintComponent ( Graphics g )
   {
      super.paintComponent( g );
      g.setColor( faceColor );                // face
      g.fillOval( 0, 0, width, height );

      g.setColor( Color.black );              // outline of face
      g.drawOval( 0, 0, width, height );

      g.fillRect( width/4, height/3, width/5, 6 ); // left eye
      g.setColor( Color.blue );                  // right eye
      g.fillOval( width-width/3, height/4, width/10, height/6 );

      g.setColor( Color.red );              // mouth
      g.fillArc( width/4, height/2, width/2, height/3, 180, 180 );
   }
public void setColor( Color newColor )
{
      faceColor = newColor;
   }
}
```

The applet class using Example 10-4 is listed in Example 10-5.

EXAMPLE 10-5

```
import java.awt.*;
import javax.swing.*;

public class SmileyApplet  extends JApplet
{
    Smiley smiles;
    JButton button;
    JTextField tf;
    public void init( )
    {
        smiles = new Smiley2( 200, 200 );      // create a Smiley object
        smiles.setColor( Color.MAGENTA );      // change the color
            // setPreferredSize is in Smiley class, so no need to do
            //   it here!
            // create button and text field
        button = new JButton( "go!" );
        tf = new JTextField( 10 );
            // add to applet
        setLayout( new FlowLayout( ) );
        add( button );
        add( smiles );
        add( tf );
    }
}
```

Advanced Concept

When creating methods, we can have more than one with the same name for even more flexibility in customization. This applies to our regular methods as well as constructors. This concept is called *overloading* methods. For example, we could define two constructors—one that takes two integer values for the size and another constructor with no parameters where we use default values for the size of the component. We have actually used this ability already in many calls to the add method to add our components to the applet. Sometimes we have set a JButton as a parameter, sometimes a JTextField—yet every time we called the same method: add. The following example is a modified snippet of the Smiley class with two constructors defined. If our applet program creates a Smiley object with two parameters, it will call the first constructor Smiley s = new Smiley (350, 350), and if we create a Smiley object with no parameters, it will call the second constructor defined: Smiley s = new Smiley ( );.

(continues)

Advanced Concept, cont.

```java
import java.awt.*;
import javax.swing.*;
public class Smiley extends JPanel
{
   Color faceColor;         // declare variable as an instance variable
   int  width, height;
   public Smiley( int w, int h )
   {
      width = w;
      height = h;
   }
   public Smiley(  )
   {
      width = 300;
      height = 300;
   }
   public void paintComponent ( Graphics g )
   {
       . . . .
   {
}
```

> Overloaded constructor—two constructors with a different number of parameters

Method overloading is when we write multiple methods in the same class with the same name. There are three rules that we need to follow to overload a method:

1. Different *number* of parameters
2. Different *data types* of parameters
3. Different *ordering of the data types* of the parameters

The following is an example:

```java
public class Overloading
{
   public int add( int a, int b )
   {
      return a + b;
   }
   public int add( int a, int b, int c )
   {
      return   a + add( b, c );
   }
   public int add( int a, int b, int c, int d )
   {
      return add( a, b ) + add( c, d );
   }
}
```

> Make use of methods that you have already written.

Advanced Concept, cont.

We can also overload constructors by following the same rules, as shown in Example 10-6.

EXAMPLE 10-6

```
public class Account
{
    String name;
    double balance;
    int ID;
    public Account( )
    {
        this( "unknown", -1, 0.0 );
    }
    public Account( String n, int id )
    {
        this( n, id, 0.0 );
    }
    public Account( String n, int id, double b )
    {
        name = n;
        ID = id;
        balance = b;
    }
}
```

> this( ) calls another constructor in this class that matches based on the parameters.

10.2.2 Font Tricks

Now that we can create our own little components by extending the JPanel class, we can revisit some of the drawing techniques that we learned in Chapter 2 and extend them. For example, we can learn how to create our own funky fonts by working with the drawString method. We will look at two font examples: a shadow font and an outline font.

Shadow Font   To create our own shadow font, we first need to create a separate class that extends the JPanel class:

```
public class FontShadow extends JPanel
{
    String txt;          // instance variable to hold the text to be
                         //   displayed
                         // constructor, text to display as a parameter
    public FontShadow( String val )
    {
        txt = val;
    }
```

```
    public void paintComponent ( Graphics g )
    {
        super.paintComponent( g );
                                // draw code here
    }
}
```

The name of our class is called FontShadow, and we will need to reference this in our applets whenever we want to create a shadow font text. The method FontShadow is called a *constructor* method, which gets called when our applet does the following:

```
FontShadow fs;
fs = new FontShadow( "text" );
```

To customize our component, we want to call the FontShadow with specific text to be displayed. We need to keep track of this information, so we store it in an *instance variable* named txt. Now we need to add some methods in our paint method to draw the shadow text. First change the font by calling the setFont method. Then change the color to the shadow color. Next draw the shadow by calling the drawString method twice (for extra shadow effect). Then change the color for the text color, and drawString again for the text. The final class is displayed in Example 10-7:

EXAMPLE 10-7

```
import java.awt.*;
import javax.swing.*;
public class FontShadow extends JPanel
{
    String txt;
    public FontShadow( String val )
    {               // change background color
        setBackground( Color.yellow );
        txt = val;
    }
    public void paintComponent( Graphics g )
    {
        super.paintComponent( g );
        g.setFont( new Font ( "SansSerif", Font.BOLD, 16 ) );
        g.setColor( Color.BLACK );     // can change shadow color
        g.drawString( txt, 4, 21 );
        g.drawString( txt, 5, 22 );
        g.setColor( Color.RED );       // can change text color
        g.drawString ( txt, 3, 20 );
    }
}
```

Note: we can change the color for the background, shadow, and text. A good exercise would be to make this class more customizable by allowing users to call methods to set the background color, text color, and shadow color.

Now we need our applet to use this class we created. We can do this in Example 10-8 by creating FontShadow components just like we create JButtons and JLabels.

EXAMPLE 10-8

```
import java.awt.*;
import javax.swing.*;
public class FontShadowEx extends JApplet
{
    FontShadow fshad;
    public void init( )
    {
        fshad = new FontShadow( "Elizabeth Sugar Boese" );
        fshad.setPreferredSize( new Dimension( 190, 30 ) );
                                    // must define its size

        setLayout( new FlowLayout( ) );
        add( fshad );
    }
}
```

Outline Font   Drawing an outline around the text is fairly similar to creating a shadow text, but this time we need to draw the text one pixel left and up, left and down, right and up, and right and down. Doing so gives the effect of an outline around the text, which is drawn last in a different color. This approach is implemented in Example 10-9.

EXAMPLE 10-9

Example 10-9 is based on the same code as Examples 10-7 and 10-8 but draws an outline.

```
import java.awt.*;
import javax.swing.*;
public class FontOutlineEx extends JApplet
{
    FontOutline fshad;
    public void init( )
    {
        fshad = new FontOutline( "Elizabeth Sugar Boese" );
        fshad.setPreferredSize( new Dimension( 190, 30 ) );
                                    // define size

        setLayout( new FlowLayout( ) );
        add( fshad );
    }
}
```

(continues)

Example 10-9 (continued)

```
import java.awt.*;
import javax.swing.*;
public class FontOutline extends JPanel
{
    String txt;
    public FontOutline( String val )
    {
        setBackground( Color.YELLOW );   // can change background color
        txt = val;
    }
    public void paintComponent( Graphics g )
    {
        super.paintComponent( g );
        g.setFont( new Font ( "SansSerif", Font.BOLD, 16 ) );
        g.setColor( Color.BLACK );      // can change shadow color
        g.drawString( txt, 3, 19 );
        g.drawString( txt, 3, 21 );
        g.drawString( txt, 5, 19 );
        g.drawString( txt, 5, 21 );
        g.setColor( Color.RED );        // can change text color
        g.drawString( txt, 4, 20 );
    }
}
```

How would you create a hollow font—just an outline of text?

10.2.3 Background Image

We can create a second class that extends JPanel and create a paintComponent method where we paint an image or draw shapes (e.g., Chapter 2) as a background for the panel. In this class we can draw an image as a backdrop in the paintComponent method by using the drawImage method. Then we can use this class in other classes, adding components to it like we do to any JPanel. In Example 10-10 and Example 10-11, it is written to center the image within the size of the panel. Note: You cannot make a call to getImage inside a class that does not extend JApplet. This method is accessible only by classes that extend JApplet (via inheritance).

EXAMPLE 10-10

```
import java.awt.*;
import javax.swing.*;
public class ImgBackground extends JApplet
{
    JLabel myplay, name;
    Image img;
    ImgPanel ipanel;
```

```
   public void init( )
   {
      myplay = new JLabel( "My Fun Playground" );
      name = new JLabel( "Java Rules" );
      myplay.setForeground( Color.YELLOW );
      name.setForeground( Color.RED );
      img = getImage( getCodeBase( ), "nepal.jpg" );
      ipanel = new ImgPanel( img );

      myplay.setFont( new Font( "Serif", Font.BOLD, 20 ) );
      ipanel.setLayout( new GridLayout( 2, 1 ) );
      ipanel.add( myplay );
      ipanel.add( name );
      add( ipanel );
   }
}
```

> ImgPanel is just like JPanel—setLayout and add components to it.

EXAMPLE 10-11

```
import java.awt.*;
import javax.swing.*;
public class ImgPanel extends JPanel
{
   Image img;
   public ImgPanel( Image ic )
   {
      img = ic;
   }
   public void paintComponent( Graphics g )
   {
      super.paintComponent( g );
      if ( img != null )                    // make sure that the image exists
      {
         int imgWidth = img.getWidth( this ); // find the width of the image
         int panelWidth = this.getWidth( );   // find the width of the panel
         int x = ( panelWidth - imgWidth ) / 2;  // calculate x to center the
                                                 //    image
         int imgHeight = img.getHeight( this );  // find the height of the
                                                 //    image
         int panelHeight = this.getHeight( );    // find the height of the
                                                 //    panel
         int y = ( panelHeight - imgHeight ) / 2; // calculate y to center the
                                                  //    image
                     // paint the image
         g.drawImage( img, x, y, img.getWidth( this ), img.getHeight( this ), this );
      }
   }
}
```

> Use this separate class—send the Image when you create an instance.

10.2.4 Customized Field Set

We can create a second class that extends JPanel and put a group of components inside it. Then we can reference this class whenever we want that group of components in our program. For example, a common set of fields is for a person's address. We could create a separate class that extends JPanel that handles creating all these fields for us. Then in our applet class, we could instantiate this new component twice—once for a person's mailing address and once for the billing address (or more times if the person has work/school/home addresses, etc.).

Example 10-12 shows the class that extends JPanel with all these components. We named it AddressFields.

EXAMPLE 10-12

```java
import java.awt.*;
import javax.swing.*;
public class AddressFields extends JPanel
{
    // instance variables
    JLabel name, street, city, state, zip;
    JTextField tf_name, tf_street, tf_city, tf_state, tf_zip;

    public AddressFields( )            // constructor
    {
        // initialize the instance variables
        name = new JLabel( "Name:", JLabel.RIGHT );
        street = new JLabel( "Street:", JLabel.RIGHT );
        city = new JLabel( "City:", JLabel.RIGHT );
        state = new JLabel( "State:", JLabel.RIGHT );
        zip = new JLabel( "ZIP:", JLabel.RIGHT );
        tf_name = new JTextField( 20 );
        tf_street = new JTextField( 20 );
        tf_city = new JTextField( 20 );
        tf_state = new JTextField( 20 );
        tf_zip = new JTextField( 20 );
    // add to the panel
        setLayout( new GridLayout( 5, 2 ) );
        add( name );      add( tf_name );
        add( street );    add( tf_street );
        add( city );      add( tf_city );
        add( state );     add( tf_state );
        add( zip );       add( tf_zip );
    }
}
```

Example 10-13 is the applet code that makes use of our newly created AddressFields component.

EXAMPLE 10-13

```
import java.awt.*;
import javax.swing.*;
public class AddressApplet extends JApplet
{
   JLabel homeAddress, billingAddress;
   AddressFields home, billing;
   public void init( )
   {
      homeAddress = new JLabel( "Home Address" );
      billingAddress = new JLabel( "Billing Address" );
      home = new AddressFields( );
      billing = new AddressFields( );
      setLayout( new BoxLayout( getContentPane( ), BoxLayout.Y_AXIS ) );
      add( homeAddress );
      add( home );
      add( billingAddress );
      add( billing );
   }
}
```

We have now gone through examples that extend the JPanel class and either draw like we did in Chapter 2 or use layout managers and components from Chapters 4 and 5. We can also create our own customized versions of components that already exist beyond using JPanel. For example, if we wanted to use a lot of JButtons with a particular image and remove the borders/content area/focusPainted/etc., we could create a helper class that extends JButton. Then in our applet class, instead of creating JButtons, we will create our fancy buttons that act just like regular JButtons but have the appearance that we desire. Examples 10-14 and 10-15 demonstrate this. Regular methods that we call on JButton such as setFocusPainted and setContentAreaFilled still work. Our class *inherits* all the methods from JButton.

EXAMPLE 10-14

```java
import java.awt.*;
import javax.swing.*;
public class FancyButton extends JButton
{
   public FancyButton( Image img, String text )
   {
      setIcon( new ImageIcon( img ) );
      setText( text );
      setHorizontalTextPosition( JButton.CENTER );
      setForeground( Color.white );
      setBorderPainted( false );
      setContentAreaFilled( false );
      setFocusPainted( false );
   }
}
```

EXAMPLE 10-15

```java
import java.awt.*;
import javax.swing.*;
public class FancyButtonApplet extends JApplet
{
   Image img;
   FancyButton home, portfolio, contact;
   public void init( )
   {
      setLayout( new FlowLayout( ) );
      img = getImage( getCodeBase( ), "buttonGreen.png" );
      home = new FancyButton( img, "Home" );
      portfolio = new FancyButton( img, "Portfolio" );
      contact = new FancyButton( img, "About Us" );
      add( home );  add( portfolio );   add( contact );
   }
}
```

Advanced Concept

Writing classes is the heart of object-oriented programming. Classes help us manage our programs into small modules. Each class maintains data specific for the class and contains the methods that affect those data variables. Methods that return the value of a data variable are called *getter* or *accessor* methods. Methods that set or change the value of one of the data variables are called *setter* or *mutator* methods. *Constructor* methods are called when we create an instance of the class via the new operator. Other methods in a class are called *helper* methods.

To properly set up a class, we should usually declare our instance variables private. Doing so prevents other classes from having direct access to change their values; instead, these classes would have to go through one of the methods that we define in our class to be able to change the data variable. This is a good practice because we could add error checking within the method, which we could not do if the variable had public access.

The following is the basic structure of a *helper* class:

```
public class <classname>    // class header
{
    // instance variables
    // constructors
    // getter methods
    // setter methods
    // helper methods
}
```

> *Helper* classes do not extend JApplet; therefore they cannot be run. They can extend JPanel, JComponent, etc., or nothing at all.

A more fleshed out class structure follows:

```
public class <classname>    // class header
{
    // instance variables
    private <type>  <instanceVariable1>;
    private <type>  <instanceVariable2>;
        ...
    // constructors
    public  <classname> ( <parameterList> )
    {
    }
    // getter methods
    public <returnType> get<instanceVariableName>( )
    {
        return <instanceVariableName>;
    }
}
```

> Instance variables should be private to adhere to encapsulation.

> Constructors have no return type.

> *Getter* method return types must match the data type of the variable being returned.

(continues)

```
        // setter methods
        public void set<instanceVariableName>( <type>
                                               <parameterName> )
        {
            <instanceVariableName> = <parameterName>;
        }
    }
```

Let us build an example class. We want to develop a program that keeps track of the courses that we are taking this semester. We need a class to keep track of each course that we are taking. To keep it simple, we are going to record just the title of the course and the number of credits. In our Course class, we need *getter* and *setter* methods for our instance variables, because our instance variables should be declared private. A listing of our Course class is shown in Example 10-16 and the applet class is shown in Example 10-17.

EXAMPLE 10-16

Constructor method name matches the name of the class and has no return type.

title is a String data type, so its getter method's return type is String.

```
public class Course
{
    private int numCredits;                     // instance variable
    private String title;                       // instance variable
    public Course( String name, int nCredits )  // constructor
    {
        title = name;
        numCredits = nCredits;
    }
    public String getTitle( )                   // getter method
    {
        return title;
    }
    public int getNumCredits( )                 // getter method
    {
        return numCredits;
    }
    public void setTitle( String t )            // setter method
    {
        title = t;
    }
    public void setNumCredits( int nc )         // setter method
    {
        numCredits = nc;
    }
```

Advanced Concept, cont.

```java
public String toString( )          // returnStr is a local variable
{
    String returnStr = title;
    returnStr += " ( " + numCredits + " ) ";
    return returnStr;
}
}
```

> We do not print things by using System.out.println inside the toString method.

EXAMPLE 10-17

```java
import java.awt.*;
import javax.swing.*;
public class CourseApplet extends JApplet
{
    Course math, history, cs;
    JList list;
    DefaultListModel model = new DefaultListModel( );
    public void init( )
    {
        math = new Course( "Calculus", 4 );  // call constructor method in
                                             //   Course
        history = new Course( "History", 3 );
        cs = new Course( "Java", 4 );
        list = new JList( model );
        model.addElement( math.toString( ) );
        model.addElement( history.toString( ) );
        model.addElement( cs.toString( ) );
        setLayout( new FlowLayout( ) );
        add( list );
    }
}
```

Applet ...
Applet
Calculus (4)
History (3)
Java (4)
Applet started.

Troubleshooting

Common errors:

My code will not compile.	Remember that you can run only the class that extends JApplet. The class that extends JPanel or another component (or nothing) is not an applet and cannot execute.
	Make sure that the constructor in the helper class is the same name as the class name, which also matches the name of the file. Also, there is no return type on the constructor methods.
	Making calls to getImage and getCodeBase for images is available only via the JApplet class. Load your images inside your class that extends JApplet and send these images to your helper class as parameters to methods (see ImgBackground Examples 10-10 and 10-11). If you want to load images inside a separate class that does not extend JApplet, you need to pass as a parameter a reference to the JApplet class from the class that does extend JApplet and make calls to getImage and getCodeBase via this variable (e.g., app.getImage( )). See Example 13-3.
	When using the drawing methods from Chapter 2, put it inside a paintComponent method (not paint, as we did in Chapter 2). Also, the first line in the method must be super.paintComponent(g);, where g is your Graphics variable name.
My helper class is not displaying.	Make sure that you instantiate it inside your applet class and then add it to the applet or a JPanel that is added to your applet. Try changing the background color of your JPanels and/or your helper class to see if you can see where it is going or supposed to go.
	Helper classes usually default to a width and height of zero. Make sure that you call setPreferredSize or setBounds on your helper class variable after you instantiate it inside your helper class.
Nothing is displayed, but my applet class properly instantiates and adds the helper class to the applet.	Ensure either that the paintComponent method is listed exactly as specified in the text (Java is case sensitive) and has the first line in the method calling the super.paintComponent, or if you are using components inside an init method, make sure that your applet class calls the init method directly: helperClassVariable.init( );.

SUMMARY

- We can create our own classes as helper classes to our programs. These helper classes do not extend JApplet but may extend JPanel, another component, or nothing at all.
- Each class that we create can maintain its own list of instance variables and methods.
- When extending the JPanel, we can customize the background of the panel by using the Graphics methods inside a paintComponent method.
- Calling the new operator on a class will call the constructor method in the class.

- The constructor method header differs from other method headers. There is no return data type defined, and the name of the method must match the name of the class.
- We can create several constructors depending on our needs. Therefore, we could have one constructor that takes no parameters and another constructor that takes an ImageIcon as a parameter. This is called *overloading* the method. The program can figure out which method to call based on the parameters sent to the method.
- When extending a component such as the JPanel, we need to set the preferred size of the component—otherwise, it will default to a size of zero. We can set the preferred size either in the applet on our component variable or inside the constructor of our custom component.
- We can extend almost any component, but the most common ones are JPanel and JComponent.

EXERCISES

1. True or false? The JPanel component is useful for creating your own components, because you can use the paintComponent method to draw it any way you like.

2. When you create a separate class by using the JPanel, how does this class specify that it inherits from the JPanel class?

3. What happens to your program if you create a JPanel object (or use an extension such as the Smiley class) and you do *not* call the setPreferredSize method?

4. What other stylized fonts can you create by extending the JPanel class?

5. When we use the new operator to create an object, what is the method that gets called?

6. When you call the method setPreferredSize, what parameters do you need to send to it?

7. Take your drawings from Chapter 2 and put them into a separate class that extends the JPanel class, and then add them to your applet with other buttons and labels, etc.

8. Create an applet that instantiates three FontOutline objects and add them to the applet.

9. Modify the ImgPanel class to stretch the image to fit the size of the JPanel instead of centering it.

10. Write a class that extends the JComponent class that keeps track of information for a movie. Maintain instance variables for the title, director, year released, and an image. Write your own paintComponent method in this class that draws the image and then displays the title, director, and release

year. In your applet class, instantiate several Movie objects for different movies and add each to your applet.

11. Create a Logo class that displays your name with some shapes as your own personal logo. Add it to the bottom of all your applets.

12. Create an applet with nine Smiley objects, each with different colors for face, eyes, and mouth. Use GridLayout to display in a 3 × 3 grid. Use a method for creating each Smiley that takes the various colors as parameters.

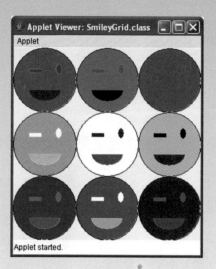

Swing Components II

 **Overview**

This chapter explores a variety of extra components and enhanced options we can add to our applets. We begin with JTabbedPane which makes it easy to include a tabbed interface to our applets. Next we discuss how to add tooltips to our components. Then we explore various border options we can apply to our JPanels and other containers. We then explain how to add audio files, which can either play when the applet starts or when a user clicks a button or other event. Next we discuss pop-up windows with JFrame and pre-set dialog boxes. Last, we cover how to use MediaTracker to ensure our applets load all images before running.

 JTabbedPane

JTabbedPane allows us to have tabs for the user to click to view different components. The tabs can be placed on any side—top, left, bottom, or right—by specifying the location when we create the JTabbedPane. We can create a JTabbedPane in two ways:

```
JTabbedPane tabpane;                        // declare the JTabbedPane

tabpane = new JTabbedPane( );               // tabs on top
tabpane = new JTabbedPane( tabLocation );   // tabs where specified
```

The first instantiation defaults the tabs on the top, as shown in **FIGURE 11-1**. The second one allows us to choose the location of the tabs, which can be one of the following:

- JTabbedPane.LEFT
- JTabbedPane.RIGHT
- JTabbedPane.TOP
- JTabbedPane.BOTTOM

FIGURE 11-1   JTabbedPage with tabs on the top.

When adding components to each tab, we call the method addTab. There are several formats for calling addTab:

```
JTabbedPane tabpane;
tabpane = new JTabbedPane( );

tabpane.addTab( tabText, component );
tabpane.addTab( tabText, ImageIcon, component );
tabpane.addTab( tabText, ImageIcon, component, toolTipText );
```

The tabText is the text that is displayed on the actual tab. If an ImageIcon is specified, it will be displayed with the text on the tab. The component will be added to the pane for when the tab is selected—**only one component can be added to each of these tab panes**. This component is added to the pane in BorderLayout. CENTER (therefore, the component will be stretched both horizontally and vertically). Example 11-1 shows an example of a JTabbedPane with three tabs. The third tab has both an image on the tab and a tooltip. Notice how the button on the first pane is proportionally sized to the image, whereas the button shown on the second pane is stretched in both directions. This first tab placed the button into a JPanel by using FlowLayout and added the panel to the pane instead of adding the button directly to the pane, which automatically stretches via BorderLayout.CENTER.

> We can add only one component to each pane in JTabbedPane. Consider putting multiple components inside a JPanel and add that to the JTabbedPane.

> Components added to a pane of JTabbedPane are added as BorderLayout.CENTER. To control the look of the pane, add the component to a JPanel and add that to the JTabbedPane.

EXAMPLE 11-1

```
import java.awt.*;
import javax.swing.*;
public class JTabEx extends JApplet
{
    JButton b_China, b_Germany;
    JLabel flowers;
    JPanel panel;
    JTabbedPane tabpane;
    Image img1, img2, img3;
```

(continues)

Example 11-1 (continued)

```
ImageIcon iconWindow, iconStatue, iconFlowers;
public void init( )
{
    tabpane = new JTabbedPane( );
    img1 = getImage(getCodeBase( ), "Window.jpg" );
    img2 = getImage(getCodeBase( ), "Statue.jpg" );
    img3 = getImage(getCodeBase( ), "Flowers.jpg" );
    iconWindow = new ImageIcon( img1 );
    iconStatue = new ImageIcon( img2 );
    iconFlowers = new ImageIcon( img3 );
    b_China = new JButton( "", iconWindow );
    b_Germany = new JButton( "What an idea!",
                                        iconStatue );
    flowers = new JLabel( iconFlowers );
    panel = new JPanel( );
    panel.add( b_China );


      // add tabs
    tabpane.addTab( "China", panel );
    tabpane.addTab( "Germany", b_Germany );
    tabpane.addTab( "Slovakia", iconFlowers,
                                flowers, "Slovakia" );


    add( tabpane, BorderLayout.CENTER );   // add tabbed pane
                                           //  to applet
  }
}
```

We can also have the tabs on the left, as shown in **FIGURE 11-2**, by specifying the location when we create the JTabbedPane.

```
JTabbedPane tabpane;
tabpane = new JTabbedPane( JTabbedPane.LEFT );
```

FIGURE 11-2 JTabbedPane with tabs on the left.

Switching between tabs can be done several ways. The easiest is by the user simply clicking on the arrow keys. This approach works automatically without our programming anything, as long as the JTabbedPane currently has the focus either by the user's clicking on the JTabbedPane or by calling the method .requestFocus( ) on your JTabbedPane variable. We can also add key mnemonics by calling the method .setMnemonicAt(paneNum, keyCode). Remember that pane numbers start counting at 0, and the keyCode is the same as the ones explained in Chapter 8 on events. Example 11-2 demonstrates another option of using buttons inside each pane to switch to either the next tab or the previous tab.

EXAMPLE 11-2

```
import java.awt.*;
import javax.swing.*;
import java.awt.event.*;
public class JTabbedSwitch extends JApplet implements ActionListener
{
    JTabbedPane pane = new JTabbedPane( );
    JButton prev2 = new JButton( "Back" ), prev3 = new JButton( "Back" );
    JButton next1 = new JButton( "Next" ),  next2 = new JButton( "Next" );
    public void init( )
    { // add listeners
        prev2.addActionListener( this );
        prev3.addActionListener( this );
        next1.addActionListener( this );
        next2.addActionListener( this );
        // first pane: no previous tab, has next tab
        JPanel panel1 = new JPanel( new FlowLayout( ) );
        JLabel label1 = new JLabel( "Here is some fine text " );
        panel1.add( label1 );
        panel1.add( next1 );
        pane.add( "one", panel1 );
        // second pane: has previous and next buttons
        JPanel panel2 = new JPanel( new FlowLayout( ) );
        JLabel label2 = new JLabel( "Whhoooooeeeee!" );
        panel2.add( prev2 );
        panel2.add( label2 );
        panel2.add( next2 );
        pane.add( "two", panel2 );
        // third pane: has previous button only
        JPanel panel3 = new JPanel( new FlowLayout( ) );
        JLabel label3 = new JLabel( "yeaoswers!" );
        panel3.add( prev3 );
        panel3.add( label3 );
        pane.add( "three", panel3 );
        add( pane );            // add to applet
    }
```

(continues)

Example 11-2 (continued)

```
public void actionPerformed( ActionEvent ae )    // handle button events
{
    Object obj = ae.getSource( );                    // get the object that
                                                     //   caused the event
    int tabindex = pane.getSelectedIndex( );  // determine which tab index
                                                     //   is currently selected
    if ( obj == prev2 || obj == prev3 )        // check which object caused
                                                     //   the event
        pane.setSelectedIndex( tabindex-1 );   // go back one tab
    else if ( obj == next1 || obj == next2 )  // check if event was caused
                                                     //   by next button
        pane.setSelectedIndex( tabindex+1 );   // go forward one tab
}
}
```

We can also modify the colors of the tabs on our JTabbedPane. We can specify the color of the currently selected tab with a call to the user interface's put method.

> Change the color to any color (see Chapter 2).

```
UIManager.put( "TabbedPane.selected",
               new javax.swing.plaf.ColorUIResource( Color.BLUE ) );
```

To change the background color of each tab, we call the method .setBackgroundAt and specify the index of the tab that we want to change and the color we want to make the background.

```
// set the color for each tab
tabpane.setBackgroundAt( 0, Color.RED );
tabpane.setBackgroundAt( 1, Color.YELLOW );
tabpane.setBackgroundAt( 2, Color.GREEN );
```

> The first tab is identified at index 0.

If we want to change the background color to be the same for all the tabs, we can set up a for loop.

```
for ( int i=0; i<numTabs; i++ )
        tabpane.setBackgroundAt( i, Color.RED );
```

To change the color of the text, we could either use HTML code when specifying the text on the tab or call the method .setForegroundAt in a similar way as changing the background color.

```
// set font color for each tab
tabpane.setForegroundAt( 0, Color.MAGENTA );
```

11.3 ToolTips

Tooltips are mini-popups that display some information when the user's cursor hovers for a moment over a particular component (**FIGURE 11-3**). All we need to do to

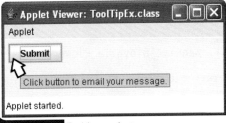

FIGURE 11-3 Tooltip on a button.

set the tooltip information for a component is to call the method .setToolTipText(toolTipTextString) on the component.

```
component.setToolTipText( String )
```

Examples:

```
JButton submit;
submit = new JButton( "Submit" );
submit.setToolTipText( "Click button to email your message." );

Image img;
ImageIcon ic;
JLabel label;
img = getImage( getCodeBase( ), "me.gif" );
ic = new ImageIcon( img );
label = new JLabel( ic );
label.setToolTipText( "Image of me and friend" );
```

Change the background color of the tooltip box by specifying the color of your choice in the following code:

```
UIManager.put( "ToolTip.background", Color.GREEN );
```

For JTabbedPane, we can specify the tooltip text when we add each tab with the addTab method.

```
tabpane.addTab( tabText, ImageIcon, Component, toolTip );
```

The partial code that follows demonstrates how to add a tooltip for a tab in JTabbed-Pane as shown in **FIGURE 11-4**.

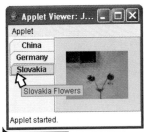

FIGURE 11-4 JTabbedPane with a tooltip on the tab.

```
JTabbedPane tabs;
tabs = new JTabbedPane( );
...
    tabs.addTab( "Slovakia", null, panel, "Slovakia Flowers" );
```

Note: More code is necessary to get Figure 11-4.

null specifies no image on the tab.

where we specify `null` to designate no image on the tab and `panel` is the JPanel with the stuff that goes into the tab pane.

11.4 Borders

We can add borders to any JComponent that we create, including a JPanel. Borders add no functionality; they merely add decor to our applets. There are a few steps that we need to do to get borders to appear, some dependent on the type of border that we want. For all borders, we have to import the `javax.swing.border` package:

```
import javax.swing.border.*;
```

Now we need to decide what type of border we want. We will need to call a method on the BorderFactory class to create the actual Border object (these are explained in more detail later). There are many types of borders:

- line (in any color)
- etched (raised or lowered)
- bevel (raised or lowered)
- title (line, etched: raised or lowered; bevel: raised or lowered)
- matte (uses an image)

Once we create the border, we can add it to a component by calling the `setBorder` method:

```
JPanel pane;
pane = new JPanel( );
pane.setBorder( Border );
```

Example 11-3 shows a basic line border.

EXAMPLE 11-3

```
import java.awt.*;
import javax.swing.*;
import javax.swing.border.*;
public class BorderEx extends JApplet
{
    JPanel panel;
    JLabel text, textImg;
    Image img;
```

```
    public void init( )
    {
        setLayout( new FlowLayout( ) );
        panel = new JPanel( );
        text = new JLabel( "<HTML>Multiple<BR>lines<BR>require<BR>HTML" );
        img = getImage( getCodeBase( ), "Bike.jpg" );
        textImg = new JLabel( "Bikes!", new ImageIcon( img ), JLabel.LEFT );
        panel.add( text );
        panel.add( textImg );
        Border lineborder = BorderFactory.createLineBorder( Color.RED );
        panel.setBorder( lineborder );
    }
}
```

11.4.1 Line Border

Create a line border in color (Example 11-3):

```
Border lineborder = BorderFactory.createLineBorder( Color.RED );
panel.setBorder( lineborder );
```

11.4.2 Etched Border

Create an etched border, raised (**FIGURE 11-5**):

```
Border etchedBorder = BorderFactory.createEtchedBorder(
                                        EtchedBorder.RAISED );
panel.setBorder( etchedBorder );
```

Create an etched border, lowered (**FIGURE 11-6**):

```
Border etchedBorder = BorderFactory.createEtchedBorder(
                                        EtchedBorder.LOWERED );
panel.setBorder( etchedBorder );
```

FIGURE 11-5 Raised etched border.

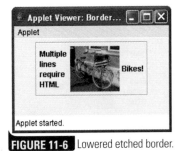

FIGURE 11-6 Lowered etched border.

11.4.3 Bevel Border

Create a bevel border, raised (**FIGURE 11-7**):

```
Border bevelBorder = BorderFactory.createRaisedBevelBorder( );
panel.setBorder( bevelBorder );
```

Create a bevel border, lowered (**FIGURE 11-8**):

```
Border bevelBorder = BorderFactory.createLoweredBevelBorder( );
panel.setBorder( bevelBorder );
```

11.4.4 Titled Border

Create a title border (**FIGURE 11-9**):

```
TitledBorder title = BorderFactory.createTitleBorder(
                                        "Favorite Things" );
panel.setBorder( title );
```

11.4.5 Matte Border

Matte borders allow us to specify an image to go around the component. Images can be any size, but some look better than others. A good idea for a matte image is a pattern to create a type of frame.

Create a matte border (**FIGURE 11-10**):

```
Image borderimg = getImage( getCodeBase( ), "ViewSm.png" );
ImageIcon bordericon = new ImageIcon( borderimg );
Border matteBorder = BorderFactory.createMatteBorder( -1,-1,-1,-1,
                                        bordericon );
panel.setBorder( matteBorder );
```

> The -1 values represent a proportional size for the image. We can specify a specific size for the top, left, bottom, and right side of the matte in that order.

FIGURE 11-7 Raised bevel border.

FIGURE 11-8 Lowered bevel border.

FIGURE 11-9 Tilted border.

FIGURE 11-10 Matte border.

11.5 Audio

Java supports five different types of sound files:

- AIFF
- AU
- WAV
- MIDI
- RMF

> *Note: Java does not naturally support mp3 files, but you can download and install third-party software that does. Doing so, however, takes some work and is not covered in this book.*

To play sounds, we can simply get the sound file with the getAudioClip method and then play it by calling the play method.

```
AudioClip  clip;
clip = getAudioClip( getCodeBase( ), audioFilename );
clip.play( );
```

Example 11-4 loads an audio file and plays it once through.

EXAMPLE 11-4

```
import java.awt.*;
import javax.swing.*;
import java.applet.*;
public class AudioPlay extends JApplet
{
    String audioFilename = "mySounds.mid";
    AudioClip ac;
    public void init( )
    {
        ac = getAudioClip( getCodeBase( ), audioFilename );
        ac.play( );
    }
}
```

AudioClip is in the java.applet package.

getCodeBase determines the file path location.

There are three methods we can call on our AudioClip:

- play   play the sound file once through
- loop   play the sound file continually
- stop   stop playing the file

We can have our audio file loop so that it continually plays over and over again instead of playing through once and stopping. To continually loop, we call the loop method on our AudioClip object.

Example:

From the preceding code, replace

```
ac.play( );
```

with

```
ac.loop( );
```

Whether playing a long audio file or looping an audio file, we should be sure that we stop playing when the user leaves our applet page. To do this, we need to code a method named stop in our applet, which is automatically called when the user leaves our web page with our applet. In this method, we need to reference the AudioClip object. First we need to verify that it has been created by checking to see that it is not equal to null, and if it is not, then we should call the stop method on our AudioClip variable. Example 11-5 demonstrates a looping audio and use of the stop method. Example 11-6 is an example of a guitar tuner where a specific audio file is played based on which button is clicked.

EXAMPLE 11-5

```
import java.awt.*;
import javax.swing.*;
import java.applet.*;
import java.awt.event.*;
public class LoopAudio extends JApplet
{
    String audioFilename = "happyDaze.wav";
    AudioClip ac;
                                    Note: This code will work only if
                                    you declare your AudioClip object
                                    at the top of your program.
    public void init( )
    {
        ac = getAudioClip( getCodeBase( ), audioFilename );
        ac.loop( );              // loop instead of play
    }
    public void stop( )
    {
        if( ac != null )         // cannot stop it if it is not running
            ac.stop( );
    }
}
```

We need to write a `stop( )` method if we are looping our audio—otherwise, the audio will continue playing even after the user has left your applet website.

EXAMPLE 11-6

```java
import java.awt.*;
import javax.swing.*;
import java.applet.*;
import java.awt.event.*;
public class GuitarTune extends JApplet implements ActionListener
{
    AudioClip  s1, s2, s3, s4, s5, s6;
    JButton E1, A, D, G, B, E2;
    public void init(  )
    {
        setLayout( new FlowLayout( ) );
        setupSounds( );
        E1 = new JButton( "E" );
        A = new JButton( "A" );
        D = new JButton( "D" );
        G = new JButton( "G" );
        B = new JButton( "B" );
        E2 = new JButton( "E" );
        setupButton( E1 );
        setupButton( A );
        setupButton( D );
        setupButton( G );
        setupButton( B );
        setupButton( E2 );
    }

    public void setupSounds( )
    {
        s1 = getAudioClip( getCodeBase( ), "snd6.au" );
        s2 = getAudioClip( getCodeBase( ), "snd5.au" );
        s3 = getAudioClip( getCodeBase( ), "snd4.au" );
        s4 = getAudioClip( getCodeBase( ), "snd3.au" );
        s5 = getAudioClip( getCodeBase( ), "snd2.au" );
        s6 = getAudioClip( getCodeBase( ), "snd1.au" );
    }
```

(continues)

Example 11-6 (continued)

```
public void setupButton( JButton btn )
{
   btn.addActionListener( this );
   add( btn );
}
public void actionPerformed( ActionEvent ae )
{
   Object src = ae.getSource( );
   if ( src == E1 )
       s1.play( );
   else if ( src == A )
       s2.play( );
   else if ( src == D )
       s3.play( );
   else if ( src == G )
       s4.play( );
   else if ( src == B )
       s5.play( );
   else if ( src == E2 )
       s6.play( );
   }
}
```

11.6 JFrame

JFrame allows us to open a new window. The default JFrame is demonstrated in Example 11-7.

EXAMPLE 11-7

```
import javax.swing.*;
public class JFrameDefault extends JApplet
{
   JFrame frame;
   public void init( )
   {
      frame = new JFrame( "Testing JFrame stuff" );
      frame.setSize( 200, 100 );
      frame.setVisible( true );
   }
}
```

> To see the frame, we must specify the size and visibility. The `setVisible` method makes sure that the frame is visible.

When we create the `JFrame`, we specify the title that is to appear in the top of the window.

```
JFrame frame;
frame = new JFrame( text );
```

For example:

```
JFrame newframe;
newframe = new JFrame( "Testing JFrame stuff" );
```

By default, we see that the new frame window appears in the top-left corner of our screen. We can specify a better location by calling the `setLocation` method on our frame object. For example, we can set the frame to appear 500 pixels to the right and 600 pixels down from the upper-left corner of the screen:

```
frame.setLocation( 500, 600 );
```

The default layout manager for the frame is `BorderLayout`. We can change the layout manager as we have done before:

```
frame.setLayout( new FlowLayout( ) );
frame.setLayout( new GridLayout( 1, 2 ) );
```

There are five major steps to get the frames to work. Although there are additional things that we could specify, these are the core steps that we will want to do at a minimum each time that we use `JFrame` components.

1. Create the frame.

```
JFrame frame;
frame = new JFrame( "FrameDemo" );
```

2. Set layout manager.

```
frame.setLayout( new BorderLayout( ) );
```

3. Create components and put them in the frame.

```
JButton go = new JButton( "Go for it!" );
frame.add( go, BorderLayout.SOUTH );
```

4. Size the frame.

```
frame.pack();
```

OR

```
frame.setSize( 200, 500 );
```

> Calling the `.pack( )` method will size the frame on the basis of the minimum size to fit all the components added to the frame.

5. Show it.

```
frame.setVisible(true);
```

> JFrame is invisible by default.

Other steps that we may want to consider include setting the location of the frame, changing the look and feel, and adding events. Example 11-8 creates a JFrame and displays it. The pack method call makes the frame just wide enough to fit the text in the bottom of the frame and high enough for each component to display properly. Example 11-9 uses button click events to trigger when to display the frame.

EXAMPLE 11-8

```java
import java.awt.*;
import javax.swing.*;
public class JFrameStuff extends JApplet
{
    JFrame frame;
    JLabel myname, universe;
    JButton go, skiing;
    public void init( )
    {
        //1. Create the frame.
        frame = new JFrame( "FrameDemo" );
        //2. Set layout manager.
        frame.setLayout( new BorderLayout( ) );
        //3. Create components and put them in the frame.
        myname = new JLabel( "<HTML>My <BR>Stuff", JLabel.CENTER );
        go = new JButton( "Go for it!" );
        skiing = new JButton( "Do you like skiing too?" );
        universe = new JLabel( "I live at the borders of the universe "
            + " where fact and fiction collide" );
        frame.add( myname, BorderLayout.NORTH );
        frame.add( go, BorderLayout.WEST );
        frame.add( skiing, BorderLayout.EAST );
        frame.add( universe, BorderLayout.SOUTH );
        //4. Size the frame.
        frame.pack( );
        //5. Show it.
        frame.setVisible( true );
    }
}
```

EXAMPLE 11-9

```java
import java.awt.*;
import javax.swing.*;
import java.awt.event.*;
public class JFrameEvents extends JApplet
      implements ActionListener
{
   JFrame frame;
   JPanel buttonspane;
   JButton Bots, Swazi, Thai;
   Image botsImg, zebraImg, thaiImg;
   ImageIcon icon;
   JLabel label;

   public void init( )
   {
      setLayout( new BorderLayout( ) );
      setupImages( );
      setupButtons( );
   }
   public void setupButtons( )
   {
      Bots = new JButton( "<HTML>Botswana<BR>animals" );
      Swazi = new JButton( "Swaziland Zebra" );
      Thai = new JButton( "Thailand" );
      Bots.addActionListener( this );  // add listeners
      Swazi.addActionListener( this );
      Thai.addActionListener( this );

      buttonspane = new JPanel( new GridLayout( 3, 1 ) );
      buttonspane.add( Bots );
      buttonspane.add( Swazi );
      buttonspane.add( Thai );
      add( buttonspane, BorderLayout.CENTER );
   }
   public void setupImages( )
   {
      botsImg = getImage( getCodeBase( ), "Botswana.jpg" );
      zebraImg = getImage( getCodeBase( ), "Swazi_Zebra.jpg" );
      thaiImg = getImage( getCodeBase( ), "Thailand.jpg" );
      icon = new ImageIcon( botsImg );  // starting image
      label = new JLabel( icon );
   }
```

(continues)

Example 11-9 (continued)

```
public void actionPerformed( ActionEvent ae )
{
    Object src = ae.getSource( );
    //1. Create the frame.
    frame = new JFrame( "FrameDemo" );
    //2. Set layout manager.
    frame.setLayout( new BorderLayout( ) );
    //3. Create components and put them in the frame.
    if( src == Bots )
    {
            icon.setImage( botsImg );
            label.setIcon( icon );
    }
    else if ( src == Swazi )
    {
            icon.setImage( zebraImg );
            label.setIcon( icon );
    }
    else if ( src == Thai )
    {
            icon.setImage( thaiImg );
            label.setIcon( icon );
    }
    frame.add( label, BorderLayout.CENTER );
    //4. Size the frame.
    frame.pack( );
    //5. Show it.
    frame.setVisible( true );
}
}
```

11.7 Dialog Boxes

Sometimes it is useful to have a popup dialog box appear like the JFrame. Although we could use JFrame to create our own customized version of a popup dialog, we can also make use of the ones that come standard with the Java libraries. We will first look at the simplest dialog boxes that have only an "OK" button and a message. These are shown in **TABLE 11-1** with the code to display them.

TABLE 11-1 Examples of Standard Dialog Boxes With Only 'OK' Button Option

Dialog Box Display	Code to Display Dialog Box	Type

Title Goes Here
? Do you agree?
OK
	```// question icon```
	```JOptionPane.showMessageDialog(null,```
	``` "Do you agree?",```
	``` "Title Goes Here",```
	``` JOptionPane.QUESTION_MESSAGE);```
		Question

Title Goes Here
(i) Agree!
OK
	```// information icon```
	```JOptionPane.showMessageDialog(null,```
	``` "Agree!",```
	``` "Title Goes Here",```
	``` JOptionPane.INFORMATION_MESSAGE);```
		Information

Title Goes Here
(X) There's been an error
OK
	```// information icon```
	```JOptionPane.showMessageDialog(null,```
	``` "There's been an error",```
	``` "Title Goes Here",```
	``` JOptionPane.ERROR_MESSAGE);```
		Error

Title Goes Here
⚠ Warning! Something went wrong!
OK
	```// warning icon```
	```JOptionPane.showMessageDialog(null,```
	``` "Warning! Something went wrong!",```
	``` "Title Goes Here",```
	``` JOptionPane.WARNING_MESSAGE);```
		Warning

Title Goes Here
Message for you.
OK
	```// no icon```
	```JOptionPane.showMessageDialog(null,```
	``` "Message for you.",```
	``` "Title Goes Here",```
	``` JOptionPane.PLAIN_MESSAGE);```
		Message (no icon)

We can also have dialog boxes that give the user options, such as "Yes", "No," and "Cancel," or we can customize the buttons to our own values. We still make use of the JOptionPane and specify which buttons to display. We can record which option the user selects, which is returned as an int from the method call to showOptionPane. Commonly, we then set up an if statement to analyze the result, matching it to one of the constants in the JOptionPane class. **TABLE 11-2** shows several example options and the code for each.

With the showConfirmDialogs, we usually want to know which option the user picked. We store the value returned from the method call into an int variable (e.g.,

TABLE 11-2   Examples of Dialog Boxes With Options

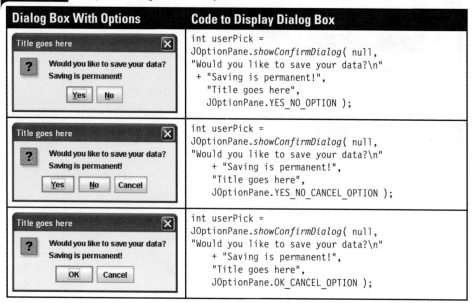

Dialog Box With Options	Code to Display Dialog Box
Title goes here — Would you like to save your data? Saving is permanent! [Yes] [No]	```int userPick = JOptionPane.showConfirmDialog(null, "Would you like to save your data?\n" + "Saving is permanent!", "Title goes here", JOptionPane.YES_NO_OPTION);```
Title goes here — Would you like to save your data? Saving is permanent! [Yes] [No] [Cancel]	```int userPick = JOptionPane.showConfirmDialog(null, "Would you like to save your data?\n" + "Saving is permanent!", "Title goes here", JOptionPane.YES_NO_CANCEL_OPTION);```
Title goes here — Would you like to save your data? Saving is permanent! [OK] [Cancel]	```int userPick = JOptionPane.showConfirmDialog(null, "Would you like to save your data?\n" + "Saving is permanent!", "Title goes here", JOptionPane.OK_CANCEL_OPTION);```

userPick in the examples in Table 11-2). We can then write an if-else statement to determine which option was selected:

```
if ( userPick == JOptionPane.YES_OPTION )
        StatusLabel.setText( "yes!" );
else if ( userPick == JOptionPane.NO_OPTION )
        StatusLabel.setText( "no!" );
else if ( userPick == JOptionPane.OK_OPTION )
        StatusLabel.setText( "OK!" );
else if ( userPick == JOptionPane.CANCEL_OPTION )
        StatusLabel.setText( "cancel" );
```

If we wanted to add components to the dialog box, such as combo boxes, radio buttons, or text fields, we could do so through more customization of setting up our JOptionPane by calling the method showInputDialog. However, we can also implement our own customized dialog boxes by creating a JFrame and adding our components to the JFrame, adding ActionListeners to the buttons, and handling the event of a button click to read any input that the user may have entered in our entry fields.

11.8 MediaTracker

When we create an applet with lots of images or some large images, it can take a while to load all the images. By default the applet will try to start to run even though the images are not all loaded yet. This can result in some of the images not appearing at all on our applets. The proper way to ensure that our images are fully loaded before running our applets is to load them into a MediaTracker object and then tell the applet to wait for all the images to load before continuing. We can do this by loading the images into the MediaTracker with the addImage method call, and then in the start method, we force our applet to ensure that all images have loaded. This code can produce exceptions, and therefore we need to put them inside something called a try . . . catch block. Example 11-10 shows how to work with the MediaTracker. This example is merely a structure for setting up and using the MediaTracker to load the images—the program does not actually display anything.

EXAMPLE 11-10

```java
import java.awt.*;
import javax.swing.*;
public class MediaTrackerEx extends JApplet
{
    Image one, two, three, four;
    MediaTracker imgTracker;
    public void init( )
    {
        loadImages( );
    }
    public void start( )
    {
        try
        {
            imgTracker.waitForAll( );
        }catch (Exception e )
        { }
    }
    public void loadImages( )
    {
        imgTracker = new MediaTracker( this );
        one = getImage( getCodeBase( ), "one.gif" );
        two = getImage( getCodeBase( ), "two.gif" );
        three = getImage( getCodeBase( ), "three.gif" );
        four = getImage( getCodeBase( ), "four.gif" );
        imgTracker.addImage( one, 1 );
        imgTracker.addImage( two, 2 );
        imgTracker.addImage( three, 3 );
        imgTracker.addImage( four, 4 );
    }
}
```

Troubleshooting

Common errors:

My code will not compile.	If you are using borders, you need to add the import statement: `import javax.swing.border.*;`.
	If you are using `AudioClip`, you need to add the import statement: `import java.applet.*;`.
JFrame does not appear.	Make sure that you call the method `.setVisible( true )` on your `JFrame` because, by default, it is set to invisible.
	Make sure that you call the method `.pack( )` or `.setBounds( )` to define the size of the `JFrame`; otherwise, it defaults to zero by zero.
	Sometimes the `JFrame` pops up behind your other windows. Flip through your open windows and see if you can find it. If you did not move its location, look in the top-left corner of your screen.
I am not getting feedback as to which button a user selected in a `JOptionPane`.	Make sure that you have an `int` variable equal to the value returned from the call to the `JOptionPane` method.
	Try printing out the value of the result. It should be an integer. In your `if-else` structure, make sure that you have two equal signs to check for equality. Be sure to check equality to one of the `JOptionPane` constants.

SUMMARY

- Tabs can be added to a JTabbedPane on top, left, bottom, or right.
- Only one component can be added to a tab in JTabbedPane. To have multiple components displayed in a tab, put them inside a JPanel and add the JPanel to the tab.
- The pack method on a JFrame will size the frame on the basis of the minimum size required to fit all the components in the JFrame.
- Call the method setVisible on the JFrame when it is ready to be displayed.
- Add tooltips to Swing components by calling the setToolTipText method on the object for which we want a tooltip.
- Add tooltips to JTabbedPane panes when we call the addTab method by specifying the text on the tab, an ImageIcon (or null for none) for the tab, the panel to go inside the pane, and the text for the tooltip.
- Create borders by using the BorderFactory class in the javax.swing.border package.
- Add borders by using the setBorder method.

- Types of borders include line, etched, bevel, titled, matte, and empty.
- Etched and bevel borders can be either raised or lowered.
- Java supports five types of audio files: AIFF, AU, WAV, MIDI, and RMF.
- To access an audio file, call the method `getAudioClip` in a similar way to `getImage`.
- To play audio files, call either `play` or `loop` on the `AudioClip` object.
- Call the `stop` method on the `AudioClip` object to stop it from playing.
- Write a `stop` method that stops all `AudioClips` from running when the user leaves your applet.
- `JOptionPane` is used for dialog popup windows and has many customizable options.
- `MediaTracker` can be used to ensure that all images load before the applet continues.

EXERCISES

1. True or false? On a JTabbedPane, you can only put tabs on the top or left side of the pane.
2. What method is called to add a component to a JTabbedPane?
3. On a JTabbedPane, what happens when you try to directly add two components to the same tab?
4. What is the default placement for tabs in a JTabbedPane?
5. How do you add a button to a tab in JTabbedPane but keep the button's dimensions appropriate?
6. JFrames use what layout manager by default?
7. What is the purpose of the pack( ) method for a JFrame?
8. What are the five steps for producing a window frame?
9. True or false? JFrames can pop up based on a button click.
10. True or false? You can program a JFrame to pop up as soon as the applet loads.
11. What is the purpose of the method setVisible for JFrames? What happens if you do not call setVisible(true) on your JFrame?
12. Fill in the blanks so that this program displays a JFrame:

```
import java.awt.*;
import javax.swing.*;
public class xyz extends JApplet
{
    JFrame frame;
    JLabel  name;
```

```
public void init( )
{
    frame = new _____( "Title" );
    frame._____( new FlowLayout( ) );
    name = new JLabel( "Cookie Monster" );
    frame._____( name );
    frame.pack( );
    frame._____( true );
}
}
```

13. True or false? You can have tooltips on a JPanel object.

14. What method do you call on a component when you want to set the border to a matte border object that you previously created?

15. True or false? You can make a border with an image.

16. True or false? You can make borders that look raised like a button or lowered like they are carved into the component.

17. How do you add a tooltip to each pane in JTabbedPane?

18. True or false? You can change the color of a line border.

19. What three things do you need to do to get a border?

20. Can you add a border object (e.g., Border from the examples) directly to an applet?

21. What sound file extensions can be played using the standard Java class libraries?

22. True or false? You cannot have two different audio files playing at the same time.

23. Why do we need to implement a stop method if we are running our audio file by using loop?

24. Do we need a stop method if we just run the audio file with play?

25. Add images to the guitar tuner so that it looks like the actual guitar strings. Add different images for when the user clicks on a string to make it look like it is being "plucked" (Example 11-6).

26. Write an applet of quiz questions. When the user selects a particular difficulty and topic, pop up the quiz question inside a JFrame. When the user answers in the JFrame, pop up another JFrame letting the user know whether or not he answered the question correctly. Extend this to be a full Jeopardy-style or Family Feud–style applet.

27. Add tooltips and borders to your applets that you made from the components and/or layouts chapter (favorite movies/songs/party invitation/etc.).

28. Create an applet of your résumé by using `JTabbedPane`. Add tabs for your education, work experience and/or portfolio, contact information, and photos.

29. Create an applet that loads 10 of your photos in a large size. Try to run the applet to display the images. Then implement the `MediaTracker` to ensure that all the images load before running the applet.

Collections

12

12.1 List Data Structures

Many times when we are programming we need to handle a group of items. Instead of creating separate variables for each one, it is more convenient for us to have one reference variable for all of them. This system also allows us more flexibility to easily change the number of items in the group. For example, when we create a list of things that we need at the supermarket, we label our list "Grocery List" and then list each item. We do not want to write out "Grocery list item 1, Grocery list item 2, Grocery list item 3," etc. In programming we use lists all the time. There are websites that now allow you to create a grocery list and order items to be home-delivered. At the university, we have a list of students in the course, a list of students' quiz scores, exam scores, etc. For all these list examples, we will store all the values in an array where we will have only one variable name to reference all the items in the list. We will also see some clever code techniques that we can implement based on using one of these collections data structures. The two data structures that we will look at are arrays and `ArrayList`.

12.2 Arrays

An array is a data structure that can hold a list of items. We can have a list of numbers, Strings, buttons, etc. One limitation is that when we create an array, all the elements in the array must be of the same data type that we declared it. Therefore, we cannot have `int`s and buttons in the same array.

We can depict arrays graphically as a bunch of boxes with the elements in each box. We can then number each box with an *index* value, to designate where the element is in the array.

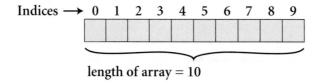

The indices start at zero. Therefore, if we have *n* elements in an array, the last element is at index $n - 1$.

12.2.1 Array Declaration

We use brackets to declare an array. We can place the brackets either after the data type or after the variable name.

```
int[ ] grades;        JButton[ ] buttons;    // after data type
int grades[ ];        JButton buttons[ ];    // after variable name
```

Declaration does not initialize the values. Currently there is nothing at buttons[0]. We still need to initialize the array and then initialize each element in the array.

12.2.2 Array Initialization

When instantiating an array, we need to specify the maximum size of our list. We do this by putting the size in brackets as follows:

```
grades = new int[3];
buttons = new JButton[4];
```

Doing so differs from creating a new JButton, where we say

```
button = new JButton( "txt" );
```

Note also how we can create a list of primitives, like an array of int. This step initializes a list (array) of the specified size. We have not yet initialized each element in the list.

> Arrays indices start at zero. The last element in an array is at the array.length − 1.

Array Element Initialization   Next we need to initialize each element in the array. We can do this one of two ways: manually or with a loop.

Example of manually:

```
grades[0] = 89;        buttons[0] = new JButton( "A" );
grades[1] = 92;        buttons[1] = new JButton( "B" );
grades[2] = 95;        buttons[2] = new JButton( "C" );
                       buttons[3] = new JButton( "D" );
```

Array of JButton objects

Example of using a loop:

Array of int

```
for( int i=0; i<3; i++ )
    grades[i] = i;
```

What are the values in the array after the loop executes?

Shortcut Initializer List   We also have the option to declare and initialize our list all at once if we know what we want in it. We do this by using braces to designate the values inside the list.

The following two examples illustrate this:

```
int[ ] grades = { 89, 92, 95 };
```
← Semicolon at the end

```
JButton buttons[ ] = { new JButton( "A" ), new JButton( "B" ),
                       new JButton( "C" ), new JButton( "D" ) };
```

Length   One of the most important things to know about arrays is the *length* of an array. We can access this information by referring to the constant length on the array.

For example, from the preceding examples:

```
grades.length      ← returns 3
buttons.length     ← returns 4
```

> *Note: there are no parentheses after length.*

This concept is useful when we want to walk through all the elements in an array. For example, if we want to calculate the average of all the grades, we need to loop through the array to calculate:

```
int sum = 0;
for( int i=0; i < grades.length; i++ )
        sum = sum + grades[i];
double average = (double)sum / grades.length;
```

Another example, if we had an array of buttons that we wanted to add to a JPanel:

```
JPanel pane = new JPanel( new GridLayout( 4, 1 ) );
for( int i=0; i<buttons.length; i++ )
{
        buttons[i].addActionListener( this );
        pane.add( buttons[i] );
}
add( pane );
```

The code in Example 12-1 displays a new quote each time that the user clicks on the button. The quotes are stored in a String array. Each time the button is clicked, we randomly select a new quote from the array to display.

EXAMPLE 12-1

```java
import java.awt.*;
import javax.swing.*;
import java.awt.event.*;
import java.util.*;
public class RandomQuoter extends JApplet
    implements ActionListener
{
    JButton next;
    JLabel label;
    Random random = new Random( );
    String[ ] quotes =
    {
        "What's up, doc?",
        "Have you any Grey Poupon?",
        "Can you hear me now?",
        "<HTML><CENTER>What is the average ground speed"
            +" <BR> of an unladen swallow?",
        "As you wish"
    };
    public void init( )
    {
        setLayout( new BorderLayout( ) );
        next = new JButton( "Next!" );
        next.addActionListener( this );
        label = new JLabel( "Good morning!", JLabel.CENTER );
        label.setFont( new Font( "Serif", Font.BOLD, 16 ) );
        add( next, BorderLayout.NORTH );
        add( label, BorderLayout.CENTER );
    }
    public void actionPerformed( ActionEvent ae )
    {
        Object obj = ae.getSource( );
        if( obj == next )
        {
            int index = random.nextInt( quotes.length );
            label.setText( quotes[index] );
        }
    }
}
```

Example 12-2 shows the use of an array of images and buttons to walk through the images.

EXAMPLE 12-2

```java
import java.awt.*;
import javax.swing.*;
import java.awt.event.*;
public class SlideShowUsingButtons extends JApplet implements ActionListener
{
    Image[ ] photos;        // array of all your images
    ImageIcon icon;         // images need to be in an ImageIcon
    JLabel imgLabel;        // and stored into a JLabel
    int currentIndex = 0;   // which image index is currently displayed
    JButton prev, next;
  public void init( )
  {
    setLayout( new FlowLayout( ) );
    photos = new Image[4];              // load the images into memory
    photos[0] = getImage( getCodeBase( ), "Cambodia.jpg" );
    photos[1] = getImage( getCodeBase( ), "Czech.jpg" );
    photos[2] = getImage( getCodeBase( ), "NewZealand.jpg" );
    photos[3] = getImage( getCodeBase( ), "Poland.jpg" );
    icon = new ImageIcon( );
    imgLabel = new JLabel( );
    imgLabel.setHorizontalAlignment( JLabel.CENTER );    // center images
    prev = new JButton( "Prev" );
    next = new JButton( "Next" );
    setupIcon( 0 );          // initialize setup to first display first image (index 0)

    add( prev );   // add components to applet
    add( imgLabel );
    add( next );
    prev.addActionListener( this );          // add listeners
    next.addActionListener( this );
  }
  public void setupIcon( int index // method changes image in label
  {                 // and modifies next/previous buttons to be enabled/disabled
    currentIndex = index;
    icon.setImage( photos[index] ) ;
    imgLabel.setIcon( icon );
    prev.setEnabled( true ); // default both buttons to enabled
        next.setEnabled( true );
    if( index == 0 )
        prev.setEnabled( false );
        if( index == photos.length-1 )
            next.setEnabled( false );
  }
  public void actionPerformed( ActionEvent ae )
  {
    Object obj = ae.getSource( );
    if( obj == next )
        setupIcon( currentIndex+1 );         // otherwise just increment the index
    else
        setupIcon( currentIndex-1 );    // otherwise just increment the index
    repaint( );                         // Show the change.
  }
}
```

> Previous button is disabled at start.

> Back button is disabled at end.

> We need the repaint method call to ensure that the applet updates the display.

Example 12-3 is first listed (on the left) without using arrays, and the second list (right) uses an array for all the buttons. Notice the differences between the two. This example shows how using an array can save coding effort. How much code is necessary to expand each of these programs to handle 20 buttons? Which one would be easier to work with?

EXAMPLE 12-3

```java
import java.awt.*;
import javax.swing.*;
import java.awt.event.*;
public class ButtonNoArr extends JApplet
                    implements ActionListener
{
    JLabel label;
    JButton mybuttons1 = new JButton( "one" );
    JButton mybuttons2 = new JButton( "two" );
    JButton mybuttons3 = new JButton( "three" );
    JButton mybuttons4 = new JButton( "four" );
public void init( )
    {
        setLayout( new FlowLayout( ) );
        label = new JLabel( "Hello" );
        add( label ) ;
        mybuttons1.addActionListener( this );
        mybuttons2.addActionListener( this );
        mybuttons3.addActionListener( this );
        mybuttons4.addActionListener( this );

        add( mybuttons1 );
        add( mybuttons2 );
        add( mybuttons3 );
        add( mybuttons4 );
    }
    public void actionPerformed( ActionEvent ae )
    {
        Object obj = ae.getSource( );
        if( obj == mybuttons1 )
        {
            label.setText ( "first button" );
        }
        else if( obj == mybuttons2 )
        {
            label.setText( "second button" );
        }
        else if( obj == mybuttons3 )
        {
            label.setText( "third" );
        }
        else if( obj == mybuttons4 )
        {
            label.setText( "fourth" );
        }
    }
}
```

```java
import java.awt.*;
import javax.swing.*;
import java.awt.event.*;
public class ButtonArr extends JApplet
                    implements ActionListener
{
    JLabel label;
    JButton[ ] mybuttons =
    {
        new JButton( "one" ),
        new JButton( "two" ),
        new JButton( "three" ),
        new JButton( "four" )
    };
    public void init( )
    {
        setLayout( new FlowLayout( ) );
        label = new JLabel( "Hello" );
        add( label ) ;

        for( int x=0; x < mybuttons.length; x++ )
        {
            mybuttons[x].addActionListener( this );
            add( mybuttons[x] );
        }
    }
    public void actionPerformed( ActionEvent ae )
    {
        Object obj = ae.getSource( );
        if( obj == mybuttons[0] )
        {
            label.setText( "first button" );
        }
        else if( obj == mybuttons[1] )
        {
            label.setText( "second button" );
        }
        else if( obj == mybuttons[2] )
        {
            label.setText( "third" );
        }
        else if( obj == mybuttons[3] )
        {
            label.setText( "fourth" );
        }
    }
}
```

Loop works no matter how many buttons are in the array.

The example on the right can be optimized using another array for the text to be set in the label. Create a `String` array at the top of the class with "first button", "second button", "third", and "fourth". Then in the `actionPerformed` method, change it to loop through the buttons; once a match is found, the index of the matching button matches the index into our `String` array. Therefore, we can set the text on our label to the string matching the index of the selected button. The code is shown in Example 12-4:

EXAMPLE 12-4

```
import java.awt.*;
import javax.swing.*;
import java.awt.event.*;
public class ButtonArr extends JApplet    implements ActionListener
{
    JLabel label;
    JButton[ ] mybuttons = { new JButton( "one" ),  new JButton( "two" ),
                         new JButton( "three" ), new JButton( "four" ) };
    String[ ] text = { "first button", "second button", "third", "fourth" };
    public void init( )
    {
        setLayout( new FlowLayout( )  );
        label = new JLabel( "Hello" );
        add( label ) ;
        for( int x=0; x < mybuttons.length; x++ )
        {
            mybuttons[x].addActionListener( this );
            add( mybuttons[x] );
        }
    }
    public void actionPerformed( ActionEvent ae )
    {
        Object obj = ae.getSource( );
        for( int x=0; x<mybuttons.length; x++ )
            if( obj == mybuttons[x] )
                label.setText ( text[x] );
    }
}
```

This is a great example of clever programming. We can use this in a multitude of ways, for example, matching a button to an image or matching a button to an image and audio file and text. Create arrays for each item, where the indices match up within each array. Then when we figure out which button was selected, we know the index into each array: the image, the text, or the audio to play.

Applet Viewer: ButtonArr.class
Applet
Hello one   two   three   four
Applet started.

x is the correct index for the button array as well as the `String` text array.

We can also create a sliding puzzle with one "blank" spot. The user clicks on picture fragments adjacent to the blank spot to move them around until he can finally produce the correct picture. Example 12-5 will automatically divide up the image into a 4 × 4 grid.

EXAMPLE 12-5

```java
import java.awt.*;
import javax.swing.*;
import java.awt.event.*;
import java.awt.image.*;
public class SlidingPuzzle extends JApplet  implements ActionListener
{
    Image image;
    ImageIcon icon;
    JButton buttons[ ], blankButton;
    JPanel grid, spots[ ];
    int currentBlankSpot;
    public void init( )
    {
        setLayout( new FlowLayout( ) );
        buttons = new JButton[16];
        grid = new JPanel( new GridLayout( 4, 4) );
        setupPanels( );
        setupImage( );
        grid.setSize( 400, 400 );
        add( grid );
    }
    public void setupPanels( )
    {
        spots = new JPanel[16];
        blankButton = new JButton( " " );
        blankButton.setBackground( Color.BLACK );
        for( int i=0; i<spots.length; i++ )
        {
            spots[i] = new JPanel( new BorderLayout( ) );
            grid.add( spots[i] );
        }
    }
    public void setupImage( )
    {
        image = getImage( getCodeBase( ), "GalapagosTurtlesSquare.gif" );
        MediaTracker tracker = new MediaTracker( this );
        tracker.addImage( image, 1 );
        try { tracker.waitForAll( );
        } catch( Exception e ) { }
          BufferedImage bimage = new BufferedImage(
      image.getWidth( null ), image.getHeight( null ), BufferedImage.TYPE_INT_ARGB );
        Graphics g = bimage.getGraphics( );
        g.drawImage( image, 0, 0, this );
```

(continues)

Example 12-5 (continued)

```
    int width = image.getWidth( this );
    int height = image.getHeight( this );
    System.out.println( width + " h = " + height );
    int count = 0;
    for( int i=0; i<4; i++ )
      for( int j=0; j<4; j++ )   // do not display last one; this is the
                                 //  blank spot
      {
          BufferedImage window = bimage.getSubimage(
                               i*width/4, j*height/4, width/4, height/4 );
          setupButton( count++, window );
      }
    // override the last button with the blank spot
    spots[ spots.length-1 ].add( blankButton );
    currentBlankSpot = spots.length-1;
}
public void setupButton( int id, Image img )
{
    buttons[id] = new JButton( new ImageIcon( img ) );
    buttons[id].addActionListener( this );
    buttons[id].setMargin(new Insets( 0, 0, 0, 0 ) );
    buttons[id].setContentAreaFilled( false );
    spots[id].add( buttons[id], BorderLayout.CENTER );
}
public void actionPerformed( ActionEvent ae )
{
    Object src = ae.getSource( );
    for( int i=0; i<buttons.length; i++ )
    {
        if( buttons[i] == src )
            if( currentBlankSpot - 1 == i || currentBlankSpot - 4 == i
                || currentBlankSpot + 1 == i || currentBlankSpot + 4 == i )
            {
                                                   // exchange spots with blank
                spots[ currentBlankSpot ].removeAll( );
                spots[ i ].removeAll( );

                spots[ currentBlankSpot ].add( buttons[ i ] );
                spots[ i ].add( blankButton );

                buttons[ currentBlankSpot ] = buttons[ i ];
                buttons[ i ] = blankButton;
                currentBlankSpot = i;
                repaint( );
                return;                            // must have this here
            }
    }
  }
}
```

Example 12-6 handles the button state, maintaining a look of "selected" for the selected button.

EXAMPLE 12-6

```
import java.awt.*;
import javax.swing.*;
import java.awt.event.*;
public class JButImg extends JApplet implements ActionListener
{
   JButton[ ] buttonArray = new JButton[3];
   public void init( )
   {
     setLayout( new GridLayout( 3, 1 ) );
     setupButton( 0, "About Me" ); // set up each button by calling setupButton
                                    //   method
     setupButton( 1, "Resume" );   // send it the number of the button in the array
     setupButton( 2, "Hobbies" );
   }
   public void setupButton( int buttonNum, String name )
   {
     Image img = getImage( getCodeBase( ), "buttongr.gif" );
     ImageIcon ic = new ImageIcon( img );
     buttonArray[buttonNum] = new JButton( name, ic );
                 // place the text on top of the image
     buttonArray[buttonNum].setHorizontalTextPosition( JButton.CENTER );
     buttonArray[buttonNum].setBorderPainted(false); // remove border around the
                                                      //   button
           // no spacing between the contents of the button and the edge
     buttonArray[buttonNum].setMargin( new Insets(0, 0, 0, 0 ) );
     buttonArray[buttonNum].setForeground( Color.white ); // set the font color to
                                                          //   white
     buttonArray[buttonNum].addActionListener( this );    // listen for clicks
         // when user presses the button, have the icon color change
     buttonArray[buttonNum].setPressedIcon(
             new ImageIcon( getImage( getCodeBase( ), "buttonbrite.gif" ) ) );
         // when user selects the button, have the icon color change
     buttonArray[buttonNum].setSelectedIcon(
             new ImageIcon( getImage( getCodeBase( ), "buttongray.gif" ) ) );
         // when user rolls the mouse over the button, have the icon color change
     buttonArray[buttonNum].setRolloverIcon(
             new ImageIcon( getImage( getCodeBase( ), "buttonred.gif" ) ) );
         // when user rolls the mouse over a SELECTED button, have the icon color
         //   change
     buttonArray[buttonNum].setRolloverSelectedIcon(
             new ImageIcon( getImage( getCodeBase( ), "buttondim.gif" ) ) );
         // do not draw the regular button background
     buttonArray[buttonNum].setContentAreaFilled( false );
```

(continues)

Example 12-6 (continued)

```
        buttonArray[buttonNum].setFocusPainted( false );
        add( buttonArray[buttonNum] );    // add to applet
    }
    public void actionPerformed( ActionEvent ae )
    {
        Object obj = ae.getSource( );
        if( obj instanceof JButton )
        {                                  // deselect button that is currently selected
            for( int i=0; i<buttonArray.length; i++ )
                if( buttonArray[i].isSelected( ) )
                        buttonArray[i].setSelected( false );
            JButton button = ( JButton ) obj;
            button.setSelected( true ); // set the button that was just clicked to
                                        //    selected
        }
    }
}
```

12.3 Arrays and JTable

Arrays are going to help us display graphical tables in our applets, which look similar to spreadsheets. Before we can learn how to create tables in applets, we first need to expand our knowledge of arrays. So far, we have looked at single-dimensional arrays. We also need to look at two-dimensional (2-D) arrays.

12.3.1 2-D Arrays

A 2-D array is similar to a 1-D array, but we now have two dimensions. We still designate using the square brackets, [and], but we have two sets of brackets.

Example:

```
int[ ][ ] grades;       String data[ ][ ];
```

Just as for the 1-D arrays, we still need to create the actual array and specify the dimensions—the number of rows and columns. The first set of brackets is used to designate the number of rows, and the second set of brackets is for the number of columns.

Example:

```
grades = new int[2][3];   // two rows, three columns
data = new String[5][4];  // five rows, four columns
```

Remember: Java starts counting at zero.

We can assign values to each cell in the array manually, by again specifying the exact row and column for a particular cell.

Example:

```
grades[0][1] = 89;          // row zero, column 1
data[4][3] = "Good";        // last row 4, last column 3
```

Similar to the 1-D array, we can also initialize the entire thing all at once by using the braces for an initializer list: the outer braces for the row and the inner sets of braces for each column. The following code

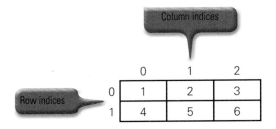

```
int[ ][ ] grades = {  {1, 2, 3},  {4, 5, 6}  };
```

creates the following array:

```
        Column indices
           0    1    2
      0    1    2    3
      1    4    5    6
Row indices
```

Common 2-D array references and their values include the following:

grades[1][2]   references the int cell with the value 6
grades.length   references the number of rows, which is 2
grades[0].length   references the length of the first row's 1-D array, which is 3
grades[1].length   references the length of the second row's 1-D array, which is 3
grades[0]   references the 1-D array in the first row (int [ ])

Examples using the preceding references:

```
int gradeVal = grades[1][2];          gradeVal is equal to 6
int numRows = grades.length;          numRows is equal to 2
int numCols = grades[0].length;       numCols is equal to 3
int[ ] row1 = grades[0];              row1 is equal to the 1-D array {1, 2, 3}
```

This next example shows a 2-D array of Strings. The following code

```
Object data[ ][ ] = {  { "Liz", "Skiing", "Fort Fun", "21" },
                        { "C. M.", "Cooking", "Denver", "56" },
                        { "Oscar", "Mtn Biking", "Mars", "19" },
                    };
```

creates the following array:

		Columns			
		0	**1**	**2**	**3**
Rows	**0**	Liz	Skiing	Fort Fun	21
	1	C. M.	Cooking	Denver	56
	2	Oscar	Mtn Biking	Mars	19

Common references and their values based on the previous 2-D String array include the following:

data[1][2]	references the int cell with the value "Denver"
data.length	references the number of rows, which is 3
data[0].length	references the length of the first row's 1-D array, which is 4
data[1].length	references the length of the second row's 1-D array, which is 4
data[0]	references the 1-D array in the first row (int [ ])

12.3.2 JTable

Now that we can do both 1-D and 2-D arrays, we can put together a JTable. A table requires both a 1-D and a 2-D array—the 1-D array for the column headings displayed at the top of the table and a 2-D array for the actual data inside the table. The column headings have to be Strings, but our data array can be of type Object where we could put Strings, checkboxes, or even images inside them. Of course, adding different types adds to the complexity of creating the table, but having such flexibility available is great.

Let us start with a simple example, creating a table with just Strings. We will use the data example listed previously. First we need to create the column headings:

```
String[ ] colHeadings = { "Name", "Sport", "Location", "Age" };
```

Then we can use the data variable listed earlier:

```
Object data[ ][ ] = {   { "Liz", "Skiing", "Fort Fun", "21" },
                        { "C. M.", "Cooking", "Denver", "56" },
                        { "Oscar", "Mtn Biking", "Mars", "19" },
                      };
```

> Note: we cannot store an int or any other primitive data type directly into a JTable—
> convert it to a String first or use the Integer class.

To create our table:

```
JTable table;
table = new JTable( data, colHeadings );
```

To get the headings to display properly, we also have to do two more things. The first is to set the viewable area of the table (based on pixels—width and height):

```
table.setPreferredScrollableViewportSize( new Dimension( 500, 70 ) );
```

Then we need to put the table into a scroll pane so that users can view all of it, in case the rows and columns do not fit within the viewport size:

```
        // Create the scroll pane and add the table to it.
JScrollPane scrollPane = new JScrollPane( table );

        // Add the scroll pane to this panel.
panel.add( scrollPane );
```

Put JTables into a JScrollPane and add the JScrollPane to the applet to ensure that the JTable displays properly.

Example 12-7 is a complete program creating a table.

EXAMPLE 12-7

```
import java.awt.*;
import javax.swing.*;
public class JTableData extends JApplet
{
   String[ ] colHeadings = { "Name", "Sport", "Location", "Age" };

   Object data[ ][ ] = {   { "Liz", "Skiing", "Fort Fun", "21" },
                           { "C. M.", "Cooking", "Denver", "56" },
                           { "Oscar", "Mtn Biking", "Mars", "19" },
                      };
   JScrollPane scrollPane;
   JTable table;

   public void init( )
   {
      table = new JTable( data, colHeadings );
      table.setPreferredScrollableViewportSize( new Dimension( 400, 70 ) );
      // Create the scroll pane and add the table to it.
      scrollPane = new JScrollPane( table );
      add( scrollPane );  // add the scrollPane to the applet.
   }
}
```

Coloring   We can also have too much fun with colors on our tables. Example 12-8 explores several opportunities for coloring different aspects of our tables.

EXAMPLE 12-8

```java
import java.awt.*;
import javax.swing.*;
public class JTableDataColor extends JApplet
{
    String[ ] colHeadings = { "Name", "Sport", "Location", "Age" };
    Object data[ ][ ] = {   { "Liz",   "Skiing", "Fort Fun", "21" },
                            { "C. M.", "Cooking", "Denver", "56" },
                            { "Oscar", "Mtn Biking", "Mars", "19" },
                         };
    JScrollPane scrollPane;
    JTable table;
    public void init( )
    {
        table = new JTable( data, colHeadings );
                        // change the color of the column headings
        table.getTableHeader( ).setBackground( Color.RED );
        table.getTableHeader( ).setForeground( Color.YELLOW );
                        // change colors of the selected row
        table.setSelectionBackground( Color.ORANGE );
        table.setSelectionForeground( Color.WHITE );
        table.setGridColor( Color.GREEN ); // change color of grid lines
            // specify which grid lines to display (default is show)
        table.setShowHorizontalLines( true ); // this is the default
        table.setShowVerticalLines( false );
                        // change the color of the data cells
        table.setBackground( Color.BLUE );
        table.setForeground( Color.CYAN );
    table.setPreferredScrollableViewportSize( new Dimension( 400, 70 ) );
    scrollPane = new JScrollPane( table );
    add( scrollPane );
    }
}
```

Only horizontal lines are displayed.

The last row is highlighted, with orange background and white foreground.

Applet Viewer: JTableDataCol.

Applet

Name	Sport	Location	Age
Liz	Skiing	Fort Fun	21
C. M.	Cooking	Denver	56
Oscar	Mtn Biking	Mars	19

Applet started.

Change the color of the grid lines

```
table.setGridColor( Color.GREEN );
```

Change the width of each column

```
table.setAutoResizeMode( JTable.AUTO_RESIZE_OFF );
table.getColumnModel( ).getColumn( 0 ).setPreferredWidth( 50 );
table.getColumnModel( ).getColumn( 1 ).setPreferredWidth( 200 );
table.getColumnModel( ).getColumn( 2 ).setPreferredWidth( 100 );
```

Fix the width to a set size

```
table.getColumnModel( ).getColumn( 0 ).setPreferredWidth( 50 );
table.getColumnModel( ).getColumn( 0 ).setMinWidth( 50 );
table.getColumnModel( ).getColumn( 0 ).setMaxWidth( 50 );
```

Make the cells uneditable

```
JTable table;
DefaultTableModel dfmodel = new DefaultTableModel( data, roster )
{
        public boolean isCellEditable( int row, int column )
        {
            return false;
        }
};
table = new JTable( dfmodel );
```

Change the colors of the column headings

```
DefaultTableCellRenderer head = new DefaultTableCellRenderer( );
head.setBackground( Color.YELLOW );
head.setForeground( Color.BLUE );
table.getColumnModel( ).getColumn( 0 ).setHeaderRenderer( head );
table.getColumnModel( ).getColumn( 1 ).setHeaderRenderer( head );
table.getColumnModel( ).getColumn( 2 ).setHeaderRenderer( head );
// continue for each column
```

Other Features   There are many additional features for JTables, but it starts to get very complex very fast. We learned the basics for most uses of tables, which should suffice.

12.4 ArrayList

ArrayList is a data structure that also allows us to keep track of a group of items. Just as for the array, we do not add the ArrayList to the applet as a display component. It is a data structure to help organize our program, not a component that we add to an applet. However, it is quite different from an array. For instance, we can store only objects inside an ArrayList—so we cannot put int, double, boolean, or char types in an ArrayList. Another difference is that we do not have to specify the maximum size of the list. ArrayList will dynamically grow and shrink as needed. To create an ArrayList, we need to reference the java.util package:

```
import java.util.*;
```

We create an instance of ArrayList by calling the new operator. We should also specify what type of objects we are going to put into the ArrayList by designating the data type in angle brackets. For example, if we are creating a list of String objects, we would use the <String> notation. The following code examples declare ArrayList variables designating a particular data type.

```
ArrayList<String>  mylist;
mylist = new ArrayList<String>( );

ArrayList<ImageIcon> iconList;
iconList = new ArrayList<ImageIcon>( );

ArrayList<JButton> buttonList;
buttonList = new ArrayList<JButton>( );
```

We can add any Object data type to an ArrayList. Therefore, primitive data types need to be wrapped inside an Object data type. To add items to the list, we call the add method.

```
mylist.add( aButton );
iconList.add( anImageIcon );
buttonList.add( aJButton );
intlist.add( new Integer( intVal ) );
dbllist.add( new Double( doubleVal ) );
chrlist.add( new Character( charVal ) );
```

To access elements in the list, call the get method. The get method takes the index as a parameter (remember—Java starts counting at zero).

```
String s = mylist.get( index );
JButton b = buttonList.get( index );
int i = ( intlist.get( index ) ).intValue( );  // get int value
double j = ( doublelist.get( index ) ).doubleValue( );
```

To remove items from the list we can call the `remove` method with either the object we want removed or the index of the element we want to remove from the list:

```
iconList.remove( 0 );    // remove first element
buttonList.remove( aJButton );
```

When we walk through the list of elements in the `ArrayList`, we need to know the size of the list. We can call the `.size( )` method on the `ArrayList` variable to tell us the exact number of elements in the list.

```
int numElements = iconList.size( );
```

> `.size( )` on `ArrayList` returns the number of elements in the list. `.length` on an array returns the maximum size of the list.

When considering whether to use an array or an `ArrayList`, determine whether or not the items in the list are going to change through the course of the program. For example, if we have a program that randomly selects a quote to display (e.g., Example 12-1 `RandomQuoter` presented earlier in this chapter), then using an array is the better option (arrays are faster than manipulating an `ArrayList`). If, however, we modify this quote program to display each quote only once, then we might prefer to use an `ArrayList` and remove the quote from the list after we display it to the user. Example 12-9 demonstrates this new version of the program using an `ArrayList` instead of an array.

EXAMPLE 12-9

```
import java.awt.*;
import javax.swing.*;
import java.awt.event.*;
import java.util.*;
public class RandomQuoterAL extends JApplet
    implements ActionListener
{
    JButton next;
    JLabel label;
    Random random = new Random( );
    ArrayList<String> quotes;
    public void init( )
    {
        setLayout( new BorderLayout( ) );
        quotes = new ArrayList<String>( );
        quotes.add( "What's up, doc?" );
        quotes.add( "Have you any Grey Poupon?" );
        quotes.add( "Can you hear me now?"  );
```

Applet Viewer: Ra...
Applet
Next!

Good morning!

Applet started.

Applet Viewer: Ra...
Applet
Next!

What is the average ground speed of an unladen swallow?

Applet started.

(continues)

Example 12-9 (continued)

```
    quotes.add( "<HTML><CENTER>What is the average ground speed"
        + " <BR> of an unladen swallow?" );
    quotes.add( "As you wish" );

    next = new JButton( "Next!" );
    next.addActionListener( this );
    label = new JLabel( "Good morning!", JLabel.CENTER );
    label.setFont( new Font( "Serif", Font.BOLD, 16 ) );
    add( next, BorderLayout.NORTH );
    add( label, BorderLayout.CENTER );
    }
    public void actionPerformed( ActionEvent ae )
    {
        Object obj = ae.getSource( );
        if( obj == next )
        {
            if( quotes.size( ) > 0 )
            {
                int index = random.nextInt( quotes.size( ) );
                label.setText( quotes.get( index ) );
                quotes.remove( index );
            }
            else                                // ran out of quotes
                label.setText( "I have nothing more to say." );
        }
    }
}
```

12.5   Differences Between Arrays and ArrayList

What are the differences between arrays and ArrayList? Remember that an ArrayList is implemented using arrays; the difference is that the ArrayList provides us with a bunch of methods that implement features that would otherwise be a lot of code for us to write if we were using an array. In general, if we are using a list of a fixed size we would want to use an array for efficiency. If our list is going to change a lot—especially through inserting and deleting elements—it would make our life much easier if we chose to implement with an ArrayList. **TABLE 12-1** shows some of the differences between arrays and ArrayList.

TABLE 12-1   Comparisons Between Arrays and `ArrayLists`

Characteristic	Arrays	ArrayList
Size	Static	Dynamic
Method to access size	`.length`	`.size( )`
Get/remove elements	`arrayname[i]`	Cast result from `.get(i)` or `.remove(i)`
Data type	Objects and primitives	Objects only
Insert/remove element	You program it	Method call
Speed	Faster	Slower
Implementation		Using arrays

case study

One of the best situations for implementing arrays is when we have many buttons in our applet. Usually there are a lot of method calls that we need on each button, so setting up an array can make it a lot easier to implement. The following example is based on a ski wax DVD tutorial website. First we need to think through the design. A full image is provided for the backdrop (**FIGURE 12-1**), which we can make a background image by using the `ImgPanel` we worked with earlier in the chapter on classes. Then we need to display the buttons in the top-right corner, in a `JPanel` by using `GridLayout` inside the `ImgPanel` in `BorderLayout.NORTH`. For the text, we can display that in the

FIGURE 12-1   Image backdrop for tuning website. Courtesy of Luke Scanlon, 5311 Studios.

case study, cont.

BorderLayout.WEST region. If we set the preferred size of our ImgPanel, we will not need to put anything inside BorderLayout.CENTER.

Example 12-10 is the code for this case study.

JPanel GridLayout with 3 rows and 1 column

JLabel in BorderLayout.WEST with EmptyBorder around it

Courtesy of Luke Scanlon, 5311 Studios.

EXAMPLE 12-10

```java
import java.awt.*;
import javax.swing.*;
import java.awt.event.*;
import javax.swing.border.*;
public class Tuning2 extends JApplet implements ActionListener
{
    Image background;
    ImgPanel mainPanel;
    JButton[ ] buttons;
    Color redColor = new Color( 189, 33, 38 );
    JLabel theText;
    JPanel menu, menuNorthPanel;
    String [ ] texts =
    {
        "<HTML><B><U>Chapters</U></B><BR><BR>Chapter 1: Equipment"
            + "<BR><BR>Chapter 2: Base Prep"
            + "<BR><BR>Chapter 3: Edge Sharpening"
            + "<BR><BR>Chapter 4: Waxing"
            + "<BR><BR>Chapter 5: Brushing and Polishing"
            + "<BR><BR>Chapter 6: Extras",
        "<HTML><B><U>Guarantee</U></B><BR><BR>"
```

```
              + "If you are not completely satisfied that this DVD"
              + "<BR>tutorial that explains how to properly tune your gear,"
              + "<BR>simply return it and we will refund 100% of the"
              + "<BR>purchase price, and we can still be friends.  The"
              + "<BR>information contained in this material has been"
              + "<BR>compiled from 25 years of professional tuning"
              + "<BR>experience.  Sharp edges and fast wax cocktails"
              + "<BR>have allowed us to outrun the masses for years,"
              + "<BR>and we're certain you will be able to do the same",
      "<HTML><B><U>Contact Us</U></B><BR><BR>http://www.tuning101dvd.com"
              + "<BR><BR>If you have any questions, <BR>feel free to contact us at:"
              + "<BR><BR>info@tuning101dvd.com"
   };
   public void init( )
   {
      doBackground( );
      doMenu( );
      doText( );
   }
   public void doBackground( )
   {
      background = getImage( getCodeBase( ), "tuning101website.jpg" );
      mainPanel = new ImgPanel( background );
      mainPanel.setLayout( new BorderLayout( ) );
      mainPanel.setPreferredSize( new Dimension( 800, 600 ) );
      setLayout( new BorderLayout( ) );
      add( mainPanel, BorderLayout.CENTER );
   }
   public void doMenu( )
   {
      menu = new JPanel( new GridLayout( 3, 1, 50, 10 ) );
      buttons = new JButton[3];
      buttons[0] = new JButton( "Chapters" );
      buttons[1] = new JButton( "Guarantee" );
      buttons[2] = new JButton( "Contact Us" );
      for ( int i=0; i<buttons.length; i++ )
      {  buttons[i].addActionListener( this );
         buttons[i].setFocusable( false );
         buttons[i].setForeground( redColor );
         menu.add( buttons[i] );
      }
      menuNorthPanel = new JPanel( new FlowLayout( FlowLayout.RIGHT ) );
      menuNorthPanel.add( menu );
      menu.setOpaque( false );
      menuNorthPanel.setOpaque( false );
      mainPanel.add( menuNorthPanel, BorderLayout.NORTH );
   }
```

(continues)

case study, cont.

Example 12-10 (continued)

```
public void doText( )
{
    theText = new JLabel( texts[0] );      // display chapters when starts
    theText.setFont( new Font( "Serif", Font.PLAIN, 14 ) );
    theText.setForeground( redColor );
    Border margins = BorderFactory.createEmptyBorder( 0, 50, 0, 0 );
    theText.setBorder( margins );
    mainPanel.add( theText, BorderLayout.WEST );
}
public void actionPerformed( ActionEvent ae )
{
    Object src = ae.getSource( );
    if ( src == buttons[0] )
      theText.setText( texts[0] );
    else if ( src == buttons[1] )
      theText.setText( texts[1] );
    else if ( src == buttons[2] )
      theText.setText( texts[2] );
}
}
```

Troubleshooting

Common errors:

My code will not compile.	When initializing an array, you need to specify the maximum size inside square brackets.
	When you are referencing a cell in an array, the data type of the element in the array is the base data type of the array (e.g., a cell in an integer array is an integer).
	2-D arrays can reference either the 1-D row array (single brackets) or single cell in the array (accessed by specifying the row and then the column). Note how you are referencing the data.
	The length of the array is accessed by referencing .length on the array variable, not .length( ) like we do with Strings.
I get an "array out of bounds" exception error.	Remember that the indices start counting at zero.
	Check all references to the array (including loops) to ensure that you are not trying to access an element of the array past the last element or an index that is negative.
	In a 2-D array, we reference the row in the first set of square brackets and the column in the second set. Make sure that you do not have this reversed.
	There is no way to directly access a column in the array. Instead, you will need to loop through the array for each row to access each element in a column.

SUMMARY

- An array is a data structure than can hold a list of items.
- All elements in an array must be of the same data type.
- Indices are used to reference each item in an array. Indices start at zero.
- Arrays are declared with the data type of the elements to be stored in the array and square brackets.
- When initializing an array, the maximum size must be specified.
- The .length on an array gives the size of the array.
- The last element in an array can be accessed at index array.length − 1.
- An initializer list is when the array is declared and initialized in one step, specifying each element within braces.
- 2-D arrays contain rows and columns of data.
- JTable is made up of a 1-D array for the column headings and a 2-D array for the cells in the table.
- JTables must be stored in a JScrollPane and the method setPreferredScrollableViewportSize called to display correctly.
- The JTable can be customized heavily, though some features become complex to implement.
- The ArrayList is also a data structure to maintain a list of items, but the size is dynamic.
- Stepping through an array or ArrayList is usually done using a for loop.

EXERCISES

1. The indices of an array always start with what value?
2. Which of the following are legal? Circle all that apply.
   a. int vals[ ] = (4, 2, 1);
   b. char vals[ ] = new char[3];
   c. JButton controls[ ] = { "Up", "Down", "Left", "Right" };
3. Which loop should you use to walk through an array?
4. True or false? You can have an array of primitive values.
5. What is the index of the last element in any array? For example, an array named values.
6. In the Slideshow example in the lecture notes, how does the program know when it is at the end of the list of photos? (Example 12-2)
7. True or false? The column headings for a JTable are stored in a String variable.
8. True or false? Column headings in a JTable are in a 2-D array.

Answer questions 9–13 based on the following code:

```
String[ ] skiing = { "Beaver Creek",
        "Breckenridge", "Copper", "Jackson Hole", "Vail" };
```

9. What is the index of `Vail` in the array?

10. Write an expression that refers to the string `Copper` within the array.

11. What is the value of the expression `skiing.length`?

12. What is the index of the last item in the array?

13. What is the value of the expression `skiing[3]`?

14. Which loop should you use to access each item in an array?

15. In the Slideshow example presented, remove the call to the `repaint` method. What happens?

16. In the Slideshow example presented, add comments explaining how the `setupIcon` method works.

17. Change the Slideshow example presented such that the buttons are never disabled. Instead, once the user selects the "next" button and the slideshow is at the end of the list of images, have it start over with the first image.

18. Change the Slideshow example presented to store an array of `ImageIcon` objects with the appropriate `Images` instead of an array of `Image` objects.

19. True or false? You can store integers and booleans directly into cells of a `JTable`.

20. How would you create an array of three buttons containing the numbers 1–3?

21. How would you create a new `JTable` with your column headings in the variable named `colHeadings` and your data in a variable named `data`?

22. Why is it preferred to use an array rather than an `ArrayList` for a slideshow?

23. Would you use an array or `ArrayList` for a program that maintains an inventory of your mp3 files?

24. Write a method called `find` that takes an `ArrayList` of `Strings` and a `String` keyword and returns the index into the `ArrayList` where the keyword appears in the `ArrayList`.

25. Write a method called `sort` that takes an `int` array and returns a new array with the list in sorted order.

26. Write a method named `getMaximum` that takes an `int` array and returns the maximum value in the array.

27. Write a method named `getMaximum` that takes an `ArrayList` containing `Integer` objects and returns the maximum value in the list.

28. Write a method named `getAvgLength` that takes an array of `Strings` as a parameter and returns the average length of all the `Strings`.

29. Write a method named getAverage that takes an array of ints as a parameter and returns the average of all the numbers.

30. Write a method that takes an int array and returns a new array with the values in reverse order.

31. Write a method that takes an array of ints as a parameter and prints out each value on the same line with each value separated with a comma (e.g., 10, 4, 9, 5, 1).

32. Write a method that takes an int array and reverses the elements in this array. This method should not return anything.

33. Write a method that takes an ArrayList of Strings and returns a new ArrayList with the values in reverse order.

34. Write a method that takes an ArrayList of Integer objects and reverses the elements in this ArrayList. This method should not return anything.

35. Modify the slide puzzle to have a button that, when clicked, will solve the puzzle. This can either just display the correct ordering (easy problem) or go through the motions following the rules of clicking on adjacent tiles to the blank spot (difficult problem).

36. Convert the following code from using an ArrayList to an array:

```java
public class ArrayListEx1
{   ArrayList<String> names = new ArrayList<String>( );
    public void addName( String n )  { names.add( n ); }
    public String getName( int index )
    {
        return names.get( index );
    }
    public void printList( )
    {
        for( int i=0;  i<names.size( ); i++ )
        {
            if( i != 0 )
                System.out.print( ", " );
            System.out.print(  names.get( i ) );
        }
    }
}
```

Suggestion: Write a class named *Toolbox* that contains all your methods, so if you ever need to use one of these methods, you can simply refer to this class that you have written.

Threads and Timer

13

13.1   Threads

Threads allow multiprocessing—when two or more things can be occurring at the same time—to occur. When we run a program, a single thread automatically starts to run the program. To run two or more things simultaneously, we need to create a second (or more) thread(s). For example, if we want to perform a slideshow while the user is typing inside a JTextArea, we need to use a separate thread for the slideshow. If we did not use a second thread, the applet would hang while we ran through the code for the slideshow.

There are four steps to get Threads to work:

1. The class needs to implement the Runnable interface.

   ```
   implements Runnable
   ```

2. Create a Thread.

   ```
   Thread runner;
   runner = new Thread( this );
   ```

3. Start the Thread.

   ```
   runner.start( );
   ```

4. Create a method named run.

   ```
   public void run( )
   {
   }
   ```

When we use threads we put the code inside the run method. Usually we want the code to loop. We can set up the loop as an infinite loop.

```
public void run( )
{
      while( true )
      {
            // code
      }
}
```

We can also use the method sleep in the Thread class to simulate a delay:

```
Thread.sleep( delayInMilliseconds );
```

To use this method, we need to put it within a try ... catch block to catch any exceptions (errors) that may occur (usually put the try ... catch around the while(true) loop):

```
try {
      Thread.sleep( delayInMilliseconds );
} catch( Exception exc )    {  }
```

TABLE 13-1 Applet Methods and When They Are Executed

Method Header	Description
`public void init( )`	Initialize our applet; called only once
`public void start( )`	Starts our applet running; start up necessary threads
`public void stop( )`	Applet is no longer being displayed; stop our threads from running

(We can also use a Timer—see next section).

When working with threads we also need to handle the different states that the applet may be in. Because applets are intended to be run embedded within a web page, the user may leave our applet to go to another web page. It is our responsibility to ensure that our applet stops using resources that we reserved for our applet to run. We also need to ensure that our applet will display correctly again if the user were to return to our applet page. To keep track of all these different states of our applet, Java applets provide specific methods for each situation as shown in **TABLE 13-1**. When we first run our applet, we need to initialize it by calling the `init` method. The `init` method is executed only once—when the applet first loads. Then the `start` method is called. This is where we should start our threads. The `start` method is called each time that our applet is to run. We also need to implement a `stop` method that is called when the user leaves our applet page. We need to stop our threads from running inside this `stop` method.

An outline sketch of a program using Threads is listed in Example 13-1.

EXAMPLE 13-1

```
import java.awt.*;
import javax.swing.*;
public class className extends JApplet implements Runnable
{
    Thread thread;
    public void init( )
    {
        // put code here
    }
    public void start( )
    {
        thread = new Thread( this );
        thread.start( );
    }
```

(continues)

Example 13-1 (continued)

```
    public void run( )
    {
        while( true )
        {
            // put code here
            try {
                Thread.sleep( 500 );
            }
        catch( Exception e ) { }
        }
    }
    public void stop( )
    {
        if ( thread != null )
        {
            thread.stop( );
            thread = null;
        }
    }
}
```

First verify that the variable thread is not null to prevent a null exception error.

If you are using more than one Thread, there are possibilities of synchronization issues if two or more Threads are trying to access the same component. There are ways of synchronizing methods to handle these situations, but these are beyond the scope of this book.

◼ 13.1.1 Slideshow

We will look at two examples of a slideshow that automatically displays the next image. Example 13-2 adds the slideshow code within an applet with other components as well. Example 13-3 shows how we can separate the slideshow into a separate class and reference it within our applet class (e.g., extend JPanel class).

EXAMPLE 13-2

```java
import java.awt.*;
import javax.swing.*;
public class SlideShow extends JApplet implements Runnable
{
    int SPEED = 1000;        // how fast to rotate through images
    Image[ ] photos;         // array of all your images
    ImageIcon icon;          // images need to be in an ImageIcon
    JLabel imgLabel;         // and be stored into a JLabel
    int currentIndex = 0;    // which image index is currently displayed
    Thread  runner;
    public void init( )
    {
        photos = new Image[4];        // load the images into memory
        photos[0] = getImage( getCodeBase( ), "Australia.jpg" );
        photos[1] = getImage( getCodeBase( ), "Budapest.jpg" );
        photos[2] = getImage( getCodeBase( ), "Galapagos.jpg" );
        photos[3] = getImage( getCodeBase( ), "Nepal.jpg" );
        icon = new ImageIcon( );
        imgLabel = new JLabel( );
        imgLabel.setHorizontalAlignment( JLabel.CENTER );
        setupIcon( 0 );       // initialize setup to display first image (index 0)
        add( imgLabel );      // add label to applet
    }
    public void start( )
    {
        runner = new Thread( this );             // start a thread to time it
        runner.start( );
    }
    public void setupIcon( int index )           // changes the image in the label
    {
        currentIndex = index;
        icon.setImage( photos[index] );
        imgLabel.setIcon( icon );
        validate( );
    }
    public void run( )
    {
        try {
            while( true ) {
            if( currentIndex == photos.length-1 )  // if at the last one,
                setupIcon( 0 );                     // start over with index 0
            else
                setupIcon( currentIndex+1 );        // else increment index
                repaint( );                         // Show the change.
                Thread.sleep( SPEED );
            }
        } catch( InterruptedException ie ) { }
    }
}
```

We need our code in the run method inside a `try ... catch` block to handle errors.

The `Thread.sleep` waits for *x* milliseconds.

Another way to work with a slideshow is to put the code for the slideshow in a separate class and then add this class to the applet. Doing so makes the code more manageable, with everything related to the slideshow in its own separate file, and simplifies the code required inside the applet.

EXAMPLE 13-3

```java
import java.awt.*;
import javax.swing.*;
public class SlidesApplet
            extends JApplet
{
    Slides  myslideshow;
    public void init( )
    {
        myslideshow = new Slides( );
        myslideshow.init( this );
        setLayout( new FlowLayout( ) );
        add( myslideshow );
    }
}
```

```java
import java.awt.*;
import java.awt.event.*;
import javax.swing.*;
public class Slides extends JPanel implements Runnable
{
    int SPEED = 1000; // how fast to rotate through images
    Image[ ] photos;  // array of all your images
    ImageIcon icon;   // images need to be in ImageIcon
    JLabel imgLabel;  // and be stored into a JLabel
    Thread runner;
    int currentIndex = 0;  // current image index displayed

    public void init( JApplet app )
    {
        photos = new Image[4];        // load the images into memory
        photos[0] = app.getImage( app.getCodeBase( ), "Australia.jpg" );
        photos[1] = app.getImage( app.getCodeBase( ), "Budapest.jpg" );
        photos[2] = app.getImage( app.getCodeBase( ), "Galapagos.jpg" );
        photos[3] = app.getImage( app.getCodeBase( ), "Nepal.jpg" );
        icon = new ImageIcon( );
        imgLabel = new JLabel( );
        imgLabel.setHorizontalAlignment( JLabel.CENTER );
        setupIcon( 0 );           // initialize to display first image (index 0)
```

```
        add( imgLabel );        // add label to applet
        runner = new Thread( this ); // start a thread to time it
        runner.start( );
    }
    /** change the image in the label     */
    public void setupIcon( int index )
    {
        currentIndex = index;
        icon.setImage( photos[index] );
        imgLabel.setIcon( icon );
        validate( );
    }
    public void run( )     // time the slideshow
    {
      try {
        while(true) {
            if( currentIndex == photos.length-1 )    // if  at  the last one,
                setupIcon( 0 );              // start over with index 0
            else                             // otherwise just increment the index
                setupIcon( currentIndex+1 );
            repaint( );                      // Show the change.
            Thread.sleep( SPEED );
        }
      } catch( InterruptedException ie ) { }
    }
}
```

13.1.2 Animation

This next example shows how we can animate our own drawings. We will put our drawing code in a separate class that extends JPanel that implements threads and then we will add it to our applet. To prevent it from redrawing the whole thing each time, we will draw only over a small area where the eye is. To do this, when we wink, we first fill in the eye with yellow and then draw the wink. Example 13-4 contains the code that extends JPanel, and Example 13-5 is the applet.

EXAMPLE 13-4

```
import java.awt.*;
import javax.swing.*;
public class Smiley extends JPanel implements Runnable
{
    int size = 50;
    int leftEyeX = ( int )( size*0.25) ;
    int eyeWidth = size/7;
```

(continues)

Example 13-4 (continued)

```
int eyeHeight = size/6;
int rtEyeX = ( int )( size*0.75-eyeWidth );
int eyeY = ( int )( size/3 );
boolean winking = false;
public void run( )
{
  while( true )
  {
    repaint( );
    try {
        Thread.sleep( 500 );              Sleep for 500 milliseconds and
    }                                     then redraw.
    catch( Exception e ) { }
  }
}
public void paintComponent ( Graphics g )
{
    super.paintComponent( g );            First color over the black eye in
    g.setColor( Color.YELLOW );           yellow, and then draw the wink.
    g.fillOval( 0, 0, size, size );
    g.setColor( Color.BLACK );
    g.drawOval( 0, 0, size, size );   // outline
    g.fillOval( leftEyeX, eyeY, eyeWidth, eyeHeight ); // left eye
    if( winking )
    {                                     Decide what to draw—either a
                                          wink or a full eye.
            g.setColor( Color.YELLOW );
            g.fillOval( rtEyeX, eyeY, eyeWidth, eyeHeight );   // right eye
            g.setColor( Color.BLACK );
            g.fillRect ( rtEyeX, eyeY+eyeHeight, eyeWidth, 2 );
            winking = false;
    }
    else
    {
            g.fillOval( rtEyeX, eyeY, eyeWidth, eyeHeight );   // right eye
            winking = true;
    }
    g.setColor( Color.RED );
    g.fillArc( 10, eyeY+eyeHeight, size-20, 20, 180, 180 );
  }
}
```

EXAMPLE 13-5

```
import java.awt.*;
import javax.swing.*;
public class Wink extends JApplet
{
    Smiley sm;
    Thread t;
    JLabel title, leftside;
    public void init( )
    {
        setLayout( new FlowLayout( ) );
        title = new JLabel( "<HTML><FONT SIZE=+2 COLOR=BLUE>Gooood Mornin'!" );
        leftside = new JLabel( "<HTML>This goes <BR>to show<BR>some"
                    + "fun<BR>animation!" );
        add( title );
        add( leftside );
        sm = new Smiley( );     // work the smile
        sm.setPreferredSize( new Dimension( 55, 55 ) );
        add( sm );
    }
    public void start( )
    {
        t = new Thread( sm );
        t.start( );
    }
}
```

We do not need to do any thread code in the Wink applet class. All the thread work is done in the Smile class. This makes it easy for us to add two smiley faces on our applet, both animated.

13.2 Timers

Timers are useful for repeating steps at particular intervals. Timers can be used to create progress bars, custom clocks, and timed animation, similar to using Threads. Timers are based on event processing, so it is important that the code to be run from a Timer event can be executed quickly to enable the system to handle the next event. Threads do not have this limitation and therefore are ideal for more time-intensive code processing.

We create a Timer object by specifying the delay count as an integer in milliseconds and the listener for the ActionEvent:

```
Timer timer;
timer = new Timer( delay, this );
```

Just as for threads, we then need to start the timer:

```
timer.start( );
```

After the delay in milliseconds, the actionPerformed method is called. Therefore, just like when we listen for events on buttons, we need to implement the Action-Listener.

There are six steps to get Timers to work:

1. Import the package to handle ActionEvent events.

```
import java.awt.event.*;
```

2. Specify that we are listening for events.

```
public class xyz extends JApplet implements ActionListener
```

3. Add an actionListener method.

```
public void actionPerformed( ActionEvent ae )
```

4. Create a Timer object.

```
Timer timer;
timer = new Timer( delay, this );
```

5. Start the timer.

```
timer.start( );
```

6. (Optional) Stop the timer. If you want the timer to stop, call the stop method. For example, you may want to stop the Timer in the actionPerformed method after the first time it expires. If you do not ever call stop on the Timer, it will continue to trigger an ActionEvent after every time interval you specified for the delay.

```
timer.stop( );
```

If we are listening for ActionEvents from multiple objects (e.g., buttons), recall that we can use the instanceof operator to differentiate between them:

```
Object src = actionEvent.getSource( );
if ( src instanceof Timer )
    ...
else if ( src instanceof JButton )
    ...
```

We can also check to see if the source that caused the event is a specific timer by checking for equality with ==. For example, if we have two Timer object variables named timer1 and timer2:

```
Object src = actionEvent.getSource( );
if ( src == timer1 )
    ...
else if ( src == timer2 )
    ...
```

We may have other code to handle buttons in the same `actionPerformed` method. This approach works by setting up an `if-else` structure. Either use the `instan-ceof` operator to differentiate between Timer and JButton or JList events, or check for the source of the event matching to one of your variables. For example, the `actionPerformed` method may have the following:

```java
public void actionPerformed( ActionEvent ae )
{
    Object src = ae.getSource( );
    if ( src == timer )
        myLabel.setText( "Time out!" );
    else if ( src == button1 )
        myLabel.setText( "Submitting your results" );
    else if ( src == buttonStopTimer )
        timer.stop( );
}
```

An example of using a Timer is to perform a countdown. In Example 13-6, every 800 milliseconds the JLabel is updated with the next lower number. Once the countdown reaches zero, the label displays "Blastoff!" and the Timer is turned off.

EXAMPLE 13-6

```java
import java.awt.*;
import javax.swing.*;
import java.awt.event.*;
public class TimedClock extends JApplet
        implements ActionListener
{
    JLabel countdown;
    int count = 10;
    Timer timer;
    int DELAY = 800;    // delay in milliseconds
    public void init( )
    {
        setLayout( new FlowLayout( ) );
        countdown = new JLabel( String.valueOf( count ) );
        countdown.setFont( new Font( "Serif", Font.BOLD, 46 ) );
        add( countdown );
        timer = new Timer( DELAY, this );
        timer.start( );
    }
    public void actionPerformed( ActionEvent ae )
    {
        Object src = ae.getSource( );
```

(continues)

Example 13-6 (continued)

```
        if( src == timer  && count > 0 )
        {
                count = count - 1;
                countdown.setText( String.valueOf( count ) );
        }
        if( count == 0 )
        {
                countdown.setText( "Blastoff!" );
                timer.stop( );
        }
    }
}
```

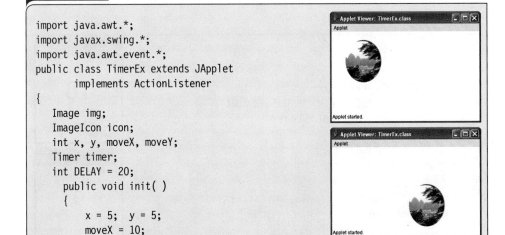

Example 13-7 displays an image traveling around the applet, bouncing off the borders, using a Timer.

EXAMPLE 13-7

```
import java.awt.*;
import javax.swing.*;
import java.awt.event.*;
public class TimerEx extends JApplet
       implements ActionListener
{
    Image img;
    ImageIcon icon;
    int x, y, moveX, moveY;
    Timer timer;
    int DELAY = 20;
      public void init( )
      {
          x = 5;  y = 5;
          moveX = 10;
          moveY = 5;
          img = getImage( getCodeBase( ), "gocart.png" );
          timer = new Timer( DELAY, this );
          timer.start( );
      }
    public void paint ( Graphics g )
    {   // clearRect clears a small portion of the screen to prevent flicker
        g.clearRect( x, y, img.getWidth( this ), img.getHeight( this ) );
        x = x + moveX;
        y = y + moveY;
        g.drawImage( img, x, y, this );
    }
```

```
public void actionPerformed( ActionEvent ae )
{
    if( x <= 0 || x >= this.getWidth( ) - img.getWidth( this ) )
        moveX = moveX * -1;
    if( y <= 0 || y >= this.getHeight( ) - img.getHeight( this ) )
        moveY = moveY * -1;
    repaint( );      // force a call to the paint method
}
}
```

Troubleshooting

Common errors:

My code will not compile.	The call to `Thread.sleep( ms )` must be within a `try . . . catch` block to catch any errors that may occur.
Thread does not work.	Thread require you to tell it when to begin. Be sure to call the `.start( )` method on your Thread variable.
Thread does not work.	Timers require you to tell them when to begin. Be sure to call the `.start( )` method on your Timer variable.
Timer/Thread goes too fast.	When creating the timer, you specify the delay time in milliseconds. Change the number to a bigger value.
My Thread does not stop when I leave the web page with my applet.	Create a `stop` method that forces the thread to stop.

SUMMARY

- Threads allow us to process multiple things at the same time.
- There are four steps required for adding threads: (1) specify that the class implements the `Runnable` interface, (2) create a Thread, (3) start the thread, and (4) write a method named `run` to handle what happens.
- Use `Thread.sleep` to create a delay in the animation.
- Put the code in the `run` method within a `try ... catch` block to handle errors that may occur.
- Slideshows can be written within the applet class or inside a separate class that extends the `JPanel` class.
- Timers are useful for repeating steps at particular intervals.
- Threads are preferred over Timers when the processing will take a while.
- Timers create `ActionEvents`, so we handle the Timer delay inside the `actionPerformed` method.

EXERCISES

1. Animate one of the drawings from Chapter 2.

2. Animate the Smiley face to speak in synchrony with sound.

3. Change the Wink animation such that it redraws the whole screen instead of just the eye each time. What is the difference in performance when you run the program now?

4. Implement the Wink animation with a Timer instead of Threads. How does this change the performance?

5. True or false? A slideshow of images could be implemented with either a Thread or a Timer.

6. True or false? Using Threads triggers ActionEvent events.

7. True or false? We send the number of seconds for which we wish to delay to the Thread.sleep method.

8. True or false? Threads allow us to process multiple things at the same time.

9. True or false? Timers are useful for repeating steps at particular intervals.

10. What is the interface that we need to implement to get Threads to work?

11. What is the name of the method that you are required to write if you implement the Runnable interface?

12. What type of code block do you need in which to put your call to Thread.sleep?

13. When a program calls Thread.sleep, in what unit of measurement is the delay expressed?

14. What method do you call on your thread to get the thread to begin running?

15. What listener does the Timer use?

16. Write an applet that shows a clock, which updates the second hand every second, the minute hand every minute, and the hour hand every hour. Make use of the Calendar class to figure out the current time.

17. Create an applet that is a stopwatch, where the user can enter an amount of time to wait before the alarm should go off. Either play sound for an alarm bell and/or pop open a JFrame with flashing text.

Inheritance

14

"The artist is the person who invents the means to bridge between biological inheritance and the environments created by technological innovation."
—Marshall McLuhan

14.1 Overview

Each class that we have written so far has made use of a programming concept called *inheritance*. Inheritance is a way to extend the functionality of another class. It enables us to reuse code, which saves us lots of time. We can also modify portions of the functionality for our customization. For example, in Chapter 10 we created separate classes that extend JPanel. We were inheriting all the functionality of a JPanel and adding to that functionality by drawing the backdrop (or adding all the components for the address example). In Examples 10-3 and 10-4, we extended the functionality by adding extra methods. Now we can create classes that extend *any* object. We inherit all the functionality of the original object, and we can modify and add functionality to our customized version of it.

We designate inheritance by using the Java keyword extends in the class header. Java allows only single inheritance, so we can only ever extend one thing. The following are some example class headers using inheritance:

```
public class FancyButton extends JButton
public class AddressFields extends JPanel
```

> Classes that do not explicitly extend anything extend the Object class by default.

```
public class SchoolAddress extends AddressFields
public class HomeAddress extends AddressFields
public class BillingAddress extends AddressFields
```

> All three classes extend our custom class AddressFields from Chapter 10.

```
public class Sprite
public class BadGuy extends Sprite
public class Player extends Sprite
public class Weapon extends Sprite
```

> A Sprite is commonly used in games for any object that may move.

We can show diagrams of the relationships between each of these classes to get a clear picture of how the inheritance is set up. **FIGURE 14-1** shows an inheritance tree

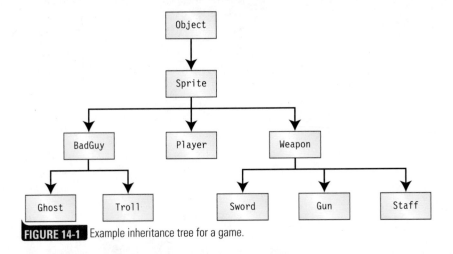

FIGURE 14-1   Example inheritance tree for a game.

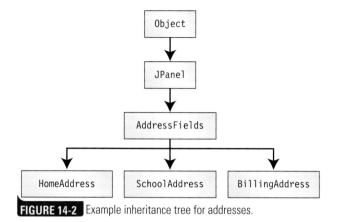

FIGURE 14-2 Example inheritance tree for addresses.

for a game and **FIGURE 14-2** demonstrates the inheritance for AddressFields. All objects inherit from the root-level class Object. The Object class in Java contains some basic methods that we make use of. Classes at the end of the tree are called *leaves* and inherit from all classes above it. For example, the Sword class inherits everything from the Weapon, Sprite, and Object classes.

14.2 AddressFields **Example**

Let us take a look at Figure 14-2 in more detail. We implemented the class AddressFields in Chapter 10 in Example 10-12. AddressFields extends the JPanel class and creates JLabels and JTextFields for the name, street, city, state and ZIP code. We can extend this class to customize it for different types of addresses, such home versus school versus billing. For example, if it is a home address, we may want to add checkboxes to determine whether they can receive post mail, packages, or both at that address. In the SchoolAddress class, we may want to include fields for dates of when that address is valid. For billing, we may want to include their billing phone number. We can update our class diagram and add the method responsibilities of each class. In **FIGURE 14-3** we add the data values that we want to keep track of for each class. Here is a perfect example where we could modify our design to create the titled border inside AddressFields instead of copying the same code in each of the subclasses (this is left as an exercise for you). **FIGURE 14-4** shows the output of the applet class in Example 14-1 and the supporting classes HomeAddress in Example 14-2, SchoolAddress in Example 14-3, and BillingAddress in Example 14-4.

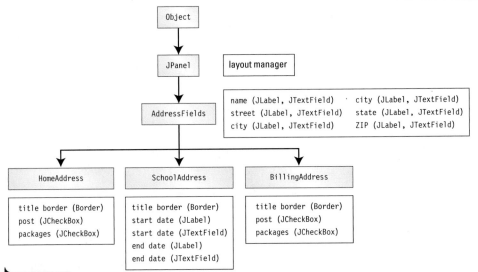

FIGURE 14-3 Data values for each class in inheritance tree.

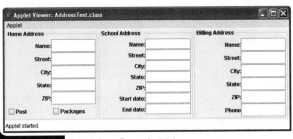

FIGURE 14-4 Output from Example 14-1.

EXAMPLE 14-1

```java
import java.awt.*;
import javax.swing.*;
public class AddressTest extends JApplet
{
    HomeAddress home;
    SchoolAddress school;
    BillingAddress billing;
    public void init( )
    {
        setLayout( new GridLayout( 1, 3 ) );
        home = new HomeAddress( );
        school = new SchoolAddress( );
        billing = new BillingAddress( );
        add( home );
        add( school );
        add( billing );
    }
}
```

EXAMPLE 14-2

```java
import java.awt.*;
import javax.swing.*;
import javax.swing.border.*;
public class HomeAddress extends AddressFields
{
    Border titled;
    JCheckBox post, pkg;
    public HomeAddress( )
    {
        setLayout( new GridLayout( 6, 2 ) );
        init( );
    }
    public void init( )
    {
        titled = new TitledBorder( "Home Address" );
        setBorder( titled );
        setupMailOptions( );
    }
    public void setupMailOptions( )
    {
        post = new JCheckBox( "Post" );
        pkg = new JCheckBox( "Packages" );
        add( post );
        add( pkg );
    }
}
```

EXAMPLE 14-3

```java
import java.awt.*;
import javax.swing.*;
import javax.swing.border.*;
public class SchoolAddress extends AddressFields
{
    Border titled;
    JTextField tf_phone;
    JLabel start, end;
    JTextField tf_start, tf_end;
    public SchoolAddress( )
```

(continues)

Example 14-3 (continued)

```
  {
     setLayout( new GridLayout( 7, 2 ) );
     init( );
  }
  public void init( )
  {
     titled = new TitledBorder( "School Address" );
     setBorder( titled );
     start = new JLabel( "Start date:", JLabel.RIGHT );
     end = new JLabel( "End date:", JLabel.RIGHT );
     tf_start = new JTextField( 20 );
     tf_end = new JTextField( 20 );
     add( start );
     add( tf_start );
     add( end );
     add( tf_end );
  }
}
```

EXAMPLE 14-4

```
import java.awt.*;
import javax.swing.*;
import javax.swing.border.*;
public class BillingAddress extends AddressFields
{
  Border titled;
  JLabel phone;
  JTextField tf_phone;
  public BillingAddress( )
  {
     setLayout( new GridLayout( 6, 2 ) );
     init( );
  }
  public void init( )
  {
     titled = new TitledBorder( "Billing Address" );
     setBorder( titled );
     phone = new JLabel( "Phone", JLabel.RIGHT );
     tf_phone = new JTextField( 20 );
     add( phone );
     add( tf_phone );
  }
}
```

If we add events to our applet class and want to get the street the user entered from each address group, we can do so by referencing the street text field via each address variable. For example:

```
String schoolStreet = school.tf_street.getText( );
String homeStreet = home.tf_street.getText( );
```

14.3 Sprite Examples

Another example that we will look at is the use of a `Sprite` class. `Sprite`s are objects that are displayed that need to maintain information about their location (*x, y* coordinates), size (width and height), image, and visibility. These are commonly used in game programs as well as animation programs. We can then build on our `Sprite` class to customize it specifically for various types of objects, such as bad guys, and the player who might also need to keep track of her health points, current weapon yielded, inventory, etc. Other objects in the game will have their own attributes, such as coins that have an amount of value, food items that may have text associated with them as well as how many health points they add when consumed, weapons that have an amount of damage that they inflict when hitting a player/bad guy, etc. **FIGURE 14-5** shows the class diagram outline, with lots of options for you to expand on.

Let us start with the `Sprite` class. We will keep track of things that all movable objects need in our program, such as the image to display, the (*x, y*) coordinates for the location, and whether the item is currently visible. There are many reasons to make an item invisible; for example, we may want to show the coins only when the

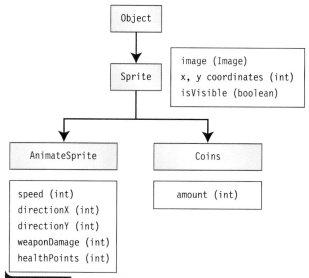

FIGURE 14-5 `Sprite` class inheritance tree with data values.

player passes through a secret door, presses the right button, or kills a particular bad guy who then "drops" the coins; or when the player does "pick up" the coins, then the coins go into the player's inventory and are no longer displayed on the screen.

To make our class easily usable, we will create some methods that we can call from our subclasses. For the image, we will want a method to set the image to use setImage. When we set the image, we will also modify our isVisible variable to be true so that when we go to draw this object, it will draw it. The setLocation method allows us to move our object to a new location and modifies our instance variables for the *x* and *y* coordinates of our object. We also want to be able to see if our object intersects with another object—such as the player who intersects with the coins and hence picks them up, or the monster and player who intersect and a fight breaks out (or the player dies). Two useful methods for programming this are a method to automatically calculate the dimensions of the object by determining the width and height of the image and another method to determine whether this object intersects with another's boundaries. The code for the Sprite class is in Example 14-5.

When we create our Sprite class, it is not necessary for us to have it extend anything. We could have it extend JComponent or perhaps JLabel or JPanel, but we could also handle all the drawing to the screen ourselves. When we create a class that does not extend anything, it automatically extends the Object class, which is the root of all classes in Java. Remember that Java is an object-oriented language, so all data types that are not one of the eight primitive data types all extend the Object class.

EXAMPLE 14-5

```java
import java.awt.*;
import javax.swing.*;
public class Sprite
{
    Image image;
    int x, y;
    boolean isVisible;
    public Sprite( )
    {
        isVisible = false;
        image = null;
    }
    public Sprite( Image i )
    {
        isVisible = true;
        image = i;
        x = 10;
        y = 10;
    }
```

```
      public void setImage( Image img )
      {
          image = img;
          isVisible = true;
      }
      public void setLocation( int _x, int _y )
      {
          x = _x;
          y = _y;
      }
      public Rectangle getDimensions( )
      {
          return new Rectangle( x, y, image.getWidth(null),
                                image.getHeight(null) );
      }
      public boolean intersects( Sprite s )
      {
          return getDimensions( ).intersects( s.getDimensions( ) );
      }
      public void setVisible( boolean vis )
      {
          isVisible = vis;
      }
      public void paintComponent( Graphics g )
      {
          if ( isVisible )
                g.drawImage( image, x, y, null );
      }
}
```

When we create the Coins class (Example 14-6), we can extend the Sprite class from Example 14-5. This means that we inherit all the instance variables and methods from the Sprite class. The only new details that we are going to create for the Coins class are to keep track of the amount the coins are worth. We will add a constructor class to initialize the amount of the coins, as well as methods to get the value and set the value.

EXAMPLE 14-6

```java
import java.awt.*;
import javax.swing.*;
public class Coins extends Sprite
{
    int amount;
    public Coins( int amt )
    {
        amount = amt;
    }
    public int getAmount( )
    {
        return amount;
    }
    public void setAmount ( int amt )
    {
        amount = amt;
    }
}
```

For the player and monsters in our minigame, we will need to keep track of more information than we have listed in the Sprite class. We need to know how fast the player/monster moves during each round as well as keep track of the direction that it is heading. This way we can also create several easy methods for us to call in our main game class to make it move up, down, left, or right. We also need to keep track of the health points, so that when the points get down to zero or below, that entity is "dead." To enable a "fight," we will create a method called hit to inflict damage on the entity.

Because both players and monsters need this information, we will create a class that extends the Sprite class with this information, called AnimateSprite. We could then extend the AnimateSprite to create the Player and Monster classes, but for now we will instantiate both our player and monsters from the AnimateSprite class. Example 14-7 contains the code for the AnimateSprite class.

EXAMPLE 14-7

```java
import java.awt.*;
import javax.swing.*;
public class AnimateSprite extends Sprite
{
    int speed=5;
    int directionX = 1, directionY = 1;
    int healthPoints = 100;
    final boolean DEAD = false;
```

```
    final boolean ALIVE = true;
    public void moveUp( )
    {
        y -= speed;
    }
    public void moveDown( )
    {
        y += speed;
    }
    public void moveLeft( )
    {
        x -= speed;
    }
    public void moveRight( )
    {
        x += speed;
    }
    public int getHealthPoints( )
    {
        return healthPoints;
    }
    public void setHealthPoints( int hp )
    {
        healthPoints = hp;
    }
    public boolean hit( int amt )
    {
        healthPoints -= amt;
        if ( healthPoints < 0 )
                return DEAD;
        else
                return ALIVE;
    }
}
```

Our last class for this base game example is the class that extends JApplet. This is our main driver class that makes use of all the other helper classes that we just created. We will start off with our instance variables that we need:

```
AnimateSprite user;
AnimateSprite monster, troll;
Coins ten, twenty;
Thread thread;
Random random;
```

The `init` method gets called when the applet begins to execute, so we will initialize all our instance variables. Doing so includes loading the images for each of our entities, setting up the event handling for listening for arrow keys, and starting up a thread. We will also make use of the `Random` class from the `java.util` package so that we can randomly move the monsters around.

```
public void init( )
{
    random = new Random( );
    user = new AnimateSprite( );
    user.setImage( getImage( getCodeBase( ), "player.gif" ) );
    monster = new AnimateSprite( );
    monster.setImage( getImage( getCodeBase( ), "monster.gif" ) );
    monster.setLocation( 250, 250 );
    troll = new AnimateSprite( );
    troll.setImage( getImage( getCodeBase( ), "troll.gif" ) );
    troll.setLocation( 350, 350 );
    setupCoins( );
    setFocusable( true );
    addKeyListener( this );
    thread = new Thread( this );
    thread.start( );
}
public void setupCoins( )
{
    ten = new Coins( 10 );
    twenty = new Coins( 20 );
    ten.setLocation( 400, 350 );
    twenty.setLocation( 450, 50 );
    ten.setImage( getImage( getCodeBase( ), "coins.gif" ) );
    twenty.setImage( getImage( getCodeBase( ), "coins.gif" ) );
}
```

Within the `paint` method of our applet class we will draw the scene. For now, we will clear the screen and then redraw it each time by calling the `clearRect` method. This approach does cause some flicker, and we will address how to fix that in the next chapter on game programming. Just like in Chapter 2, the order in which we cause each component to draw will affect the way it looks on the screen when one entity is overlapping another. The last component drawn is the one that displays on top of the others. In the following code, we implement the check for the player colliding with the monster (not the troll or the coins). We can make use of the methods that are anywhere within the hierarchy of inheritance of the class `AnimateSprite`. We also demonstrate how to access a variable directly within the inheritance hierarchy when we specify `monster.x`, `monster.y`, and `monster.weaponDamage`. Example 14-8 has the full code listing for the applet class.

```java
public void paint( Graphics g )
{
    g.clearRect( 0, 0, this.getWidth( ), this.getHeight( ) );
    ten.paintComponent( g );
    twenty.paintComponent( g );
    monster.setLocation( random.nextInt( 10 ) - 5 + monster.x,
                              random.nextInt( 10 - 5 + monster.y ) );
    monster.paintComponent( g );
    user.paintComponent( g );
    if ( user.intersects( monster ) )
    {
        boolean alive = user.hit( monster.weaponDamage );
        if ( ! alive )
        {
            g.setFont( new Font( "Serif", Font.BOLD, 26 ) );
            g.drawString( "YOU LOSE!", 20, 100 );
            thread.interrupt( );   // stop thread; game is over
        }
    }
}
```

EXAMPLE 14-8

```java
import java.awt.*;
import javax.swing.*;
import java.awt.event.*;
import java.util.*;
public class MiniGame extends JApplet implements Runnable, KeyListener
{
    AnimateSprite user;
    AnimateSprite monster, troll;
    Coins ten, twenty;
    Thread thread;
    Random random;
    public void init( )
    {
        random = new Random( );
        user = new AnimateSprite( );
        user.setImage( getImage( getCodeBase( ), "player.gif" ) );
        monster = new AnimateSprite( );
        monster.setImage( getImage( getCodeBase( ), "monster.gif" ) );
        monster.setLocation( 250, 250 );
        troll = new AnimateSprite( );
        troll.setImage( getImage( getCodeBase( ), "troll.gif" ) );
        troll.setLocation( 350, 350 );
        setupCoins( );
        setFocusable(true);
        addKeyListener( this );
```

(continues)

Example 14-8 (continued)

```
      thread = new Thread( this );
      thread.start( );
   }
   public void setupCoins( )
   {
      ten = new Coins( 10 );
      twenty = new Coins( 20 );
      ten.setLocation( 400, 350 );
      twenty.setLocation( 450, 50 );
      ten.setImage( getImage( getCodeBase( ), "coins.gif" ) );
      twenty.setImage( getImage( getCodeBase( ), "coins.gif" ) );
   }
   public void keyPressed( KeyEvent ke )
   {
      int key = ke.getKeyCode( );
      if ( key == KeyEvent.VK_UP )
         user.moveUp( );
      else if ( key == KeyEvent.VK_DOWN )
         user.moveDown( );
      else if ( key == KeyEvent.VK_LEFT )
         user.moveLeft( );
      else if ( key == KeyEvent.VK_RIGHT )
         user.moveRight( );
   }
   public void keyReleased( KeyEvent ke ) { }
   public void keyTyped( KeyEvent ke ) { }
   public void update( Graphics g ) { paint( g ); }
   public void paint( Graphics g )
   {
      g.clearRect( 0, 0, this.getWidth(), this.getHeight( ) );
      ten.paintComponent( g );
      twenty.paintComponent( g );
      monster.setLocation( random.nextInt( 10 ) - 5 + monster.x,
                              random.nextInt( 10 - 5 + monster.y ) );

      monster.paintComponent( g );
      user.paintComponent( g );
      if ( user.intersects( monster ) )
      {
         boolean alive = user.hit( monster.weaponDamage );
         if ( ! alive )
         {
            g.setFont( new Font( "Serif", Font.BOLD, 26 ) );
            g.drawString( "YOU LOSE!", 20, 100 );
            thread.interrupt( );          // stop thread; game is over
         }
      }
   }
}
```

```
   public void run( )
   {
      try
      {
         while( true )
         {
            repaint( );
            Thread.sleep( 10 );
         }
      } catch( Exception e ) { }
   }
}
```

Troubleshooting

Common errors:

My code will not compile.	Be sure to save all the class files before compiling.
	Check to see that the class extends the appropriate class that is desired.
	Making calls to getImage and getCodeBase are available only through the class that extends JApplet. If you are trying to load your images in other classes, you need to pass a variable reference to the JApplet class to access those methods. More information on how to do this is available in the Chapter 12 Slideshow example.
	When calling a method from a separate class, you need to reference the variable to call the method: e.g., variableName.methodName( ).
	Make sure that your methods are all declared with the public visibility modifier. There are other visibility modifiers such as private, protected, and the default that restrict which classes can access those methods (and are beyond the scope of this text).
Nothing displays.	Make sure that you either add the objects to the applet or draw them.

SUMMARY

- Inheritance enables the reuse of code.
- Inheritance is declared on the class header with the Java keyword extends.
- Classes can extend (inherit) directly from only one other class.
- Classes inherit all methods and variables from all classes above it in the hierarchy.
- Classes that do not extend any class automatically extend the Object class.

- Methods and variables written anywhere at or above the inheritance hierarchy of a particular class are "inherited" and can be referenced as if they were declared within the class.

EXERCISES

1. From what class does a class inherit if it does not *extend* anything?

2. True or false? To inherit from more than one class, separate each one with a comma after the keyword extends.

3. True or false? Methods are inherited only from the one class above in the hierarchy.

4. Add to the game applet a way for the player to be able to pick up the coins and add them to his inventory. Make sure that monsters do not pick up the coins.

5. Extend the AnimateSprite class to create a class for a player and a separate class for bad guys. Determine all the data variables that are distinct between the two and implement any methods required. Modify the applet class to make use of your new classes.

6. Create a Weapon class that extends the Sprite class and add it into the game applet. Enable the player and monsters to be able to wield a weapon. Create several *instances* of your Weapon class for different types of weapons that do different amounts of damage.

Game Programming

15

*If life is a game,
why not create your own?*

15.1   Overview

There are many different types of games that we could program, and they all fall into different styles for development. Arcade games, tic-tac-toe, pinball, pong, adventure, and point-and-shoot are various game types that use different programming structures to develop. I will introduce game programming here to give you some of the basics to get you started.

Most games deal with three essential ingredients: a game world, player control, and brains for intelligent behavior. The game world involves the backdrop, borders/walls, objects that may be either consumed or held, and entities that may be either good or bad for the player. Player control is the method of interaction for the player to be involved in the game, which can include keyboard keys, mouse movements, and joystick actions. The last ingredient for a game is the brains—intelligent behavior for entities that the computer must control in the game.

When we develop a game, we should use multiple classes to help simplify development and maintain modularity. Doing so will help us test small portions of code to ensure that they work correctly and will enable us to reuse code in multiple games. For example, if we first write a Breakout game that makes use of a `Ball` object, when we want to develop a Pong game we can reuse our code for the `Ball` class with minimal, if any, changes.

15.1.1 Game World

The game world provides the fundamental view of the game for the player. It is responsible for displaying the world with the walls and boundaries defined. It should also maintain information about the entities and objects in the game, as well as an instance of the player object.

The design of the base world can be done with drawing methods on the applet or working with components and using a `null` layout structure. In the examples provided in this chapter, we will look at building a world based on drawing to the applet. When we draw to the applet, we will need to prevent flicker from occurring, so we will make use of a `BufferedImage` to draw all the items offscreen first before overlaying the current applet screen with the final version of our image.

There are multiple ways to keep track of the entities in the game, as we will discuss during our exploration of creating a dungeon game. Arrays and `ArrayLists` are good data structures for keeping track of items in our game, including monsters, weapons, and coins.

15.1.2 Player Control

We need to handle the users' interaction to control the player in the game. Usually we implement the `KeyListener` to handle different keystrokes that the user types to move the player. The code to maintain information about the player is usually implemented in a separate class, called a `Sprite` (we will see this in the dungeon example). On the basis of the key that is pressed, we need to move the player on the screen.

15.1.3 Brains

Each game needs to define some objective that the player is trying to accomplish to win the game. Part of the brains of a game is coordinating this effort—has the player rescued the princess and escaped to the exit with her safely? Has the player knocked out all blocks in the Breakout game? Some games have monster enemies that can harm the player if the two collide or fight. Monsters that do not move at all are not very interesting to play against, so it is best if we can somehow program each monster to move differently around the game world.

15.1.4 Flicker

Before we begin writing games, we need to learn how to get rid of the flicker problem. When the screen is to be redrawn, it is first cleared before the program attempts to redraw the screen. This clearing and redrawing is usually not fast enough, so our eyes detect what we call a flicker of white as the screen is cleared before it is completely redrawn. The fix to this is to work on an offscreen image where we update the screen as we want it and then draw on top of the current screen instead of erasing it first. Example 15-1 demonstrates this approach by having an offscreen image where the backdrop and player image are drawn before redrawing on the viewing screen occurs. The applet moves the player's image wherever the user's mouse roams.

EXAMPLE 15-1

```
import java.awt.*;
import javax.swing.*;
import java.awt.event.*;
public class BufImages extends JApplet implements MouseMotionListener
{
    Image offscreen;            // offscreen image to prevent flicker
    Graphics offscreenGrp;      // graphics for offscreen image - draw here first
    Image player;               // image for player - moves where mouse is
    int x, y;                   // coordinates for player - where mouse is
    public void init( )
    {   resize( 300, 300 );
        offscreen = createImage( 300, 300 );       // create offscreen image
                            // get graphics for drawing on offscreen image
        offscreenGrp = offscreen.getGraphics( );
        player = getImage( getCodeBase( ), "zil.gif" );
        addMouseMotionListener(this);
    }
```

(continues)

Example 15-1 (continued)

```
public void paint( Graphics g )
{
    // draw to the offscreen image first
    offscreenGrp.setColor( Color.CYAN );
    offscreenGrp.fillRect( 0, 0, 300, 300 );
    offscreenGrp.setColor( Color.GREEN );
    offscreenGrp.fillRect( 0, 290, 300, 10 );
    offscreenGrp.drawImage( player, x, y, this );
    // draw offscreen image to applet
    g.drawImage( offscreen, 0, 0, this );
}
public void mouseMoved( MouseEvent me )
{
    x = me.getX( ) - 50;
    y = me.getY( ) - 50;
    repaint( );
}
public void mouseDragged( MouseEvent me ) { }
}
```

Image courtesy of Luke Scanlon, 5311 Studios.

15.2 Breakout Game

We will start with a simple old game called Breakout (**FIGURE 15-1**). Breakout is a form of the Pong game, where the user has a paddle that can move horizontally across the bottom of the screen. The objective of the game is to knock out all the blocks. Let us build this game incrementally, the way a programmer would approach it.

There are multiple different solutions to this same program, but we will explore one way here. Let us start off by programming the blocks. Our initial program will look similar to what we did in Chapter 2. However, we will need to keep track of each block so that we can remove it when it is hit by the ball. To keep track of each block, we will create a Rectangle object:

```
Rectangle rec = new Rectangle( x, y, width, height );
```

We will need to store them all inside a list. Doing so will make it easy for us to repaint the screen each time by writing a loop through the list and drawing each Rectangle object. Because our list will be dynamic, in that we want it to shrink as we remove Rectangle objects from the list when hit, we should use a data structure called ArrayList instead of choosing an array. Arrays do not allow us to easily remove things from the list; ArrayList makes it easy.

To create an ArrayList object, we declare and instantiate it similar to other objects:

```
ArrayList  blocks;
blocks = new ArrayList( );
```

To populate the list with all our blocks, we will need to write a loop inside a loop. The outer loop should create each of the rows in our game—notice in the top image of **FIGURE 15-1** that we start with three rows of blocks. The inner loop will keep track of our columns—in our game, we have 10 columns across. Because we need to create our Rectangles for each block inside the loop, we can make our loops keep track of the *x* and *y* coordinates of where the next block should begin. To do this, we will need to also figure out what the size of each block should be. That gives us a loop that looks like the following:

```
public void buildBlocks( )
{
    int sizeOfBlock = width / numBlocks;
    int heightOfBlock = 15;
    for( int rows=0; rows<width; rows += sizeOfBlock )
    {
        for( int cols=0; cols<numRows*heightOfBlock; cols += heightOfBlock )
        {
            Rectangle r = new Rectangle( rows, 80+cols, sizeOfBlock-2, heightOfBlock-2 );
            blocks.add( r );
        }
    }
}
```

> The 80 is the number of pixels from the top that we want the first row to be displayed.

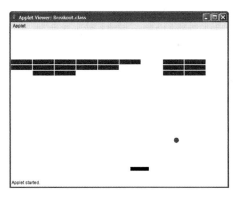
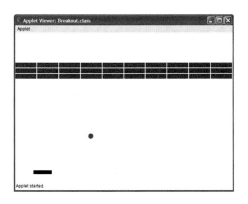
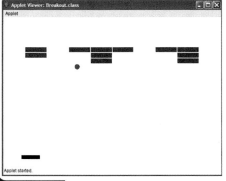
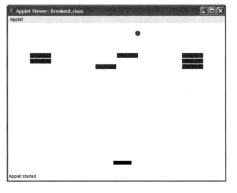

FIGURE 15-1 Example output during Breakout game.

Inside our `paint` method, we can walk through our list of blocks and display each one by calling the `fillRect` method on the `Graphics` object. The code for Part I of our Breakout game appears in Example 15-2.

EXAMPLE 15-2

```java
import java.awt.*;
import javax.swing.*;
import java.util.*;        // for ArrayList
public class BreakoutPart1 extends JApplet
{
    ArrayList blocks;
    int width, height;      // dimensions of applet
    int numBlocks = 10;     // number of blocks horizontally
    int numRows = 3;        // number of rows
    public void init( )
    {
        blocks = new ArrayList( );
        width = getWidth( );
        height = getHeight( );
        buildBlocks( );
    }
    public void buildBlocks( )   // create all the blocks and store in list
    {
        int sizeOfBlock = width / numBlocks;
        int heightOfBlock = 15;
        for ( int rows=0; rows<width; rows += sizeOfBlock )
          for ( int cols=0; cols<numRows*heightOfBlock; cols += heightOfBlock )
          {
            Rectangle r = new Rectangle(
                          rows, 80+cols, sizeOfBlock-2, heightOfBlock-2 );
            blocks.add( r );
          }
    }
    public void paint( Graphics g )
    {
        g.clearRect( 0, 0, width, height );         // clear screen
        g.setColor( Color.RED );
        for (int i=0; i<blocks.size( ); i++ )       // color remaining blocks
        {
            Rectangle r = ( Rectangle )blocks.get( i );
            g.fillRect( r.x, r.y, r.width, r.height );
        }
    }
}
```

The next step is to create a ball and have it move around the screen, bouncing off the walls. When we create a ball, we will need to know the (x, y) coordinates of the ball's location; the size (ball has same size for width and height); the speed in pixels, which is how many pixels the ball moves each time the screen is redrawn; and the width and height of the screen so that we can bounce the ball off the walls of the screen.

To create a bounce off a wall, we will create a method named move that first adjusts the *x* and *y* coordinates of the ball and then checks to see if these coordinates are beyond the area of the screen. If the ball is past the left side of the wall, then the *x* value is less than zero. If it is greater than the applet's width, it is past the right side. Usually in a real Breakout game, once the ball drops below the screen the ball is "out" and either the game ends or a new ball comes into play (depending on the exact rules of this game's variation). We are going to keep the ball in play for now, bouncing off the bottom of the screen as well. You can configure this program differently however you like. When the ball bounces off a wall, we will change the direction of the ball by inversing the direction: direction = (-1) * direction. This way, whenever we move, we will add the speed * direction to the *x* coordinate, which will direct the ball for us. Example 15-3 is our Ball class. We do not need this class to extend anything. We will not add it to the applet; instead, we will make calls from the applet class to the paint method inside the Ball class to paint it on the screen.

EXAMPLE 15-3

```java
import java.awt.*;
public class Ball
{
    int x, y, size, speed;
    int dirX, dirY;
    int appletWdt, appletHgt;
    public Ball( int _x, int _y, int _size, int _speed, int w, int h )
    {
        x = _x;            // (x, y) coordinates of ball
        y = _y;
        size = _size;      // width and height are same size
        speed = _speed;    // speed is number of pixels to move each time
        dirX = 1;          // direction is either +1 to go right or -1 to go left
        dirY = 1;          // direction is either +1 to go down or -1 to go up
        appletWdt = w;     // applet width
        appletHgt = h;     // applet height
    }
    public void paint( Graphics g )        // called from applet
    {
        g.setColor( Color.BLUE );
        g.fillOval( x, y, size, size );
    }
    public void move( )
    {                                  // move ball according to speed and direction
        x = x + speed * dirX;
        y = y + speed * dirY;
```

(continues)

Example 15-3 (continued)

```
        if ( x < 0 )                 // hit left boundary, change direction
            dirX = 1;
        else if ( x > appletWdt )    // hit right boundary, change direction
            dirX = -1;
        if ( y < 0 )                 // hit top boundary, change direction
            dirY = 1;
        else if ( y > appletHgt )    // hit bottom boundary, change direction
            dirY = -1;
    }
}
```

To use this Ball class in our program, we will add some code to create the Ball object and to paint it. To keep the ball moving, we will need a Thread running that continuously moves and repaints the ball. We also need to check to see if the ball collides with one of our Rectangle blocks. Example 15-4 adds the Ball object to our Breakout game.

EXAMPLE 15-4

```
import java.awt.*;
import javax.swing.*;
import java.util.*;
public class BreakoutPart2 extends JApplet  implements Runnable
{
    ArrayList blocks;
    int width, height;  // dimensions of applet
    int numBlocks;      // number of blocks horizontally
    int numRows;        // number of rows - 1 is least difficult; 5 is more
                        //   difficult
    // Part II
    Thread thread;
    Ball ball;
    public void init( )
    {
        numBlocks = 10;
        numRows = 3;
        blocks = new ArrayList( );
        width = getWidth( );
        height = getHeight( );
        buildBlocks( );
        // Part II
        ball = new Ball( 50, 120, 15, 5, width, height );
    }
```

```
public void start( )
{
   thread = new Thread( this );
   thread.start( );
}
public void buildBlocks( )
{
   int sizeOfBlock = width / numBlocks;
   int heightOfBlock = 15;
   for ( int rows=0; rows<width; rows += sizeOfBlock )
     for ( int cols=0; cols<numRows*heightOfBlock; cols += heightOfBlock )
     {
      Rectangle r=new Rectangle( rows, 80+cols, sizeOfBlock-2, heightOfBlock-2 );
        blocks.add( r );
     }
}
public void paint( Graphics g )
{
   g.clearRect( 0, 0, width,height );         // clear screen
   ball.paint( getGraphics( ) );              // paint ball
   g.setColor( Color.RED );
   for (int i=0; i<blocks.size( ); i++ )      // color remaining blocks
   {
      Rectangle r = ( Rectangle )blocks.get( i );
      g.fillRect( r.x, r.y, r.width, r.height );
   }
}
public void run( )
{
   while( true )
   {
      ball.move( );
      checkForCollision( );
      repaint( );
      try {
          Thread.sleep( 15 );
      }catch( Exception ex ) { }
   }
}
public void checkForCollision( )
{
   Rectangle ballR = new Rectangle( ball.x, ball.y, ball.size, ball.size );
   for( int i=0; i<blocks.size( ); i++ )
   {
      Rectangle r = ( Rectangle )blocks.get( i );
      if ( r.intersects( ballR ) )
      {
         blocks.remove( r );
```

(continues)

Example 15-4 (continued)

```
            ball.dirX = -1 * ball.dirX;
            ball.dirY = -1 * ball.dirY;
            return;
        }
     }
   }
}
```

The next step would be to add the user's paddle and allow the user to move left or right based on the arrow keys. This is similar to the code from the example of the character walking around based on KeyEvents from the chapter on events.

One thing you might notice is that there is a lot of flicker occurring when we run our game applet. We can fix this by first drawing to an offscreen BufferedImage and then drawing the BufferedImage to the applet. The only difference is inside the paint method. Start with the paint method as follows,

```
public void paint( Graphics grph )
   {
       BufferedImage buffer = new BufferedImage( width, height,
                                     BufferedImage.TYPE_INT_RGB );
       Graphics g = buffer.getGraphics( );
```

keeping the rest of the code in the paint method the same. Then at the end of the paint method we draw the buffered image on to the applet screen as follows:

```
   grph.drawImage( buffer, 0, 0, this );
```

Example 15-5 is the final version of the Breakout game with the user paddle added and the flicker removed.

EXAMPLE 15-5

```
/* Breakout - Final version  -    add paddle and remove flicker problems  */
import java.awt.*;
import javax.swing.*;
import java.util.*;
import java.awt.event.*;
import java.awt.image.*;
public class Breakout extends JApplet  implements Runnable, KeyListener
{
   ArrayList blocks;
   int width, height;      // dimensions of applet
   int numBlocks;          // number of blocks horizontally
   int numRows;            // number of rows - 1 is least difficult; 5 is more
                           //  difficult
```

```
Rectangle paddle;
int speed;
Thread thread;
Ball ball;
Image buffer;
public void init( )
{
   resize( 600, 400 );
   numBlocks = 10;
   numRows = 3;
   blocks = new ArrayList( );
   width = getWidth( );
   height = getHeight( );
   buildBlocks( );
   paddle = new Rectangle( 50, height-30, 50, 10 );
   addKeyListener( this );
   speed = 10;
   buffer = createImage( width, height );
   ball = new Ball( 50, 120, 15, 5, width, height );
}
public void start( )
{
   if ( thread == null )
      thread = new Thread( this );
   thread.start( );
   setFocusable( true );
}
public void buildBlocks( )
{
   int sizeOfBlock = width / numBlocks;
   int heightOfBlock = 15;
   for( int rows=0; rows<width; rows += sizeOfBlock )
      for( int cols=0; cols<numRows*heightOfBlock; cols += heightOfBlock )
      {
         Rectangle r = new Rectangle( rows, 80+cols, sizeOfBlock-2,
                                      heightOfBlock-2 );
         blocks.add( r );
      }
}
public void paint( Graphics g )
{
   Graphics bg = buffer.getGraphics( );
   bg.setColor( Color.WHITE );
   bg.fillRect( 0, 0, width, height );
   ball.paint( bg );
   bg.setColor( Color.RED );
```

(continues)

Example 15-5 (continued)

```
      for ( int i=0; i<blocks.size( ); i++ )
      {
          Rectangle r = ( Rectangle )blocks.get( i );
          bg.fillRect( r.x, r.y, r.width, r.height );
      }
      bg.setColor( Color.BLACK );
      bg.fillRect( paddle.x, paddle.y, paddle.width, paddle.height );
      g.drawImage( buffer, 0, 0, this );
  }
  public void run( )
  {
    while( true )
    {
        ball.move( );
        checkForCollision( );
        repaint( );
        try {
            Thread.sleep( 15 );
        }catch( Exception ex ) { }
    }
  }
  public void checkForCollision( )
  {
    Rectangle ballR = new Rectangle( ball.x, ball.y, ball.size, ball.size );
    for ( int i=0; i<blocks.size( ); i++ )
    {
      Rectangle r = ( Rectangle )blocks.get( i );
      if ( r.intersects( ballR ) )
      {
          blocks.remove( r );
          ball.dirX = -1 * ball.dirX;
          ball.dirY = -1 * ball.dirY;
          return;
      }
    }
    if ( ballR.intersects( paddle ) )      // check for paddle collision
    {
        ball.dirX = -1 * ball.dirX;
        ball.dirY = -1 * ball.dirY;
    }
  }
  public void keyTyped( KeyEvent ke ) { }
  public void keyReleased( KeyEvent ke ) { }
```

```
public void keyPressed( KeyEvent ke )
{
    int code = ke.getKeyCode( );
    if( code == KeyEvent.VK_LEFT )
        paddle.x -= speed;
    else if( code == KeyEvent.VK_RIGHT )
        paddle.x += speed;
}
}
```

These are the basics of programming games similar to Pong, missile command/ asteroids, etc. A good exercise would be to modify this program to a two-person Pong game.

15.3 Dungeon Games

There are different styles of dungeon games: full-screen view of dungeon (e.g., Pac Man), scrolling to different rooms via top–down view (e.g., Zelda) or via first-person view (e.g., Doom), or a scrolling left–right background (e.g., Super Mario Brothers). Some of the core programming for any style is the same, such as using something called Sprites to maintain information about the player. There are two different approaches to drawing the scene for any game: use painting techniques with a buffered image or use components (classes that extend JComponent to create custom components). We will explore the use of the painting methods and a buffered image.

As we saw during the Breakout game, the BufferedImage is important to prevent flicker in the drawing of the graphics. In our dungeon game we will also first draw the image to a BufferedImage object before drawing on the applet screen.

We are going to create a dungeon game where we can see the full maze from the top. For the first step in developing our game, we will define the walls where the player cannot go as Rectangle objects (like the Breakout game) stored in an ArrayList and check for collisions of the player with each wall every time we move. The code in Example 15-6 is our starting point, where we draw the walls and set up the thread for processing the graphics.

EXAMPLE 15-6

```java
import java.awt.*;
import javax.swing.*;
import java.awt.image.*;
import java.util.*;
public class Game extends JApplet implements Runnable
{
    int width, height;       // dimensions of game
    ArrayList<Rectangle> walls;
        // screenBuf = draw background, then player, and then entities in layers
    Image backgroundBuf, screenBuf;
    Graphics2D background;
    Thread thread;
    public void init( )
    {
        width = this.getWidth( );
        height = this.getHeight( );
        walls = new ArrayList<Rectangle>( );
        buildWalls( );
    }
    public void start( )
    {
        if ( thread == null )
            thread = new Thread( this );
        thread.start( );
    }
    public void stop( )
    {
        if ( thread != null )
            thread.interrupt( );
        thread = null;
    }
    public void buildWalls( )
    {
        // create Rectangle objects and store in ArrayList walls
        int wallThickness = 10;
        walls.add( new Rectangle( 0, 0, width, wallThickness ) );   // top
        walls.add( new Rectangle( 0, 0, wallThickness, height ) );  // left
        walls.add( new Rectangle( width-wallThickness, 0, wallThickness, height ) );
                                                                   // right
        walls.add( new Rectangle( 0, height-wallThickness, width, wallThickness ) );
                                                                   // bottom

        walls.add( new Rectangle( 0, 100, 100, wallThickness ) );   // left
        // bottom wall structure
                                                        // vertical on left
        walls.add( new Rectangle( 50, height-wallThickness-120, wallThickness, 70 ) );
                                                        // horizontal top
```

Applet Viewer: Game0.class
Applet
Applet started.

```
        walls.add( new Rectangle( 50, height-wallThickness-120, width-150,
                            wallThickness ) );      // horizontal bottom
        walls.add( new Rectangle( 50, height-wallThickness-50, width-120,
                            wallThickness ) );
        walls.add( new Rectangle( 200, height-230, wallThickness, 130 ) );// vertical
                                                                    // on right
    }
    public void paintWalls( )
    {
        backgroundBuf = createImage( width, height ); // backdrop and walls
        background = ( Graphics2D )backgroundBuf.getGraphics( );
        background.setColor( Color.black );
        background.fillRect( 0, 0, width, height );
        background.setColor( Color.gray );
        for ( int i=0; i<walls.size( ); i++ )
        {
            Rectangle r = ( Rectangle )walls.get( i );
            background.fillRect ( r.x, r.y, r.width, r.height );
        }
    }
    public void paint( Graphics g )
    {
        g.drawImage( screenBuf, 0, 0, this );
    }
    public void run( )
    {
        paintWalls( );
        screenBuf = createImage( width, height );
        Graphics gapplet = ( Graphics2D )screenBuf.getGraphics( );

        while( true )
        {                           // first draw background on buffer
            gapplet.drawImage( backgroundBuf, 0, 0, this );
                                    // then draw player on buffer
            repaint( );             // draw buffer to applet
            try {
                Thread.sleep( 10 );
            } catch( Exception ex ) { stop( ); }
        }
    }
}
```

Our next step is to add the player. To maintain information about the player, such as the image to display and the location, direction, and speed, we will set up a separate class called Sprite (this generic class is not called "Player" because we can use the same class to create monsters and other entities we want in our game). Key components of Sprite include the image, *x* and *y* coordinates, speed, and direction. Example 15-7 is the code for setting up a Sprite and Example 15-8 incorporates it into our main applet.

EXAMPLE 15-7

```java
import java.awt.*;
import javax.swing.*;
public class Sprite
{
    Image image, up, down, left, right, stand;
    int x, y, lastX, lastY;
    int speed = 5;
    int directionX = 1, directionY = 1;
    public Sprite( Image i )      // all images are the same
    {
        image = i;  stand = i; up = i; down = i; left = i; right = i;
        x = 10;   lastX = 10;
        y=10;    lastY = 10;
    }
    public Sprite( Image i, Image u, Image d, Image l, Image r )
    {
        image = i;  stand = i;  up = u; down = d; left = l; right = r;
        x = 10;   lastX = 10;
        y=10;    lastY = 10;
    }
    public void setLocation( int _x, int _y )
    {
        lastX = x;  lastY = y;
        x = _x;
        y = _y;
    }
    public Rectangle getDimensions( )
    {
        return new Rectangle( x, y, image.getWidth( null ),
                              image.getHeight( null ) );
    }
    public void stopMoving( )
    {
        image = stand;
    }
    public void moveUp( )
    {
        image = up;
        lastX = x;  lastY = y;
        y -= speed;
    }
    public void moveDown( )
    {
        image = down;
        lastX = x;  lastY = y;
        y += speed;
    }
```

Separate image objects allow us to customize the look of the character (player or monster). Use animated GIFs to make it look like it is walking/flying.

```
    public void moveLeft( )
    {
        image = left;
        lastX = x;   lastY = y;
        x -= speed;
    }
    public void moveRight( )
    {
        image = right;
        lastX = x;   lastY = y;
        x += speed;
    }
    public void paintComponent( Graphics g )
    {
        g.drawImage( image, x, y, null );
    }
    public void undoMove( )
    {
        x = lastX;
        y = lastY;
    }
}
```

> Keep track of the last (*x, y*) coordinates when moving in case an undo is necessary because of a collision.

EXAMPLE 15-8

```
import java.awt.*;
import javax.swing.*;
import java.awt.event.*;
import java.awt.image.*;
import java.util.*;
public class Game extends JApplet implements Runnable, KeyListener
{
    int width, height;      // dimensions of game
    ArrayList<Rectangle> walls;
    Image backgroundBuf, screenBuf; // screenBuf = draw background, then player, and
                                    // then entities in layers
    Graphics2D background;
    MediaTracker track;
    Sprite player;
    Thread thread;
    public void init( )
    {
        loadImages( );
        width = this.getWidth( );
        height = this.getHeight( );
```

(continues)

Example 15-8 (continued)

```java
        walls = new ArrayList<Rectangle>( );
        buildWalls( );

        player.setLocation( 50, 50 );

        addKeyListener( this );
    }
    public void start( )
    {
        try {
                track.waitForAll( );
        } catch ( Exception e ) { };
        if ( thread == null )
                    thread = new Thread( this );
        thread.start( );
        setFocusable( true );
    }
    public void loadImages( )
    {
        track = new MediaTracker( this );
        Image img = getImage( getCodeBase( ), "stand_front.gif" );
        Image back = getImage( getCodeBase( ), "walk_back.gif" );
        Image front = getImage( getCodeBase( ), "walk_front.gif" );
        Image right = getImage( getCodeBase( ), "walk_right.gif" );
        Image left = getImage( getCodeBase( ), "walk_left.gif" );

        track.addImage( img, 2 );       track.addImage( back, 6 );
        track.addImage( front, 3 );  track.addImage( left, 4 );
        track.addImage( right, 5 );

        player = new Sprite( img, back, front, left, right );
    }
    public void buildWalls( )
    {
        // create Rectangle objects and store in ArrayList walls
        int wallThickness = 10;
        walls.add( new Rectangle( 0, 0, width, wallThickness ) );       // top
        walls.add( new Rectangle( 0, 0, wallThickness, height ) );      // left
        walls.add( new Rectangle( width-wallThickness, 0, wallThickness, height ) );
                                                                        // right
        walls.add( new Rectangle( 0, height-wallThickness, width, wallThickness ) );
                                                                        // bottom

        walls.add( new Rectangle( 0, 100, 100, wallThickness ) );       // left
                                                            // bottom wall structure
        walls.add( new Rectangle( 50, height-wallThickness-120, wallThickness, 70 ) );
                                                            // vertical on left
        walls.add( new Rectangle( 50, height-wallThickness-120, width-150,
                            wallThickness ) );              // horizontal top
```

```
          walls.add( new Rectangle( 50, height-wallThickness-50, width-120,
                                   wallThickness ) );        // horizontal bottom
          walls.add( new Rectangle( 200, height-230, wallThickness, 130 ) );
                                                             // vertical on right
}

public boolean checkCollisionWalls( Rectangle entityAura )
{
     for ( int i=0; i< walls.size( ); i++ )
     {
               if ( entityAura.intersects( walls.get( i ) ) )
                          return true;
     }
     return false;
}
public void paintWalls( )
{
     backgroundBuf = createImage( width, height );        // backdrop and walls
     background = ( Graphics2D )backgroundBuf.getGraphics( );
     background.setColor( Color.black );
     background.fillRect( 0,0, width, height );
     background.setColor( Color.gray );
     for ( int i=0; i<walls.size( ); i++ )
     {
               Rectangle r = ( Rectangle )walls.get( i );
               background.fillRect( r.x, r.y, r.width, r.height );
     }
}
public void keyReleased( KeyEvent ke )
{
     player.stopMoving( );
}
public void keyPressed( KeyEvent key )
{
     int code = key.getKeyCode( );
     if( code == KeyEvent.VK_UP || code == KeyEvent.VK_8 )
         player.moveUp( );
     else if( code == KeyEvent.VK_RIGHT )
         player.moveRight( );
     else if( code == KeyEvent.VK_LEFT )
         player.moveLeft( );
     else if( code == KeyEvent.VK_DOWN || code == KeyEvent.VK_2 )
         player.moveDown( );
     if ( checkCollisionWalls( player.getDimensions( ) ) )
   player.undoMove( );
}
```

> Walk through `ArrayList` and check for `Rectangle`s intersecting with either the player or other entity's dimensions.

(continues)

Example 15-8 (continued)

```java
    public void keyTyped( KeyEvent ke ) { }
    public void paint( Graphics g )
    {
         g.drawImage( screenBuf, 0, 0, this );
    }
    public void update( Graphics g )
    {
         paint( g );
    }
    public void run( )
    {
         paintWalls( );
         screenBuf = createImage( width, height );
         Graphics gapplet = ( Graphics2D )screenBuf.getGraphics( );
      while( true )
      {
         gapplet.drawImage( backgroundBuf, 0, 0,  this ); // first draw background on
                                                          //  buffer
         player.paintComponent( gapplet );   // then draw player on buffer
         repaint( );        // draw buffer to applet
         try {
            Thread.sleep( 10 );
         } catch( Exception ex ) { stop( ); }
      }
    }
}
```

Now we can have our player move around the dungeon space, with custom graphics based on the direction the player is walking. Now let us add a way for the player to get out of the dungeon. Let us create a fairy flying around the dungeon. When the player runs into the fairy, he gets his wish—to find the door out of the dungeon. We can reuse the Sprite class for the fairy, but we will have to add some "brains" to have the computer automatically move the fairy around. We will also add a check for collisions with the player, and once they collide, we will display an exit for the player. The exit will be a Thing object (Example 15-9) and we will copy the Sprite class and modify it a bit for all objects in our game (e.g., the exit, coins, and food). We could also implement this where the Sprite class extends the Thing class through inheritance.

EXAMPLE 15-9

```java
import java.awt.*;
import javax.swing.*;
public class Thing
{
    Image image;
```

> Use the visible variable to determine whether or not to display the item. For the exit, display only after the player collides with fairy. For coins, do not display once the player picks them up.

```
    int x, y;
    boolean visible = false;
    public Thing( Image i )
    {
        image = i;
        x = 0;
        y = 0;
    }
    public void setLocation( int _x, int _y )
    {
        x = _x;
        y = _y;
    }
    public void setVisible( boolean b )
    {
        visible = b;
    }
    public boolean isVisible( )
    {
        return visible;
    }
    public Rectangle getDimensions( )
    {
        return new Rectangle( x, y, image.getWidth( null ),
                            image.getHeight( null ) );
    }
    public void paintComponent( Graphics g )
    {
        if ( visible )
                g.drawImage( image, x, y, null );
    }
}
```

EXAMPLE 15-10

```
import java.awt.*;
import javax.swing.*;
import java.awt.event.*;
import java.util.*;
public class Game extends JApplet
                implements Runnable, KeyListener
{
    int width, height;          // dimensions of game
    ArrayList<Rectangle> walls;
    Image backgroundBuf, screenBuf;   // screenBuf = draw background, then
                                      //    player, and then entities in layers
```

(continues)

Courtesy of Luke Scanlon, 5311 Studios.

Example 15-10 (continued)

```
MediaTracker track;
Sprite player;
Sprite fairy;
Thing exit;
Thread thread;
Random random;
public void init( )
{
loadImages( );
width = this.getWidth( );
height = this.getHeight( );

walls = new ArrayList<Rectangle>( );
buildWalls( );

    player.setLocation( 50, 50 );
    fairy.setLocation ( width-70, height-70 );
    random = new Random( );
addKeyListener( this );
}
public void start( )
{
    try {
       track.waitForAll( );
    } catch ( Exception e ) { };

if ( thread == null )
    thread = new Thread( this );
thread.start( );
setFocusable( true );
}
public void loadImages( )
{
    track = new MediaTracker( this );
    Image img = getImage( getCodeBase( ), "stand_front.gif" );
    Image back = getImage( getCodeBase( ), "walk_back.gif" );
    Image front = getImage( getCodeBase( ), "walk_front.gif" );
    Image right = getImage( getCodeBase( ), "walk_right.gif" );
    Image left = getImage( getCodeBase( ), "walk_left.gif" );

    track.addImage( img, 2 );     track.addImage( back, 6 );
    track.addImage( front, 3 );  track.addImage( left, 4 );
    track.addImage( right, 5 );

    player = new Sprite( img, back, front, left, right );
    img = getImage( getCodeBase( ), "Fairy.gif" );
    fairy = new Sprite( img );
```

```
      fairy.speed = 2;
      exit = new Thing( getImage( getCodeBase( ), "door.jpg" ) );
}
public void buildWalls( )
{
   // create Polygon or Rectangle objects and store in ArrayList walls
   int wallThickness = 10;
   walls.add( new Rectangle( 0, 0, width, wallThickness ) );  // top
   walls.add( new Rectangle( 0, 0, wallThickness, height ) ); // left
   walls.add( new Rectangle( width-wallThickness, 0, wallThickness,
                             height ) );                       // right
   walls.add( new Rectangle( 0, height-wallThickness, width,
                             wallThickness ) );                // bottom

   walls.add( new Rectangle( 0, 100, 100, wallThickness ) );  // left
                                              // bottom wall structure
   walls.add( new Rectangle( 50, height-wallThickness-120, wallThickness,
                             70 ) );                // vertical on left
   walls.add( new Rectangle( 50, height-wallThickness-120, width-150,
                             wallThickness ) );         // horizontal top
   walls.add( new Rectangle( 50, height-wallThickness-50, width-120,
                             wallThickness ) );      // horizontal bottom
   walls.add( new Rectangle( 200, height-230, wallThickness, 130 ) );
                                               // vertical on rt

   exit.setLocation( 50+wallThickness, height-wallThickness-50-60 );
}
public boolean checkCollisionWalls( Rectangle entityAura )
{
   for ( int i=0; i< walls.size( ); i++ )
   {
        if ( entityAura.intersects( walls.get( i ) ) )
            return true;
   }
   return false;
}
public boolean checkCollisionFairy(  )
{
   return player.getDimensions( ).intersects( fairy.getDimensions( ) );
}
public void paintWalls(  )
{
   backgroundBuf = createImage( width, height );   // backdrop and walls
   background = ( Graphics2D )backgroundBuf.getGraphics( );
   background.setColor( Color.black );
   background.fillRect( 0, 0, width, height );
   background.setColor( Color.gray );
```

(continues)

Example 15-10 (continued)

```
     for ( int i=0; i<walls.size( ); i++ )
     {
          Rectangle r = ( Rectangle )walls.get( i );
          background.fillRect ( r.x, r.y, r.width, r.height );
     }
}
public void keyReleased( KeyEvent ke )
{
   player.stopMoving( );
}
public void keyPressed( KeyEvent key )
{
   int code = key.getKeyCode( );
   if( code == KeyEvent.VK_UP || code == KeyEvent.VK_8 )
        player.moveUp( );
   else if( code == KeyEvent.VK_RIGHT )
        player.moveRight( );
   else if( code == KeyEvent.VK_LEFT )
        player.moveLeft( );
   else if( code == KeyEvent.VK_DOWN || code == KeyEvent.VK_2 )
        player.moveDown( );
   if ( checkCollisionWalls( player.getDimensions( ) ) )
   player.undoMove( );
}
public void keyTyped( KeyEvent ke ) { }
public void paint( Graphics g )
{
   g.drawImage( screenBuf, 0, 0, this );
}
public void update( Graphics g )
{
   paint( g );
}
public void run( )
{
     paintWalls( );
     screenBuf = createImage( width, height );
     Graphics gapplet = (Graphics2D )screenBuf.getGraphics( );

     while( true )
     {
        gapplet.drawImage( backgroundBuf, 0, 0, this );
                                     // first draw background on buffer
        if ( ! exit.isVisible( ) && checkCollisionFairy( ) )
     // exit not yet visible, check if collision with fairy has occurred
           exit.setVisible( true );
        exit.paintComponent( gapplet );
        moveFairy( );
```

> The order in which we draw to the applet is important. Draw the player last to be displayed on top of other things like the exit.

```
        fairy.paintComponent( gapplet ); // draw the fairy
        player.paintComponent( gapplet );        // then draw player on buffer
        if ( exit.isVisible( ) && player.getDimensions( ).intersects(
                                              exit.getDimensions( ) ) )
        {
            gapplet.setFont( new Font( "Serif", Font.BOLD, 42 ) );
            gapplet.setColor( Color.WHITE );
            gapplet.drawString( "YOU WIN!", 60, 120 );
        }
        repaint( );     // draw buffer to applet
        try {
            Thread.sleep( 10 );
            } catch( Exception ex ) { stop( ); }
        }
    }
    public void moveFairy( )
    {
        boolean badLocation = true;     // keep track of whether we found a
                                        //  good location or not
        int numTries = 10;              // give up after a while to prevent
                                        //  infinite loop
        while( badLocation && numTries > 0 )
        {
            int newx = random.nextInt( fairy.speed );
                // generate a new random coordinate according to speed of fairy
            int newy = random.nextInt( fairy.speed );
            if ( random.nextInt( 2 ) == 0 )        // change direction in x
                newx = -1 * newx;
            if ( random.nextInt( 2 ) == 0 )
                newy = -1 * newy;
            fairy.setLocation( fairy.x + newx, fairy.y + newy );
            if ( checkCollisionWalls( fairy.getDimensions( ) ) )
                fairy.undoMove( );
            else
                badLocation = false;
            numTries = numTries -1;
        }
    }
}
```

Now we have gone through a fundamental structure for building a dungeon game. Here are some hints on how to expand on this game structure. The biggest decision is to decide what we want the purpose of the game to be—is it to collect the most coins? Is it to find a princess and rescue her? Is it to collect all the gems/keys/other in each room before exiting? Can bombs be used to break walls to create doorways out?

If we want to maintain a list of items that the user picks up, the ideal data structure is an `ArrayList`. The `ArrayList` allows us to easily add and remove items from the list. If each item is of type `Thing`, we can cast our `ArrayList` to hold `Thing`:

```
ArrayList<Thing> list;
list = new ArrayList<Thing>( );
```

Even though each "thing" is quite different (coins vs gems vs food vs keys), we can still use the same `Thing` class for each. Another option is to extend the `Thing` class for specific types of things, such as food, which is consumable and can be used to maintain health points. This approach is a good option if we create monsters in a game (use `Sprite` class) and when the player collides with a monster, he loses some health points (but does not necessarily die). To extend the `Thing` class, we use the extends keyword:

```
public class Food extends Thing
```

When we extend a class, we inherit all the methods and variables defined in the parent class. We can also *override* some methods from our parent class that we inherited by defining the method header the same as the one in the class that we inherited but by writing a different body inside the method.

To implement weapons in the game, create a new class that extends the `Thing` class. Add methods for how many points each hit takes off on a monster (be sure to modify the `Sprite` class such that each entity loses some health points each time it collides with something). For each `Sprite`, we could structure it such that the entity can pick up only one weapon at a time. Instead of maintaining the weapons in an `ArrayList`, add one instance variable to keep track of the weapon currently in use. We could program it such that when the player picks up a new weapon, he automatically drops his current weapon to replace it.

If we have a nice graphics background image for a dungeon, we could easily implement this in the current program (**FIGURE 15-2**). Instead of drawing the walls in the `ArrayList`, have the background paint the background image. Be sure that the walls in the `ArrayList` match the coordinates of the walls in the image so that the rest of the code works the same. Create an instance variable at the top of the applet class for the image of the backdrop:

```
Image bkdrop;
```

Read the image within the `loadImages` method and add it to the `MediaTracker`. Then modify the `paintWalls` method to draw the image instead of drawing each of the `Rectangle` objects in the `ArrayList`. Replace the method as follows:

```
public void paintWalls( )
{
    backgroundBuf = createImage( width, height );
    background = ( Graphics2D )backgroundBuf.getGraphics( );
    background.drawImage( bkdrop, 0, 0, width, height, this );
}
```

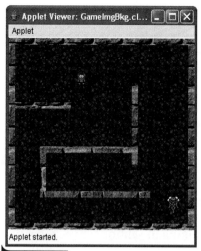

FIGURE 15-2 Dungeon game with images for the background. Courtesy of Luke Scanlon, 5311 Studios.

If we want to create a big dungeon with lots of rooms, we should restructure the code to create a Room class that keeps track of each room. We could write code to automatically create dynamic room structures, but doing so takes some serious thought. We would need to ensure that the walls do not completely block off a section (unless we want that). The Room class should maintain the ArrayList of walls and should contain a method to handle collision checks given a Rectangular dimension.

SUMMARY

- Game programming requires the use of threads to continuously repaint and handle user interaction events such as key presses.
- To prevent flicker, paint the screen to an offscreen BufferImage first before painting on the actual applet.
- Dungeon games can be created as a full maze view from the top, scrolling left to right either top–down view or first-person view.
- Order of painting on the screen is important—the last thing painted will be on top of the rest.
- Games with players and other entities usually maintain information about the entity in a class called Sprite. The Sprite class should maintain all information about the entity—the image, coordinate location, dimensions, speed, direction, objects picked up, weapon, etc.
- ArrayList is a good data structure to maintain a list of items that may be added or removed frequently through the program, such as blocks in a Breakout game and objects picked up in a dungeon game.

- Classes can be extended to add functionality for specific types of objects. Extending a class enables us to reuse the code for multiple other classes that inherit from it.
- `MediaTracker` is useful for ensuring that all images are loaded before starting the applet.
- Start the thread in the `start` method of the applet.
- The `Random` class can be used to randomly select a number. Calls to `nextInt` can take a parameter to specify a restriction that the random number be between 0 and the number −1 (non-inclusive).
- Calls to `getImage` can be done only inside the class that extends `JApplet` (method is defined in the `JApplet` class).
- Check for collisions between two entities/objects by calling the method intersects on two `Rectangle` objects containing the entities'/objects' coordinates and width/height dimensions.
- `Thread.sleep` is used to pause the program for a specified number of milliseconds. Calls to the `sleep` method must be inside a `try ... catch` block to catch interrupts that may occur.
- Writing a method with the same method header as a parent class is called *overriding*.

EXERCISES

1. Modify the Breakout game to use images instead of drawing red blocks.
2. Why should we use an `ArrayList` instead of an array for each block in the Breakout game?
3. Why should we use `BufferedImage` instead of drawing directly onto the applet?
4. How do we check for collisions between two entities/objects?
5. True or false? When we write a `paintComponent` method, we are overriding the method from our parent class.
6. Modify the Breakout game to have two levels—slow and fast. Change the speed of the ball in play accordingly.
7. Modify the dungeon game such that when the game ends, the user cannot move the player anymore and the fairy stops moving. Tell the user that she can press the space bar to start again. If the user presses the space bar, allow the user to restart the game.
8. Add a monster to the dungeon game. Give the monster a different algorithm for moving around the maze. If the player collides with the monster, end the game.
9. Add a second room to the dungeon game, such that when the user goes through the door, the new dungeon room appears.

10. Expand the dungeon game to enable the player to pick up weapons that he finds in the dungeon. Allow only one weapon to be held by the player at a time. When the user presses the letter *a*, have the weapon attack whatever is in front of the player. If the weapon collides with a monster, kill the monster.

11. Modify the dungeon game to display a nice graphical dungeon (create an image of the dungeon in a graphics program). Make sure that the walls match up to the wall coordinates in the image so that the code works as it is.

Internet Applications

16

16.1 Internet

The Internet allows us to share information across the world. We can incorporate our applets on the Internet by embedding them inside a web page. We can also display web pages inside our applet.

16.1.1 Key Terms

When discussing the Internet, we use some key terms. First and foremost, when using a browser to view web pages, we specify the location of the web page by entering the uniform resource locator (URL). The URL begins with the protocol used (http, https, ftp, telnet, etc.) followed by the Internet address and path to the file name.

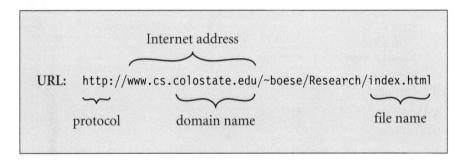

URL   The URL is the full path to some file or directory on the Internet, which includes the protocol, Internet address, and path.

Protocol   *Protocol* is defined as a set of rules. The protocols used in Internet applications determine how to handle the data. The most common protocol is http (hypertext transfer protocol). This protocol defines how to transfer web pages between the server and the computer that wishes to display the page. An extension to http is https, which is a secure version of http and used frequently for secure credit card transactions and account access. Another common protocol is called ftp (file transfer protocol), which is used to copy files from one computer to another computer or network. We will use ftp to upload our files to an Internet host so we can run our applets on the Internet.

Domain Name   The domain name is the base of an Internet address that is unique on the Internet. Anyone can buy a domain name that is not currently registered by someone else.

Internet Address   The Internet address is the full address to a computer or network established on the Internet. The Internet address ends with the domain name but may have other computers or networks listed before the domain name (e.g., the cs network in the preceding URL). The Internet address maps to a four-digit IP address that uniquely identifies itself on the Internet.

16.1.2 Hyperlinks

Web pages are usually coded in HTML code: hypertext markup language. HTML is made up of tags in angle brackets, < >. We discussed some HTML tags in previous chapters to incorporate customizations of our components. HTML web pages may also have an additional tag that is called a *hyperlink*. This is a tag that enables the user to click on either some text or an image and be redirected to a different web page.

16.2 JEditorPane

Do you want to display an HTML page from the Internet inside your applet? Now you can. The JEditorPane is designed specifically for this purpose. Unfortunately, it is a lot more complicated than our other components that we have been working with, but if we follow the guidelines it should not be too difficult. To start off, let us look at a basic example of displaying the website for our coffee club in Example 16-1.

EXAMPLE 16-1

```
import java.io.*;
import java.awt.*;
import javax.swing.*;
import javax.swing.event.*;
public class JEditorPaneEx extends JApplet
        implements HyperlinkListener
{
    JEditorPane pane;
    String sPath;
    JScrollPane scrollPane;
    public void init( )
    {
        setLayout( new BorderLayout( ) );

        sPath = "http://www.coffeeClubOfTheWorld.com/";
        setupURL( sPath );

        pane.setEditable( false );
        pane.addHyperlinkListener( this );
        scrollPane = new JScrollPane(pane);
        add( scrollPane, BorderLayout.CENTER );
    }
```

(continues)

Example 16-1 (continued)

```java
public void setupURL( String url )
{
    if( pane == null )
        pane = new JEditorPane( );
    try {
        pane.setPage( url );
    }
    catch( IOException ioe )
    {
        pane.setText ( "Error accessing web page: " + url );
    }
}
public void hyperlinkUpdate( HyperlinkEvent event )
{
    if( event.getEventType( ) == HyperlinkEvent.EventType.ACTIVATED )
    {
        setupURL( String.valueOf( event.getURL( ) ) );
    }
}
}
```

Now let us take a look at the new code. First off, we are working with a JEditorPane component. In Example 16-1 we declared pane as our JEditorPane variable.

```java
JEditorPane pane;
```

Inside the setupURL( ) method, we want to create a new JEditorPane if one has not been created yet. Therefore, we first check to see if it is null (the first time that we run the applet). If it is null, we can instantiate it:

```java
if( pane == null )
        pane = new JEditorPane( );
```

The next step is to set the web page into the JEditorPane. We do this by calling the method setPage on the JEditorPane variable and send it the String for the URL of the web page. *Note: The URL must begin with http://.*

```java
pane.setPage( url );
```

Notice how this method call is inside a try ... catch block. Try ... catch blocks are Java's way of handling errors that are thrown (yes, Java actually *throws* errors around). When we want to execute some code that potentially might cause a major error, called an *exception*, we need to wrap the code inside a try ... catch block to be able to catch the error, which we call an exception.

In our example, the call to the setPage method might cause a major error, so it is inside the try ... catch block. If an error does occur, such as if the URL is invalid, then the code inside the catch block is executed. In our example, if an error occurred, the text displayed in the JEditorPane would contain "Error accessing web page:" and the URL attempted, instead of the intended web page.

```
try {
      pane.setPage( url );
}
catch( IOException ioe )
{
      pane.setText( "Error accessing web page: " + url );
}
```

The JEditorPane needs to be displayed inside a JScrollPane to display properly. We have worked with JScrollPane before with JList, JTextArea, and JTable. Put the JEditorPane object in the JScrollPane and then add the JScrollPane to the applet.

```
JScrollPane scrollPane = new JScrollPane( pane );
```

The last thing that we need to write is how to handle clicks on links inside the web page that is displayed. To do this, there are four things that we need to do (similar to other events that we have worked with).

1. First, we need to specify that we are listening for these types of events:

   ```
   implements HyperlinkListener
   ```

2. These events are inside the javax.swing.event package, so we need an import statement at the top of our program:

   ```
   import javax.swing.event.*;
   ```

3. Now we need to specify that we want to listen for HyperLinkEvents on our JEditorPane component:

   ```
   pane.addHyperlinkListener( this );
   ```

4. Finally, we need to implement the required method for implementing the HyperlinkListener, which is the hyperlinkUpdate method

   ```
   public void hyperlinkUpdate( HyperlinkEvent event )
   {
         if( event.getEventType( ) ==
             HyperlinkEvent.EventType.ACTIVATED )
             setupURL( String.valueOf( event.getURL( ) ) );
   }
   ```

Inside this hyperlinkUpdate method, we check to see if the user is clicking on a link. If so, we want to call our setupURL method that we previously wrote to change the web page in our JEditorPane, based on the URL clicked—event.getURL( ). Example 16-2 uses buttons to determine which web page is displayed.

The URL must begin with http:// when displaying a web page in a JEditorPane.

EXAMPLE 16-2

```java
import java.io.*;
import java.awt.*;
import java.awt.event.*;
import javax.swing.*;
import javax.swing.event.*;

public class JEditorPaneExBtn extends JApplet
        implements HyperlinkListener, ActionListener
{
    JEditorPane pane;
    JPanel toppane;
    String coffee = "http://www.coffeeClubOfTheWorld.com";
    String art = "http://www.newArtPerspectives.com/";
    String health = "http://completeHealthTherapy.com/";
    JScrollPane scrollPane;
    JButton b_coffee, b_art, b_health;

    public void init( )
    {
        setLayout( new BorderLayout( ) );
        setupButtons( );
        setupURL( health );
        pane.setEditable( false );
        pane.addHyperlinkListener( this );
        scrollPane = new JScrollPane( pane );
        add( scrollPane, BorderLayout.CENTER );
    }
    public void setupButtons( )
    {
        b_coffee = new JButton( "Coffee" );
        b_art = new JButton( "Art" );
        b_health = new JButton( "Health" );
        b_coffee.addActionListener( this );
```

```
            b_art.addActionListener( this );
            b_health.addActionListener( this );
            toppane = new JPanel( new FlowLayout( ) );
            toppane.add( b_coffee );
            toppane.add( b_art );
            toppane.add( b_health );
            add( toppane, BorderLayout.NORTH );
    }
    public void setupURL( String url )
    {
            if( pane == null )
                    pane = new JEditorPane( );
            try {
                    pane.setPage( url );
            }
            catch( IOException ioe )    {
                pane.setText( "Error accessing " + "web page: " + url );
            }
    }
    public void hyperlinkUpdate( HyperlinkEvent event )
    {
        if( event.getEventType( ) == HyperlinkEvent.EventType.ACTIVATED )
                setupURL( String.valueOf( event.getURL( ) ) );
    }
    public void actionPerformed( ActionEvent ae )
    {
        Object src = ae.getSource( );
        if( src == b_coffee )
                setupURL( coffee );
        else if( src == b_art )
                setupURL( art );
        else if( src == b_health )
                setupURL( health );
    }
}
```

Note: Not all web pages display properly using JEditorPane.

16.3 Hosting Your Applet on the Internet

The first step to hosting our applet on the Internet is to get our applet ready without using an IDE such as Eclipse. If you are not using an IDE and have been creating HTML files already to display your applets, then you can skip this step. (This step was introduced in Chapter 1.) There are three steps to get your applets up on the Internet.

Step 1. Set up the HTML file.

- Create a file (in your text editor).
- Enter the following HTML code, changing the XYZ to the name of your class.

```
<HTML>
   <BODY>
      <APPLET CODE=XYZ.class WIDTH=500 HEIGHT=500>
      </APPLET>
</BODY></HTML>
```

Modify the width and height to the size you want in pixels.

This code should be saved in a file named exactly "index.html" in lower-case letters.

> When using images, we must first load the image into the applet by calling `getImage` before putting into an `ImageIcon` object; if you try to use `ImageIcon icon = new ImageIcon( "img.gif" )` it will not work once you put it up on the Internet.

Although Microsoft allows you to mismatch the cases of letters on your file names for images and audio files, this will not work when you load your applet on the Internet. Make sure the cases in your code match exactly to the filename.

Step 2. Find a host.

A host is a web server that stores your files and enables web surfers to find your web page and run your applet. You can use either a free hosting site or pay for hosting.

Hosting for free

There are many places to put up web pages for free. Check with your school to see if it provides space, or search the Internet for options. Some of the free hosting places such as Geocities (Yahoo) will put an advertisement on the upper-right side of your web page. It is a small price that you pay to get a free space on the Internet. Here are a few other options to look at:

- University accounts
- Googlepages.com
- Geocities (http://geocities.yahoo.com; free, but they put ads up on your pages)
- http://www.doteasy.com
- http://members.freewebs.com/index.jsp

Buy a domain name

If you are really gung-ho about your applets and want to own your own domain name, you can purchase a domain from a registrar. When purchasing a domain name, ensure that you have full rights to the domain name and that you are not merely leasing the name (in case your site becomes famous, you would hate to have them turn around and charge you more for leasing your domain name). Many registrars also offer some hosting space for your website if you buy a domain name from them. If you buy a cheap package it may not have enough space if you have a lot of large image files and/or sound files. Some places you can buy a domain name and host your applet:

- Register.com
- Registar.com
- Aplus.net
- GoDaddy.com

Step 3. Upload files.

Upload the `index.html`, all the `.class` files, and all the image and sound files necessary to make your applet work (you do not need to upload the .java files). Optionally, you can create a jar file (Chapter 17), which makes it much easier to upload if you have a lot of files.

Make sure that your code referencing the image and audio file names matches the actual file name (case sensitive—this is important because Windows allows any case, so it may work fine on your own computer and not work at all when you upload it to the Internet).

Note: if your project reads in from a local file (not a URL) or writes to a file not using CGI, you need to remove that code before it will work on the Internet (see Security section of Chapter 17).

16.4 Applet Parameters

We can allow easy customization of our applets by initializing our variables through parameters that we set in our HTML file. We define each parameter in an HTML `param` tag with the `name` attribute identifying each parameter and the `value` tag containing what the value should be. These tags must be defined between the applet open and close tags. Then we change our applet to read these parameter values. An HTML file example is listed next, with three customizations: the color of the background, color of the text, and text for the title displayed at the top of the applet.

```
<HTML>
    <BODY>
        <APPLET CODE=XYZ.class WIDTH=500 HEIGHT=500>
            <PARAM NAME=bkcolor VALUE="0000FF">
            <PARAM NAME=textcolor VALUE="AAAA00">
            <PARAM NAME=title VALUE="Lizzie's Playground">
        </APPLET>
    </BODY></HTML>
```

Use standard HTML hex values for colors: RRGGBB red green blue.

Easiest way to parse colors is to read in hex values (commonly used in HTML).

Use double quotes for text with spaces in it.

Inside our Java program, we can access the parameters we defined in the HTML file by calling the method getParameter and specifying the name of the parameter in parenthesis.

```
getParameter( "bkcolor" )
getParemeter( "title" )
```

The value is returned as a String. Recall that we can convert Strings to numbers by calling either Integer.parseInt(String) or Double.parseDouble(String). Example 16-3 contains the Java code to read in the parameters from the preceding HTML code.

EXAMPLE 16-3

```
import java.awt.*;
import javax.swing.*;
public class AppParams extends JApplet
{
    JPanel bkgrnd;
    JLabel heading;
    public void init( )
    {
        bkgrnd = new JPanel( );
        bkgrnd.setBackground( new Color( Integer.parseInt(
                        getParameter( "bkcolor" ), 16 ) ) );
        heading = new JLabel( getParameter( "title" ) );
        heading.setForeground( new Color( Integer.parseInt(
                        getParameter( "textcolor" ), 16 ) ) );
        bkgrnd.add( heading );
        setLayout( new BorderLayout( ) );
        add( bkgrnd, BorderLayout.CENTER );
    }
}
```

Applet View...

Applet

Lizzie's Playground

Applet started.

16.5 Configuration Files

Another way for us to customize our programs without changing the source code is to make use of configuration files. These are simple text files that contain a "name=value" on each line of the file. Inside our Java program, we can read through this file and set our variables according to the values in our config file. An example of a config file using the same parameters as the preceding example is Example 16-4. The Java program that reads the config file is in Example 16-5.

EXAMPLE 16-4

```
title=My Favorite Playground
bkcolor=0000FF
textcolor=AAAA00
```

EXAMPLE 16-5

```
import java.awt.*;
import javax.swing.*;
import java.io.*;
import java.net.*;
public class ConfigFile extends JApplet
{
    JPanel bkgrnd;
    JLabel heading;
    Color backcolor, textcolor;
    String titletext;
    String configFilename = "config.txt";
    public void init( )
    {
        String config = readConfigFile( );
        parseConfig( config );
        bkgrnd = new JPanel( );
        bkgrnd.setBackground( backcolor );
        heading = new JLabel( titletext );
        heading.setForeground( textcolor );
        bkgrnd.add( heading );
        setLayout( new BorderLayout( ) );
        add( bkgrnd, BorderLayout.CENTER );
    }
```

> Be sure that your config file is in the same directory as your .class files.

(continues)

Example 16-5 (continued)

```
public void parseConfig( String cfg )
{
    String[ ] lines, tokenkey;
    lines = cfg.split( "\n" );
    for( int i=0; i<lines.length; i++ )
    {
        tokenkey = lines[i].split( "=" );
            // remove newline at end
        String value = tokenkey[1].substring( 0, tokenkey[1].length( ) -1 );
        if ( tokenkey[0].equals( "bkcolor" ) )
            backcolor = new Color( Integer.parseInt( value, 16 ) );
        else if ( tokenkey[0].equals( "textcolor" ) )
            textcolor = new Color( Integer.parseInt( value, 16 ) );
        else if ( tokenkey[0].equals( "title" ) )
            titletext = value;
    }
}
public String readConfigFile( )
{   String content;
    try {
        URL target = new URL( getCodeBase( ), configFilename );
        URLConnection con = target.openConnection( );
        con.connect( );
        byte b[ ] = new byte[1024];            // byte array
        int nbytes;      // number of bytes read in
        String retVal = new String( );
        BufferedInputStream in = new BufferedInputStream(
                                        con.getInputStream( ), 2048 );
        while( (nbytes = in.read( b, 0, 1024 ) ) != -1 ) // while there is more
                                                         //  to read
        {     content = new String( b, 0, nbytes );    // get 1024 bytes of
                                                       //  data
            retVal += content;
        }
        in.close( );          // close connection
        return retVal;
    } catch ( Exception e )     {   return "Error reading config file";   }
    }
}
```

Callout: Method to parse the String containing the contents of the config file.

Callout: split method on Strings returns an array dividing the String according to a delimiter.

Callout: Read in the entire config file. You should not need to change this code for reading in any file.

16.6 Applets and Email

Applets have restrictions placed on them to prevent malicious activity. Therefore, for us to have our applet email us a message, we will need to make use of a CGI program. CGI programs execute on the server, as opposed to our applets that are executing on the user's computer.

The CGI program that we will use in this example is written in the Perl programming language. To use this program, we need an account on a UNIX/Linux system (you may need to ask your network administrator how to get the program to work on your specific system setup). The name of the file is also system specific, whether it ends with .pl or .cgi. Many systems require all CGI programs to be in a specific directory, such as the cgi-bin directory. The Perl version is in Example 16-6.

EXAMPLE 16-6

```perl
#!/usr/bin/perl
use CGI ':standard';

my $outfile  = "mailing.out";
my $sendmail = "/usr/sbin/sendmail -t";
my $reply_to = "Reply-to: boese\@cs.colostate.edu\n";
my $subject  = "Subject: Applet Message\n";
my $to       = "To: boese\@cs.colostate.edu\n";
my $content  = param( 'message' );

print header;        # required first set of lines
print "Thanks!";

open( SENDMAIL, "|$sendmail" ) or die "Cannot open $sendmail: $!";
print SENDMAIL $reply_to;
print SENDMAIL $subject;
print SENDMAIL $to;
print SENDMAIL "Content-type: text/plain\n\n";
print SENDMAIL $content;
close( SENDMAIL );
```

> Change to the absolute path to the Perl program on your system and the absolute path to the sendmail program.

> Change the Reply-to and To email addresses to your own.

To make use of our CGI program, we need to encode our message before we send it. We are using the GET protocol (as opposed to POST), which will encode the message at the end of the URL. In Example 16-7, we will also read a status from the server, which is "Thanks!" (or "Error" if there is a problem). In our example, we display this in a JLabel to the user.

EXAMPLE 16-7

```java
import java.awt.*;
import javax.swing.*;
import java.awt.event.*;
import java.net.*;
import java.io.*;
```

(continues)

Example 16-7 (continued)

```
public class mailApplet extends JApplet implements ActionListener
{
   JTextArea msg;
   JLabel messageLabel, status;
   JButton submit;
   public void init( )
   {
      messageLabel = new JLabel( "Enter your message: " );
      status = new JLabel( );
      msg = new JTextArea( 5, 20 );
      submit = new JButton( "Submit" );
      submit.addActionListener( this );
      setLayout( new FlowLayout( ) );
      add( messageLabel );       add( msg );       add( submit );       add( status );
   }
   public void actionPerformed( ActionEvent ae )
   {
      Object src = ae.getSource( );
      if ( src == submit )
      {
         String message = msg.getText( );
         String s = sendMail( "http://www.cs.colostate.edu/~boese/cgi-bin/
                              mailer.cgi?message=",message );
         status.setText( s );
      }
   }
   public String sendMail( String fullPath, String msg )
   {
      try
      {
         String enc = URLEncoder.encode( msg, "UTF-8" );
         URL target = new URL( fullPath + enc );
         String content;
         URLConnection con = target.openConnection( );       // open connection
         con.setUseCaches( false );
         con.setDefaultUseCaches( false );
         byte b[ ] = new byte[ 1024 ];       // byte array
         int nbytes;       // number of bytes read in
         String retVal = new String();
         BufferedInputStream in = new BufferedInputStream( con.getInputStream( ),
                                                            2048 );
         while( (nbytes = in.read( b, 0, 1024 ) ) != -1 )// while there is more data
                                                         //  to read
         {
            content = new String( b, 0, nbytes );       // get 1024 bytes of data
                                                         //  from file
            retVal += content;
         }
```

> Change the URL to where your CGI program is. Keep the ?message=" part.

```
        in.close( );      // close connection
        return retVal;
    }
    catch( Exception e )
    {
        return "Error " + e.toString( );
    }
  }
}
```

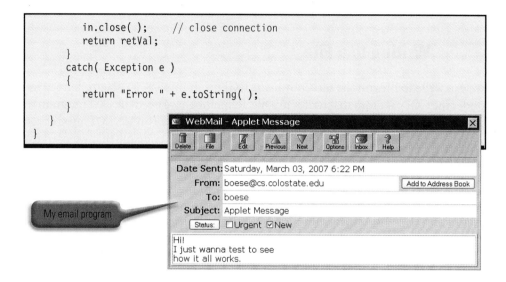

PHP is another language for writing CGI programs. It is more platform independent, so the code provided should work on any system (UNIX/Linux/Windows/Mac/etc.) The PHP version of the email program is in Example 16-8, where your applet should specify the URL for this file that ends with the .php extension.

EXAMPLE 16-8

```php
<?php
    $request_method = $_SERVER["REQUEST_METHOD"];
    if ( $request_method == "GET" ) {
            $query_vars = $_GET;
    }
    elseif ( $request_method == "POST" ) {
            $query_vars = $_POST;
    }
    reset ( $query_vars );
    $emailbody = "New Form Submission: ";
    while ( list ( $key, $val ) = each ( $query_vars ) ) {
            $emailbody = "$emailbody \n  $key = $val" ;
    }
    $emailto = 'info@coffeeClubOfTheWorld.com';        Change to your
    $emailfrom = 'info@coffeeClubOfTheWorld.com';       email address.
    $subject = "New Form Submission";
    mail ( $emailto, $subject, $emailbody, "From: $emailfrom" );
?>
```

16.7 Writing to a File

We can write to files on the server by using CGI programs as well. Example 16-9 includes the CGI program that writes to a file. Remember, we need the CGI program to be set to read, write, and execute permissions for the owner (on UNIX/Linux: chmod u=rwx writeFile.cgi). You can use the same Java source code file that we used for the email example in this chapter—just change the name of the CGI program. The CGI program in Perl is in Example 16-9, and Example 16-10 is PHP.

EXAMPLE 16-9

```perl
#!/usr/bin/perl
use CGI ':standard';

my $outfile = "mailing.out";

print header;   # required first set of lines

# Write to file
open( OUT, ">>$outfile" ) or print( "Couldn't open $outfile: $!" );
if ( param( 'message' ) )
{
    print OUT param( 'message' ),"\n";
}
close( OUT );

print "Thanks!";
```

File name of where to store the information

Use ">" instead of ">>" if you want to rewrite the file—e.g., store a new "High Score".

'message' is the name of the parameter being sent.

EXAMPLE 16-10

```php
<?php
    $request_method = $_SERVER["REQUEST_METHOD"];
    if( $request_method == "GET" ){
      $query_vars = $_GET;
    } elseif ( $request_method == "POST" ){
      $query_vars = $_POST;
    }
    reset( $query_vars );
    $file = $_SERVER['DOCUMENT_ROOT'] . "/form_";
    $fp = fopen( $file,"a" );
      fputs( $fp,"--------------------\n" );
```

```
   while ( list ( $key, $val ) = each ( $query_vars ) ) {
     fputs( $fp,"$key = $val\n" );
   }
   fclose( $fp );
?>
```

We can make use of this CGI program to write to a file and then use the example of reading a config file to read the data file back into our applet. For example, with a little change to the read-from-a-config-file example, we could create a voting program that displays the results as a bar graph in our applet. We could also maintain our own bulletin board by recording the users' messages and then reading the file back and displaying the file appropriately within our applet. There are many programs that we can write now with the ability to read and write files on the server.

Troubleshooting

Common errors:

I am not getting any email.	Make sure that you changed the email in the program to point to your own email. If you are using the Perl version of the CGI program, make sure that there is a backslash before the @ sign in the email address.
	When you make a call to the `sendmail` method, make sure that you pass as a parameter the correct location of your CGI program. Also make sure after the URL that you add `?message="`, e.g., `"sendMail(" http://www.cs.colostate.edu/~boese/cgi-bin/ mailer.cgi?message=",message );` with your own URL in place of mine.
Perl script is giving an error.	The first line in a Perl script specifies the location of the Perl program. Make sure that matches to where it is in your system. You can check on Linux/Mac by typing "which perl". If it does not exist, then ask your system administrator for help.
Config file is not working.	When running your applet on the Internet, make sure that the permissions are set for "other" to be readable.
	Make sure that there are no extra blank lines at the end of the file.
	Java is case sensitive—ensure that all names match.
	Put the config file in the same location where your `.class` and `.html` files are.
The links in my `JEditorPane` do not work.	Make sure that you invoke the method `.addHyperlinkListener( this )` on your `JEditorPane`.
The `JEditorPane` is not displaying properly.	Some web pages do not display properly in `JEditorPane`. For example, it does not support HTML frames or Flash programs.

| I get "Applet not initialized" when I run my applet on the Internet, though it works fine offline. | Java is case sensitive and although some systems (e.g., Windows) will allow you to name your files in either case and still be able to match them, most hosting websites do not allow this. You must name the files identically. You also cannot have spaces and some other particular characters in your file names. Keep it simple and rely on alphanumeric and the underscore characters only in your file names. |
| | Although offline we can shortcut loading images into our applet by skipping the call to getImage and simply doing `new ImageIcon( "file.gif" )`, this approach does not work when applets run on the Internet. Go back to Chapter 4 and follow the steps to properly add images to your applet. |

SUMMARY

- The URL is the full path to some file or directory on the Internet. This includes the protocol, Internet address, and path.
- *Protocol* is defined as a set of rules.
- Internet protocols are used to determine how to handle the data.
- Common Internet protocols include http, https, and ftp.
- The domain name is the base of an Internet address that is unique on the Internet.
- Domain names can be bought if they are not currently registered by someone else.
- The Internet address is the full address to a computer or network established on the Internet.
- Hyperlink tags in a web page enable the user to click on either some text or an image and be redirected to a different web page.
- `JEditorPane` can display HTML tags and web pages from the Internet.
- `JEditorPane` implements the `HyperLinkListener`.
- When setting the web page to display in a `JEditorPane`, the call to `setPage` must be within a `try . . . catch` block in case there is a problem accessing the web page.
- To handle the links within a web page displayed in a `JEditorPane`, we must listen for the `HyperlinkEvent` and change the URL of the page being displayed.
- There are some websites that allow people to create web pages (with or without applets) on the Internet for free.
- Applets on the Internet cannot attempt to read local files—files can be read only via http requests.

- The HTML file to embed an applet must define the applet's width and height and include an end tag for the applet tag.
- The HTML file to embed an applet must reference the .class file, not the .java file.
- When uploading files to a website, be sure to upload all required image files and the bytecode (.class file) for the applets.
- CGI programs need to have read, write, and execute permissions for the owner.

EXERCISES

1. Name the URL of a website where you can buy a domain name.
2. In http://www.cs.colostate.edu/~cs150/syllabus.html, what is the protocol? What is the Internet address? URL? Domain name?
3. What is the .java file? What is the .class file?
4. Fill in the missing blanks in the following HTML code:

```
<HTML><BODY>
<APPLET _____ = "myApplet . _____"
width=200 height= 200 >
</_____> </HTML>
```

5. True or false? The four parts to a URL include protocol, host name, path name, and file name.
6. From the URL http://www.jujo.uno.com/helpstuff/faq.html, match the following:

_____ Domain name   a. www.jujo.uno.com

_____ Protocol   b. http

_____ URL   c. uno.com

               d. com

               e. helpstuff/faq.html

               f. www.jujo.uno.com/helpstuff/faq.html

               g. http://www.jujo.uno.com/helpstuff/faq.html

7. What happens if you do not listen for Hyperlink events and you display a web page in a JEditorPane—does the page display correctly? What happens when you click on a link within the page?
8. Create a JEditorPane in an applet and instead of displaying a web page from the Internet, set the text of the pane with some HTML tag formatting.
9. True or false? When setting the web page to display in a JEditorPane, if the http:// is left off, it will default to use http:// for the protocol.

10. True or false? The try . . . catch block used for setting the page to display in a JEditorPane is not necessary if you simply set the text of the JEditorPane.

11. True or false? When the user clicks on a link in a web page displayed inside a JEditorPane, a HyperlinkEvent occurs.

12. Create an applet that has four buttons on the left side, one for each of your favorite college football teams. Add a JEditorPane in the center of the applet that correctly displays the main web page for the football team selected.

13. Extend the email example to handle two text fields entered by the user.

14. Write an applet with a CGI program that allows users to vote for one of three JRadioButton options. Record each result in a file on the server. Include a button that then reads the data file and displays a histogram or pie chart of all the votes.

Java

17.1 Java

Java was originally designed for small appliances, such as smart toasters and cell phones. However, as the WWW came to popularity, Java became one of the fore-front languages that could be displayed by web browsers, which has partially led to its popularity. Java started out as a small language, which also made it relatively easy to learn. It is now growing into a robust language with many complex features. In the following sections we explore some of the advantages and disadvantages of the Java language.

17.1.1 Simplicity

Java also became popular as a first language in learning programming because of its simplicity. Some of the complex aspects of languages like C and C++ are automatically taken care of in Java. For example, memory management can be a nightmare to figure out in a C/C++ program, where the programmer must allocate and deal-locate memory lest the program be susceptible to memory leaks, but is automatically handled in Java via object creation and automated *garbage collection*. Java also removed some of the complexity of other languages such as operator overloading, multiple inheritance, and automatic coercions.

17.1.2 Small Language—Or Is It?

Although initially the Java language was small, and it was easy to learn the entire language, it has increasingly become larger and more complex, with new versions coming out almost annually. Being a small language used to be one of Java's selling points. However, as the language grows with more spectacular features, it has be-come a bit disadvantageous as a learning language, requiring more knowledge and programming to make it work. Keeping students up to date with the current version of Java and a textbook to match it has also become somewhat problematic.

17.1.3 Graphics

Java has graphics capabilities that are easier than those of C/C++, but they still lag behind the ease of languages such as Flash and Visual Basic. The graphics also enable Java to be displayed within a web page. Graphical programming tends to be more enticing to students as a learning language as well, because the visual feedback is considered more rewarding than programs that result in only text output.

17.1.4 Object-Oriented Language

Java is an object-oriented language, meaning that everything (except the eight primi-tive data types) is an object. Objects store data values and methods related to the data together in the same class. Object-oriented languages help facilitate code reuse, either through inheritance or by instantiating several objects. For example, our `FontOutline` class will work with whatever text that we send to it, such that we need not change the Java code but can instantiate the class several times with different text.

17.1.5 Platform Independent

Java can be compiled on any machine type and then executed on any other machine type if there is an interpreter for the machine. This feature is a huge benefit over other languages and a fundamental aspect on how applets work over the Internet (review Chapter 1 for more details). However, with platform independence also comes a disadvantage—Java is slow. It is slower than other languages that are compiled directly into machine code, which can then execute right away. Java first needs its *bytecode* to be *interpreted*, where the interpreter translates to machine code and then executes.

> **Advanced Concept**
>
> Although Java usually compiles to bytecode, there are special Java compilers that will compile the source code straight to machine code for a specific machine type. This method will not work for applets on the Internet but can help optimize Java applications that will be executed only on a specific machine type.

17.1.6 Multithreading

Multithreading is the ability to simulate running many processes simultaneously. The CPU, which handles computer instructions, switches between all running processes fast enough that it appears to the user that they are all being executed at the same time. This feature prevents one process from holding up all other processes from having a chance to run. Java supports threads, which allows multiple tasks to be executing at the same time. This is how many animation techniques and processor-intensive code can be executed without freezing the view to the users.

17.1.7 Security

Web browsers that run Java applets impose certain security restrictions to prevent malicious code from wreaking havoc on a system. Some of the restrictions include the following:

- Applets cannot read or write files on the computer running the applet.
- Applets cannot create network connections to other computers.
- Applets cannot start a program on the computer that is running the applet.
- Applets cannot read system properties on the computer that is running the applet.

- Windows that are displayed from an applet are displayed differently than windows from an application so that the user knows where it came from.

17.2 Modifying and Using Free Applets

There are many free applets available. Some also provide the source code and allow you to modify them as you like. Be sure to read the copyright, licensing, and agreements before you use one of these applets.

Follow these steps to use an example free applet from the Java Boutique website:

1. Go to http://java.internet.com.
2. Find an applet that you want to use. Make sure that it includes the java source code, not just the .class files.
3. Download the files (if it is a .zip file, you will need to extract the contents of the file).
4. Copy the .java file(s) into your IDE (e.g., Eclipse). The easiest way to do this is to open the file in Notepad (Windows) or Kwrite (Linux), select all the text and copy it, and then paste it into a new class inside your IDE. Alternatively, you can import the files into your IDE.
5. Compile and run the Java applet.
6. You can usually modify the parameters in the HTML code to customize the applet, or look at the code itself and modify it as you need.

17.3 Other Features from Third-Party Libraries

We can enhance our Java applets through the use of third-party libraries. Some of these are available for free, whereas others cost money. The bigger catch is that users that view your website with your applet can usually do so only if they too have downloaded and installed the libraries or a runtime interpreter for these additional functionalities.

Some of the available features include the following:

- 2D graphics
- 3D graphics
- Virtual reality

- Video
- Accessing databases
- MP3 playback
- Music manipulation
- Creating applications for cell phones

17.4 Graphics2D

Graphics2D is a more advanced and more complex class for drawing. It extends the methods that we learned in Chapter 2. There, we saw an introduction to using Graphics2D to enable antialiasing to allow us to make our drawing curves more smooth. We can also use color dithering, stroke thickness and stroke patterns, fill patterns, transparency, and much more.

To use Graphics2D, we cast our Graphics object to a Graphics2D object and then call all our methods on this Graphics2D object. To cast to Graphics2D, we will do one of the following, depending on if we are using the paint method for a JApplet class or the paintComponent method inside a class that extends JPanel or other component.

```
public void paint( Graphics g ) // paint method inside JApplet class
{
      Graphics2D  g2d = ( Graphics2D ) g;
}
// paintComponent method when extending JPanel or other classes
public void paintComponent( Graphics g )
{
      super.paintComponent( g );
      Graphics2D  g2d = ( Graphics2D ) g;
}
```

We can create a gradient fill by creating a GradientPaint instance and calling the method setPaint on our Graphics2D object. The *x1* and *y1* coordinates define where color1 begins, *x2* and *y2* coordinates define the end point for color2, and the boolean value specifies whether the color is cyclic (repeating) if true, or if the colors are available only within the range of the two coordinate sets if the boolean value is false. In Example 17-1 we create an ellipse with a gradient fill from blue to white.

```
GradientPaint gp = new GradientPaint(
      x1, y1, color1,
      x2, y2, color2, booleanIsCyclic );
```

EXAMPLE 17-1

```java
import java.awt.*;
import javax.swing.*;
import java.awt.geom.*;
public class Graphics2DEx extends JApplet
{
   public void paint( Graphics g )
   {
      Graphics2D g2 = ( Graphics2D ) g;
      int x = 15, y = 10, w = 50, h = 50;
      Ellipse2D ellipse = new Ellipse2D.Double( x, y, w, h );
      GradientPaint gp = new GradientPaint( x, y, Color.blue,
                                            w, h, Color.white,
                                            false);
      g2.setPaint( gp );     // fill with gradient
      g2.fill( ellipse );
   }
}
```

> If the shape is drawn outside the coordinate ranges defined for the GradientPaint and the cyclic value is false, then the shape is drawn clear and you will not see it.

Gradient fill depends on the coordinates that you specify for the gradient and where you draw your object. For example, if we set up a GradientPaint object as:

```java
GradientPaint( 50, 75, Color.yellow, 95, 95, Color.blue, true );
```

the gradient will repeat over the space, where yellow begins at (50, 75) and morphs to blue by (95, 95) and the pattern then repeats throughout the space as shown in **FIGURE 17-1**. The selection of blue and yellow that appears is dependent on where the circle is drawn. Example 17-2 demonstrates this gradient based on the location of filled circles drawn, and Example 17-3 based on using BasicStroke.

FIGURE 17-1   Demonstration of a gradient fill.

EXAMPLE 17-2

```java
import java.awt.*;
import javax.swing.*;
import java.awt.geom.*;
public class Graphics2DEx extends JApplet
{
    public void paint( Graphics g )
    {
        Graphics2D g2 = ( Graphics2D ) g;
        int x = 15, y = 10, w = 50, h = 50;
        Ellipse2D ellipse = new Ellipse2D.Double( x, y, w, h );
        Ellipse2D ellipse2 = new Ellipse2D.Double( x+w, y, w, h );
        GradientPaint gp = new GradientPaint( 50, 75, Color.yellow,
                                    95, 95, Color.blue,
                                    true );
        g2.setPaint( gp );     // fill with gradient
        g2.fill( ellipse );
        g2.fill( ellipse2 );
        g2.fill( new Ellipse2D.Double( x+w+w, y, w, h ) );
    }
}
```

When we are working with the Graphics2D object, we utilize specific 2D shapes for drawing. The following code lists some of the common shapes that can be created and then sent to the fill or draw method on a Graphics2D object.

```java
Ellipse2D.Double( x, y, width, height )
Rectangle2D.Double( x, y, width, height )
RoundRectangle2D.Double( x, y, width, height, cornerArcWidth,
                          CornerArcHeight )
Line2D.Double( x1, y1, x2, y2 )
Arc2D.Double( x, y, width, height, startAngle, arcAngle, type )
```

where type is either

```java
Arc2D.OPEN
Arc2D.CHORD
Arc2D.PIE
```

EXAMPLE 17-3

```java
import java.awt.*;
import javax.swing.*;
import java.awt.geom.*;
public class Graphics2DStroke extends JApplet
```

(continues)

Example 17-3 (continued)

```
{
    public void paint( Graphics g )
    {
        Graphics2D g2 = ( Graphics2D ) g;
        int x = 15, y = 10, w = 50, h = 50;
        Ellipse2D ellipse = new Ellipse2D.Double( x, y, w, h );
        Ellipse2D ellipse2 = new Ellipse2D.Double( x+w+20, y, w, h );
        GradientPaint gp = new GradientPaint( 50, 75, Color.yellow, 95,
                                              95, Color.blue, true );
        g2.setPaint( gp );    // fill with gradient
        g2.setStroke( new BasicStroke( 8 ) ); // outline is 8 pixels
        g2.draw( ellipse );
        // Stroke with a gradient.
        g2.setStroke( new BasicStroke( 20 ) ); // outline is 20 pixels
        g2.draw( ellipse2 );
    }
}
```

17.5 Jar Files

A useful tool when creating applets with many files is to archive them together into one file. Although we could do this with the zip and tar utilities, we should use the *jar* program provided with our Java Development Kit because we can have our applets reference jar files. This makes it faster for a user to download and run our applet. Our jar files must end with the extension .jar and can contain all our .class files, image files, and audio files to make our applet work.

To create a jar file, go to a term window in Linux/Mac or command prompt in Windows and change directory until you are in the same directory where all your files are located. Type the following to create a jar file:

```
jar cvf  jarFileName.jar *
```

Doing so will create a jar file with all the files in that directory (the "*" is a wildcard for all files). We could also list each file individually instead of using the *, as in the following example:

```
jar cvf  jarFileName.jar Project.class Logo.class logo.gif sd.au
```

If you are using an IDE, look for the option to create a jar file and follow the instructions in the IDE.

To reference our jar file in our HTML file, we need to add
ARCHIVE="jarFileName.jar", as shown in the following full HTML file example:

```
<HTML>
   <BODY>
      <APPLET CODE=XYZ.class ARCHIVE="files.jar"
            WIDTH=500 HEIGHT=500>
         </APPLET>
   </BODY></HTML>
```

Now when you upload your applet to the Internet, you need upload only two files:
your jar file and the html file.

SUMMARY

- Java was originally intended for small appliances but became popular
  when applets were enabled to be embedded in web pages.
- Java is an object-oriented language. Other than the eight primitive data
  types, everything else is stored as an object. This approach leads to better
  code reuse and code modularity.
- Some of the complex features in other programming languages were omit-
  ted from the Java language, which made it a simpler language to learn.
- Java is platform independent, which means that the compiled code (bytecode) can be executed on any type of system. The disadvantage to this is
  that each machine needs to first interpret the code to machine code before
  executing, causing Java programs to run slower than other languages like
  C/C++.
- Multitasking enables a single CPU to handle multiple tasks by swapping
  between them until each finishes.
- Through threads, Java supports multitasking to enable many tasks to
  execute "simultaneously."
- Applets have restrictions placed on them to prevent malicious activity on a
  client computer running the applet.
- There are many free applets available on the Internet that can be down-
  loaded and modified.
- There are additional third-party libraries that can be imported into pro-
  grams to extend the functionality.
- We could write our own third-party libraries to share with others.
- Jar files are like zip files; we can archive many files together to store inside
  one file and reference them in an HTML page.
- Graphics2D adds additional features, including stroke thickness, gradient
  patterns, and gradient strokes.

EXERCISES

1. Why can applets on the Internet not write to files?

2. Name the URL of a website where you can buy a domain name.

3. What does it mean for a computer language to be object oriented?

4. Why is Java considered to be easier to program in than other languages such as C++?

5. Why is security an issue for applets on the Internet? How is Java secure?

6. Why is Java slower than other languages?

7. If your computer has only one processor (CPU), how could more than one task be executing at the same time?

8. How does Java enable multitasking?

9. What are third-party libraries? What are they used for?

10. Go to the website http://java.internet.com and find an applet with source code available. Download the source code and any additional required files and modify the applet before putting it on your own web page.

11. Put all the files you need to run your applet into a jar file. Create the HTML file to reference your jar file and upload it to the Internet.

12. Convert the examples in Chapter 2 to use `Graphics2D`, implementing thicker strokes and gradient fills.

Debugging

*The code that is the most difficult to debug
is the code that you know cannot possibly be wrong.*

Sometimes when we are working on a programming project, figuring out what is wrong with it is difficult. Even an IDE like Eclipse sometimes does not specify an error, or the message it gives us does not help us figure it out. We have many methods in our bigger programs, and figuring out where the problem is can be confusing.

When we are trying to fix errors in our program, we are *debugging* our code. There are three types of errors that we can have in our code: syntax (or compile-time) errors, runtime errors, and logical errors.

Syntax errors are when we have violated the Java grammar for programs. This category includes when we forget a semicolon at the end of a statement, leave out a brace, or try to put a method inside another method. If we are running an IDE like Eclipse, it will usually be able to detect and show us these errors before we attempt to run our program. If there are syntax errors, do not try to execute the program—it either will not work at all or will try to execute an *old* version and will deceive you as to what your code is doing. Always make sure that all syntax errors are fixed before proceeding with development.

The second type of error is a *runtime* error. This type of error occurs when the program compiles fine but then crashes when we try to run it. The program may run partly before crashing and may even run for an hour before it crashes. These are usually more dynamic errors such as a division by zero or an error that is not caught via an exception handler. Check the console window for the location of where the error most probably occurred. There may be many errors listed, so be sure to find the first listing of your program name.

The third error type is called a *logical* error. This is when the program compiles and runs fine, but there is an error in the output. Sometimes this is as simple as a misspelled word, but sometimes it is more complicated, like a calculation that always results to zero. Another logical error is when components do not appear correctly or do not appear at all. This is where the debugging techniques below may be helpful.

There are several methods that we can try to debug our code, depending on what is wrong with it. If our code is getting stuck somewhere (e.g., an infinite loop), a helpful method is to print out values to the console window throughout the program. Then we can see where it stops printing and what the last thing was that printed and narrow down how much code we need to look at for the error. If the problem is that the output is incorrect from some calculation we did, we can try printing out all our variables used in the calculation to start narrowing down why the calculation did not work. This approach could help us determine whether the variable was not correctly assigned a value from reading a JTextField, whether integer division occurred, or if a division by zero occurred. If our problem is that a certain component or JPanel does not seem to be appearing on the applet, we could temporarily set the background color of our component and see if it displays, and where. A more advanced debugging technique is to make use of a debugger. If we are using an IDE such as Eclipse, there is a debugger built into the IDE.

Designators

One way to help figure out what is going on in our program is to use System.out. println statements to print out a designator of where we are in our code. For example, we may add print statements to print out the alphabet (in expected order), the name of the method we are currently in, or an identifying phrase of what the next statement is about to do. In Example A-1, we print out the alphabet:

EXAMPLE A-1

```
/* Example showing how to loop through a list of items stored in a List object
 * @author : E.S.Boese  */
import java.awt.*;
import javax.swing.*;
public class Debugging extends JApplet
{
    JList list;
    DefaultListModel model;
    JTextArea textarea;
    public void init( )
    {
            System.out.println( "A" );
            setLayout( new FlowLayout( ) );
            System.out.println( "B" );
            setupList( );
            System.out.println( "C" );

            textarea = new JTextArea( 5, 10 );
            add( textarea );
            System.out.println( "D" );

            addListItemsToTextarea( );
            System.out.println( "E" );
    }
    public void setupList( )
    {
            System.out.println( "F" );
            model = new DefaultListModel( );
            list = new JList( model );
            model.addElement( "Milk" );
            model.addElement( "Cookies" );
            model.addElement( "Eggs" );
            add( list );
            System.out.println( "G" );
    }
```

(continues)

Example A-1 (continued)

```java
public void addListItemsToTextarea( )
{
        System.out.println( "H" );
        for( int i=0; i<model.getSize( ); i++ );
                        // getSize returns the number of items in the list
        {
           System.out.println( "I" );
           textarea.append( ( String )model.get( i ) );
                                        // grab the item at index i
           textarea.append( "\n" );
        }
        System.out.println( "K" );
    }
}
```

Now when we run our program, we see that it does not fully work. The list items are not being added to the textarea. The System.out.println statements actually print output to the console window. The output from our example is as follows:

```
A
B
F
G
C
D
E
```

The print statements H, I, and K are never called. This realization can help determine that the method addListItemsToTextarea is never called. We just need to add a call to this method to fix the problem.

Another example of this use follows in Example A-2, which leads to an infinite loop:

EXAMPLE A-2

```java
import java.awt.*;
import javax.swing.*;
public class Infinite extends JApplet
{
    JTextArea textarea;
    public void init( )
    {
        System.out.println( "A" );
        textarea = new JTextArea( 3, 10 );
        System.out.println( "B" );
        int i=10;
```

```
            System.out.println( "C" );
            while( i<100 )
                    textarea.append( i + "\n" );
                    System.out.println( "D" );
                    i = i+1;
            System.out.println( "E" );
            add( textarea );
            System.out.println( "F" );
    }
}
```

Which prints out the following:

    A
    B
    C

This output can help you realize that the code is in an infinite loop and that the problem is somewhere after the printing of C and before D or E print statements.

 ## A.2 Printing Values

Another use of print statements for debugging is to print out the values of our variables to see if they are what we think they are before we do our calculations, as in Example A-3.

EXAMPLE A-3

```
import java.awt.*;
import javax.swing.*;
import java.awt.event.*;
public class DebugValue extends JApplet
                implements ItemListener
{
    double cat = 4;
    double dog = 10;
    double horse = 350;
    double costOfItem = 0;
    double quantity;
    JComboBox list;
    JTextField qty;
    JLabel price;
    public void init( )
```

Applet Viewer: DebugValue.cl
Applet
[3]   dog ▼ 0.0
Applet started.

Output to console window:

qty=3.0
cost=0.0
total=0.0

(continues)

Example A-3 (continued)

```
{
    setLayout( new FlowLayout( ) );
    qty = new JTextField( 4 );
    list = new JComboBox( );
    price = new JLabel( "0.0" );
    list.addItem( "cat" );
    list.addItem( "dog" );
    list.addItem( "horse" );
    list.addItemListener( this );
    add( qty );
    add( list );
    add( price );
}
public void itemStateChanged( ItemEvent ie )
{
    Object src = ie.getSource( );
    if( ie.getStateChange( )==ItemEvent.SELECTED )
    {
        if( src == list )
        {
            quantity = Integer.parseInt( qty.getText( ) );
            System.out.println( "qty=" + quantity );
            System.out.println( "cost="+costOfItem );
            double totalCost = costOfItem * quantity;
            System.out.println( "total=" + totalCost );
            price.setText( "" + totalCost );
        }
    }
}
}
```

> Here we can see the variable costOfItem is not the correct value. So the total cost is calculating to zero because costOfItem is zero. We can go back and add the necessary code to fix the problem, now that we know what the problem is.
>
> *Exercise: Can you fix the code?*

A.3 Color-Coding Components

Another method for debugging our graphical interface is to color-code our panels. When we are having problems with our components not appearing or not appearing correctly, it is sometimes helpful to change the background colors of our components to try to determine where the problem may be. If we make each JPanel a different color, we can see where each panel is being displayed. This approach can also help immensely when we write a separate class that extends the JPanel class, in case we forgot to set the size of this new component.

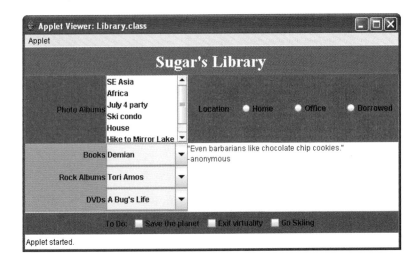

For example, in Chapter 5 we covered design. The example of the Library applet had vibrant colors in each section of the applet, which helps make it clear where each component is. Although this is probably not how we want our final version of the library to look (we prefer to have most, if not all, regions the same background color), this technique is helpful for debugging code when components seem to be in the wrong place or are the wrong size.

> When changing the background color of components, remember that some components are transparent by default, so you may need to call .setOpaque(true) on the component before the call to .setBackground(color) will work.

 ## Debuggers

An advanced option for debugging is to use a debugger. These are usually integrated into IDEs, so if you are using an IDE such as Eclipse, you can make use of it. Debuggers help you set breakpoints in the code, display values of variables in the code, step through the code line by line or from breakpoint to breakpoint, and they have many other features to help us debug our code. Because each IDE has a different setup for debugging, we leave it to you to explore the help available for your IDE in this regard.

SUMMARY

- Debugging is the process of fixing errors in the code.
- There are three types of errors: syntax or (compile-time) errors, runtime errors, and logical errors.
- Syntax errors are violations of Java grammar rules.
- Runtime errors are errors that cause the program to crash during execution.
- Logical errors occur when the program compiles and runs fine, but there are errors in the output produced.
- Use of the `System.out.println` statement to print locations in the code is one way to figure out where the problems are occurring. `System.out.println` prints output to the console window.
- Printing out the value of variables helps debug problems where calculations are not correct.
- If components are not showing up or are appearing incorrectly, temporarily change the background color of components to check the size and location of the components and panels.
- For more advanced debugging, make use of a debugger.

EXERCISES

1. Put an infinite loop into a large program and use the debugging techniques to see how they can help you find the problem.
2. Which debugging technique is best for figuring out why a calculation keeps evaluating to zero?
3. Which debugging technique is best for figuring out why a particular component is not showing up on the applet?
4. What is a debugger? How do you use one?
5. Write an entire class named `Debug` that keeps track of an `int` value for the level of debugging desired. Create constants for three different levels: CLASS, METHOD, or VARIABLE, where CLASS is the highest level and VARIABLE is the lowest. Create a constructor that initializes the level of debugging and a mutator method to change the level. Then create a method called `printDebug` that takes an `int` for the level of the request and a `String` to be printed. In this method, if the level is equal to or higher than the debugging level (instance variable), then print the `String` parameter. If not, the method should not do anything. Then integrate this method into a program that you have written, where you instantiate this class at the beginning of your program and each method calls your `printDebug` method with the name of the method as a parameter, and each method that changes the value of a variable calls the `printDebug` method with the value of the variable as the parameter.

Java API

B

Methods provided are a subset of the standard Java API.

`ActionEvent`
Constructors
- Generated from button clicks

Useful methods:
- `Object getSource( )`
  - · Returns a reference to the object that generated the event

`ArrayList`
Constructors
- `ArrayList list = new ArrayList( )`

Useful methods:
- `Object get( index )`
  - · Returns the element at the specified index—cast to appropriate type
- `int size( )`
  - · Returns the number of elements in the list

`AudioClip`
Constructors
- None—call method `getAudioClip` on applet

Useful methods:
- `void loop( )`
  - · Plays the audio clip continuously
- `void play( )`
  - · Plays the audio clip once through
- `void stop( )`
  - · Stops playing the audio clip

`BasicStroke`
Constructors
- `BasicStroke stroke = new BasicStroke( w )`
  - · Creates a new `Stroke` object with a stroke width of (w)

Useful methods:
- `Stroke createStrokedShape( Shape )`
  - · Takes a Shape as a parameter to define the style for drawing the stroke and returns the `Stroke` object

`Border`
see `BorderFactory`

`BorderFactory`
Constructors
- None

Useful methods:

- `Border createBevelBorder( type )`
  - Creates a Border object with a bevel where the type can be either `BevelBorder.LOWERED` or `BevelBorder.RAISED`
- `Border createBevelBorder( type, highlightColor, shadowColor )`
  - Creates a Border object with a bevel where the type can be either `BevelBorder.LOWERED` or `BevelBorder.RAISED` and the `highlightColor` is the color for the outer edge and the `shadowColor` for the inner edge
- `Border createEmptyBorder( top, left, bottom, right )`
  - Creates an empty border to take up space on the basis of the number of pixels specified for each region
- `Border createEtchedBorder( type )`
  - Creates a Border object with an etched look where the type can be either `EtchedBorder.RAISED` or `EtchedBorder.LOWERED`
- `Border createLineBorder( Color )`
  - Creates a Border object with the specified color
- `Border createLineBorder( Color, thickness )`
  - Creates a Border object with the specified color and thickness
- `Border createTitledBorder( Border, String )`
  - Creates a Border by using the style defined in the parameter Border with text specified in the `String` parameter
- `Border createTitledBorder( Border, String, titleJustification, titlePosition )`
  - Creates a Border by using the style defined in the parameter Border with text specified in the `String` parameter, where `titleJustification` specifies how the title is displayed and can be `TitledBorder.LEFT`, `TitledBorder.CENTER`, or `TitledBorder.RIGHT`, and `titlePosition` specifies where the title is located with respect to the component where the values are `TitledBorder.ABOVE_TOP`, `TitledBorder.TOP`, `TitledBorder.BELOW_TOP`, `TitledBorder.ABOVE_BOTTOM`, `TitledBorder.BOTTOM`, or `TitledBorder.BELOW_BOTTOM`
- `Border createTitledBorder( Border, String, titleJustification, titlePosition, Font, Color )`
  - Same as the previous with addition of specifying the font and color of the text
- `MatteBorder createMatteBorder( top, left, bottom, right, ImageIcon )`
  - Creates a matte border that is based on an image in an `ImageIcon` that is repeated around the component. Specify how many pixels to display for each region: top, left, bottom, right.

BorderLayout
Constructors

  — `BorderLayout layout = new BorderLayout( );`
   · Creates a new layout manager instance

Useful methods:

  — `void add( component, location )`
   · Where location is `BorderLayout.NORTH`, `BorderLayout.SOUTH`, `Borderlayout.WEST`, `BorderLayout.EAST`, or `BorderLayout.CENTER`
   · Adds the component to the region specified. Only one component may be added to each region.

BoxLayout
Constructors

  — `BoxLayout layout = new BoxLayout( target, axis );`
   · Creates a new layout manager instance where target is the container that the box layout is to be applied (`getContentPanel( )`) and `axis` is either `BoxLayout.X_AXIS` or `BoxLayout.Y_AXIS`

BufferedImage
Constructors

  — `BufferedImage bi = new BufferedImage( w, h, imageType )`
   · Creates a new `BufferedImage` with a width of (w) and height of (h) and the `imageType` is `TYPE_INT_RGB`

Useful methods:

  — `Graphics2D createGraphics( )`
   · Returns a `Graphics2D` object to use to draw on the `BufferedImage`
  — `flush( )`
   · Stop optimizing and flush output to the screen

ButtonGroup
Constructors

  — `ButtonGroup bg = new ButtonGroup( )`
Useful methods:

  — `void add( Button )`
   · Adds a button to the group such that only one in the group may be selected at a time

Calendar
Constructors

  — None

Useful methods:

- `Calendar getInstance( )`
  - Returns an instance of `Calendar` based on current date/time
- `int get( int )`
  - Returns the specified part of date/time where the parameter can be `Calendar.HOUR`, `Calendar.MINUTE`, `Calendar.SECOND`, `Calendar.HOUR_OF_DAY`, `Calendar.TIME`, `Calendar.DATE`, `Calendar.MONTH`, or `Calendar.YEAR`.

`Color`

Constants

    `Color.BLACK`

    `Color.BLUE`

    `Color.CYAN`

    `Color.DARK_GRAY`

    `Color.GRAY`

    `Color.GREEN`

    `Color.LIGHT_GRAY`

    `Color.MAGENTA`

    `Color.ORANGE`

    `Color.PINK`

    `Color.RED`

    `Color.WHITE`

    `Color.YELLOW`

Constructors

- `Color c = new Color( red, green, blue );`
  - Creates a `Color` object with specified red, green, and blue

`DefaultListModel`

Constructors

- `DefaultListModel model = new DefaultListModel( );`
  - Creates a new model for a `JList`

Useful methods:

- `void addElement( Object )`
  - Adds the `Object` (`String`, `ImageIcon`, etc.) to the end of the list
- `void add( int, Object )`
  - Adds the `Object` (`String`, `ImageIcon`, etc.) to position of int in the list

- `void clear( )`
    - Removes all items from the list
- `boolean contains( Object )`
    - Returns `true` or `false` whether or not the `Object` is already in the list
- `Object get( index )`
    - Returns the item at the specified index (parameter), returns the item as an `Object` (cast to specific type)
- `int getSize( )`
    - Returns the number of elements in the list
- `void remove( index )`
    - Removes the element at the specified index

`Double`
Constructors

- `Double d = new Double( number )`
    - Creates an instance of `Double` object with the specified number

Useful methods:

- `double Double.parseDouble( String )`
    - Returns a `double` type of the number stored in the `String`

`FlowLayout`
Constructors

- `FlowLayout layout = new FlowLayout( );`
    - Creates a new layout manager instance with center horizontal alignment
- `FlowLayout layout = new FlowLayout(alignment);`
    - Creates a new layout manager instance where alignment is `FlowLayout.LEFT`, `FlowLayout.RIGHT`, or `FlowLayout.CENTER`
- `FlowLayout layout = new Flow Layout(alignment, horizGap, vertGap)`
    - Creates a new layout manager instance where alignment is `Flowlayout.LEFT`, `Flowlayout.RIGHT`, or `Flowlayout.CENTER`, and `horizGap` and `vertGap` specify the number of pixels between components horizontally and vertically

`FocusEvent`
Useful methods:
- `Object getSource( )`
    - Returns the object that caused the event

Font
Constructors
- Font f = new Font(type, style, size) ;
  - Creates a new Font where type is "Serif", "Sanserif" or "Mono-spaced", style is Font.PLAIN, Font.BOLD, Font.ITALIC or Font.BOLD+Font.ITALIC and size is in points (e.g. 12 for 12 pt font)

Graphics
Constructors
- None
Useful methods:
- void clearRect(x, y, w, h)
  - Clears the rectangle at coordinates (x, y) with the width (w) and height (h) by filling it with the background color
- void draw3Drect(x, y, w, h, boolean)
  - Draws a 3-D rectangle outline that appears *raised* if boolean is true or *sunken* if false
- void drawArc(x, y, w, h, startAngle, arcAngle)
  - Draws the outer arc according to where it lies if an ellipse were drawn from the coordinates (x, y) with a width of (w) and height of (h) and the angle based on $0°$ drawn out from the center of the ellipse directly to the right, and the arcAngle is drawn by going counterclockwise.
- void drawImage(Image, x, y, this)
  - Draws the image with the top-left corner at the coordinates (x, y). The this keyword specifies that the current class is handling the drawing of the image and will always be this for what is covered in this book.
- void drawImage(Image, xd1, yd1, xd2, yd2, xs1, ys1, xs2, ys2, this)
  - Draws the image with the top-left corner at the coordinates $(xd1, yd1)$ scaled to fit within coordinates $(xd2, yd2)$ [bottom-right corner] where the coordinates $(xs1, ys1)$ represent the top-left corner of the source image [where to start to draw on the original image, allows for cropping] and the coordinates $(ys1, ys2)$ represent the bottom-right corner of the source image.
- void drawLine(x1, y1, x2, y2)
  - Draws a line from the coordinates $(x1, y1)$ to coordinates $(x2, y2)$
- void drawOval(x, y, w, h)
  - Draws an oval/ellipse whose top-left corner is at coordinates (x, y) with a width of (w) and height of (h) such that the bottom-right corner is at coordinates $(x + w, y + h)$

– void drawPolygon(Polygon)
  · Draws the figure defined by the sequence of points in the Polygon object. The order of the points added to the Polygon defines the shape, as it connects the points in sequential order.

– void drawRect(x, y, w, h)
  · Draws the outline of a rectangle with the top-left corner at coordinates (x, y) with a width of (w) and a height of (h)

– void drawRoundRect(x, y, w, h, arcWidth, arcHeight)
  · Draws the outline of a rectangle with the top-left corner at coordinates (x, y) with a width of (w) and a height of (h), where the corners are rounded based on the number of pixels specified for the arcWidth and arcHeight.

– void drawString(String, x, y)
  · Draws the text specified in the String starting at the coordinates (x, y), where the coordinates define the bottom-left of the text.

– void fill3DRect(x, y, w, h, boolean)
  · Paints a 3-D rectangle that appears raised if boolean is true or sunken if false

– void fillArc(x, y, w, h, startAngle, arcAngle)
  · Fills the arc on the basis of where it lies if an ellipse were drawn from the coordinates (x, y) with a width of (w) and height of (h) and the angle based on 0° drawn out from the center of the ellipse directly to the right, and the arcAngle is drawn by going counterclockwise.

– void fillOval(x, y, w, h)
  · Fills an oval/ellipse whose top-left corner is at coordinates (x, y) with a width of (w) and height of (h) such that the bottom-right corner is at coordinates $(x + w, y + h)$

– void fillPolygon(Polygon)
  · Fills the figure defined by the sequence of points in the Polygon object. The order of the points added to the Polygon defines the shape, as it connects the points in sequential order.

– void fillRect(x, y, w, h)
  · Fills the outline of a rectangle with the top-left corner at coordinates (x, y) with a width of (w) and a height of (h)

– void fillRoundRect(x, y, w, h, arcWidth, arcHeight)
  · Fills the outline of a rectangle with the top-left corner at coordinates (x, y) with a width of (w) and a height of (h), where the corners are rounded based on the number of pixels specified for the arcWidth and arcHeight.

– void setColor(Color)
  · Sets the current painting color to the specified color

- void setFont(Font)
  - Sets the current painting font to the specified font

Graphics2D

Constructors

- None

Useful methods:

- void clearRect(x, y, w, h)
  - Clears the rectangle at coordinates (x, y) with the width (w) and height (h) by filling it with the background color
- void draw(Shape)
  - Draws the outline of a Shape, where Shape can be one of the following Shape objects: Arc2D, Area, CubicCurve2D, Ellipse2D, GeneralPath, Line2D, Polygon, QuadCurve2D, Rectangle, Rectangle2D, RectangularShape, RoundRectangle2D
- void draw3DRect(x, y, w, h, boolean)
  - Draws a 3-D rectangle outline that appears raised if boolean is true or sunken if false
- void drawArc(x, y, w, h, startAngle, arcAngle)
  - Draws the outer arc according to where it lies if an ellipse were drawn from the coordinates (x, y) with a width of (w) and height of (h) and the angle based on $0°$ drawn out from the center of the ellipse directly to the right, and the arcAngle is drawn by going counterclockwise
- void drawImage(Image, x, y, this)
  - Draws the image with the top-left corner at the coordinates (x, y). The this keyword specifies that the current class is handling the drawing of the image and will always be this for what is covered in this book.
- void drawImage(Image, xd1, yd1, xd2, yd2, xs1, ys1, xs2, ys2, this)
  - Draws the image with the top-left corner at the coordinates $(xd1, yd1)$ scaled to fit within coordinates $(xd2, yd2)$ [bottom-right corner], where the coordinates $(xs1, ys1)$ represent the top-left corner of the source image [where to start to draw on the original image, allows for cropping] and the coordinates $(ys1, ys2)$ represent the bottom-right corner of the source image.
- void drawLine(x1, y1, x2, y2)
  - Draws a line from the coordinates $(x1, y1)$ to coordinates $(x2, y2)$
- void drawOval(x, y, w, h)
  - Draws an oval/ellipse whose top-left corner is at coordinates (x, y) with a width of (w) and height of (h) such that the bottom-right corner is at coordinates $(x + w, y + h)$

- void drawPolygon(Polygon)
  - Draws the figure defined by the sequence of points in the Polygon object. The order of the points added to the Polygon defines the shape, as it connects the points in sequential order.
- void drawRect(x, y, w, h)
  - Draws the outline of a rectangle with the top-left corner at coordinates (x, y) with a width of (w) and a height of (h)
- void drawRoundRect(x, y, w, h, arcWidth, arcHeight)
  - Draws the outline of a rectangle with the top-left corner at coordinates (x, y) with a width of (w) and a height of (h), where the corners are rounded based on the number of pixels specified for the arcWidth and arcHeight.
- void drawString(String, x, y)
  - Draws the text specified in the String starting at the coordinates (x, y), where the coordinates define the bottom-left corner of the text.
- void fill(Shape)
  - Paints the Shape, where Shape can be one of the following Shape objects: Arc2D, Area, CubicCurve2D, Ellipse2D, GeneralPath, Line2D, Polygon, QuadCurve2D, Rectangle, Rectangle2D, RectangularShape, RoundRectangle2D
- void fill3DRect(x, y, w, h, boolean)
  - Paints a 3-D rectangle that appears raised if boolean is true or sunken if false
- void fillArc(x, y, w, h, startAngle, arcAngle)
  - Fills the arc on the basis of where it lies if an ellipse were drawn from the coordinates (x, y) with a width of (w) and height of (h) and the angle based on $0°$ drawn out from the center of the ellipse directly to the right, and the arcAngle is drawn by going counterclockwise.
- void fillOval(x, y, w, h)
  - Fills an oval/ellipse whose top-left corner is at coordinates (x, y) with a width of (w) and height of (h) such that the bottom-right corner is at coordinates $(x + w, y + h)$
- void fillPolygon(Polygon)
  - Fills the figure defined by the sequence of points in the Polygon object. The order of the points added to the Polygon defines the shape, as it connects the points in sequential order.
- void fillRect(x, y, w, h)
  - Fills the outline of a rectangle with the top-left corner at coordinates (x, y) with a width of (w) and a height of (h).

– void fillRoundRect(x, y, w, h, arcWidth, arcHeight)
- Fills the outline of a rectangle with the top-left corner at coordinates (*x, y*) with a width of (*w*) and a height of (*h*), where the corners are rounded based on the number of pixels specified for the arcWidth and arcHeight.

– void setBackground(Color)
- Sets the background color

– void setColor(Color)
- Sets the current painting color to the specified color

– void setFont(Font)
- Sets the current painting font to the specified font

– void setPaint(Paint)
- Sets the paint attribute for drawing and filling

– void setRenderHint(RenderingHints.KEY, hintValue)
- Sets the value of a single preference for rendering

– void setStroke(Stroke)
- Sets the stroke for painting

GridLayout
Constructors

– GridLayout layout = new GridLayout(rows, cols);
- Creates a new layout manager instance with specified number of rows and columns

HyperlinkEvent
Constructors

– None

Useful methods:

– getEventType( )
- Returns the type of the event which is either HyperlinkEvent.ACTIVATED, HyperlinkEvent.ENTERED, or HyperlinkEvent.EXITED

– URL getURL( )
- Returns the URL of the hyperlink

ImageIcon
Constructors

– ImageIcon icon = new ImageIcon(Image)
- Creates a new ImageIcon object with the specified image

Useful methods:

– Image getImage( )
- Returns the image of the icon

    — void setImage(Image)
       · Changes the image of the icon

`Integer`
Constructors

    — Integer i = new Integer(number)
       · Creates an instance of `Integer` object with specified number
Useful methods:

    — Integer.parseInt(String)
       · Returns an `int` type of the number stored in the `String`

`ItemEvent`
Constructors

    — Generated from selecting/deselecting radio buttons/checkboxes/lists
Useful methods:

    — Object getSource( )
       · Returns a reference to the object that generated the event
    — int getStateChange( )
       · Returns the type of selection/deselection (e.g., `ItemEvent.SELECTED` or `ItemEvent.DESELECTED`)

`JApplet`
Constructors

    — None
Useful methods:

    — AudioClip getAudioClip(getCodeBase( ), filename)
       · Gets an `AudioClip` from the file system
    — Image getImage(getCodeBase( ), filename)
       · Gets an image from the file system

`JButton`
Constructors

    — JButton b = new JButton( )
       · Creates a new button with neither text nor image
    — JButton b = new JButton(ImageIcon);
       · Creates a new button with an image
    — JButton b = new JButton("happy");
       · Creates a new button with the text "happy"
    — JButton b = new JButton("happy", ImageIcon);
       · Creates a new button with the text "happy" and an image in an `ImageIcon` object

Useful methods:
- void setBackground(Color)
  - · Sets the background color
- void setBorderPainted(boolean)
  - · If boolean is true, the line border around the button is painted
  - · If boolean is false, the border is not painted
- void setContentAreaFilled(boolean)
  - · If boolean is true, the background of the button is painted
  - · If boolean is false, the background is not painted
- void setDisabledIcon(ImageIcon)
  - · Sets the image to display when the button is disabled
- void setEnabled(boolean)
  - · Enables (boolean is true) or disables (boolean is false) the button
- void setFocusPainted(boolean)
  - · Draws box around component if it has focus (boolean is true) or not if boolean is false
- void setForeground(Color)
  - · Changes the text color of all text on the button
  - · *(Use HTML to change only parts of the text)*
- void setHorizontalTextPosition(JButton.POSITION)
  - · Sets where the text should be placed with respect to the image
  - · POSITION is one of: LEFT, CENTER, or RIGHT
- void setOpaque(boolean)
  - · Sets background as transparent (boolean is false) or solid (boolean is true)
- void setMargin(new Insets(0, 0, 0, 0))
  - · Sets the buffer between the image/text and the border of the button
  - · Inset parameters are ordered as: top, left, bottom, right
- void setPressedIcon(ImageIcon)
  - · Sets which image to display when mouse presses on the button
- void setRolloverIcon(ImageIcon)
  - · Sets which image to display when mouse rolls over the button
- void setSelectedIcon(ImageIcon)
  - · Sets which image to display when button is selected
- void setVerticalTextPosition(JButton.POSITION)
  - · Sets where the text should be placed with respect to the image
  - · POSITION is one of: TOP, CENTER, or BOTTOM

JCheckBox

Constructors

- JCheckBox cb = new JCheckBox( );
  - · Creates a new checkbox with no text or image
- JCheckBox cb = new JCheckBox(ImageIcon);
  - · Creates a new checkbox with an image in an ImageIcon object
- JCheckBox cb = new JCheckBox(ImageIcon, true);
  - · Creates a new checkbox with an image and initially selected
- JCheckBox cb = new JCheckBox("happy");
  - · Creates a new checkbox with the text "happy"
- JCheckBox cb = new JCheckBox("happy", true);
  - · Creates a new checkbox with the text "happy" and initially selected
- JCheckBox cb = new JCheckBox("happy", ImageIcon);
  - · Creates a new checkbox with the text "happy" and an image in an ImageIcon object

Useful methods:

- String getText( )
  - · Returns the text of the checkbox
  - · String theText = cbox.getText( );
- boolean isSelected( )
  - · Returns whether or not the checkbox is selected
- void setBackground(Color)
  - · Sets the background color
- void setEnabled(boolean)
  - · Enables (boolean is true) or disables (boolean is false) the checkbox
- void setFocusPainted(boolean)
  - · Draws box around component if it has focus (boolean is true) or not if boolean is false
- void setOpaque(boolean)
  - · Sets background as transparent (boolean is false) or solid (boolean is true)
- void setSelectedIcon(ImageIcon)
  - · Set which image to display when checkbox is selected

JComboBox

Constructors

- JComboBox droplist = new JComboBox( );
  - · Creates an empty combo box

    – JComboBox droplist = new JComboBox(array);
      · Creates a list based on the array

Useful methods:

    – int getItemCount( )
      · Returns the number of items in the list
      · int numItemsInList = combolist.getItemCount( );

    – int getSelectedIndex( )
      · Returns the index of the selected item
      · int selectedIndex = combolist.getSelectedIndex( );

    – Object getSelectedItem( )
      · Returns the selected item as an Object
      · String selectedText = (String)combolist.getSelectedItem( );

    – void removeItem(Object obj)
      · Removes the object from the list
      · combolist.remove("sad");

    – void removeItemAt(int index)
      · Removes the object at the specified index
      · combolist.remove(2);

    – void setBackground(Color)
      · Sets the background color

    – void setEditable(boolean flag)
      · Determines whether the combo box is editable
      · combolist.setEditable(true);

    – void setEnabled(boolean)
      · Enables (boolean is true) or disables (boolean is false) the combo box

    – void setOpaque(boolean)
      · Sets background as transparent (boolean is false) or solid (boolean is true)

JEditorPane

Constructors

    – JEditorPane pane = new JEditorPane( );
      · Creates a new editor pane

Useful methods:

    – void setPage(URL)
      · Displays the web page at the URL specified

    – void setText(String)
      · Puts the String into the editor pane (can use HTML formatting)

JFrame

Constructors

– JFrame f = new JFrame( );

  · Creates a new frame window

– JFrame f = new JFrame(String);

  · Creates a new frame window with String as the title of the window

Useful methods:

– void add(Object)

  · Adds the Object to the frame based on the layout manager specified

– void pack( )

  · Sizes the JFrame to fit the components displayed within the frame

– void setSize(int w, int h)

  · Sets the width (w) and height (h) of the frame

– void setLayout(layoutManager)

  · Sets the layout manager for the frame

– void setLocation(int x, int y)

  · Sets the upper-left corner of the screen of where to display the frame

– void setVisible(boolean)

  · Shows the frame (boolean is true) or hides the frame (boolean is false)

JList

Constructors

– DefaultListModel model = new DefaultListModel( );
  JList list = new JList(model);

  · Creates a list based on a default model, such that we can add items to the model

– JList list = new JList(array);

  · Creates a list based on the array

Useful methods:

– int getSelectedIndex( )

  · Returns the index of the item that is selected

– Object getSelectedValue( )

  · Returns the object that is selected

– void setBackground(Color)

  · Sets the background color

– void setEnabled(boolean)

  · Enables (boolean is true) or disables (boolean is false) the list

- void setOpaque(boolean)
  - · Sets background as transparent (boolean is `false`) or solid (boolean is `true`)
- void setVisibleRowCount(number)
  - · Sets the preferred number of visible rows
- void setSelectionMode(int mode)
  - · where mode can be:
    `ListSelectionModel.SINGLE_SELECTION`
    `ListSelectionModel.MULTIPLE_INTERVAL_SELECTION` (default)

JPanel
Constructors
- JPanel pane = new JPanel( )
  - · Creates a new panel with the default layout manager
- JPanel pane = new JPanel(layoutManager)
  - · Creates a new panel with the specified layout manager

Useful methods:
- void add(component)
  - · Adds the component to the panel using the layout manager
- void setBackground (Color)
  - · Changes the background color of the panel
- void setLayout(layoutManager)
  - · Sets the layout manager to the one specified
- void setOpaque(boolean)
  - · Sets whether or not the panel is transparent (boolean is `false`) or solid (boolean is `true`—default)

JRadioButton
Constructors
- JRadioButton rb = new JRadioButton(ImageIcon);
  - · Creates a radio button with an image in an `ImageIcon` object
- JRadioButton rb = new JRadioButton("red");
  - · Creates a radio button with the text "red"
- JRadioButton rb = new JRadioButton("blue", true);
  - · Creates a radio button with the text "blue" and is initially selected

Useful methods:
- String getText( )
  - · Returns the text for the radio button
- boolean isSelected( )
  - · Returns whether or not the radio button is selected

−void setBackground(Color)

   · Sets the background color

−void setEnabled(boolean)

   · Enables (boolean is true) or disables (boolean is false) the radio button

−void setForeground(Color)

   · Sets the font color

−void setFocusPainted(boolean)

   · Draws box around component if it has focus (boolean is true) or not if boolean is false

−void setOpaque(boolean)

   · Sets background as transparent (boolean is false) or solid (boolean is true)

−void setSelectedIcon(ImageIcon)

   · Sets which image to display when radio button is selected

JScrollPane

Constructors

−JScrollPane p = new JScrollPane(Object);

   · Creates a scroll pane with scrollbars with Object inside it

JTabbedPane

Constructors

JTabbedPane pane = new JTabbedPane ( );

   · Creates a tabbed pane instance

−JTabbedPane pane = new JTabbedPane (location);

   · Creates a tabbed pane with tabs at location where location is JTabbedPane.TOP (default), JTabbedPane.LEFT, JTabbedPane.BOTTOM, or JTabbedPane.RIGHT

Useful methods:

−void addTab(text, component)

   · Adds the component to the tab with text on the tab

−void addTab(text, ImageIcon, component)

   · Adds the component to the tab with text and image on the tab

−void addTab(text, ImageIcon, component, tooltip)

   · Adds the component to the tab with text and image on the tab and tooltip text when mouse hovers on tab

JTable

Constructors

−JTable table = new JTable(data, colHeadings);

   · Creates a new JTable component with the data as a 2-D array and colHeadings as a 1-D array

Useful methods:
  - `void setBackground( Color )`
    · Changes the background color of the table
  - `void setForeground( Color )`
    · Changes the text color in the table
  - `void setGridColor( Color )`
    · Changes the color of the grid lines
  - `void setPreferredScrollableViewportSize( Dimension )`
    · Sets the viewable width and height of the table (the rest must be scrolled within a `JScrollPane`)
  - `void setSelectionBackground( Color )`
    · Changes the background color of selected entry
  - `void setSelectionForeground( Color )`
    · Changes the foreground color of selected entry
  - `void setShowHorizontalLines( boolean )`
    · Show horizontal lines (`true`—default) or not (`false`)
  - `void setShowVerticalLines( boolean )`
    · Show vertical lines (`true`—default) or not (`false`)

`JTextArea`
Constructors
  - `JTextArea ta = new JTextArea ( );`
    · Creates a text area with a default number of columns
  - `JTextArea ta = new JTextArea ( 5, 60 );`
    · Creates a text area with five rows and 60 columns
  - `JTextArea ta = new JTextArea ( "I love JaVa" );`
    · Creates a text area with the text "`I love JaVa`" inside the text box
  - `JTextArea ta = new JTextArea ( "Java rocks", 4, 10 );`
    · Creates a text area with the text "`Java rocks`" inside the text box, which has four rows visible (height) and 10 columns visible (width)
Useful methods:
  - `void append( String )`
    · Adds the `String` to the end of the text inside the text area box
  - `int getLineCount( )`
    · Returns the number of lines in the text area box
  - `String getText( )`
    · Returns the text that is inside the box
  - `void setBackground( Color )`
    · Sets the background color

- void setEnabled(boolean)
  - Enables (boolean is `true`) or disables (boolean is `false`) the button
- void setFont(Font f)
  - Set the font for the text box
    ```
    Font fnt = new Font( "Serif", Font.BOLD, 18 );
    textField.setFont( fnt );
    ```
- void setLineWrap(boolean)
  - Sets whether to wrap at edge of text area box (boolean is `true`) or not (boolean is `false`)
- void setOpaque(boolean)
  - Sets background as transparent (boolean is `false`) or solid (boolean is `true`)
- void setText(String)
  - Enters the text in the `String` into the text box (use \n for new lines)
    ```
    ta.setText( "I like to learn java\nFun" );
    ```
- void setWrapStyleWord(boolean)
  - Wraps at edge of text area box based on word (boolean is `true`) or not (boolean is `false`)

JTextField

Constructors

- JTextField tf = new JTextField( );
  - Creates a text field with a default (0) number of columns
- JTextField tf = new JTextField(2);
  - Creates a text field with two columns (good for states: NC, IL)
- JTextField tf = new JTextField("I love JaVa");
  - Creates a text field with the text "I love JaVa" inside the text box
  - Size of box will fit exactly to the text
- JTextField tf = new JTextField("Java rocks", 10);
  - Creates a text field with the text "Java rocks" inside the text box, which has 10 columns visible (width)

Note: A column width is the size of the capital letter W in the current font.

Useful methods:

- String getText( )
  - Returns the text that is inside the box
    ```
    String theText = JTextField.getText( );
    ```
- void setBackground(Color)
  - Sets the background color

— void setEnabled(boolean)
  · Enables (boolean is true) or disables (boolean is false) the button
— void setFont(Font f)
  · Set the font for the text box
```
        Font fnt = new Font( "Serif", Font.BOLD, 18 );
        JTextField.setFont( fnt );
```
— void setForeground(Color c)
  · Sets the color of the text
— void setOpaque(boolean)
  · Sets background as transparent (boolean is false) or solid (boolean is true)
— void setText(String)
  · Enters the text in the String into the text box
```
        JTextField.setText( "I like to learn Java" );
```

KeyEvent
Constructors
— Generated from keyboard presses
Useful methods:
  — int getKeyCode( )
    · Returns the key pressed (e.g., arrow keys: KeyEvent.VK_UP, KeyEvent.VK_DOWN, KeyEvent.VK_LEFT, KeyEvent.VK_RIGHT)
  — Object getSource( )
    · Returns a reference to the object that generated the event

MouseEvent
Constructors
— Generated from mouse enter/exit/press/release/click
Useful methods:
  — Object getSource( )
    · Returns a reference to the object that generated the event
  — int getX( )
    · Returns *x* coordinate of mouse
  — int getY( )
    · Returns *y* coordinate of mouse

MouseMotionEvent
Constructors
— Generated from mouse move/drag

Useful methods:

- Object getSource( )
  - Returns a reference to the object that generated the event
- int getX( )
  - Returns *x* coordinate of mouse
- int getY( )
  - Returns *y* coordinate of mouse

Polygon

Constructors

- Polygon p = new Polygon( )
  - Creates a new Polygon object

Useful methods:

- void addPoint(x, y)
  - Adds the coordinate (*x, y*) to the list of coordinates defining the Polygon object.
- boolean contains(x, y)
  - Returns true if the coordinates (*x, y*) are within the boundary of the Polygon or false if they are not
- boolean contains(Point)
  - Returns whether the coordinates (*x, y*) are within the boundary of the Polygon
- boolean intersects(x, y, w, h)
  - Returns whether the region defined by the coordinates (*x, y*) and width of (*w*) and height of (*h*) overlap with the Polygon

Random

Constructors

- Random r = new Random( )
  - Creates an instance of Random based on the current timestamp

Useful methods:

- int nextInt( )
  - Returns the next pseudorandom number as an integer
- int nextInt(num)
  - Returns the next pseudorandom number between 0 and (num − 1)

Rectangle

Constructors

- Rectangle r = new Rectangle(x, y, width, height);
  - Creates a new Rectangle object

Useful methods:

    — `boolean contains( Rectangle )`
       · Returns `true` or `false` based on whether the `Rectangle` is inside the other

    — `boolean intersects( Rectangle )`
       · Returns `true` or `false` based on whether the `Rectangle` intersects with the other

`String`

Constructors

    — `String s = new String( text );`
       · Creates a new `String` object based on the text

    — `String s = text;`
       · Creates a new `String` object based on the text (shortcut way)

Useful methods:

    — `char charAt( index )`
       · Returns a character at the specified index in the string

    — `boolean contains( String )`
       · Returns `true` if the string contains the parameter string somewhere within the text, otherwise returns `false`

    — `boolean equals( String )`
       · Returns `true` if the two strings are identical (case sensitive) or `false` otherwise

    — `int indexOf( charOrString )`
       · Returns the index of where the character or `String` sequence first appears

    — `String valueOf( number )`
       · Returns a `String` object of the number

`Stroke`
see `BasicStroke`

`Thread`

Constructors

    — `Thread thread = new Thread( this );`
       · Creates a new thread

Useful methods:

    — `static void sleep( num )`
       · Pauses execution for num milliseconds

    — `void start( )`
       · Starts the thread, calls the run method

– `void stop( )`

· Stops the thread

`Timer`

Constructors

– `Timer timer = new Timer ( delay, this );`

· Creates a new timer that triggers after delay in milliseconds

Useful methods:

– `void start( )`

· Starts the timer

– `void stop( )`

· Stops the timer

Symbol Index

Word Index

A

"About Us" guideline, 116
absolute value function, 136
ActionEvents, 172–176, 305
ActionListener, 170, 172, 306
actionPerformed method, 180, 276, 306, 307
addHyperlinkListener, 361, 373
addItem method, 83
addKeyListener, 180
add method, 286
addPoint method, 30
AddressFields, 313–317, 314f
addTab method, 245
algorithm, defined, 211
angle brackets, use of, 286
animation, 208–209, 303–305
  Sprite class and, 317
  timed, 305
anotherMethod, 50
anti-aliasing, 37, 38f, 41
API (application programming interface), 7
applet coordinate system, 20f
applets, 6, 7–14
  adding components to (*See* Swing components)
  ArrayList, 286–288
  class declaration, 9
  drawing on (*See* drawing)
  enhancements, 191–197
  events, procedure for working, 170–171
  graphical tables for arrays, 280–285
  header comments, 8
  HTML file, 10
  images, 262–263
  import statements, 7–8
  keeping track of states of, 299
  modifying/using free applets, 380
  mouse listener, adding, 184–185
  paint method, 9–10
  running an example of (Linux and Macintosh), 12–14
  running an example of (Windows), 10–12
  seasonal weather example, 157–165, 157f

applications, 6
arcs, drawing, 29–30
arithmetic operators, 133–134
  mathematical operations, 133t
  mathematical operator shortcuts, 134t
array
  array declaration, 271
  ArrayList and, differences, 288–289, 289t
  initialization, 271–280
  JTable and, 280–285
array initialization, 271–280
  elements, 271
  length, 272
  shortcut list, 272
array declaration, 271
ArrayList structures, 286–288, 330, 352
assembly language, 3
assignment, performing, 47–48
AudioClip method, 253
audio files, 253–256
  AudioClip object, 254
  loops, 254
  stop method, 254

B

background color, changing, 248
background image, creating, 232–233
bevel borders, 252
binary representation, 3
binary to decimal, converting, 211
BlueJ (graphical IDE), 13
boolean, 46, 129, 147
booleanExpression, 202, 204
BorderFactory class, 250
BorderLayout, 101–107, 102f, 104f, 257
borders, 250–252
BoxLayout, 109–111
braces, use of, 130, 147, 149, 154, 180, 202, 210, 272, 281
brackets, use of, 271, 280
Breakout, 330–339, 331f
break statement, 154
BufferedImage, 328, 336, 339